The Official History of

SURREY
COUNTY
CRICKET CLUB

THE CHRISTOPHER HELM COUNTY CRICKET HISTORIES

Series Editors:
Peter Arnold and Peter Wynne-Thomas

DERBYSHIRE
John Shawcroft, with a personal view by Bob Taylor

GLAMORGAN
Andrew Hignell, with a personal view by Tony Lewis

HAMPSHIRE
Peter Wynne-Thomas, with a personal view by John Arlott

KENT
Dudley Moore, with a personal view by Derek Underwood

MIDDLESEX
David Lemmon, with a personal view by Denis Compton

WORCESTERSHIRE
David Lemmon, with a personal view by Basil D'Oliveira

The Official History of

SURREY
COUNTY
CRICKET CLUB

David Lemmon

**With a personal view by
PETER MAY**

CHRISTOPHER HELM

London

© 1989 David Lemmon and Peter May
Christopher Helm (Publishers) Ltd, Imperial House,
21–25 North Street, Bromley, Kent BR1 1SD

ISBN 0-7470-2010-8

A CIP catalogue record for this book is available from the British Library

Typeset by Cotswold Typesetting Ltd, Gloucester
Printed and bound in Great Britain by Biddles Ltd, Guildford, Surrey

CONTENTS

A PERSONAL VIEW
Peter May

MY ASSOCIATION WITH SURREY BEGAN when I was in my last year at school. I had been scoring well for Charterhouse, and when the County arranged a match at Farncombe, not far from the school, in 1947, I was invited to play. The game was one of several which were played in aid of the Surrey Centenary Appeal. The Centenary was in 1945, but it was not celebrated until the following year because of the war, and in 1946 and 1947, matches and functions were arranged to try and raise money for the Club which had suffered greatly when The Oval was requisitioned for use as a prisoner-of-war camp and for other military activities during the war years.

In the match at Farncombe, I played alongside Errol Holmes, the County Captain at the time, Laurie Fishlock, Stan Squires, Eddie Watts and the Bedser twins who were to become great friends of mine. Some days after this game I had a letter from the Surrey secretary Brian Castor, an active and resourceful administrator and a good friend to cricket and later to me, asking me to throw in my lot with Surrey. I was flattered and delighted to agree, and it is a decision which I have never regretted for a moment.

I was born in Berkshire and played a little for that county during the school holidays, but the attraction of first-class cricket was strong, and I received only encouragement and sympathy from Berkshire when Surrey approached me. My schooling at Charterhouse, which is in Surrey, gave me the necessary qualification, for the laws governing representing a county were much stricter in those days than they are today, and I found that the link between Surrey and Berkshire was a firm one. The Bedsers, Geoff Kirby, reserve to Arthur McIntyre, and the late and much-missed Ken Barrington were all born in Berkshire while Graham Roope has, of course, played for the county in recent years.

I learned later that, after the match at Farncombe, Brian Castor had spoken to both Errol Holmes and Stan Squires, a most respected senior professional, and sought their opinion of me, and they had confirmed that he should approach me on behalf of Surrey because they said I reminded them of Douglas Jardine. Having agreed to throw in my lot with Surrey in 1947, I was not able to play for them, save in one second-eleven match in 1948, until 1950, for I spent two years in the Royal Navy on national service and then went up to Cambridge.

At the end of the summer term in 1950, I was invited by Michael Barton to join the Surrey side, and I played my first Championship match against Gloucestershire at Bristol. Far from suffering from any resentment on the part of my colleagues that one of them had to stand down to make room for me, I received nothing but help and encouragement. If everyone was fit, the two senior professionals, Laurie Fishlock and Jack Parker, would take it in turns to stand down to accommodate me. They did so without complaint and were only too eager to offer advice and encouragement. I received nothing but kindness.

I realised very quickly how much help I needed, for, in my first game, I was out for 1 and 1. I fell victim to the great Tom Goddard in my first innings. He was 50 years old and

I

seemed something of an awesome figure. He had massive hands and turned his off-breaks prodigiously, encouraged at the time by the Bristol wicket. In my first Championship innings, I shouldered arms to a ball from him which pitched well outside the off stump and I was bowled in front of my pads. I realised very soon that I would have to learn to bat against top quality spin bowling, for in my first few weeks in the Surrey side, I came up against players like Appleyard and Wardle of Yorkshire and Jenkins and Howorth of Worcestershire, all of whom gave much thought to the game and were always encouraged by the sight of a novice.

We finished the season well in 1950 and earned a share of the Championship, which delighted us, for the County had not known success for 36 years. We did not realise then that, ten years later, a shared Championship would be something of a disappointment to us.

I was able to play little in 1951, which was Michael Barton's last as captain. He did a fine job. He was much respected and did much to lay the foundation for subsequent successes.

I was in my final year at Cambridge in 1952 and rejoined the Surrey side in mid-July when I was fortunate enough to hit my first Championship century at The Oval in the match against Kent. Stuart Surridge took seven wickets in the first innings of that match and, at the close, he and Tom Clark won the game for us by two wickets in the last over. Surridge was a magnificent captain. His enthusiasm was unlimited and infectious, and he consistently got the best out of all of his men. I learned so much from him, and what I learned was not restricted to captaincy or cricket. As a player, he was always doing something, hitting quick runs, taking a vital wicket or making a breath-taking catch close to the wicket. He was inspiring in every sense of the word, and he even seemed in touch with the elements on occasions, glowering at approaching cloud and halting its progress until Surrey had completed victory.

There were times when I, and others, suspected that he had gone mad, such as on the occasion when he declared at 92 for three against Worcestershire. There was general incredulity, but we won by an innings, and he was proved right, again.

Of course, the success would not have come had Surridge not had some fine players at his command. I cannot think that any county has ever possessed a better attack than Laker, Lock, Loader, Surridge and the Bedsers. They were indignant at suggestions that their triumphs were due to the help that they received from The Oval wickets and were quick and right to point out that they took as many wickets away from The Oval as at the great ground itself and that visiting bowlers found The Oval no great comfort.

There were also some very fine players in that Surrey side who did not receive all the praise or recognition that they should have done, men like Dave Fletcher, a consistent opening batsman, Tom Clark, a fine stroke-player and useful spin bowler, and Bernard Constable, neat and tidy, a wonderful player of spin and a marvellous cover point.

When I look back on those days the quality which I remember above all others is the wonderful team spirit that Surridge created. Whatever one did, it was for the side, and a brisk 20 or 30 on a damp day or a good catch was valued as highly as a century made in conditions favourable to the batsman when there were no pressures upon him. Surrey were essentially a family, and there was a feeling of pride and excitement running right through the Club. Surridge was confident from the start that we would win the Championship five years in succession so was Monty Garland-Wells who had an accumulator on us winning the title for seven years in a row. After four years, he accepted a settlement from the bookmakers to cancel the bet, and with the proceeds he made the typical gesture of throwing a celebratory party for us at The Oval.

Monty was just one of the old players who supported us through those years. Sir Jack Hobbs, a dear and kindly man, and Errol Holmes, a prophet of joy and sportsmanship, were members of the committee, and Andrew Sandham and Herbert Strudwick were on the staff so that we were always linked to the glories of the past and acutely aware of the traditions which we had to uphold. It is a quality which the Club has not lost. Former players have continued to involve themselves in the administration, and at The Oval today, you will find Raman Subba Row, Michael Barton, Alf Gover, Geoff Arnold, Chris Waller, Alec and Eric Bedser, former secretary Geoff Howard, Stuart Surridge, Maurice Allom and Dennis Cox among those working away for the future good and prosperity of Surrey cricket.

The Club has a great history and tradition of which all who have been part of Surrey in any capacity are justifiably proud. I feel honoured to think that I have been one of them.

PROLOGUE TO THE OVAL

IF ANY COUNTY HAS A RIGHT to claim pre-eminence in cricket, that county is Surrey. Formed in 1845, Surrey County Cricket Club is the oldest of the county clubs in that it has undergone no traumatic reformation since that date. Surrey can lay claim to being the first Champions, unofficial, 1864, and the first Champions, official, 1890. Men of Surrey were on England's first overseas tour, to North America, 1859, and Surrey provided the captain, H. H. Stephenson, of the first England side to tour Australia in 1861–62. The first 50 hit by an England batsman in a Test match came from Jupp of Surrey.

Long before those days, in 1598, John Derrick gave one of the earliest, if not the earliest, written testimonies to cricket being played in England when, in a dispute over a plot of land in Guildford, believed to have been somewhere near the top of what is now North Street, he gave evidence in a court case that, half a century earlier, at the 'free schoole of Guldeford', he did 'runne and play there at creckett'.

It was Surrey who staged the first Test match in England, the first Football Association Cup Final and the first Rugby Union International match to be played in England. Surrey were the first, and only, side to win the Championship seven years in succession, the first county side to engage in a tied match twice, and the first side to win a county match in one day.

In more recent years, they have pioneered pop concerts and Australian Rules Football at a cricket venue, and the only man to take all ten wickets in a Test match innings was a bowler from Surrey. In the distant past, they can almost certainly claim to have been associated with the first streaker.

On 24 June 1748, the landlord of the Hand and Flower in Kent Street Road advertised in the *Penny London Morning Advertiser*:

> On Monday, June 27th, on Walworth Common (Surrey) High Kent v the Black Swan Club in Long Lane, Southwark. After the match a Holland Smock will be run for by two women stark naked, one the noted Mary Weaver of the Borough, the other Sarah Lucas from Rotherhithe.

Cricket was being played in Surrey before this time, for, in the *Post Man*, 25 June 1709, it was stated that:

> On Wednesday the 29th instant will be play'd a famous match of Cricket at Dartford Brimph for £50 by Kent and Surrey.

It would be wrong to assume that this was a contest between two sides fully representative of the counties concerned, for it was customary for eleven men of a town or village to adopt the name of their county, but this is the first record of a match where the two sides have come from different counties.

By 1730, cricket was being played on Mickleham and Epsom Downs and at Croydon, while, in July 1730:

> A great cricket-match was played on Merrow Downs, near Guildford, between the Duke of Richmond's and Mr Andrews's – eleven men on each side – which was won by the latter. There were present the Right Honble. Lord Onslow, and Lord Middleton, Sir Peter Soame, Mr Steed, and a great many other persons of distinction.

Mr Andrews came from Sunbury in Middlesex, and a month before the game referred to above, it was noted that 'a great cricket-match was played at Richmond Green between Surrey and Middlesex, which was won by the former'.

F. S. Ashley-Cooper, the great cricket historian and statistician, in his record of matches between Middlesex and Surrey, counts three other matches as being played between the two sides in 1730, at the Artillery Ground and on Kennington Common, but it is likely that he included the matches played between Surrey and London in August 1730.

> A great cricket-match was played at Kennington Common, between eleven young gentlemen of London against the same number of Surrey: it was thought to be one of the completest matches that ever was played; the London side won by 1 notch. The same gentlemen played again on the following Monday, and was in the Artillery Ground, where the Londoners likewise won; but 'twas said the Surrey gentlemen are desirous of saving their credit if possible, and it is to be played the third time, which will be on the following Friday, in the Artillery Ground.

Kennington Common, now the Park, is, of course, just across the road from The Oval while Walworth Common, another great centre for Surrey cricket in the early part of the eighteenth century, has long since been built upon. It occupied the area close to the junction of Albany Road and Portland Street, Walworth, now covered by Faraday Street, Mann Street and Westmoreland Road.

The London Club which played at the Artillery Ground, situated in Middlesex, was the most prestigious cricket club of its time, boasting the Prince of Wales and the Duke of Cumberland among its members and having at least five Surrey men as its leading players. These five were John Frame, Thomas Faulkner, Stephen Dingate, and John and Joseph Harris. They were all in the Surrey side which beat England by two wickets at Dartford Brent in 1749.

Frame was only 16 at the time, and he later became renowned as a fast bowler. He was to play for England against Hambledon in 1774 and was described by John Nyren, the Hambledon chronicler, as 'an unusually stout man for a cricketer'.

The difficulties of granting authenticity to any side which labelled itself 'Surrey', however, can be seen from the account of the match between Eleven of Kent and Eleven of Surrey at Duppas Hill, near Croydon, in July 1731. Surrey are reported to have won the match and interestingly, though not uniquely, to have fielded a side all eleven of whom bore the same name, Wood.

The game played at this time was very different from the game we know today. The over consisted of four balls, and the wicket consisted of two stumps, 22 inches high and 6 inches apart, surmounted by a single bail. Matches were generally played out in a day, and runs were notched on a stick, hence the term 'notches'. Bowling was mostly fast and low, under-arm, and the bat was curved at the end like a hockey stick. The earliest bat now known to have survived belonged to James Chitty of Knaphill in Surrey, and it is housed at The Oval. It is dated 1729.

Certainly at this time, clubs were coming into existence all over the county, Addington, Barnes, Cheam, Chertsey, Esher, Mitcham, Croydon, Kingston, Richmond, Wandsworth and Moulsey Hurst among them. Addington became one of the strongest of clubs, and Thomas Faulkner of London and Surrey, whom we have mentioned above, was one of their most noted performers as a batsman and fast bowler. He was also a very good boxer.

One of the reasons for the growth of interest in cricket was the patronage the game received from members of the aristocracy. Seen initially as a pastime for the lower orders, cricket, at the beginning of the eighteenth century, gained the approval of men of wealth and influence, notably Frederick Louis, Prince of Wales, son of George II.

He was, as we have mentioned, the principal dignitary in the London Club, and his patronage of Surrey, whose elevens he mostly selected, was generous and beneficial. His interest and presence excited the interest and presence of others. In September 1731, when Kingston played the county of Surrey at Moulsey Hurst, near Hampton Court, 'some thousands of persons of both sexes were present'.

Two years later, also at Moulsey Hurst, when Surrey beat Middlesex by three 'notches', the Prince, who was accompanied by 'several persons of distinction', was so pleased with what he saw that he gave each man a guinea. He also awarded a silver cup to the winners of a match between Kent and his own side, and his own side were the victors.

It is doubtful that the 'Surrey men and other country men on the Prince's side' were the same eleven who represented Croydon against London at Duppas Hill. The Croydon side became rather unpopular in September 1734, because, as was reported:

> A great cricket-match was lately to have been played between the gentlemen of London and Croydon, but the latter having been regaled with a good dinner, &c., gratis, withdrew, and have not since been heard of.

The Londoners advertised that they wished to play one more game before the season was over and would play anyone, except Croydon, whom they had an ill opinion of as men.

The Prince's men would not have run away, for their patron cared for them well, and he would often arrange matches at £1,000 a side. Money and betting played an important part in the matches so that when Surrey beat Kent on Kennington Common in 1736 'a great deal of money was lost and won upon the occasion'.

The games, too, were not without incident. In the match above on Kennington Common, 'three soldiers apprehended a Kentish man for deserting; but the populace, hearing of the matter, joined and rescued the deserter out of their hands, and after a severe discipline let them go about their business'. The crowd could grow ugly, producing scenes more violent than anything about which there are complaints today, and, at a single-wicket match between a man of Mitcham and one of Wandsworth in 1737:

> John Smith, a mechanic, for many years foreman to Mr Strong, a painter in Doctors Commons, died of a wound he received by a cut from a stone yesterday at the cricket-match on Kennington Common, when the mob outrageously threw dirt, dung, &c., on account of people entering the line.

Matches at Kennington Common were invariably watched by large crowds. So great were the numbers on occasions that accidents would occur as when the Prince of Wales's Surrey side lost to the Duke of Dorset's Kent side in June 1737:

> There was a pavilion erected for his Royal Highness, who was accompanied by several persons of distinction. The press was so great on the occasion that a poor woman, by the crowd bearing upon her, unfortunately had her leg broke, which being related to his Royal Highness he was pleased to order her ten guineas.

It has been estimated that during the Prince's period of interest and patronage, approximately 1730 to 1750, Surrey played some 36 eleven-a-side matches of which 13 were won, 8 lost, 5 drawn and 10 are unaccounted for. The Prince himself died in 1751. His death was caused by an abscess which had formed as the result of a blow from a cricket ball which he had received when playing on the lawn at his residence in Cliveden House in Buckinghamshire. The abscess which formed internally burst some months later and killed him. Horace Walpole put the blow down to a tennis ball, but that is hardly likely, and most historians claim the Prince as one of cricket's early fatalities.

While Faulkner, Fame, Harris and the rest were at their height the ladies of Surrey were also to the fore, and, in August 1745, there was the first account of a ladies' match, inevitably in Surrey:

> The greatest cricket-match that ever was played in the south part of England was on Friday, the 26th of last month, on Gosden Common, near Guildford, in Surrey, between eleven maids of Bramley and eleven maids of Hambleton, dressed all in white. The Bramley maids had blue ribbons and the Hambleton maids red ribbons on their heads. The Bramley girls got 119 notches and the Hambleton girls 127. There was of both sexes the greatest number that ever was seen on such an occasion. The girls bowled, batted, ran, and catched as well as most men could do in that game.

Although cricket thrived all over the county in the second half of the eighteenth century, the force of the county side diminished with the passing of the patron. Eleven poulterers played eleven butchers on Kennington Common, and Kingston and Richmond were locked in close combat on Richmond Green. In October 1767, a match

> was played near Croydon, for 200 guineas, by a farmer with a gold-laced hat and ten others with silver-laced hats, against eleven gentlemen of the Hambledon Club, which was won by the latter by a majority of 262 notches. It was remarkable that the Hambledon Club got two new hands from Hampshire, who kept in three hours and a half and got 192 notches, the greatest thing ever known.

The same month, Hambledon played 'a set of gentlemen belonging to a club in Surrey' at Broad-Halfpenny Down and won by 224 runs. Power had moved from Kent, Surrey and London to a small village in Hampshire, yet even that village was dependent upon men of Surrey.

If we look at the Surrey side which beat Kent by 35 runs on 11 and 12 June 1773, at Laleham-Burway, near Chertsey, we will notice that four of them were stalwarts of the Hambledon side, foremost among them being Edward Stevens, always referred to as Lumpy.

There are various reasons given as to how Lumpy became known by that name. One version gives the reason as being a peculiarity in his bowling action, another because he once ate a whole apple pie at a Hambledon Club dinner and a third because of his physique. Whatever the reason, Lumpy was the most renowned bowler of his time and one of the first great Surrey cricketers. He was employed as a gardener by the Earl of Tankerville, a patron of the game, who also employed another Surrey stalwart, William Bedster, as butler.

John Nyren, the chronicler of Hambledon cricket, in *The Young Cricketer's Tutor and Cricketers of My Time*, published in 1833, writes of Lumpy, as one of the four 'principal bowlers who were usually opposed to' Hambledon:

> Beyond all the men within my recollection Lumpy would bowl the greatest number of length balls in succession. His pace was much faster than Lord Beauclerc's, but he wanted his Lordship's general knowledge of the game.

Lumpy delighted in bowling people out and would always choose a spot to pitch the wickets which would aid his shooter, much to the chagrin of his side who would have preferred 'a rising spot to bowl against, which would have materially increased the difficulty of the hitter'. It was Lumpy's propensity for bowling straight and fast that brought about a change in the regulations of the game.

Playing for Five of England against Five of Hambledon in May 1775, Lumpy was bowling to last man John Small (senior) with 14 runs needed to win. Three times he bowled right through Small's wicket, but with no middle stump to be knocked over, Small survived and obtained the 14 runs. Many thought that this was very hard on Lumpy, and a third stump was later added. 'Lumpy was a short man, round-shouldered, and stout. He had no trick about him, but was as plain as a pike-staff in all his dealings.'

Another of the great Surrey cricketers with a Hambledon connection was Richard Francis. Nyren relates excitedly his discovery of Francis in Hambledon:

> One day I met him in the street of Hambledon, and ran to tell our General that the famous Francis had come to live among us; he could scarcely believe me – perhaps for joy. This was the luckiest thing that could have happened to us, for Brett had just about the same time left off playing. Francis was a fast *jerker*; but though his delivery was allowed to be fair bowling, still it was a jerk. We enlisted him immediately, for we all knew what he could do, having seen him play on the Surrey side against us.

Francis was a gamekeeper who played for Hambledon for several years. He had played for Kent as well as Surrey, and as the century drew to its close he was to be found playing in Essex.

9

Thomas 'Shock' White, John Wells and Harry and Tom Walker were other Surrey men to assist Hambledon. Two other notables were Yalden and William Beldham.

William Yalden, born in 1739, was wicket-keeper for Surrey and England in their matches against Hambledon and Kent in the second half of the century, and for Hambledon, too, although perhaps his time with them was a little before their great days. He was a tall, thin, dark, agile man who once jumped a fence, it is said, and fell flat on his back while taking a catch. He was particularly adept at keeping to Lumpy's shooters, and, like Lumpy, he worked on the Earl of Tankerville's estate. Nyren was not too keen on Yalden. He saw him as a man 'whose word was not always to be depended on when he had put a man out – he would now and then shuffle and resort to trick'. More forcefully, he was accused of acts of 'low cunning, as is not consistent with the character of an Englishman'.

Nyren placed Tom Sueter, the Hambledon wicket-keeper, above him, and Sueter, a builder and carpenter, subsequently played for Surrey until about 1791. On the qualities of one Surrey man, none ever disagreed. That man was 'Silver' Billy Beldham.

Beldham was born in 1766 and died in 1862 at the age of 96. Ten years before his death he had walked the seven miles from his home in Tilford to Godalming to see a match. Nyren saw him first when he was young, but the impression that Beldham made upon Nyren was the impression he made on all who saw him. It was an indelible one:

> I hardly ever saw a man with a finer command of his bat; but, with the instruction and advice of the old heads superadded, he rapidly attained to the extraordinary accomplishment of being the finest player that has appeared within the latitude of more than half a century. There can be no exception against his batting, or the severity of his hitting. He would get in at the balls, and hit them away in a gallant style; yet, in this single feat, I think I have known him excelled; but when he could cut them at the point of his bat, he was in his glory; and upon my life their speed was as the speed of thought. One of the most beautiful sights that can be imagined, and which would have delighted an artist, was to see him make himself up to hit a ball. It was the beau-ideal of grace, animation and concentrated energy.

In his *Oxford Memories*, Rev James Pycroft confirms that Beldham, who was also a fine bowler and wicket-keeper, was supreme in his day and says that 'Beldham's was a green old age. Even when between sixty and seventy he was barred in county matches.'

A player was barred when it was felt that his presence would give his side such an advantage as to make the contest uneven, but Surrey certainly included Beldham in their side when they took on England, as they did regularly from 1793 until 1810 and intermittently until 1831. Surrey more than held their own in these matches and even pitted their 11 against 13 of England in the early years. In 1809, they even lent England Beldham and still won the match at the Holt Ground, which was at Wrecclesham, near Farnham, Beldham's birthplace, and had been made for Beldham by Lord Stowell.

One of Beldham's greatest achievements was for Surrey against England at Lord's in June 1794, when he hit 72 and 102, phenomenal scoring for the time. Harry Walker hit 115 not out in the second innings, and Surrey, 223 and 259 for five, to England's 88 and 197, won with ease.

The patron of the Surrey side in this match, and in many others, was Lord Winchilsea, a keen cricketer and able performer. He set up an establishment at Moulsey Hurst in 1787 and gathered a strong side around him. Moulsey Hurst had been a noted cricket centre for some years, but was particularly fashionable at the end of the century. David Garrick, the most celebrated actor of the age, had a house close by, and the three games between Surrey and England in 1795 were played at Moulsey Hurst. The ground later became lost to cricket when it became the property of the Hurst Park Racing Company.

In the Surrey side which trounced England at Lord's in 1794 was Robert Robinson, 'three-fingered Jack'. He was born at Ash, near Farnham, in 1765 and was a tall, powerful left-hander who was able to hit the ball very hard. As a boy, he lost a finger on his right hand through fire, and, in consequence, had his bat grooved to accommodate his stunted fingers.

'Long Bob' Robinson was in the Players' side in the first game of their historic series against the Gentlemen, at Lord's, the original ground in Dorset Square, in 1806. It seems that there had been an attempt to introduce this fixture at Moulsey Hurst in 1798, but the first game between those who were paid for their cricketing endeavours and those who were not took place at Lord's eight years later, and Surrey played a significant part in it. Not only were Robinson and Tom Walker on the Players' side, but Beldham and Lambert had been loaned to the Gentlemen in an attempt to balance the sides. In fact, they tipped the scales in favour of the Gentlemen with their fine all-round play. Lambert hit 57, the first 50 in the fixture, and the Gentlemen won by an innings. The Gentlemen also won the return match a fortnight later (it was played over two days with a four-day interval in between), but this time Beldham was in the Players' side.

William Lambert, born at Burstow, first played for Surrey five years before the inaugural Gentlemen and Players match. He was an outstanding cricketer in all that he did, batting, bowling, fielding and wicket-keeping, and he was a noted single-wicket champion. Without question, he was the greatest all-round cricketer of his day.

Interestingly, Lambert, in his youth, anticipated the Gooch school of batting in that he stood at the wicket with his bat raised above his shoulder, but he jettisoned the method after he had been beaten by shooters on several occasions. As a batsman he was of the forward driving style. 'He stood with left foot a yard in advance, swaying his bat and body as if to maintain momentum, and reaching forward almost to where the ball must be pitched'. He dominated the bowling of the age and was always on the attack. Those who played with him would admit no superior, as batsman or bowler, and at Lord's, in July 1817, he created cricket history by scoring a century in each innings of a match, 107 and 157. This was the first time that such a feat had been accomplished, and it remained unchallenged in a match at Lord's for 76 years.

Lambert was not above using gamesmanship, and he won a famous single-wicket victory at Lord's in 1810 by outwitting his opponent. He and Osbaldeston were due to play Lord Frederick Beauclerk and partner, but Osbaldeston was ill and unable to take part. Lord Frederick was adamant that the game should go ahead and insisted 'Pay or play!' So Lambert played both men on his own and knew well how to frustrate Lord Beauclerk. He bowled wides right and left, and his Lordship lost his temper and then his wicket.

Unfortunately, Lambert's appetite for the prizes resulted in his downfall. In his day, matches were played for high stakes, and this often led to accusations of bribery and corruption. When England played Twenty-Two of Nottingham in 1818 it was said that Lambert had 'sold' the match and, in consequence, he was excluded from matches at Lord's and other great matches of the day after that year. He continued to play in minor matches in Surrey until he was nearly 60, and his last recorded match was in 1839.

The Surrey supremacy which had spanned the period of their great contests with the rest of England came to an end after the first decade of the nineteenth century. The great players, like Beldham, Robinson and the Walkers, were ageing, and there was no recognised county ground to act as a focal point and draw a side together. After 1796, for example, the matches between Surrey and England, apart from two at the Holt Ground, one at Dartford and one at Godalming, were all played at Lord's. The generous patrons had passed away, and the power of Surrey cricket was dispersed among several strong clubs like Montpelier, Richmond, Mitcham, Dorking and Godalming who took on England in the middle of the century.

Records of matches involving Surrey become sparse after 1815. There is mention of three games against England in 1829 and 1831, but

Surrey now had to have 'given' men (guest players) to bring them up to strength. Indeed, Surrey cricket's great days were over, and the County passed into something of an eclipse before reappearing brighter than ever in 1845.

SURREY COUNTY CRICKET CLUB – THE FORMATIVE YEARS

CHARLES BOX, ONE OF THE EARLIER cricket historians was amazed that 'a county like Surrey, with its vast acreage and numerous townships – a county famed for being first to give tongue to cricket, should have been for a period of nearly two centuries without sufficient centralising power and influence to claim for itself really and truly proper headquarters and a home.'

That Surrey came to find a 'truly proper headquarters and a home' was due to the Montpelier Club and the energetic treasurer of that club, Mr W. Baker.

The Montpelier Club had been founded in 1796 and was for some years the strongest club south of the Thames. The club played at the Beehive Tavern in Walworth, which had a pleasant cricket ground adjacent to it. The Beehive Tavern stood where we now find Lorrimore Square, Chapter Road, and it was not long the home of the Montpelier Club, for its position made it particularly attractive to property developers who were as rampant in the mid-nineteenth century as they are today. In the early months of 1844, the club found itself without a ground.

It was at this point that William Baker became most active. He looked towards the neighbouring Borough of Kennington, 'King's Town', the greater part of which was owned by the Duchy of Cornwall.

In 1611, James I had settled the Manor of Kennington and Vauxhall upon his eldest son, Henry, Prince of Wales, and the active interest of the Prince of Wales in Kennington has been maintained ever since and accounts for the presence of the Prince of Wales's feathers on the Surrey County Cricket Club badge.

On 8 January 1835, the Duchy of Cornwall had granted a lease of 99 years, dating from 27 January 1834, to the Otter family on a 'nursery and garden ground in extent about ten acres, called the Oval, with buildings thereon'. So The Oval became a market garden before it was used for cricket, and, it should be noted, the gasholders preceded the cricketers.

There was concern that the neighbourhood was losing areas on which cricket could be played so that when William Baker approached the Otter family with regard to converting The Oval into a cricket ground he was sympathetically received and negotiations went smoothly.

Baker was a highly-respected member of the local community, and he was able to negotiate a lease of 31 years with the trustees of the Otter family at a rent of £120, with another £20 a year tax. The Duchy of Cornwall was most happy to agree to the lease and the use of the ground for cricket, and the Duchy's register records that on 10 March 1845, permission was granted to convert the land into a subscription ground and to allow the proprietor to apply for a licence to sell refreshments on the premises.

Although work to convert the ground into an arena for cricket did not begin until March 1845, games of a serious nature were played at The Oval that summer. The original contract for turfing the ground was given to Mr M. Turtle of Clapham Road. It was for £300, and 10,000 turves were brought from Tooting Common.

While Baker was busy negotiating the lease of The Oval other members of the Montpelier Club, excited by this move, took the first steps towards the formation of Surrey County Cricket Club. The first game played at The Oval was on 13 May 1845, when W. Fould's XI lost to W. Houghton's XI in a one-innings match by four runs. John

Surrey Cricket Ground. The Oval in the middle of the nineteenth century.

Burrup was the only man on Houghton's side to reach double figures. This match was followed by a dinner, and good food, good drink and good company played an important part in the early months of the formation of the Surrey Club.

On 21 and 22 August, the Gentlemen of Surrey met the Players of Surrey, and the match was followed with dinner at The Horns Tavern. The main object of the match had been to lay the foundation stone of the new County Club, and the dinner at The Horns Tavern was presided over by Mr William Ward.

Ward remains one of the great figures of cricket history. It was he who purchased Lord's from Thomas Lord in 1825 and so saved the famous ground from property developers. Five years before this, he had hit 278 for MCC against Norfolk, and it was to Ward that Nyren dedicated his famous book, *The Young Cricketer's Tutor and Cricketers of My Time*. Ward, a director of the Bank of England, was to be as good a friend to Surrey as he had been to cricket in general when he saved Lord's.

On 22 August 1845, as soon as the meal at The Horns Tavern was over, approximately a hundred members from different Surrey clubs gathered together for a meeting. Ward was only presiding because Hon F. Ponsonby, who was connected with Surrey, was unable to be present. Denison, a friend of Ponsonby's, told the meeting that he and Ponsonby had often discussed the possibility of founding a Surrey County Club, but that they had felt that, without a headquarters, the work of such a club could not be carried on. The acquisition of The Oval had provided the necessary headquarters, for not only was it attractive for cricket, but it was also accessible by public transport from all parts of the capital.

Denison's speech, indeed the whole meeting, was reported in detail by the *Sunday Times*:

> He should, ere he sat down, propose a resolution, to which, from the feeling which was manifested around, he could not anticipate even a single dissentient voice. It was proposed to form a cricket club for the county of Surrey, the objects of which would mainly be to seek out and to bring together the playing strength of the county, with a view of placing Surrey in the prominent position it had for many years, in days long since passed, held in the cricket world. Allow him to ask why it was that Surrey had been for some time a dead county, as it were, in the public eye, with reference to the game? The reply was simple: it was because there had for several years – indeed, since the time of the late Mr Keen of Godalming – not been any gentleman or any club to bring out the play it possessed. They might not perhaps find, as before, another

Lambert; they might not meet another Saunders, nor another Searle; but he was enabled to say that Surrey now, as in former days – if its power were collected, but it happened to be at present very widely scattered – could produce a very formidable eleven. With the object, then, of providing the means of 'centralising' the strength of the county, he would propose as a resolution, 'That a Surrey Club be now formed'.

This proposition was seconded by the great Nicholas Felix who, although he had won much fame with Kent, was born in Camberwell in Surrey and had played for Surrey clubs before moving to Blackheath. The formation of a Surrey club appealed to him because cricket in general would profit by the creation of another county club. Felix was to play for Surrey and to continue to assist Kent.

The proposition was carried unanimously amid scenes of great excitement. Ward immediately proposed the toast of 'Success and Prosperity to the Surrey Club' and suggested that a committee of management be set up to make the necessary arrangements to make the club operative. He named the following as the committee: Hon F. Ponsonby, Hon S. Ponsonby, W. Bolland, J. Bonsor, C. Coltson, W. Denison, N. Felix, G. Hoare, C. H. Hoare, W. Houghton, H. Pickering and W. Pickering.

Ward also implored the Club to look for a good wicket-keeper.

They had no idea how important was the advantage of a first-rate man at that post. Such a man not only taught an excellent lesson for domestic life, but he taught a lesson in cricket: he taught a man to 'keep at home', a practice which was equally valuable in their respective points – keeping at home was a valuable ingredient to true domestic felicity, and it constantly, in cricket, made a man play properly.

The formal inauguration of the Club did not take place until after a second dinner held at the Horns Tavern on 18 October 1845, where the Hon Frederick Ponsonby (later Earl of Bessborough) presided. Some 70 men immediately enrolled as members of the Club, and William Denison became the first secretary.

Denison was already 44 years old and a slow round-arm bowler of note who had played for the Montpelier Club for some seasons. He was an enthusiast and a considerable writer on the game. His *Cricketer's Companion* was first published in 1844 and then annually until 1847, while his *Sketches of the Players*, one of the game's classics, was issued in 1846. He was on the staff of the *Sporting Magazine*.

William Strahan was elected first president of the Club and was a useful player as was Charles Coltson who had played for the

Gentlemen against the Players in 1843. George Brockwell, a left-handed batsman and left-arm bowler, was employed as a practice bowler in 1845 and later took charge of the ground until his retirement in 1862. His more famous nephew, also from Kingston-upon-Thames, was to serve the County well. Tom Sherman, a fast bowler, played for the Players' team against the Gentlemen of Surrey in August 1845, but he was not to assist the County until two years later.

Charles Hugh Hoare was the first captain of the Club. He was also the treasurer, played regularly and had the management of the team on the field. As well as Brockwell, Surrey engaged Martingell as a practice bowler. These two then were the first two great Surrey professionals.

Brockwell was 35 years old, short and stocky, 'a remarkably civil and good-tempered man' whose round-arm bowling was 'slow, twisting and very puzzling'. According to Haygarth, just before the ball left his hand, Brockwell would strike himself on the chest.

William Martingell was born in Nutfield in 1818. He was tall and slim, but powerful and one of the best bowlers in England. His quality was recognised by Fuller Pilch who drew Martingell, a shoemaker and gamekeeper, to Kent at a salary of £60 a year. He delivered the ball from a little below the shoulder and turned it from leg, and he was much influenced by Pilch for whom he had the greatest admiration. He first played for Kent in 1841 and continued to play for them until 1852, but this did not preclude him from assisting Surrey as well.

Both he and Felix were in the Surrey side which played MCC at The Oval on 25 and 26 May 1846. This was the first time that Surrey had taken the field as a county team, and they lost a low-scoring match although Martingell took nine wickets. Forty wickets fell for 194 runs, and MCC won by 48 runs. Surrey's first victory came in their second match, against Kent at The Oval exactly a month later. Martingell and Felix both played for Surrey so that the sides would be more balanced, but Arthur Hoare was the hero with an innings of 59. Surrey won by ten wickets.

Fixtures were few, for it should be remembered that the main purpose of a club was to offer practice facilities for its members, the more favoured of whom had special keys with which they could open the wicket gate at the Vauxhall end of the ground and gain easy access.

Initially, all had gone well and to the satisfaction of the members. From the outset The Oval was managed by W. Houghton, a chemist from Brixton Hill, who had been President of the Montpelier Club. In the initial euphoria his management had been accepted as giving all that could be desired, but by the beginning of the 1849 season, with the Club £70 in debt, it was apparent that all was not well and there was disagreement between management and the Club itself.

Hon Frederick Ponsonby forwarded the idea that the Club's financial crisis, which was serious enough to threaten its future existence, could be solved if six members were allowed to take out life-membership at £12 each. The idea was eagerly accepted, and Ponsonby himself (Lord Bessborough), W. Strahan, J. Cressingham, W. Herring, W. Mortimer and G. Raincock became the first six life members of Surrey County Cricket Club. Houghton, however, was antagonistic to the Club, and he was conducting affairs in a way that many found offensive. He staged walking matches, poultry shows and other events which lowered the character of the ground and which were not to the liking of those living close by.

The Duchy of Cornwall was deeply concerned about this lowering of the ground and of the offence being given to the neighbourhood and forbade certain events to take place. What had already taken place, however, had put the future of The Oval and the Surrey Club at risk. There were moves afoot to build on The Oval, and a bill was prepared by the solicitor of the Duchy of Cornwall to that effect. It was Prince Albert, acting for the young Prince of Wales, who intervened, and The Oval was saved.

The Club owed much to the Prince Consort and to John Burrup, who had succeeded Denison as secretary in 1848. His energy, strength and political sagacity took Surrey through a period of acute crisis. He realised that the only way in which Surrey cricket could survive was to rid itself of the association with Houghton. Accordingly, he applied himself to that task. Under his direction the executive resolved to play no more matches at The Oval and began negotiations for a ground near Coldharbour Lane, Brixton. Houghton realised he was beaten and was glad to come to terms. He handed over the lease to C. H. Hoare, A. Marshall and Henry Mortimer, acting on behalf of the Surrey County Club who obtained a new agreement for 21 years. This dated from 1855, the year in which John Burrup was succeeded as secretary by his twin brother William, and Surrey moved into a period of success on and off the field.

The off-the-field success was founded on the fact that the Club was moving towards leasing the ground directly from the Duchy of Cornwall, and for this they were to thank Henry Mortimer, who was to loan the £3,000 necessary to purchase the lease of The Oval. He was to succeed Charles Hoare as treasurer in 1869.

The on-the-field success was to have its lapses, but by 1852, Surrey were again able to play England on equal terms for the first time for 35 years. When the sides met at The Oval in June 1852, Surrey were strengthened by the loan of Clarke, Parr and Bickley and won by seven wickets, but in the return match at Lord's a month later, the three England players returned to their own side which also included

John Burrup, the County Secretary from 1848, who did much to ensure that Surrey continued to play at The Oval, which was threatened with development.

Haygarth, Box and Dean. England made 218 and dismissed Surrey for 196, but, with Martingell taking five for 31, England were bowled out for 101 in their second innings. Needing 124 to win, Surrey were 74 for five. Chester, who had hit 64 in the first innings, and Caffyn added 32 before Chester was caught and bowled by Grundy. Two more wickets fell quickly, but Heath stayed with Caffyn who won the match when he hit Grundy over the ropes for four. The victorious Surrey side is worth examining.

Charles Hoare had now handed over the captaincy to F. P. Miller, but Miller played in neither of the games against England in 1852. Hoare had been born at Mitcham in 1819 and was educated at Rugby at the time when Thomas Arnold was headmaster and was revitalising the public school system. One of Hoare's contemporaries at Rugby was Thomas Hughes whose *Tom Brown's Schooldays* chronicled Arnold's achievements in fictional form. Hoare's contribution to Surrey cricket was immense on the administrative side, for, as we have noted, he was one of the three guarantors who signed the lease of The Oval with the Duchy of Cornwall when control was wrested from Houghton, and he was treasurer of the Club until 1869.

Brockwell and Martingell, the first professionals, we have also noted and have mentioned a third, Tom Sherman. Sherman was another from Mitcham, a great cradle for Surrey cricketers, and was born in 1827. He had attracted the attention of the new county club when he was still young and became recognised as 'one of the fastest round-arm bowlers there has ever been'. He was also a very fine fielder and a capable batsman who was a little impatient and ever anxious to attack the bowling. Both his father and uncle had played for Surrey teams in the early part of the century. Tom Sherman ended his career with Surrey in 1870 and became coach at several leading schools, including both Eton and Harrow.

Nicholas Felix had played an enthusiastic part in the founding of the Surrey Club, but he was by then among the most famous of cricketers, and his appearance for Surrey against England in 1852 was among his last appearances in important cricket, for he was then nearing his 48th birthday. He was born in Camberwell, and his real name was Wanostrocht, for he was of Belgian extraction. He succeeded his father as Headmaster of Alfred House Academy, Camberwell, and first appeared at Lord's in 1828. His school was moved to Blackheath in 1832, and he made his debut for Kent two years later. He created the Catapulta, an ingenious bowling machine, is credited with having introduced batting gloves and wrote one of the most charming instructional books the game has known, *Felix on the Bat*, which was published a month before the first meeting at the Horns Tavern.

John Heath and James Chester, like Sherman, had both appeared for the Players of Surrey in the famous match against the Gentlemen which preceded the dinner at the Horns Tavern in 1845. Chester, from Kingston-upon-Thames, was a right-handed batsman whose son was also to play for Surrey. Heath was a wire-worker and carried out his trade near the Elephant and Castle. Born in Lambeth, he was a right-handed batsman who drew from Denison, in his *Sketches of the Players*, the most lavish of praises:

> Heath is one of those extraordinary men as a cricketer who ought to have spent his days at Lord's, and the only reason, it is presumed, why he is not there is, that he has no pretension as a bowler. He is a most brilliant hitter, and without exception the finest long stop that has been seen for perhaps the last forty years.

Daniel Day, a fast medium right-arm bowler and right-handed batsman, was another whom Denison singled out for special mention. Day was a very stocky man who was 'esteemed, not merely for his cricketing qualities, but for the singular respectable manner of his demeanour and conduct'. He came from Streatham, but he became groundsman at the South Hants Club in Southampton where he was also a publican.

Julius Caesar from Godalming was one of the first of The Oval crowd's great favourites. Short, sturdy and steady, he was one of the best batsmen of his day and excelled with shots on the leg side. A noted humorist and practical joker, he was also a very temperamental man who became very depressed when he was not doing well. He was born in 1830 and played for Surrey until 1867 while his elder brother, Fred, assisted the County from 1859 until 1862. Indeed, in 1850, a team of twelve Caesars lost to Eleven Gentlemen of Godalming at Broadwater Park.

Julius Caesar was one of the Surrey men who went to North America with Parr's team in 1859, and he toured Australia in 1863–64. He was involved in a tragic accident when out with a shooting party. His gun went off and killed one of the gamekeepers. Caesar never really recovered from the shock and he died at Godalming in 1878 aged 48.

The other great Oval favourite in the early days and a truly great player was William Caffyn. He was on the tours to North America and Australia mentioned above, and he also toured Australia with Stephenson's side in 1861–62. After his second tour of Australia, he accepted a coaching appointment in New South Wales and had much to do with raising the standard of cricket in the country. He returned to England in 1872 and played again for Surrey, but he was then past his best.

Caffyn was born in Reigate in 1828. His uncle, Walter Caffyn, had played for a Surrey side in 1844, but Caffyn's father was totally opposed to William taking up cricket as a profession, and wished him to pursue his work as a barber. Caffyn told how his father was so 'averse to my taking up cricket as a profession' that

> when I was selected to play for the Players of Surrey v the Gentlemen of Surrey at The Oval, he refused point blank to supply me with any money to get there. I managed to borrow half-a-crown, however, and received 10s and my expenses for playing in the match, so I felt quite rich when I returned home.

Caffyn took up a professional appointment at The Auberies on the Essex–Suffolk border, the home of Captain Caledon Alexander, in 1849, the first year in which he appeared for Surrey.

His talent was recognised immediately, for, the following year he made his first appearance for the Players against the Gentlemen at Lord's. Martingell, Chester and Day were also in the Players' side while Felix appeared for the Gentlemen, who were beaten by an innings. This was the only time that Daniel Day appeared in the fixture, and it is worth noting that although Felix is credited with having introduced the idea of batting gloves, it was Day who patented the first pair in 1827. He left instructions in his will that his bat, pads and walking stick should be buried with him.

Caffyn was a magnificent all-round cricketer although it is as a batsman that he is best remembered, for 'as a batsman his style was graceful to a degree'. He was free and attractive in style and, though noted for the cut, excelled with shots all round the wicket. He had strong and flexible wrists, and Lord Cobham told of how, in a country house match, Caffyn once cut one of his over-pitched deliveries through a large drum which, it had been supposed, was far enough away from the action to be safe from harm.

A neat, handsome, dapper cricketer who fielded brilliantly, Caffyn always wanted to be in the game. He bowled at medium pace, and although his bowling seemed to have no devil in it nor contain any great subtlety, he took hundreds of wickets and was Surrey's leading batsman and bowler for several seasons. He had an easy delivery and an appetite for bowling that left him only happy when he had the ball in his hands. For Caffyn, cricket was a joy, and he played by the maxim 'get runs or get out'. No wonder they loved him at The Oval.

The final member of the Surrey eleven which beat England in 1852 was Tom Lockyer. Like the other ten, he was born in Surrey. As we have seen, William Ward had suggested to the Club at the inaugural meeting that they must find a good wicket-keeper. In Lockyer, they found a great one who, for nearly a decade, had no superior in the country. He was the wicket-keeper chosen to tour North America in 1859 and to tour Australia with Parr's side in 1863–64.

The Rev T. O. Reay, a contributor to the first Surrey history, remembered Lockyer as:

. . . a tall, brawny man, with a pleasant smile on his honest countenance, with arms apparently covering most of the ground between short leg and short slip, such hands that the ball seemed bound to remain in them. Some called them 'saucepans'! To see him swoop a ball thrown up from long leg into the wicket with the left, and just 'run out' the batsman who was too confident of getting home, was a sight to be remembered. Even leg stump shooters did not come amiss to his grasp, and he really left longstop very little to do. Woe to the batsman if he took any liberty with Lockyer, who, though he was a little fond of playing to the gallery, never asked the umpire if he did not believe the man to be out. Occasionally he would lay down his gloves and bowl over the wicket for a few overs, but history does not record many successes, though he had his day, especially in wet weather. As a batsman he was generally good for runs, and was not in long before the bowler found his pitched up balls either flying over his head or to the 'on' or 'off'.

For many, Lockyer was the creator of modern wicket-keeping, for, until his time, it was customary for most wicket-keepers to ignore balls on the leg side, believing that it was the long stop's job to deal with them. Lockyer showed remarkable agility and, in Caffyn's opinion, took catches on the leg side which were miraculous and which no other 'keeper of the age would have attempted. Richard Daft confirmed him as 'the finest the world ever knew'.

Lockyer was a courageous, hard-working, tenacious cricketer with an unquenchable spirit, and he must have suffered some dreadful knocks at a time when protection was scanty and wicket-keepers stood up to quick bowlers on wickets which most would scorn to play upon today. It is said that once he suffered a badly-split finger but had a thimble made into which he could thrust two fingers, and with this guard and an adjusted glove, he kept for several matches. Lockyer was something of a solitary man, but a dedicated cricketer and gentle humoured, and the first in the line of great Surrey wicket-keepers.

From this eleven which achieved victory over England, there was to come the nucleus of a side which was to dominate all others in the late 1850s and early 1860s. The side could not really begin to prosper until the domestic problems had been sorted out. The battle with Houghton had scarred the Club, and when William Burrup succeeded his twin brother as secretary in 1855 Surrey could boast only some 230 members. To make matters worse, Stephenson, a new star in the firmament of Surrey cricket, and Julius Caesar declined to play for the County because of a disagreement so that fortunes were at a low ebb. Billy Burrup was undeterred. He was a man of unfailing good humour, geniality, zest and a little pomp and circumstance. It was the custom to present a bat to every amateur and a sovereign to every professional who hit a 50, and the presentation was always made by Billy Burrup at the steps of the pavilion and was accompanied by a speech. It was Billy Burrup who instituted the habit of champagne cups being taken to players on hot afternoons, and he himself always acted as cup-bearer. He was jealously proud of his county, and where his brother had saved, he now built. It was his drive that led to the erection of the pavilion in 1858.

By this time, Surrey's wounds had healed, and a prosperous age had begun to the extent that the Club's income quadrupled in the space of six years and the membership rose to nearly a thousand. In 1857, nine of ten matches were won, and the only defeat came at the hands of

Manchester, assisted by Wisden and John Lillywhite, and that by only three runs. The same year saw the first Gentlemen and Players fixture at The Oval, and the following year Surrey were unbeaten.

In that year, 1858, on 22 and 23 July, Surrey met England at The Oval. The England side was chosen by Parr and Wisden and included some of the finest players of the day: V. E. and J. Walker, Diver, Carpenter, Grundy, Willsher and Jackson. Surrey won by an innings and 28 runs, and the victory was commemorated by a marble plaque at The Oval. England were bowled out for 62 in their first innings with Stephenson and Caffyn bowling unchanged. Caffyn had four for 25, and Stephenson six for 34. Stephenson took six for 60 in the second innings, and Caffyn hit a magnificent 102.

In his memoirs, Caffyn recorded that he 'received the usual talent money, and £13 was collected for me besides. All the other Surrey players had a sovereign each given them, and Messrs Lane, Miller and Burbidge each a prize bat.' The Surrey Club gave the England professionals a dinner after the match, and Stephenson presented Billy Burrup with a light clay pipe on behalf of the team and in recognition of all that he had done to help raise the Club to a position of eminence.

From the side that had beaten England in 1852, Caffyn, Caesar,

The Old Surrey Eleven. Left to right: W. Mortlock, T. Lockyer, H. H. Stephenson, W. Caffyn, G. Griffith, Mr E. Dowson, Mr F. P. Miller, Mr C. G. Lane, Mr F. Burbidge, Julius Caesar and T. Sewell.

Lockyer, Sherman and Martingell remained. The newcomers were Miller, Lane, Stephenson, Burbidge, Griffith and Mortlock.

Fred Miller was not really a newcomer, for he had been captain of the eleven since 1851. As a captain, he was to be rivalled in years to come by Shuter, Fender and Surridge, but it is doubtful if any has surpassed him. He was the strongest of disciplinarians, but he never asked anyone to do what he would not do himself. He was born in Clapham, within a few miles of The Oval, and he later lived in a house near Clayton Street overlooking the ground. That he had considerable talent at his disposal is undeniable, but that he fused disparate personalities into a combination that was nigh invincible is also a fact. His side had absolute confidence in him and accepted his judgement and authority without question. He had no gentleness of manner, and he did not suffer fools gladly, but he played to win unflinchingly, and friend and foe knew it.

Miller was not intolerant, and he accepted human error, but his tactical grasp of the game was renowned, and Grundy, the Nottinghamshire and All-England player, was quoted as saying that Miller's captaincy was worth 50 runs in the field to Surrey.

As a batsman, Miller was resolute and determined rather than stylish, but very effective; and as a bowler, he was a very useful medium-pacer. He had few superiors as a fielder, and his lust for the game was infectious. Under him, Surrey became supreme; when he retired there was decline.

Miller was to be succeeded by his lieutenant Fred Burbidge who often led the side in 1858. In truth, Burbidge was one to whom the cares of captaincy were not suited. He was, however, a most courageous batsman and fielder. He could adapt his game to the needs of the moment, and he knew no fear.

No man could have greater claims of being a Surrey man than Charlton Lane, for he was born in the parsonage at Kennington which overlooked The Oval when it was still a market garden. He was in the eleven at Westminster School when he was 13 years old and won blues at Oxford for both cricket and rowing, a rare combination. He was a brilliant player of fast bowling, described as 'the model of a batsman' and, to Daft, 'one of the best amateur batsmen I ever saw'. His statistical record may seem moderate, but he entered the church when he came down from Oxford in 1860, and his active participation in cricket virtually ceased the following season, but he left the deepest of impressions on all those who saw him.

Heathfield Stephenson, William Mortlock and George Griffith were all members of the first England side that went to Australia in 1861–62. Following the success of Parr's side in North America, the catering firm of Spiers and Pond felt that a tour of Australia would be equally successful and profitable, and their agent, Mallam, set about contracting the leading professionals. He was empowered to offer £150 plus first-class travelling expenses, and he approached the players during the North *v* South game at Birmingham in September 1861. Parr and most of the northern contingent rejected the terms as inadequate, but Stephenson and most of the Surrey players, though not Caesar, accepted. This was to cause a rift between the players, the consequence of which we shall note later.

H. H. Stephenson, then, became, almost by default, the first captain of an England party to go to Australia. He was an exceedingly popular man who had first played for Surrey in 1854. He was born at Esher in 1833, was a first-rate batsman, an excellent wicket-keeper and, initially, a fine bowler of medium-pace off-breaks. When he retired from first-class cricket he coached at Uppingham and helped raise the standard of cricket at the school to a level never before attained.

If the Surrey eleven was meeting with unending success at this period, the county can also lay claim to a record which, although it has been equalled, will never be beaten. On 13 August 1855, at Shillinglee Park in Sussex, the seat of the Earl of Winterton, the Second Royal Surrey Militia met Shillinglee. The Surrey side was bowled out for nought, David Heather taking six wickets and Challen junior three while one man was run out. Shillinglee made 92, the Militia hit 106 in their second innings, and the match was left unfinished. The event is commemorated in the pavilion at The Oval.

Such happenings were, of course, insignificant to the rise of the County Club who, by 1859, were supreme in the land. If their record in 1860 fell considerably below that of the previous two seasons with just two victories, over Notts and Sussex to show for their endeavours, they contested only at the highest level and, to quote the purple passages of *Baily's Magazine*, they 'fought the good fight – the advancement of cricket, pluckily, skilfully, generously and well'.

The Gentlemen and Players fixture was now established at The Oval as well as at Lord's, and in the 1860 encounter, with Caffyn, Stephenson, Lockyer, Griffith, Caesar, Lane and Miller all playing, Robert Carpenter, the great Cambridgeshire professional, hit the ball out of the ground. This was the first six recorded at The Oval, for, at that time, a six could only be scored if the ball was actually hit out of the ground.

Carpenter played for the United All-England XI, one of the two great touring sides, and when they met the other great touring side, the reshaped All-England XI at Lord's in May 1860, Julius Caesar and Stephenson played for the All-England XI and Griffith, Caffyn, Lockyer and Mortlock were in the United All-England XI. Surrey supplied both wicket-keepers, Stephenson and Lockyer.

George Griffith was renowned as one of the great hitters of the age, probably the hardest hitter of the ball until the arrival of C. I. Thornton, and was immortalised in the line of verse:

If George Griffith gets a loose one, he will send it far away.

It was not Griffith, however, who was responsible for the victory at Hove in 1860, but Miller and 'Young Tom' Sewell, a clean hard-hitting batsman, who put on 154 for the first wicket. Sewell hit 62 and Miller 105. Surrey won by an innings. The quick bowling of Heartfield accounted for eight wickets in the match, but it was Caffyn's dismissal of Wells which caused the stir. In the first innings, Wells, playing a ball from Caffyn, broke the handle of his bat, and he was given out 'hit wicket' when the blade flew over his shoulder and landed on the stumps.

Caffyn played a considerable part in Surrey's victory over Notts at Trent Bridge ten days later. Surrey trailed by 87 on the first innings, but were magnificently rallied by Caffyn who went in with the score on 61 for four and hit 91. He was ninth out by which time the score had risen to 232. He finished the second day on 63 not out and runs were scored at the rate of 70 an hour while he was at the wicket. He then took six for 36, and Surrey won by 30 runs. He was always a wonderful man to have in a fight.

Baily's Magazine believed at the time that Caffyn's 91 was the best innings he ever played:

We have had the pleasure of witnessing Caffyn make his 102 against England, his 120 against the 16 of Southgate, and a majority of his other famous innings, and we feel convinced that for brilliant hitting and superb defence nothing he ever did surpassed the famous 91 he made in this match.

Inter-county matches were arousing more interest than they had done in the past, and *Baily's* was glad to find that for 1861, Surrey had increased their number of 'those "best of all matches" – county matches'. Sussex were not met in 1861, but Cambridgeshire, Kent and Yorkshire were added to the list.

Cambridge were among the strongest counties in England in the early 1860s, and included Carpenter, Diver, Tarrant and Hayward in their eleven. There were, on occasions, two Haywards in the side, Daniel and Thomas, the father and the uncle of one of Surrey's greatest of men.

The meeting between Cambridgeshire and Surrey at Fenner's in May 1861 aroused such interest that the Prince of Wales, later Edward VII, attended both days of the match. Caffyn hit 103 for

Surrey on the opening day, and Thomas Hayward 112 for Cambridgeshire on the second. The match was drawn.

Miller led Surrey in this game, but it seems that he and Burbidge now shared the captaincy. Burbidge was captain when Surrey beat Yorkshire by six wickets at The Oval although Miller was in the side, but Miller was captain, with Burbidge in the side, when Nottinghamshire were overwhelmed at The Oval.

In the Surrey side in this match was Edward Dowson, who had first played in the victory over Sussex at Hove the previous year. He was a hard hitter and a brilliant fielder, and he led Surrey in a few matches at the end of the decade. His son became a noted cricketer with the County.

The defeat, by 103 runs, of Nottinghamshire on 6, 7 and 8 June 1861 was a momentous one, not only because it was a meeting of the giants of the time – Notts numbered Grundy, Chatterton, Daft, Jackson and Parr in their side – but because it saw the introduction of the scorers' box at The Oval. It had been customary for the scorers to sit in the open or in a tent; now a covered box on wheels was introduced, and the box had a telegraph system for relaying the score. The score was changed in tens, as is often the case in club and village matches today.

Nottinghamshire were also beaten in the return match at Trent Bridge, for these were what Haygarth described as 'Surrey's best days'. Remarkably, they lost to Yorkshire at Sheffield by two wickets, but England were beaten at The Oval on 29, 30 and 31 July 1861 by 56 runs.

The matches between Surrey and England had a long and honourable tradition. After a lapse of 17 years they had been revived, at the instigation of Clarke of the All-England XI, in 1848 and they continued to draw attention and acclaim for many years even after county cricket had become the norm. They occasioned famous and infamous events. Among the most famous was the match in July 1859.

England were bowled out for 172, Caffyn taking five for 84. Surrey went in to face the fast bowling of Jackson and the round-the-wicket lobs of Vyell Walker. He bowled round the wicket because he had consistently knocked his knuckles on the stumps when bowling over. He varied his pace, mostly turned the ball from leg and was a dynamic fielder to his own bowling. He was one of seven brothers who were instrumental in founding Middlesex County Club in 1864, and three of them played for Surrey Club and Ground before the formation of the Middlesex Club.

Walker captured the first wicket when he bowled Mortlock, 'Old Stonewall', and the second when he had Miller caught at point. Burbidge was stumped, as was Caffyn, and Stephenson, Lockyer and Griffith were all caught at long on. Fred Caesar was taken at point,

Lane at short-leg and Martingell at mid-on. Before Wisden caught Martingell, Julius Caesar had been dropped, and Vyell Walker, who was in a state of high excitement, had despaired of capturing the final wicket.

With all ten wickets to his credit, Walker now proceeded to hit 108 with a five and six fours. It was the first time in the history of the game that a man had taken all ten wickets and scored a century in the same match, and it happened at The Oval where so much of the game's history was to be shaped. Surrey can look back on the game with no particular pride, for, facing the task of scoring of 432 to win, they were bowled out for 39 – Jackson six for 21, Walker four for 17.

They gained revenge in the *cripple match* of 1861 – so called because so many of the participants were suffering from ailments. Caffyn recalled that his 'knee gave way again in this match; Tom Sewell put his thumb out; Mr Burbidge had his finger knocked up; and Mudie was badly hurt by Jackson'. On top of this, Stephenson was most unwell with a stomach disorder, Mortlock had an injured thumb and V. W. Walker was very lame with a damaged knee-cap.

Surrey were 10 for three, but Dowson and Caffyn put on 132, and, as we have noted, the County went on to win by 56 runs. This was the last time that Surrey were really opposed to a full-strength England side, for, the following season, Parr and several of his northern colleagues refused to play in the match because Stephenson and his Surrey contingent had a few months earlier accepted the terms to tour Australia that they had rejected. That was not to be the only point of contention in the 1862 match.

Grundy and Willsher began England's innings with a stand of 124. Caffyn had Daft caught behind by Lockyer for nought, but Hayward and Carpenter, the Cambridgeshire pair, put on 153 for the fourth wicket. Hayward hit 117, and England finally reached 503. It was not an innings without criticism, for it lasted until 5.30 pm on the second day (play was from 12 noon to 7.00 pm with an hour's dinner break at 3.00 pm which sometimes became extended through indulgence) and Grundy's 95 occupied four hours and ten minutes, very slow for the age.

The Surrey innings began in sensational manner. Humphrey fell to V. E. Walker, who was leading the England side, for nought. The other opening bowler was Edgar Willsher of Kent. Willsher, it seems, had been told by umpire John Lillywhite that he would be no-balled if Lillywhite ever stood in a match in which Willsher bowled. Willsher had believed him to be joking. The dissension concerned Willsher's action. Bowlers had raised their arms higher and higher with the years in an effort to get the ball to lift and to turn to the off. In 1828, the hand was allowed to be raised to elbow level. In 1835, it became legal to raise it to shoulder level. Even so, there were persistent law-breakers who went unreproved.

Willsher bowled the first two of his four-ball overs without comment, but umpire Lillywhite called no-ball on the first ball of the third over, which was cut for four, and on the next six deliveries. At this point, Willsher flung down the ball and marched from the field. He was followed by the other professionals in the England side who departed before Walker, a most popular and respected man, and Hon C. G. Lyttelton could interpose.

The two amateurs and the Surrey batsmen, Mortlock and Burbidge, stayed on the field with the umpires, Tom Sewell senior and Lillywhite, until 'time' was called. A crowd of 5,000 had watched these events in something of a bemused state, and the ground was swamped when 'time' was called.

Willsher eventually apologised for leaving the ground, but Lillywhite refused to continue as umpire if he was not to be allowed to enforce the law as it stood. Street replaced him on the third day, and the match was drawn. Once again, Surrey and The Oval had been part of cricket history.

The confusion over the law was ended on 10 June 1864, when, following the match between Oxford University and MCC at Lord's, the members met in the tennis court and passed a new law which abolished the restriction on the height of the hand at the point of delivery. Sadly, the northern players whose relations with Surrey were already strained because of the dispute over the tour to Australia believed that the no-balling of Willsher had been conceived by the Surrey committee who had deliberately engaged John Lillywhite for the purpose. The vendetta continued, effectively ending matches between Surrey and a strong England eleven.

There were happier aspects for the County in 1862. In March, in Melbourne, Surrey had taken on The World. The six Surrey players in Stephenson's touring party were joined by five men, Cosstick, Bryant, Blanchard, Elliott and J. Christy, all of whom were said to be qualified for the County, and lost by six wickets to The World, a side consisting of the other members of the England party augmented by Victorians.

When Surrey played the North at The Oval at the beginning of June the name of H. Jupp appeared on the team sheet for the first time. He was to create no sensations in his first few matches, but within a year he had impressed The Oval faithful and all who saw him. For the time being Caffyn remained the hero. He took six for 42 and seven for 7 when Kent were routed at Canterbury, and he followed this with eight for 25 and two for 28 against Yorkshire at Sheffield and still finished on the losing side. His time with Surrey was drawing to its close. The following season, 1863, when Mortlock, Burbidge and

Griffith hit centuries, and Jupp reached his first 50, was, in effect, Caffyn's last for Surrey although, as we have said, he was to return nearly a decade later and play a handful of games with little success.

In 1863–64, Caffyn went with Parr's team to Australia, as did Mortlock, Julius Caesar and Lockyer, and remained there in a coaching capacity. His departure coincided with the beginning of a new era in English cricket when matches between counties became more important than ever before and when new giants of the game began to appear. The age of W. G. Grace and over-arm bowling was at hand, and the formative years of Surrey County Cricket Club were at an end.

HIGH POINT AND LEAN YEARS

THE YEAR OF 1864 IS SIGNIFICANT in the history of the game, not only for the legalisation of over-arm bowling, but also because it is the year from which we date first-class cricket, the year in which the County Championship, unofficially, came into being, and the year in which W. G. Grace appeared in an important match for the first time. In 1864, the number of first-class counties was increased from six to eight, Hampshire and Middlesex being the newcomers, and *Wisden's Cricketers' Almanack* was published for the first time.

The existence of a County Championship is, of course, debatable, for the championship was in the minds of the sporting press rather than in any official recognition. Indeed, the press could not always agree on who was the leading county, but, in 1864, there was no disagreement. Of the eight county matches they played, Surrey won six and drew two, a record unapproached by any other county. Outside county fixtures, they beat Oxford University and England and had the better of a draw with the South. No other side played as many as eleven matches. Hampshire played nine and lost them all. Sussex played eight, won five and were beaten by Surrey and Middlesex.

Surprisingly, the two drawn county matches were the first on Surrey's programme. Sussex were the first visitors to The Oval and scored 328 and 101 for two. Surrey hit 291, and there was no play on the second day. The highlight of the Surrey innings was George Griffith's knock of 86 not out. He was to prove the outstanding all-rounder of the summer, playing in 17 matches (he played for the Players, the South and the Players of the South as well as Surrey), hitting 489 runs, taking 69 wickets and making 26 catches, more than anyone else in the country.

Born at Ripley in 1833, Griffith was, by 1864, the most powerful hitter in the game as well as being one of the quicker bowlers, yet not averse to contrasting his round-arm quick bowling with some telling slow lobs. A baker by trade, he had joined the staff at The Oval in 1857, the year after he had left the Priory Park Club in Chichester, but he had left Surrey at the end of the 1863 season because of a disagreement over terms. This did not preclude him from playing for the County, and he continued to assist them until 1872. It was his six for 32 which did much to bring Surrey their first victory of the season, against Oxford University at The Oval in mid-June, but on the three days before that game, Surrey had drawn their second county match, at Sheffield.

Miller was not in the Surrey side for this game. Indeed, he played only twice in the season, and the County was led by Burbidge, but he, too, was absent from this match as were Dowson, Caesar and Lockyer. Surrey were bowled out for 195, and Yorkshire closed the first day on 36 for one. Yorkshire took a first innings lead of 41 on the second day, and Surrey ended at 19 for no wicket with Jupp on 12 and Humphrey 7. On the last day, the pair took their stand to 159 which was the highest opening partnership of the season and a Surrey first-wicket record. Humphrey was out for 74, but Jupp went on to make 110, a maiden century.

Henry Jupp was a Dorking man, and while Mortlock was 'Old Stonewall', Harry Jupp was 'Young Stonewall'. He was a powerfully built, short man, who specialised in back play and who had a tenacious and studious approach to the game. He worked his way up through the ranks to play for Surrey, and by the middle of the 1860s he was one of the finest and most reliable professional batsmen in the game. He was to form with Thomas Humphrey the first of the great Surrey opening partnerships.

Humphrey, born in 1839, was two years older than Jupp. He was another to come from Mitcham, the town which has produced so many outstanding Surrey cricketers. His first professional engagement was with Enfield in Middlesex, but he was engaged at The Oval in 1862, the year he first played for the County. With Julius Caesar troubled by gout, he became Mortlock's opening partner, but it was his partnership with Jupp which became renowned. Like Jupp, he was studious in his approach to the game, but his off-side play was free flowing, and he was one of those batsmen who appeared to have so much time to play his shots. He earned the nickname of the 'Pocket Hercules' due to the power which came from so short a frame.

Jupp and Humphrey represented the younger element in a side which was ageing and for which 1864 was the pinnacle of achievement. If one match can be chosen as the outstanding match of that *annus mirabilis*, it is the match at The Oval when Surrey gained their first win of the season in a county match.

The opponents were the formidable Notts side. Burbidge won the toss, and Surrey batted. John Jackson, fast round-arm; James Grundy, another fast round-arm, able to break the ball from the off; George Wootton, medium-pace left-arm; and Cris Tinley, lobs, constituted a menacing attack, but after the early loss of Jupp, Surrey treated them with contempt. Tom Humphrey and Mortlock added 118 for the second wicket, the only century second-wicket stand of the season, and Stephenson and Dowson added 92 for the fifth wicket, the second highest stand of the season for that wicket. Just as Notts might have thought their punishment was over, Lockyer joined Stephenson in a seventh-wicket stand of 123, which was a Surrey record.

Interestingly, this was only the second highest stand of the season, for Stephenson and Mortlock put on 169 for the seventh wicket in the Players versus Gentlemen match at The Oval in June.

Both Mortlock and Stephenson enjoyed fine seasons. Mortlock scored more runs, 855, than any other batsman in the country and was one of eight Surrey batsmen to feature in the top 20 of the first-class batting averages. Mortlock was a stylish batsman, useful slow bowler and brilliant long stop. Son of Thomas Mortlock, one of Surrey's early umpires, he was born in Clayton Street next to The Oval and lived most of his life in the vicinity. He ran a cricket outfitter's shop at Waterloo Station for some years.

Stephenson was the only batsman to hit two centuries in 1864, the other being for the Players at The Oval. He had ceased to bowl as much as he had done in the past, and, of course, kept wicket only when Lockyer emerged from behind the stumps, but he was still a fine all-round cricketer. He was an important figure in the All-England XI and is credited with the first hat-trick in cricket history – at Sheffield for the All-England XI against Hallam and Staveley in 1858. For taking three wickets with successive deliveries, Stephenson was presented with a hat by his team-mates.

Against Nottinghamshire at The Oval in 1864, he hit a century, took a wicket and went behind the stumps when Lockyer was brought on to bowl in the second innings. Nottinghamshire ended the second day on 269 for seven, but Alfred Shaw was to add only three on the last morning to his overnight score, and the visitors had to follow-on. The law in operation at the time was that a side who were trailing by 100 runs or more on the first innings had to follow-on. The matter was not in the hands of the captains.

Obviously, Surrey must have felt that they needed a fresh approach, and Lockyer joined the attack when Notts batted for a second time to produce one of the best bowling performances of his career. Remarkably, Lockyer finished second in the Surrey bowling averages for the season with 15 wickets at 14.46 runs each, and he was also the leading wicket-keeper in the country with 47 dismissals: 32 caught, 15 stumped.

The magnificent victory over Notts at The Oval which, at the time, provided a wicket far better than the one that was being provided at Lord's, was followed by the rout of Kent and by an innings victory over Sussex at Hove. In this match, Julius Caesar hit 132 not out, the highest score of the season.

The return match with Nottinghamshire at Trent Bridge was in complete contrast to the first meeting. Griffith took eleven for 84 in the match, and Surrey were left to make 62 to win. At 40 for one, all seemed well, but five wickets fell for five runs, and when last man Shepherd joined Dowson four runs were still needed. Shepherd hit a single, and Dowson struck the winning boundary.

The heights that Surrey reached in 1864 were not to be attained again for several years. The side which dominated all other counties in 1864 was a mature one, and in the next two seasons it was to move into a period of decline.

There were reasons other than age for the decline of the side. There was a weakness in bowling which leaned heavily on Griffith, and there was a problem over the captaincy. In 1865, Dowson was the only amateur to play with any regularity. Burbidge, nominally the captain, and Miller, the two seniors, played in only four matches between them. Dowson took over the captaincy in 1866, but he held the post for just a year, and Surrey were to have six official captains in the space of seven seasons.

Financially, they were the most affluent and best-supported county in the country, and in spite of their lack of success, they produced moments and players of greatness. In 1865, Thomas Humphrey hit 1,223 runs, the first man to reach four figures in a first-class season. Jupp scored 963 and followed this in 1866 with 1,140 runs. Jupp's career was to prosper with the years, but Tom Humphrey's form was never quite to fulfil the promise of those early years.

The great side began to break up, not simply as Burbidge and the great Fred Miller faded from the season, but as Lockyer ended his career and gave way to Pooley.

Edward Pooley was born in Richmond in 1838, but when he first approached Surrey for an engagement he lied about his age for fear that the Club would think him too old. He played for the colts in 1861 and was taken on as a bowler at The Oval the following season, for, as yet, he had given no indication that he was a wicket-keeper of outstanding ability. He played for Middlesex in their inaugural season, 1864, but Surrey reclaimed him in 1865 when, in fact, he appeared for both counties.

He had shown with Middlesex what a capable wicket-keeper he was, and Lockyer had been quick to recognise his talents. In his *Talks with Old English Cricketers*, A. W. Pullin related that Pooley had told him:

My introduction to wicket-keeping would be about 1863. Old Tom Lockyer's hands were bad, and the ground being very fiery he could not take his usual place behind the sticks. Mr F. P. Miller, the Surrey captain, was in a quandary as to who should relieve him, so I, saucy-like as usual, went up to him and said, 'Mr Miller, let me have

SURREY *v* NOTTINGHAMSHIRE

Played at The Oval, Kennington, 4, 5 and 6 July 1864

SURREY WON BY 10 WICKETS

SURREY	FIRST INNINGS		SECOND INNINGS	
T. Humphrey	b Wootton	75	not out	3
H. Jupp	b Jackson	6	not out	1
W. Mortlock	c Tinley b Wootton	48		
H. H. Stephenson	c Bignall b Grundy	119		
G. Griffith	c R. Daft b Tinley	17		
E. Dowson	b R. Daft	43		
*F. Burbidge	c Jackson b R. Daft	13		
†T. Lockyer	not out	108		
W. Humphrey	b Tinley	16		
T. Sewell, jnr	b Jackson	1		
W. Shepherd	b Jackson	2		
Extras	b 12, lb 7, w 1	20		0
Total		468	(for no wkt)	4

1st inns: 1-17, 2-135, 3-146, 4-188, 5-280, 6-296, 7-419, 8-456, 9-461

BOWLING	O	M	R	W		O	M	R	W
Jackson	62	20	98	3					
Grundy	28	8	61	1		0.3	0	2	0
Bignall	14	3	40	0					
Tinley	36	5	90	2					
Wootton	25	7	52	2		1	0	2	0
Oscroft	33	14	34	0					
R. Daft	22	7	36	2					
Shaw	18	5	37	0					

NOTTINGHAMSHIRE	FIRST INNINGS		SECOND INNINGS	
C. Daft	b Griffith	18	(7) b Lockyer	4
C. Brampton	c and b Griffith	20	(1) c Sewell b Lockyer	82
W. Oscroft	b Shepherd	28	c and b Stephenson	2
R. Daft	c W. Humphrey b Shepherd	56	(5) run out	29
T. Bignall	b Griffith	49	(4) lbw b Mortlock	20
*Alfred Shaw	c Shepherd b Mortlock	64	b Lockyer	6
J. Grundy	b Mortlock	21	(8) c Burbidge b Lockyer	21
R. C. Tinley	b Mortlock	8	(10) c Dowson b Lockyer	5
G. Wootton	not out	13	(2) b Sewell	7
†S. Biddulph	c Lockyer b Mortlock	1	(11) not out	1
J. Jackson	st Lockyer b Mortlock	0	(9) c and b Lockyer	3
Extras	b 2, lb 3	5	b 1, lb 3, w 4	8
Total		283		188

1st inns: 1-26, 2-53, 3-89, 4-164, 5-190, 6-228, 7-245, 8-277, 9-283
2nd inns: 1-30, 2-50, 3-97, 4-137, 5-148, 6-156, 7-161, 8-169, 9-185

BOWLING	O	M	R	W		O	M	R	W
Griffith	68	14	113	3		36	9	56	0
Shepherd	23	10	38	2		5	1	11	0
Mortlock	37	5	82	5		13	2	35	1
Sewell	13	4	24	0		12	5	15	1
W. Humphrey	4	0	19	0					
Stephenson	4	2	2	0		8	1	19	1
Lockyer						20	7	44	6

Umpires: G. Chatterton and E. Willsher

*Captain; †Wicket-keeper

a try.' 'You? What do you know about wicket-keeping? Have you ever kept wicket at all?' was Mr Miller's remark. 'No, never, but I should like to try,' I replied. 'Nonsense,' said he, when just at that moment H. H. Stephenson came up and remarked, 'Let the young 'un have a go, sir.' Mr Miller thereupon relented. I donned the gloves, quickly got two or three wickets, and became Lockyer's successor.

So began the career of one of the world's greatest wicket-keepers who, during the course of his career, which lasted until 1883, broke both thumbs and every finger of each hand, for he stood up to all bowlers, so that his hands were described at the end of his career as 'mere lumps of deformity'. A story is told of how he left the field at Lord's one day and staggered into the pavilion with three teeth knocked out. He was confronted by Jem Mace, the famous prize-fighter, who said to him: 'Pooley, I would rather stand up against any man in England for an hour than take your place behind the stumps for five minutes.'

Pooley played in Lockyer's last match. It was at The Oval in August 1866, and Middlesex beat Surrey by an innings and 70 runs. All eleven Surrey players bowled. Pooley had two stumpings and he caught and bowled Howitt; Lockyer had one stumping.

Lockyer left cricket to become a publican, first at the Prince Albert and then at the Sheldon Arms in his native Croydon. He was a good and kindly man, but he was not destined to enjoy a long life in his new occupation. He was suffering from tuberculosis, and three days before Christmas, 1869, he sat down in his chair at the Sheldon Arms and died. He was 43.

His successor, Ted Pooley, was soon to establish himself in the record books. In July 1868, Sussex came to The Oval and met Surrey on a wicket of doubtful character. In his *Companion*, Lillywhite commented:

> Sussex were the favourites at starting, as Griffith was *hors de combat*, and Southerton's dangerous assault was turned against his quondam allies, on this occasion. The wickets were not up to the usual standard of excellence, they were pitched outside the ground, artificially watered, and were as hard as a turnpike road.

Sussex won the toss and batted. By the end of the first day they had lost two of their second innings wickets, 22 wickets having fallen in the day. Southerton and James Lillywhite junior had done the damage for Sussex while John Bristow, a left-arm medium-pace bowler from Esher, produced the best bowling performance of his career to give Surrey a first innings lead of 28.

Sussex entered the second day 19 runs ahead, and they looked as if they had taken control of the game when another 23 were added before the third wicket fell, but there was a middle order collapse, and Surrey were left with the task of scoring 101 to win. This time it was Tom Sewell and James Street who were the most successful of the Surrey bowlers. Street was a fast-medium bowler who took some time to establish himself in the side, but who was to serve the County faithfully for many years and who was to open the attack with Southerton for several seasons.

The steadiness of Jupp and Mortlock proved decisive in bringing Surrey victory by seven wickets, but when all else in this match is long forgotten, the wicket-keeping of Pooley will be remembered. With six dismissals in each innings, he established a world record which has remained intact for 120 years and has been equalled only in Australia, by Tallon in 1938–39 and by Taber in 1968–69. Curiously, the closest any wicket-keeper in England has got to Pooley's record was in 1964 when, at Hove, Arnold Long of Surrey caught eleven Sussex batsmen.

Baily's Magazine lavished high praise on Pooley, but also made reference to his gamesmanship:

> The wicket-keeping of Pooley has been something marvellous, and we do not believe that even Lockyer in his best time was equal to him. It is to be regretted that being so good he should persist in the absurd tricks which gain him applause at The Oval.

Attention was very much focused on The Oval where, in 1867, Surrey were said to have the 'weakest' of teams but, *Baily's* believed,

> ... plenty of money and a magnificent ground. All that is wanted is an infusion of young blood into the somewhat elderly team that recently has buffeted against misfortune. The county of Caffyn and Lockyer and Mortlock will surely produce players not unworthy of those heroes.

Paradoxically, the revitalisation that came to Surrey came from a mature player, and not from a youngster. In his comment on the Surrey-Sussex game, Lillywhite referred to Southerton as turning against 'his quondam allies'. Southerton, born in Sussex in 1827, had played for Surrey in 1854 and 1855, but he had not bowled at that time. He subsequently represented both Sussex and Hampshire, but reappeared in the Surrey eleven in 1867 at the age of 39. He was by now an off-break bowler of considerable merit, arguably the first great spin bowler. He was a close student of the game and bowled with a cunning that made him the most formidable of opponents. He was also backed by a brilliant wicket-keeper, and the Pooley-Southerton combination became renowned and feared.

SURREY *v* SUSSEX

Played at The Oval, Kennington, 6 and 7 July 1868

SURREY WON BY 7 WICKETS

SUSSEX	FIRST INNINGS		SECOND INNINGS	
★C. H. Smith	c Pooley b Bristow	5	not out	47
C. Payne	c Pooley b Bristow	17	c Pooley b Bristow	17
Hon F. G. Pelham	lbw b Sewell	5	b Bristow	2
James Lillywhite	c Pooley b Bristow	32	st Pooley b Street	23
W. Greenhill	st Pooley b Bristow	15	b Sewell	3
H. R. J. Charlwood	c Pooley b Bristow	7	c Pooley b Sewell	0
H. Killick	c Pooley b Bristow	6	c Pooley b Sewell	2
G. Wells	c Street b Sewell	1	st Pooley b Sewell	5
C. H. Ellis	c Jupp b Bristow	4	b Sewell	0
J. Southerton	b Sewell	0	st Pooley b Street	9
H. Stubberfield	not out	4	c Nightingale b Street	9
Extras	b 1, lb 1	2	b 8, lb 3	11
Total		98		128

1st inns: 1-7, 2-16, 3-40, 4-69, 5-86, 6-87, 7-90, 8-90, 9-90
2nd inns: 1-30, 2-37, 3-70, 4-77, 5-77, 6-83, 7-87, 8-97, 9-114

BOWLING	O	M	R	W	O	M	R	W
Sewell	26.2	10	51	3	38	14	61	5
Bristow	26	8	45	7	20	8	29	2
Street					22	15	19	3
Nightingale					4	1	8	0

SURREY	FIRST INNINGS		SECOND INNINGS	
T. Humphrey	c and b Southerton	8	c Smith b Stubberfield	13
H. Jupp	c Southerton b Lillywhite	14	not out	37
†E. Pooley	c Ellis b Lillywhite	15	c Greenhill b Lillywhite	10
H. H. Stephenson	c Charlwood b Southerton	37	run out	18
W. Mortlock	c Greenhill b Lillywhite	15	not out	24
J. Bristow	c Payne b Stubberfield	0		
J. W. Noble	b Southerton	8		
★C. Calvert	c Wells b Lillywhite	13		
T. Sewell, jnr	lbw b Southerton	0		
T. Nightingale	not out	2		
J. Street	b Lillywhite	14		
Total		126	(for 3 wkts)	102

1st inns: 1-17, 2-27, 3-38, 4-80, 5-86, 6-97, 7-102, 8-104, 9-110
2nd inns: 1-15, 2-40, 3-63

BOWLING	O	M	R	W	O	M	R	W
Southerton	34	7	80	4	6	0	22	0
Lillywhite	38	19	37	5	26	10	43	1
Stubberfield	5	0	9	1	22	9	37	1

Umpires: W. H. Luck and E. Willsher

Pooley's 12 victims remains a first-class record.

★Captain; †Wicket-keeper

There were no strict qualification rules in the 1860s and Southerton appeared for three counties in one season. A week before playing for Sussex against Surrey in 1868, he had played for Surrey against Yorkshire and against Oxford University. In June 1873, the rules on qualification were introduced and ratified by the county representatives and MCC, and they were based on birth, two years' residence or family home. Southerton, 'the man of many counties', settled on Surrey, for he was landlord of The Cricketers in Mitcham and was known as the 'Mitcham Figaro'.

He took 100 wickets in a season ten times, and, in 1870, took 210 wickets at 14.63 runs each. He was, of course, involved in many notable matches. On 14 May 1872, he took four for 5 and seven for 28 as MCC were bowled out for 16 and 71, and Surrey, 49 and 39 for five, won the match in a day. Three years later, again at Lord's, he was instrumental in ending another match in a single day. Playing for the South against the North, he took the first nine wickets to fall, at a personal cost of 30 runs. The last man, Morley, was run out by W. G. Grace. When the North batted a second time, 33 in arrears, Southerton took seven for 22. Six years before this, in 1869, he had become the first man in the history of the game to take four wickets in five balls (although one account gave it as four in six). He was playing for Surrey against Lancashire at The Oval and bowled Hornby and Wright with successive deliveries. In his next over, he bowled Head and Hardcastle with consecutive balls.

In spite of possessing Southerton, the best bowler in England; Jupp, the best professional batsman; Pooley, the best wicket-keeper; and having in Strachan a most able captain and outstanding fielder, Surrey languished throughout the late 1860s and into the 1870s. George Strachan had been captain of Cheltenham College and had played for Gloucestershire. He had the makings of a fine all-rounder, and he was an astute leader who knew the game well, but he was able to captain the side for only three seasons out of four towards the end of the 1870s, and even then irregularly. Nor were the problems confined to those of captaincy, for The Oval seemed to attract controversy on several occasions.

The argument over the no-balling of Willsher by Lillywhite in 1862 we have already discussed, but there was another uproar three years later. It occurred in a late season match when Eighteen of Surrey were playing a United South of England Eleven at The Oval. There are various accounts of the match, but the main argument revolved around the dismissal of Jupp. He had proved obdurate, and, in an attempt to get him out, E. M. Grace resorted to lobs. He threw one delivery some 15 yards in the air, and Jupp hit it for two. E. M. Grace threw the next ball up even higher, and Jupp, believing it would fall behind the wicket, ignored it. The ball landed on top of the middle stump, and Jupp was out. This precursor of *Spedegue's dropper* was not to the liking of the crowd who hissed and booed and became very ugly indeed. The match was held up for about three-quarters of an hour, and E. M. Grace took a stump in his hand and said to the crowd surrounding him: 'The very first man who touches me will get the middle stump on his head'.

More seriously, the split between the Surrey Club and some of the northern professionals continued. Occasioned by the Surrey men accepting the terms to tour Australia and fuelled by the no-balling of Willsher, the dissension reached a height when Surrey beat Nottinghamshire by one wicket at The Oval in 1865, and the Notts men were incensed at umpiring decisions which had gone against them. So angry were the exchanges that neither Nottinghamshire nor Yorkshire played Surrey the following season.

It is likely that one of the causes of the rift between the parties was that the Surrey professionals were treated far better than those at other counties and were well paid, but in spite of the County's generosity, the results remained very disappointing.

If this was a depressing period for Surrey cricket, it was punctuated by moments of excitement. In 1876, Surrey and Middlesex tied a splendid match at The Oval just as they had done on the same ground eight years earlier. The 1868 match was the first tied match between two counties since the establishment of the wider county programme and first-class cricket in 1864.

The Oval in 1868 was described as 'the best public ground then in England – a light soil, drying quickly, good wickets, good light and plenty of space', and the match against Middlesex was one of high drama. The visitors had reached 111 for six and were batting one man short, as Halliwell had not arrived in time to bat, when James Street had Green caught with the last ball of one over and Vyell Walker and Howitt taken with the first two balls of the next over. This was the first hat-trick to be performed for Surrey and gave Street a permanent place in the County's history, fitting for a man who bowled many thousand balls in 15 years and was said to be so accurate that only once did he bowl a wide.

Although Middlesex had made a mere 112, they still gained a first innings lead of 19. Southerton produced one of his fine spells in the second inings, taking seven for 82, and Surrey were left needing 187 to win. Humphrey and Jupp put on 90 for the first wicket, and at 185 for seven, Surrey looked certain of victory, but two wickets fell for one run, and when the last man came to the wicket the scores were level.

The Middlesex hero had been Rutter, who had taken six wickets, but when Vyell Walker saw who the last Surrey batsman was he took

off Rutter and brought on the veteran professional Tom Hearne.
Rutter was in agreement with the move.

There was no fear of his bowling a loose ball, but it would be one
that the batsman must either play or lose his wicket. It was an
intensely exciting moment. The fieldsmen were all drawn up to
save the one – the crowd standing round in breathless silence
awaiting the result. Tom Hearne was equal to the occasion, poor
Roberts was not, and his stumps went flying at the first ball. No one
can realise the strain of cricket unless he has gone through such an
experience. The excitement on the ground was tremendous – it was
better than a win.

Poor Fred Roberts – he was a 20-year-old colt, and this was the
fourth and last match of his brief career.

For Surrey, a tie would have been most welcome at the beginning
of the 1870 season when the County established a most dismal record
by losing its first twelve matches, and only two of these by narrow
margins. In August, they rallied with wins over Middlesex,
Lancashire, Kent, Sussex and Notts. It was little comfort; earlier in the
season members had draped in black the tablet which commemorated
past glories.

Southerton took 113 wickets, 210 in all matches; Pooley and Jupp
completed 1,000 runs in all games, but nobody hit a century for
Surrey; and the reason for the August resurgence was the arrival of a
fast bowler, Walter Anstead, but his career was to be a short one, and
Surrey still searched for inspiration.

Surrey cricket was not without its moments of idiosyncrasy. It has
ever been a county rich in character and the bizarre. In July 1868, the
match between Surrey and Lancashire at The Oval was abandoned for
an hour because of the intense heat, and in the return at Old Trafford,
play was suspended because of a swarm of bees.

Surrey's propensity for record-making was again in evidence at
Thornton Heath, in 1867, when the home side were bowled out for
nought by Broad Green of Croydon, who then lost three wickets
before they scored a run. They were eventually out for 67 and won by
an innings and 18 runs.

Surrey batsmen did not always have to be bowled out. They
sometimes surrendered of their own accord. In the early, dark months
of 1870, as the defeats mounted, Surrey met MCC at The Oval, and,
facing a total of 191, they were 51 for seven. At this stage of the game,
Southerton cut a ball hard into the ground from where it bounced into
the hands of W. G. Grace at point. Southerton believed he had been
caught and left the wicket. Neither of the umpires, nor the fielders,
thought he was out, and Grace did not claim the catch, but Southerton

43

walked, and nothing could induce him to return. It was an action typical of the man, and he is recorded for immortality in the Surrey score-book as:

J. Southerton, retired, thinking he was caught, 0

That Southerton's magnificent career should coincide with one of the leanest periods in the Club's history is one of the great mysteries of cricket, but it would seem to emphasise that one great bowler, one great batsman and a great wicket-keeper are less than is needed to bring success, although they certainly brought honour.

Jupp and Southerton both played in the first Test match between England and Australia at Melbourne in March 1877. Jupp scored 63 and 4, and Southerton took three for 61. It was only later that the match was designated as the first Test match, for it began as James Lillywhite's Professional Touring XI versus the Grand Combined Melbourne and Sydney XI. Surrey should have had three players in this historic match, for Pooley was the chosen wicket-keeper of the party. Unfortunately, he had been detained in New Zealand from where the side had returned just prior to the Test.

In Christchurch, the side had played Eighteen of Canterbury, and, in a bar, on the eve of the match, Pooley had offered a local, Ralph Donkin, that he would take £1 to one shilling for every individual score of the local team that he gave correctly. Donkin fell for the trick, and Pooley then bet that each of the eighteen would fail to score. This is just what the majority of them did, and Pooley claimed £1 for each nought. Donkin refused to pay, saying he had been cheated, and a fight ensued. Pooley was later arrested and charged with assault and malicious damage. He was later acquitted and treated like something of a hero, but he had missed his one and only chance of playing Test cricket.

He had been a handsome man, not tall, but neat and tidy with longish, curly hair and slight whiskers, but he coped with cricket better than he coped with life. He suffered from rheumatic fever, but he was also his own worst enemy, and drink and gambling took their toll. Genial, likeable, he fell upon bad times and died in the workhouse in Lambeth, but he had served Surrey well until 1883 and ended his career with more than 850 dismissals to his credit.

When Southerton took the field in the first Test he was 49 years 119 days old, and he remains the oldest player to make a Test debut. Four players, W. G. Grace, Rhodes, Ironmonger and George Gunn, have played Test cricket when they were older than Southerton, but no other man has made his debut at such an advanced age. Southerton was something of a late developer, and his craft and cunning as a spinner matured with age. Stocky and strong, with thoughtful twinkling eyes, he played until 1879, after which he was appointed superintendent of the ground bowlers at The Oval. His term of office was brief for he died on 16 June 1880, some months short of his 53rd birthday:

> A conscientious worker always, a strict devotion to duty in all probability hastened his end. Though far from well, he would continue to carry out his duties in spite of gentle remonstrances. In doing this he caught a chill, with the result that Surrey cricket lost a loyal supporter and the club an honest and willing worker. It was my privilege to see a good deal of Southerton in those days. While always civil, he was independent as well as frank and fearless in his opinions. A fine judge of cricket, and with more than ordinary intelligence, his views on the game and its exponents were most instructive and reliable. A thoroughly respectable, self-reliant, good sort was James Southerton.

The writer of this appreciation was Charles William Alcock, JP, to whom Surrey, in particular, and sport, in general, owe an immeasurable debt. Educated at Harrow, he did not win a place in the School Eleven, and his cricket was restricted to club cricket for sides like Harrow Wanderers, Gentlemen of Essex and Incogniti, although he did once captain France against Germany in a match at Hamburg for some unknown reason. In *Scores and Biographies*, which was initially financed by the old Surrey skipper F. P. Miller, Haygarth describes him as 'a steady bat, a fair change fast bowler, and an excellent long stop or long field'. If his attainment at cricket was moderate, his skill at soccer was outstanding. He led England against Scotland in 1875, and it was under his leadership that Wanderers dominated the early years of the FA Cup. More than any other man, he shaped and made the game in England, and he became honorary secretary of the Football Association in 1867. He was later secretary and a vice-president. His close association with Surrey cricket began in 1872.

Billy Burrup, who had done so much good work, had begun to find the task of running both a powerful county cricket club and a prosperous business in the city too onerous. It was felt that the time had come to appoint a paid secretary, a man who would not only administer the Club, but who could also come to terms with the economic necessities of the time. The man chosen was C. W. Alcock, who had the strong backing of V. E. Walker, and at the meeting and dinner of the Committee on 6 April 1872, at the Bridge House Hotel, London Bridge, where the Club's meetings were held at that time, Alcock was formally appointed as Burrup's successor.

Billy Burrup's service to the County was not at an end, for, a year later, he was one of those who successfully obtained the Otter family's last interest in the lease of The Oval and negotiated the lease directly with the Duchy of Cornwall, thereby ending the worries as to the future of Surrey cricket. The cost was £3,000, and the money was found by Henry Mortimer, the treasurer, who was repaid by means of debentures.

When Alcock took over as secretary the economic position of the Club, a reflection of the poor form, was not good. Membership had dropped from its 1,000 plus to 57 practising and 600 ordinary members. It should be emphasised, however, that even in the 'bad' days of the early 1870s, the Surrey supporters never deserted their side, and the crowds at The Oval were good and enthusiastic. Even so, what once had been a healthy economy now gave cause for concern, and remedies were needed.

Alcock gives credit to Billy Burrup for the idea of introducing football to The Oval, but one cannot help but think that with his close connection to the game, Alcock himself was instrumental in linking the headquarters of the Surrey Club to the activities of the Football Association. For a decade all semi-finals of the FA Cup were played at The Oval, and, on 16 March 1872, a crowd of 2,000 watched Wanderers beat Royal Engineers by 1-0 to become the first winners of the trophy.

Alcock captained the Wanderers in that first final, and he refereed the final between Old Etonians and Royal Engineers in 1875. The FA Cup Final was played at The Oval until 1892 by which time the attendance had risen to 25,000 and the number of entries for the competition from 15 to 163.

International football matches, too, became a regular feature at The Oval. The first match between England and Scotland took place at the lovely Hamilton Crescent ground in Glasgow, home of the West of Scotland Cricket Club, in November 1872, and on 8 March 1873, the teams met again at The Oval, England winning 4-2. The first match between England and Wales was staged at The Oval on 18 January 1879, England winning 2-1 this time, while matches between North and South, London and Sheffield and the Universities of Oxford and Cambridge also formed part of The Oval soccer season.

The Rugby Union, too, played the first England and Scotland matches at The Oval between 1872 and 1878, and, briefly in 1880, tennis was played on the ground, for it had become most fashionable at the time. It was in that year that the racquets court was dismantled. It had been in use since the early days of the Club, but it protruded like a carbuncle from the side of the pavilion where now stands the Executive Suite and was most unsightly, yet it had served a purpose.

With the freedom given them by the fact that they now leased the ground directly from the Duchy of Cornwall, the Earl of Bessbor-

C. W. Alcock, a man of energy and vision who, when secretary of Surrey, organised the first Test match to be played in England, at The Oval. (Allsport)

ough and his colleagues were able to utilise the facilities in ways which would best benefit the Club, and in January 1885, they let a piece of ground east of the Vauxhall Gate to Michael Adams, who was to erect a roller skating rink. Roller skating was then the rage, and a handsome rink was to be erected. An asphalt floor was laid down, and there was skating for a time, but no work was started on the buildings, the craze having passed, and the County was forced to repossess the site and use the asphalt area for cricket practice when the turf was impractical.

Ten years earlier, the Montreal Lacrosse Club had been allowed to use The Oval, and behind the diversity of attractions that were now being offered, one can discern the active mind of Alcock, who grasped the economic realities of the age and made sure that Surrey cricket

47

would survive, benefit and prosper. The Oval was such a hive of activity that new members began to arrive in considerable numbers, and by the time football was ended at The Oval in the 1890s the financial position was secure and many ground improvements had been carried out. Ultimately, the crowds had grown too big, and the renovation of the outfield in 1893-94 cost £1,200. In September 1895, the members decided that there should be no more football.

It was at this time that, a new and satisfactory lease having just been negotiated, it was decided to replace the old and rather ramshackle pavilion with a new building designed by Thomas Muirhead, the architect of the pavilion which had just been constructed at Old Trafford and which was highly acclaimed. Work began on the new pavilion in 1897, and it was ready for occupation by the start of the following season.

These developments were an attempt to keep pace with the position in which cricket, and Surrey, now found themselves. As we have seen, when Alcock succeeded Burrup as secretary in 1872, Surrey's fortunes were at a low ebb. Southerton was taking many wickets, and Jupp of Dorking 'who never believes in a match being won or lost until the last wicket falls, and thinks much less of his average than of the success of his side' reigned supreme, but of success there was very little. It was, perhaps, a sign for the future that the first county match under Alcock produced a great victory over the all-amateur Gloucestershire XI for whom the future Surrey captain, Strachan, was a star performer.

The match was played at The Oval on 3 and 4 June 1872, and Surrey, trailing by 38 on the first innings, needed 110 to win. When Southerton joined Marten the score was 108 for nine, and Marten immediately turned a ball into the hands of Miles at short-leg, but unaccountably, and to the consternation of W. G. Grace and his Gloucestershire side, the catch was dropped. So distraught were they that they allowed Marten and Southerton to run a single, and this was followed by a leg-bye which won the match.

William Marten was a fast bowler who had also played for Kent and had been introduced to try to put some spark into the Surrey attack, but he was nearing the veteran stage, and he assisted Surrey for only two seasons. Caffyn had returned from Australia and played for Surrey in the game against Gloucestershire and in a few others in 1872 and 1873, but his best days were well past, and at the age of 45, he retired from the game. As he had missed a benefit by coaching in Australia, Surrey generously granted him an annuity of £39 a year.

Such successes as the one against Gloucestershire were few and far between, but the new management was striving energetically to unearth talent. On 11, 12 and 13 August 1873, against Yorkshire at The Oval, Surrey gave a first game to a young amateur, still three months short of his 18th birthday, Walter William Read. Read was destined to become one of the greatest of Surrey's batsmen, and, indeed, of England's, 'holding a high place among those nearest in merit to W. G. Grace'.

He was born in Reigate in 1855 and educated at his father's school in the town. So precocious was his cricketing talent that he was barred from the school side as being too strong for his opponents and he joined the Reigate Priory Club at the age of 13. The same year he first played against first-class bowling:

> Mr Nightingall asked my father to allow me to go to Tonbridge to play, and he placed me in that gentleman's special charge during the match. I went in first, and played against the bowling of Bob Lipscombe, at that time a member of the Kent County Eleven, and was fortunate enough to score 78 runs, not out. Lipscombe, who knocked me about a bit pretty severely during my innings, carried me into the pavilion. I was young in those days, and thoroughly tired out with the hard day's work; and on returning home after the match I was quietly left seated at the railway station with a bottle of ginger-beer and a bun for company; whilst the others, and, of course, the older members of the team enjoyed themselves in a room, after a different, although, for all I know, an equally innocent fashion. This was the first time I ever made anything like a score against first-class bowling, and it inspired me to further efforts.

Harry Jupp saw Read play in several local matches and recommended him to Alcock. It was Jupp who gave Read his first advice when he played for Surrey:

> Being young and green, I was very slow, and I shall never forget the advice given me by that veteran, Harry Jupp, who remarked: 'Now, young man, look here! The first thing you have to do if you want to be a cricketer is to keep your wicket up, and the runs are sure to come.'

Jupp was proposing the method that had made him the mainstay of the Surrey batting, although one is not entirely convinced that W. W. Read took the advice, for he was often eager to attack the bowling. The advent of Read can be seen as the beginning of the Surrey revival, although glory was still some way off and Read was able to play only in the school holiday period during his first eight seasons with Surrey because he taught at his father's school. It was not until he was appointed assistant secretary of the County in 1881 that he could give his time fully to the game. One suspects that this was another move inspired by Alcock, for one of the pressing problems was how to make it possible for amateurs of quality to play the game with any regularity.

The career of A. P. Lucas is testimony to the difficulties that the amateur of no great wealth and with a need to earn a living faced. Lucas played for Surrey from 1874 to 1882 and captained the side in 1879, yet in all that time, he played only 41 games for Surrey. He was coached at Uppingham by H. H. Stephenson and was recognised as a rare talent. He was a batsman of exquisite beauty, 'almost unique in his combination of perfect style and impregnable defence'. He was a paragon of the age, but, even in the year when nominally he was captain, he could not play regularly and shared the duties of leadership with Strachan and Shuter.

Such problems were recognised by all and caused exasperation on the part of an administration which was keen to lift Surrey cricket to its former glories. In September 1878, *Baily's Magazine* drew attention to the situation:

> . . . the absence of Mr Strachan from many matches has had a depressing effect on the team and only once has the county been represented by its strongest eleven. The elevens sent up to Nottingham and Sheffield reflected anything but credit on the county.

Two years later, the same magazine was still bemoaning the position:

> The advent of fine weather in August served to make still more manifest the extreme weakness of the bowling of Surrey. With Messrs Lucas, Strachan, J. Shuter, W. W. Read, Lindsay, Jupp, Pooley, J. M. Read, Barratt, Potter and Blamires, Surrey ought to be able to do well, but the inability of Mr Strachan and the evident disinclination of Mr Lucas to play seriously crippled the side.

Lucas moved on to Middlesex and later captained Essex. While sympathising with Surrey's plight *Baily's* was also critical, in an article by Frederick Gale, of the County recruiting men from the north. The man particularly referred to was Edward Barratt, a slow left-arm bowler from Durham.

Barratt made his mark in 1872 when, playing in his first big match, he took eight for 60 for the North against the South at Prince's. He joined the ground staff at Lord's, but transferred to The Oval and qualified for the County by residence. He made his first appearance for Surrey in 1876 and took 706 wickets for the County in the 143 matches he played for them before his retirement in 1885. He could turn the ball sharply, and although his best season for Surrey was 1883, his most memorable performance was at The Oval in 1878 when, appearing for the Players against the Australian touring team, he took all ten first innings wickets at a cost of 43 runs. The irony is that Barratt might not have been in the Players' side if the leading professionals of the day had not demanded £20 to appear in the match instead of the £10 that they were offered.

The 1878 Australian side was the first to tour England, the Aborigines excepted, and it received little encouragement at first, but victory over MCC in one day at Lord's excited interest. This was followed by a win over Yorkshire, and the Australians then came south again to meet Surrey at The Oval. Alcock relates what happened:

> The authorities at The Oval, as events proved, were utterly out of their reckoning on this occasion in preparing for the public. The increase in the price of admission to one shilling did not reduce the attendance, as had been anticipated. The glorious weather on the first day made for a big crowd of course, and with none of the spacious accommodation of to-day in the shape of banks, the limited resources of The Oval as it was then were severely taxed. By luncheon time it was estimated that over 10,000 were present, and the cry was still they come. As a matter of figures, 20,000 persons witnessed the play on the first day, and 15,000 on the second. The carriage gates, utterly unequal to resist the pressure from outside, had given way before this, and several entrances had to be improvised during the afternoon to relieve the crush. In the ground, as the afternoon advanced, the same difficulty arose. The wickets were fairly in the centre of the playing area, and in the ordinary way a good view was possible for all. But the crowd had come from curiosity rather than from a serious interest in cricket. At last the public encroached so much on the ground that the play was really interfered with. George Strachan, the Surrey captain, C. C. Clarke, among others, did their utmost to keep the people back, without success. They had come to see the Australians, they said, and would see them. Under the circumstances there was little to be done, and the game proceeded as best it could.

The Surrey executive looked in wonder as spectators circled the playing area which was reduced to half its normal size by the density of the crowd; Alcock looked on with interest and vision. The Australians won a low-scoring match by five wickets. They returned to England again two years later, but the tour was arranged late and began in strained circumstances as Lord Harris had been far from happy with the treatment he, and his team, had received in Australia the previous winter. There were suggestions that the tour should be cancelled, and several of the leading counties were unable to accommodate the Australians. There was no match at Lord's, and the two matches against Yorkshire were not arranged by the county club.

Alcock was quick to see the potential that was being wasted, and he had visions of the income that a match between England and Australia could engender. It was known that W. G. Grace was in favour, but that he had been rebuffed by MCC. The other man whose approval had to be won was Lord Harris. Alcock and the Surrey Committee saw that the most appropriate date for the match was 6, 7 and 8 September, when the Australians were due to play Sussex. Alcock was entrusted with the negotiations with both Sussex and with Lord Harris. He won the support of both, and to him and the Surrey executive must go the praise for bringing Test cricket to England. A centenary Test was played at Lord's in 1980, but it is hard to fathom for what reason.

The first Test match in England was arranged by the Surrey Club and was played at The Oval on 6, 7 and 8 September 1880. Lord Harris captained England and W. G. Grace hit 152. A. P. Lucas, the only Surrey representative, was second top scorer with 55. Facing 420, Australia were out for 149 and followed-on. Murdoch hit 153 not out, and they made 327 in their second innings. Needing 57 to win, England were 36 for five before Penn of Kent and W. G. Grace saw them home.

Such was the public interest that score-cards gave out towards the finish, and members of the public pressed around the printers' box with pieces of paper anxious to have a copy of the official score. Some 40,000 people paid to watch the first two days play. Over the next few years, Alcock was to play an important part in arranging the itinerary of the Australian tourists.

So a secretary of energy and vision, backed by a vigorous and courageous committee, had once more placed Surrey at the forefront of cricket in terms of administration and economics, but the County still lacked a team worthy of this eminence. It was, however, taking shape.

W. W. Read had been assisting the side in the summer vacation since 1873, and, in 1880, another Read, J. M. (Maurice Read), made his debut. He was an enterprising, at times unorthodox, batsman and, like his namesake, he was to bring great honour to Surrey.

The match in which Maurice Read made his debut was the game against Middlesex at Lord's on 27 and 28 May. Only two days were allotted to the game as MCC wanted the pitch for Jockeys v Huntsmen on the Saturday, a decision which caused much angry discussion. The Surrey captain in this match was John Shuter.

Shuter had first played for Surrey against Sussex at Hove on 13 and 14 August 1877. He had later played against both Kent and Gloucestershire. He did nothing significant, and few could have realised then that here was the man who would lead Surrey out of the trough.

THE SEEDS OF GREATNESS

JOHN SHUTER WAS A SURREY MAN, born at Thornton Heath on 9 February 1855, but while he was at Winchester, where he was captain of the eleven, he was invited to play for Hampshire. He did not take up the invitation, but he did play for Kent after leaving school. He did well on his two appearances for Kent, but, thankfully for Surrey, he received no further invitations to play for the hop county, and he followed his elder brother Leonard into the Surrey side in 1877.

He first captained Surrey against Notts at Trent Bridge in July 1878, when neither Strachan not Lucas was able to play, and this was the position over the next few seasons. It was not until 1882 that he became sole captain of Surrey, and he held the position until, in the early months of 1894, he decided to retire from first-class cricket. He had led Surrey for the best part of 14 years, and one can only look back in wonder at the size of his achievement. 'I think,' he wrote, 'that I may look back on those years with some feeling of pride, and with the certain knowledge that they were some of the most enjoyable of my life.'

Shuter stood five feet six inches. He was a powerful batsman, particularly on the off, and he combined his power with grace. He had no interest in averages or personal glory. His sole idea was to win the match for his side. He played in one Test match, against Australia at The Oval in 1888, when four other Surrey men, Abel, W. W. Read, Lohmann and Wood were in the side that won by an innings. Shuter opened with W. G. Grace and hit 28.

Shuter was good enough for any county side as a batsman, but it is as a captain that he will be remembered, for he will rank alongside men like Brearley, Surridge, Sellers and Robins as the greatest the game has known. He had natural gifts of leadership which set him apart from other men. He was even-tempered, of cheery disposition and had the ability to put all at ease who came in contact with him. He was scrupulously fair and impartial so that none felt his talents went unrecognised under Shuter. He knew the capabilities of his men, and the warmth of his encouragement ensured that he always got the best from them. In after years, it was said that his men would have died for him on the cricket field.

Allied to the qualities of personality which made him an outstanding leader was a judgement and knowledge of the game which few could rival. He led a side of disparate, and not universally easy, characters with intelligence and passion, and he believed solely in the principle which the weak have never dared to follow, that to

John Shuter, the captain supreme from 1880 to 1893. He continued to serve the Club till his death in 1920, less than a year after he had been appointed secretary.
(Allsport)

deserve to win a game one must be prepared to risk a good deal. A drawn game was anathema to John Shuter, and this is borne out by the fact that although Notts were considered the leading county of the first half of the 1880s, they did not win as many matches as Surrey, their status being reckoned on the fact that they lost fewer.

So positive was Shuter's approach to the game that his actions could draw attention to the absurdity of the laws and the necessity for change. At The Oval, at the end of August 1887, Surrey met Sussex in the last Championship match of the season. Surrey trailed by 45 on the first innings, but a fine stand of 97 between Maurice Read and Abel and an equally good partnership of 125 between Walter Read and Key took Surrey to a strong position. Under the existing rules, Shuter was not able to declare and give his bowlers ample time in which to bowl out the other side so he told his batsmen to surrender their wickets. This they managed to do without making their intentions obvious until Bowley, at number ten, advanced down the wicket before the ball was bowled, made no attempt to play a shot and stood rooted in the middle of the pitch as wicket-keeper Dudney took the ball. Dudney, however, declined to complete the stumping. Realising Surrey's tactics, Sussex adopted delaying measures of their own. Bean bowled eight no-balls in one over, deliberately, and the innings was only ended when Bowley trod on his wicket. By now, there were only 85 minutes left for play during which Sussex, needing 318 to win, were reduced to 61 for seven.

Shuter's effect upon the Surrey side was electric, but it would be foolish to suppose that he achieved what he did without having a highly-talented team at his disposal. As we have noted, Maurice Read, nephew of H. H. Stephenson, made his debut for Surrey in 1880 and quickly established himself in the side as a highly entertaining batsman, useful medium-pace bowler and splendid out-fielder. Well-mannered, articulate, sober and thrifty, he represented the new generation of professionals that began to emerge in the closing years of the nineteenth century. His quality was soon recognised and within two years he was in the England side against Australia at The Oval. This was the occasion when England, set to make 85 to win, were beaten by seven runs. Spofforth took 14 wickets, and *The Sporting Times* carried a mock obituary notice stating the body of English cricket would be cremated and the ashes taken to Australia. So began a famous cricket reference. Maurice Read was to play in 17 Tests, and the match against Australia at The Oval in 1893 in which he did not play was awarded to him as a benefit match. The match was played in intense heat and the gate receipts were £1,200.

In 1881, Harry Jupp, so long the backbone of the Surrey batting, retired, but his successor was already at hand. When Surrey entertained Nottinghamshire at The Oval in July 1881, they included in their side Robert Abel. He scored one and dismissed Oscroft, the Nottinghamshire captain, in each innings. Surrey won in two days.

Bobby Abel arrived at The Oval as a result of a new policy which aimed to throw off the inertia of the 1870s and bring about a change in the fortunes of the Club. W. G. Grace wrote of this new policy in *Cricket*, one of several books which appeared under his name, when he reviewed the 1881 season:

> Surrey was trying hard to recover its old position, and the Committee invited colts from all parts of the county to practise at The Oval under the eyes of good and competent judges. The old arrangement of having a colts' match once or twice a year had not produced favourable results, many a promising colt failing to do himself justice through nervousness or some other cause. Constant practice for a week or two was a better test, and showed whether they had the making of county players in them.

One of the main instigators of the scheme was former skipper Fred Burbidge who enlisted the help of Hon Robert Grimston, then at the veteran stage but ever a help to cricket. The object of the scheme was not simply to unearth young professional talent, but also to reawaken the interest of amateurs in the Club, for the late 1870s had seen little but apathy as a succession of rather mediocre captains would testify.

Bobby Abel was born in Rotherhithe in November 1857, and he played his cricket for Southwark Park. He had no illusions as to how great the gap was between club and county cricket, but he was a determined and courageous man. He impressed Burbidge and Grimston enough to be employed as a ground bowler. He played for Surrey Club and Ground and Surrey Colts, and he was called up for the game against Nottinghamshire when one of the amateurs withdrew at the last moment. He was to develop as a batsman rather than as a bowler, and his development was slow. He became a cricketer by sheer force of perseverance, and it is to the credit of Burbidge, Shuter, Alcock and the rest that they had faith in his ability when others might have weakened. That faith was amply rewarded, for the diminutive Abel – he stood less than five feet five inches – became one of the greatest of Surrey batsmen and one of the most popular. Grace wrote of him:

> As a batsman he is in the first flight, having exceptionally strong defence and patience, and for his size he hits very freely all round. His pluck and cheerfulness are really first-rate, whether they are required in fighting an uphill game with the bat or in the field.

Although he held a regular place in the Surrey side from 1882 to 1884, it was not until 1885 that Abel really established himself as a batsman, nor, until 1886, did he hit a century. By then, the Surrey side had been strengthened by some more new arrivals. George Lohmann came almost by chance, as he told W. A. Bettesworth some years later:

A friend of mine was chosen for a Colts' match at The Oval, and as I was interested in him, I went to see him play. When he was batting at the nets I bowled to him, and afterwards he asked me to bat. I had only been batting a few minutes when the then head groundsman at The Oval came up to me and said, 'You are not playing in this match (I may say that I was not in flannels) and so you have no business to be batting.' He was only doing his duty, but I was dreadfully disappointed; so I walked disconsolately away. In a few minutes Dick Humphrey came up to me and asked, 'Was that you batting in the nets just now?' I began to wonder what new crime I had committed, but when I had pleaded guilty, he said, 'Will you kindly go to the nets again – the Hon Robert Grimston wants to see you bat?' I did as I was asked and went through a sort of test performance. It seems that Mr Grimston had been watching the practice, and had noticed me, and it was through this that I afterwards played for Surrey, for I was asked to play in the Colts' match in 1884. What I have been telling you about occurred late in September 1883.

Lohmann played in a few colts' matches at the beginning of the 1884 season and met with success. He was one whose rise to the top was to be very rapid. On the morning of the Leicestershire match at The Oval in 1884, he was approached by Burbidge who told him to get some practice as he was playing. He hit 12 and nought, took two wickets and two catches in the deep field. At that time Leicestershire did not have first-class status, but Lohmann's first-class debut came a few days later when he scored 20 and 9 not out as Surrey beat Derbyshire by five wickets. Lohmann was still a few days short of his 19th birthday when he played against Derbyshire. By the end of the season, he had been recognised as a talent likely to bring great glory back to the County. The magazine, *Cricket, a Weekly Record of the Game*, edited, incidentally, by Alcock, commented:

A new colt, who seems likely to strengthen Surrey's bowling materially, was introduced this year in Lohmann. He makes the ball do a great deal, and as he uses his head well, bids fair to be a great help to the County.

In fact, Lohmann averaged 18 with the bat and captured 18 first-class wickets at 17.27 runs each. One of the greatest, but all too short, of all-round cricket careers had begun. The following season he took 106 wickets in first-class cricket and scored more than 500 runs. His biography was featured in W. G. Grace's *Cricket*, and in 1886, he was in the England side for all three Tests against the Australians. At The Oval, he took seven for 36 and five for 68 as England won by an innings. He went with Shrewsbury's team to Australia, and, at Sydney, in February 1887, he took eight for 35 and two for 52. He was the first bowler to take eight wickets in an innings in a Test match, and his eight for 35 is still a record for an English bowler in Australia. A year later, he had match figures of nine for 52 at Sydney when Australia were bowled out for 42 and 82. Lohmann was not yet 23 years old.

Fair, handsome, blue-eyed, Lohmann shot to prominence not just as a bowler, and as a slip fielder who has never been surpassed, but as a batsman who could turn the course of a game with his quick-footed aggression. Grace was adamant as to his quality in 1891 when he wrote

George Lohmann was the leading wicket-taker in England for several seasons and led the County's revival in the 1880s. Ill-health cruelly cut short his career and then his life.

'he has no superior as a bowler' and 'very good judges in Australia have said he is the best bowler that ever visited them'. Grace described him as

> above medium-pace – indeed he might almost be classed as fast – has a beautiful action, and keeps a splendid length; and he alters his pace without altering his action, which is one of the strongest characteristics of a first-class bowler. His command of the ball is half the secret of his success.

Lohmann knew his worth and pressed his point hard when it came to contracts and wages, but he threw himself into every game with an awesome zest.

Keeping wicket to Lohmann throughout his career with Surrey was Harry Wood. Pooley left the game at the end of the 1883 season and Wood kept for the County against the Australians in May 1884, and for the best part of the 16 seasons that followed. He was born in Kent and had played for that county nine times between 1876 and 1882, but, unable to gain a regular place in the side, had taken up a position as groundsman to the Streatham club and so qualified for Surrey. He was not the equal of Pooley or Lockyer, but he was a very good wicket-keeper who took a terrible battering standing up to the fast bowlers of the day. He was shorter than Bobby Abel and sported a rather extravagant moustache. He was one of those favoured by Craig, the Surrey poet:

> Good old Harry, bold and peerless,
> Calm and cool, but brave and fearless.

Wood was to keep most ably to a variety of bowlers and to stand up to them all, bar one. In his first season he had to contend with Lohmann. In his second, 1885, Bowley and Beaumont joined the attack.

Tom Bowley was from Nottinghamshire and had played for Northamptonshire, not then a first-class county, before joining Surrey. He bowled fast-medium with a rather low action, and he served Surrey well although he did not make the dramatic impact that John Beaumont did.

Beaumont was born near Huddersfield and was nearly 30 when he first played for Surrey. He had played a few games for Yorkshire in his early 20s, but when he qualified for Surrey by residence little was known of him and, unlike Bowley, he had no reputation based on past achievement.

The 1885 season opened with an innings victory over Hampshire. John Shuter hit 135, and Lohmann took seven for 13 and five for 16. Bowley did not bowl in the first innings and took three for 47 in the second. For the next match, again at The Oval, Maurice Read and Beaumont came in for Bowden and Bowley. There had, in fact, been a non-first-class match against Leicestershire following the Hampshire game, but Beaumont did not appear in that so that the game against Middlesex on 21 May was his first appearance for his adopted county.

In fairness, Middlesex were below strength. They had lost some of their established stars, and others, like C. T. Studd, Vernon and O'Brien, were not available for this match. Shuter won the toss and Surrey batted first on a wicket that was never easy because of recent rain. They were quickly in trouble at 29 for four, but Maurice Read played a glorious attacking innings to restore some sense of order to the proceedings. If Maurice Read, like his namesake, was apt to pull too often, he was always free and vigorous, and wonderfully entertaining. Finding able partners in Roller and Beaumont, he took Surrey to 166 which, in the circumstances, was not a bad score. It soon appeared to be a gigantic one.

Lohmann managed to bowl Haycraft almost immediately, but Webbe and Scott gave little indication of difficulty. Then both were bowled by Beaumont, and seven wickets fell for six runs. Williams and Burton added seven, but Beaumont had Williams lbw, and Middlesex were all out for 25. This is the lowest score ever made against Surrey in a county match by a complete eleven, although Worcestershire were also bowled out for 25 in 1954. Beaumont's debut figures were six for 11.

When Middlesex batted again they lost Haycraft at 31 and Webbe at 33, and so ended the first day's play. Rain prevented any play on the second day, and play could not begin until after lunch on the last day, the Saturday. Middlesex lost their last eight wickets for the addition of 44 runs, and Surrey won by an innings and 64 runs.

Surely no man has made a more remarkable debut for a county than Beaumont whose figures are worth recording:

16-12-11-6

37-21-37-6

Even allowing that the opposition was not of the strongest, a return of 12 for 48 is an outstanding performance, nor did it prove to be an isolated incident of success, for Beaumont topped 100 wickets for the season.

To add to the talents of Lohmann, Beaumont and Bowler were those of G. G. Jones, a medium-pace bowler who was troubled by injury and ill-health, Charles Horner, another medium-pace bowler whose playing career, ending in 1886, was all too brief, and William Eyton Roller, a most gifted all-rounder.

W. E. Roller, whose younger brother also played a few games for the County, was born in Clapham and educated at Westminster School. He went up to Cambridge, but he was given no opportunity to earn his blue, being handicapped with a broken leg for a long period. Indeed, his whole, short career was to be hampered by injury and poor health although he lived to be 91. His cricket was fashioned by the Upper Tooting and Incogniti clubs, both strong in the second half of the nineteenth century. He first played for Surrey in 1881 and became an invaluable member of the side. In 1885, he produced some outstanding feats.

The arrival of Lohmann and Beaumont, and the development of Abel had made Surrey a formidable side, though they lost both matches to Yorkshire and both to Gloucestershire. There were two draws with Notts and one with Kent and one with Lancashire. Twelve county matches ended in victory; most by a large margin. Enthusiasm abounded. On August Bank Holiday Monday, 15,663 people paid to watch Surrey play Nottinghamshire at The Oval; 10,126 were there on the Tuesday, and 2,839 on the Wednesday when rain prevented play until 12.50 pm. It is believed to be the largest crowd to have attended a county match in London.

Nottinghamshire were always a big draw at the time, for they were a strong side, and Surrey had been playing some exhilarating cricket. Lohmann and Horner had added 32 for the last wicket against Kent a week earlier and given Surrey a thrilling victory by one wicket. A fortnight before that W. W. Read and Roller had put on 169 for the fourth wicket against Sussex at Hove. Both batsmen had hit centuries, and Surrey had made 501 and won by an innings. In the first match between the two counties at The Oval, Roller and W. W. Read had also made centuries and shared a century partnership in what was an historic encounter.

Shuter won the toss. Surrey batted and were 462 for seven by the end of the day. Walter Read hit 163 in 190 minutes, and William Roller finished the day on 131. Next morning he extended his score to 204 which had been made out of 418 and included 17 fours. His 204 was the first double century to be hit for Surrey in a first-class match.

Roller's part in the game was far from finished. Sussex had reached 137 for four when he had J. B. Hide caught by Walter Read with the last ball of an over. With the first two deliveries of his next over he bowled Humphreys and Brann so completing the second hat-trick in the history of the Club. He remains the only man to have hit a double century and taken a hat-trick in the same match. He finished the innings with four for 28 and followed this with two for 16. Surrey, 631, won by an innings and 221 runs.

W. E. Roller will never be forgotten by Surrey members. One of the most impresssive of cricket portraits, Roller coming down the pavilion steps on his way to the wicket, hangs in the Long Room at The Oval. It was donated to the Club by the cricketer's mother and is a delightful reminder of a great achievement and a fine cricketer.

The exciting cricket which Surrey produced in 1885 was consistent with the increase in the County's fortunes which had taken an upward turn from the time that Shuter took over the sole captaincy in 1882, nor was the momentum to slacken. In the opinion of W. G. Grace, in 1886, 'Nottinghamshire and Surrey had a very close race for first place in county honours, and finished about equal. Both now possessed very strong teams, the Surrey committee in particular straining every nerve to obtain promising recruits'.

Surrey were, however, not equal with Nottinghamshire, for, having drawn at Trent Bridge, Surrey lost to Nottinghamshire at The Oval and were also, surprisingly, beaten by Sussex and Lancashire. Notwithstanding these setbacks, theirs was a fine record, and Alcock, quoting *The World* in *Cricket, a Weekly Record of the Game*, named his side as undisputed champions and gave some logical reasoning:

> The two counties which stand at the head of the list are undoubtedly Surrey and Nottinghamshire; the former has played perhaps the strongest eleven, notwithstanding the *laudatores temporis acti* (praise of past times) that any county has ever consistently put into the field. Of its future there can be little fear; for whereas in other counties scarcely any new talent seems to be in reserve, in Surrey there is a second eleven available, almost as good as the first, and the latter has the advantage of containing young players like Lohmann, Abel and Diver, who cannot yet in all probability have displayed their mature strength. We place Surrey, notwithstanding Nottingham's unbeaten record, unquestionably first. If the fact that an eleven had never been beaten were to be taken as conclusive evidence that the county which it represented should stand at the head of the poll, it is evident that the wisest policy for any committee would be to arrange for the fewest possible number of matches, consistent with being counted at all.

The argument was a sound one, for to aim to go through a season unbeaten in order to claim a title of leading county was hardly conducive to enterprising cricket. Alcock's assessment was that if one allowed a point for a win and a half point for a draw, Surrey were just ahead of Nottinghamshire. He was the only one to argue the point, but, in 1887, no argument was necessary.

The promise of Edwin Diver, mentioned above, was not fulfilled. A most attractive batsman with powerful off-side play, he had qualified for the County because he was a master at Wimbledon School. He first played in 1883, hit 2,643 runs in four seasons, and, at the end of the

1886 season, announced that he would in future play as a professional, severed his connection with Surrey and moved to Warwickshire. His career with Surrey was a brilliant miniature. His departure, however, produced no weakness in Surrey, who had introduced a young batsman named Brockwell to their side for a few matches in 1886.

After the success that had attended the side in 1886 there was a feeling of buoyancy in the Club. The financial position was very healthy, the Annual General Meeting was well attended and there was a sense of expectancy in the air.

The 1887 season began with victory over the Broadwater Club at Godalming where Surrey traditionally opened their season and with an innings victory over Hampshire, then not a first-class county, at The Oval. Warwickshire, too, were beaten in a non-first-class fixture before the season began in earnest with a visit to Lord's to meet Middlesex.

Webbe won the toss, and a strong Middlesex side batted first. They disintegrated before Bowley and Lohmann and were all out for 81. Surrey lost Abel without a run scored, and five men were out for 91 before Roller, who had gone in at the fall of the first wicket, found an able partner in Lohmann. They added 105 before Roller was caught in the deep. His 118 was made in two-and-a-half hours and was to be his only century at Lord's. Lohmann, enjoying a little fortune, hit well to reach 76, and it is worth remembering that Grace said of him that he was worth his place in any side for his batting and fielding alone. It also happened that he was the best bowler in the world. Surrey led by 213 on the first innings and, although no play was possible on the second day, they completed an innings victory on the Saturday.

From Lord's, Surrey travelled to Trent Bridge to meet Nottinghamshire in the first great test of strength of the season. They made one change from the side which had beaten Middlesex, Key coming in for Bowden as Abel's opening partner so that Surrey fielded what was undoubtedly their strongest side. Key was, in fact, up at Oxford so he could not assist the County regularly.

Shuter won the toss, but Surrey were soon in trouble on a wicket which 'played pretty queerly at the start'. With Surrey 27 for six, it seemed that Nottinghamshire would once more prove to be the leading county, but Maurice Read was joined by Harry Wood, always a fighter, and added 53. Nevertheless, Surrey were bowled out for 115 which hardly seemed likely to prove a winning score.

The Surrey innings had been one of hard graft, and Nottinghamshire batted in equally dour fashion. Shrewsbury and Scotton gave them a solid start with a partnership of 36, but Bowley dismissed both Shrewsbury and Barnes before the close, which came at 46 for two. On the second morning, Lohmann and Bowley bowled with great

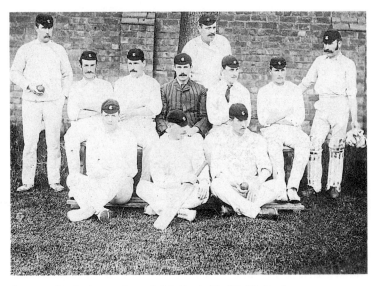

Surrey, 1887. Back row: Jones, J. M. Read, Mr W. W. Read,
Mr W. E. Roller, Beaumont (standing), Mr M. P. Bowden, Lohmann, Wood.
On ground: Henderson, Abel and Bowley.

fire. Scotton and Gunn were out without addition to their overnight score, and of the later batsmen only Mordecai Sherwin offered serious resistance. Nottinghamshire were bowled out for 89.

Abel and Key gave the Surrey second innings a fine start with a stand of 66. Then Walter Read played in incomparable style, dominating a stand of 109 with Maurice Read which went into the last morning. W. W. Read was out for 92 and Maurice Read made 28. It was at this point that Shuter's captaincy came to the fore. 'As there was every chance of winning and none of losing the later batsmen of Surrey got out, and Notts had to go in, just before lunch, with 316 to win.' Unlike Sussex two months later, Nottinghamshire did not seem to understand the Surrey tactics, for of the later batsmen, two were stumped and two hit their own wickets.

William Gunn batted with great resolution in an attempt to stave off defeat, but Lohmann scented a great victory and was not to be denied. For the second time in the match he took five wickets, and Surrey won by 157 runs with 15 minutes remaining.

This resounding win caused much comment and excitement. The Nottinghamshire approach to the game was heavily criticised, for they had now earned a reputation of batting with 'extreme caution' and seemed set on a draw from the time the first ball of a match was bowled. Shuter, on the other hand, was criticised for his orders that batsmen should give their wickets away. He was defended by a

Nottinghamshire supporter, a correspondent in *Cricket, a Weekly Record of the Game*:

> Many sharp remarks were made upon Mr Shuter's action in the recent Surrey match. There can be no doubt he was strictly within his rights, and though a Notts man myself, I think our county have brought it in a great measure upon themselves, by having practised so many times successfully the beautiful art of 'playing for a draw'. The only objection to a side getting out purposely, as Surrey did, is that a misleading record is made of both bowlers' and batsmen's averages, which would be avoided by the rule being altered so that a captain could resign the innings of his side, and put his opponents in when his judgment directed him to do so.

In the last match of the season, against Sussex at The Oval, Shuter's tactics were to be nullified by his opponents as we have described earlier in this chapter, but the agitation for declarations to be allowed continued, and in May 1889 it was agreed that captains should be allowed to declare their innings closed on the last day of a three-day match. Two years later the law was amended so that a declaration could be made after lunch on the second day.

Such problems lay in the future; for the present Surrey enjoyed an interlude of non-first-class fixtures with Warwickshire and Leicestershire and a game against Oxford University. The University were beaten by an innings, and Shuter and Walter Read hit centuries. Read was now in thrilling form. He captained England against MCC in the Centenary Match at Lord's and travelled straight from Lord's to Old Trafford where Surrey met Lancashire, who had played and won three county matches.

Hornby won the toss, and Lancashire were 108 for two at lunch. In the afternoon, Bowley and Beaumont gnawed away at the home side's batting, and the innings closed for 205. John Shuter gave his side a fine start, hitting 70 out of 104. He was out shortly before the close. Walter Read joined Roller, 15 not out overnight, the next morning, and in four hours, they added 305. Roller did not give a chance until he had made 100, when he was dropped at slip, and went on to make 120 while Read, having offered a hard chance in the deep when 82, raced to 247 which included a five and 35 fours. Lohmann pillaged 68, and Surrey, 557, won by an innings.

Meanwhile Nottinghamshire and Yorkshire were engaged in the most tedious of drawn matches. Surrey returned to The Oval to play Cambridge University, and W. W. Read followed his brilliant innings at Old Trafford with 244 not out made in 320 minutes. *Cricket* believed 'his two successive scores of over two hundred in important matches are without parallel'.

Read had been top of the first-class averages in 1883 and 1886, and he was to be in first place again in 1888. He was a most remarkable player. His cricket was founded on an innate love of the game and what Grace called 'unwearied perseverance'. He played straight until later life when he became rather obsessed by the pull, and his hitting powers were exceptional. He had few equals when it came to rapid scoring. In 1884, he had played one of the most amazing innings that Test cricket has known.

England were playing Australia at The Oval, and the visitors made 551, with Murdoch hitting 221, McDonnell 103 and Scott 102. In reply, England slipped to 181 for eight. There is disagreement as to why Walter Read was at number ten. Some suggest that he was furious at Lord Harris for batting him so low, but Ashley-Cooper would seem to be correct when he says:

> Mr Read had been rather out of form before the match commenced, and for this reason insisted, when the batting order was being drawn up, that he was not entitled to occupy a higher position than No. 10. Many were the efforts made to induce him to reconsider his decision, but he was firm and would not give way.

The Australians must have wished he had gone in earlier, for, in 113 minutes with only 36 scoring strokes, W. W. Read hit 117, the highest Test innings by a number ten batsman. He and Scotton, who had opened the innings and made 90 in 340 minutes, added 151 for the ninth wicket, which remains a record for England against Australia.

Read was a dashing player with a great power in his off-side play and was a joy to watch, but he had that seed of mastery with which few are endowed in that he was able to command the rearing ball on a doubtful wicket with apparently as much ease as he could punish an attack on the smoothest of wickets. His batting was one of the main reasons for the Surrey revival in the late 1880s.

Following the victory over Cambridge and Read's second double hundred, Surrey played Gloucestershire at Moreton-in-Marsh. The home side, fielding ten amateurs and Bendall, offered scant opposition, and with Jones taking 11 for 54, Surrey claimed another innings victory.

After six first-class victories in succession the first defeat of the season came when Oxford University won an exciting match at The Oval. Jones suffered a strain in this game which kept him out of the match against Middlesex. Surrey, below strength, played poorly and lost their first county match of the season. Fortunately, Lancashire were well beaten by Nottinghamshire at the same time. It was not, however, Lancashire who were the immediate worry, for Yorkshire, like Surrey, had lost only one match when the sides met at Bramall Lane at the beginning of July.

The matches between Yorkshire and Surrey had always been among the most attractive of the season, and Ulyett chose the 1887 fixture as his benefit. He was not to be disappointed, for more than 20,000 people paid for admission on the first two days. After a poor start in which they lost Abel for nought and Roller for 8, Surrey commanded the opening day and were all out for 301. Their innings was founded on two century partnerships, 111 between Shuter and W. W. Read for the third wicket and 105 between Lohmann and Wood for the seventh. Overnight rain and poor light put Yorkshire in a difficult position on the Tuesday, and Lohmann exploited the conditions fully, returning six for 48 and bowling out Yorkshire for 111. By the end of the day, Yorkshire were 158 for seven in their second innings, and Surrey completed victory early on the last morning, Roller taking five of the last six wickets for 35 runs.

Further honours crowded upon Surrey. At the end of June, at Chiswick Park, Key led Oxford University against Middlesex. He hit 281, the highest score of his career, and shared a seventh-wicket stand of 340 with Phillipson which, at the time, was the highest stand ever recorded in first-class cricket.

Kingsmill James Key was in his last year at Oxford and was now able to join Surrey for the rest of the season. He helped them sweep aside both Kent and Derbyshire and made a significant contribution to the second victory, hitting 97 and sharing century stands with Abel, 92, and W. W. Read, who hit 145 in 150 minutes. Now came the decisive return match with Nottinghamshire over the August Bank Holiday period. Surrey and Nottinghamshire were the giants of the nineteenth century and always met over the Bank Holiday. It is only in recent years that that tradition has been violated, but then the holiday Monday has come to mean less than it did with the longer vacations that people now enjoy.

According to *Wisden*, the attendance at The Oval on 1, 2 and 3 August 1887, in which 51,607 paid for admission, was probably the highest ever known at a cricket match in England. The contemporary account from *Cricket, a Weekly Record of the Game* tells the story of this historic match:

Neither county had quite its strength, Scotton being unable to play for Notts and Mr W. E. Roller and Jones for Surrey. Sulley, a left-handed bowler, took the place of the first-named, while Henderson and Brockwell completed the Surrey team. Sherwin won the toss for Notts, and on an excellent wicket Shrewsbury and Mr Dixon started the batting. Though the score at the fall of the first wicket was 47, the Surrey men bowled and fielded so well that the eighth wicket fell at 143, and it looked as if the Notts total would hardly exceed 160. A bad miss at extra mid-off, however, when he had

CHAPTER FOUR

only made four, gave Richardson a life, and the home team suffered heavily for the mistake, as Richardson, after the let-off, played excellent cricket, and Sherwin and he added no less than 79 for the last wicket. At the end of the first day Surrey had made 14 for the loss of one batsman (Abel), and though Messrs Shuter and W. W. Read played well, when the ninth wicket fell one run was wanted to save the follow-on. Wood, who had been obliged towards the close of the Surrey innings to retire owing to a severe injury to his hand, was, however, fortunately able to bat, and so well did Bowley and he bat, that the tenth wicket added 44, bringing the total within 36 of that of Notts. Sherwin, who had injured his wrist, was unable to keep wicket, and Gunn had to take the gloves, a great loss in a double sense – in Sherwin's absence from the wicket, and Gunn's from the long-field. The Notts eleven made several mistakes in the field, no doubt from over-anxiety, and Maurice Read was let off twice in one over, a serious mistake which in all probability enabled Surrey to save the follow-on. When Notts went in again, Shrewsbury was soon got rid of, and the best cricket was shown by Messrs Dixon and Daft, who were responsible for 86 of the 148 made at the end of the day for the loss of nine wickets. Surrey went in yesterday morning, wanting 205 to win – a heavy task at any time for a fourth innings, and particularly so against the varied bowling of Notts. Abel was caught at seven, but Messrs Shuter and Key played admirable cricket, and the two amateurs put on 70 runs before the latter was caught. Messrs Read and Shuter made another stand, and the score was 110 with only two wickets down, when Barnes was commissioned to bowl to the Pavilion wicket. So far the game had gone in favour of Surrey, but Barnes quickly dismissed Mr Shuter, who had played another splendid innings of 53, Mr Read, and Henderson, and then Notts seemed to have in turn the best of it. Surrey still wanted 78 to win when Lohmann joined Maurice Read, and during their partnership some of the very best cricket of the match was shown. Read gave a very hard chance to mid-on when he had made 23, but in spite of the excellent bowling and fielding of Notts, the score rose steadily until at 199 Read was caught in the slips for an excellent innings of 38. With only six to win Wood came in, and the newcomer adding five gave Surrey the victory at 4.40 pm by four wickets. Too much praise cannot be given to Read and Lohmann, and their pluck at the critical time determined the result. Both richly deserved the enthusiastic reception accorded to them when the game was completed. The spectators were highly elated over Surrey's success, and there was a scene of excitement such as The Oval has not seen for a long time, cheers following cheers until the various members of the winning team had dispersed.

What the report does not include, but which was mentioned by *Wisden* was that 'a great deal of bottle-throwing and other playful eccentricities were indulged in by some of the holiday crowd'.

This victory virtually assured Surrey of the title of Champion County. Gloucestershire were beaten, and Sussex by one wicket. With Wood injured, Adams kept wicket against Sussex. His first-class career consisted of only five matches, and when he came to the wicket in the second innings seven were needed, and he was the last man. He scored them all. There was defeat by Lancashire at The Oval, but this was followed by victories over Yorkshire and Derbyshire and draws with Kent and Sussex so that Surrey stood proudly as the leading county with a record reading:

P. 16, w. 12, d. 2, l. 2

It was 23 years since Surrey had last found themselves in the top position, and there was much joy. The success had come through astute planning and patience on the part of the committee, a balanced and highly capable side and intelligent and inspiring leadership.

Surrey's success had come about in spite of the fact that Roller's health had broken down early in the summer and that Jones and Beaumont missed matches through injury. Walter Read passed 1,000 runs in county matches alone, and Lohmann took 108 wickets. Significantly, Key, who could not play regularly because of his commitments at University, hit 882 runs in 19 innings. He, W. W. Read and Roller finished in the top six of the national batting averages while Jones, J. M. Read, Lohmann and Beaumont finished in the first eight among the bowlers. This was a great Surrey side, one that was to confirm its greatness over the next few seasons.

Kingsmill James Key, born at Streatham, had been playing for Surrey since 1882 when he was still at Clifton College. The following year, he and Roller had won the match against Lancashire with an eighth wicket stand of 112. For an 18-year-old, his batting in that game showed a remarkable temperament, and for his entire career he was an admirable man in a crisis. He had a solid defence, but he was never a dour player, for he had the widest range of shots and was willing to use them. He became a most able lieutenant to Shuter and was his obvious successor.

The greatest qualities of the Surrey administration in recognising players like Key, Beaumont, Abel, Lohmann and Brockwell were their perception and a patience built on the confidence in their judgement. Brockwell, like Abel, was a late developer. He first appeared in the side in 1886, but he was to command no regular place until 1891. For the time being, Surrey would field a side that would remain almost unaltered from match to match.

In 1888, they swept aside all opposition. They won the first 11 of

SURREY *v* NOTTINGHAMSHIRE

Played at The Oval, Kennington, 1, 2 and 3 August 1887

SURREY WON BY 4 WICKETS

NOTTINGHAMSHIRE	FIRST INNINGS		SECOND INNINGS	
A. Shrewsbury	c Wood b Lohmann	41	c Bowley b Beaumont	5
J. A. Dixon	c W. W. Read b Abel	30	b Lohmann	46
W. Gunn	c Wood b Bowley	4	c J. M. Read b Beaumont	2
W. Barnes	c Shuter b Lohmann	43	b Abel	17
H. B. Daft	c Lohmann b Bowley	7	b Lohmann	40
W. Flowers	c W. W. Read b Lohmann	1	c and b W. W. Read	16
W. Attewell	c Wood b Beaumont	1	c Abel b Lohmann	0
F. J. Shacklock	c Lohmann b Beaumont	15	(9) c Abel b Bowley	15
H. Richardson	not out	54	(8) c and b W. W. Read	4
J. Sulley	b Bowley	11	run out	4
*†M. Sherwin	c and b W. W. Read	34	not out	10
Extras	b 3, lb 4	7	b 7, lb 1, nb 1	9
Total		248		168

1st inns: 1-47, 2-64, 3-80, 4-105, 5-110, 6-123, 7-143, 8-149, 9-169
2nd inns: 1-31, 2-35, 3-56, 4-97, 5-130, 6-132, 7-136, 8-138, 9-143

BOWLING	O	M	R	W	O	M	R	W
Bowley	46	20	72	3	10	4	15	1
Lohmann	61	38	59	3	35	18	46	3
Beaumont	31	10	61	2	18	7	50	2
Abel	22	13	20	1	16	8	21	1
W. W. Read	5.3	2	9	1	18	3	27	2
Henderson	6	2	9	0				
Brockwell	5	1	11	0				
J. M. Read	1	1	0	0				

SURREY	FIRST INNINGS		SECOND INNINGS	
R. Abel	c Richardson b Barnes	2	c Sulley b Richardson	3
*J. Shuter	c Sulley b Richardson	44	b Barnes	53
K. J. Key	c Attewell b Barnes	0	c Sherwin b Sulley	38
W. W. Read	b Sulley	25	b Barnes	18
J. M. Read	c Shacklock b Sulley	40	c Richardson b Sulley	38
R. Henderson	c Barnes b Sulley	14	c Sherwin b Barnes	2
G. A. Lohmann	st Gunn b Attewell	17	not out	35
J. Beaumont	run out	4		
W. Brockwell	c Barnes b Sulley	4		
T. Bowley	b Attewell	36		
†H. Wood	not out	14	(8) not out	5
Extras	b 10, lb 1, w 1	12	b 11, lb 2	13
Total		212	(for 6 wkts)	205

1st inns: 1-14, 2-16, 3-76, 4-76, 5-96, 6-146, 7-152, 8-157, 9-168
2nd inns: 1-7, 2-77, 3-118, 4-123, 5-127, 6-199

BOWLING	O	M	R	W	O	M	R	W
Barnes	19	3	51	2	29.2	10	56	3
Attewell	26.2	14	43	2	17	6	22	0
Sulley	36	15	66	4	29	15	40	2
Richardson	29	16	39	1	33	16	33	1
Flowers	1	0	1	0	11	4	16	0
Shacklock					10	3	20	0
Dixon					2	1	5	0

Umpires: J. Rowbotham and C. Payne

*Captain; †Wicket-keeper

their 14 county matches. They were beaten by Lancashire, defeated Yorkshire, and the last game of the programme, against Gloucestershire at Clifton, was ruined by rain. Twelve wins and a draw in 14 matches placed them far ahead of other counties.

Shuter, Abel, Key, W. W. Read, J. M. Read, Lohmann and Beaumont played in all 14 inter-county matches. Wood and Bowley played in 13, Bowden in 12 and Henderson in 11. In effect, Surrey were able to keep practically the same eleven for every match. Jones played only once, his last game for the County, and Roller could appear in just two matches.

Montague Bowden had first played for Surrey in 1883, just after leaving school at Dulwich. If he did not quite fulfil the early hopes in him, he enjoyed a fine season in 1888, keeping wicket on several occasions and being chosen to keep for the Gentlemen at Lord's and The Oval where Surrey supplied both wicket-keepers. A few weeks after The Oval match, he hit the second and higher of his two centuries as Surrey devastated Sussex.

This match, too, was at The Oval, and Abel and Shuter gave Surrey a magnificent start with a stand of 161. Both were out at the same score, Abel for 59, Shuter for 95, but Walter Read reached a century before the end of the day which came with Surrey on 424 for five. Bowden was the other not out batsman, and he and W. W. Read took their stand to 127 the next morning. Bowden finished on 189 not out, made in 210 minutes. Surrey reached 698, their highest score at that time, and, with Lohmann taking 12 wickets, they won by an innings and 485 runs. It was typical of the dominance that they showed in 1888.

At the end of the season, M. P. Bowden went to South Africa with Major Warton's side. He played in the two Test matches, the first in which South Africa engaged, keeping wicket in the second innings of the first Test when Wood was injured and captaining England in the second Test in the absence of C. Aubrey Smith. At the age of 23 years 144 days he remains England's youngest Test captain.

He decided to stay in South Africa and set up a stockbroking firm in Johannesburg with C. Aubrey Smith, Sussex bowler, England captain and later Hollywood film star. Smith captained Transvaal in the inaugural Currie Cup match against Kimberley in April 1890, and Bowden opened the innings and kept wicket. Bowden stumped Grimmer and in the second innings, not only stumped Beech, but took two for 7 in three overs. He hit 63 and then played a match-winning innings of 126 not out in a total of 224 for four. His third first-class century was, in fact, his last first-class innings.

He trekked north with the Pioneer Column of Cecil Rhodes and for three years led an adventurous life in primitive conditions. In

February 1892 he fell heavily from his cart and died at Umtali Hospital, which was nothing more than a glorified mud hut. A man with a revolver stood guard over his body, protecting it from marauding lions, and Monty Bowden was buried in a coffin made from whisky cases.

Robert Henderson was born in the same year as Bowden and first played for Surrey in 1883. His early progress was hampered by poor health, but he won a regular place in the side in 1887 and kept it until 1893 when he began to lose form. He was an excellent batsman, a useful slow bowler and a sound fielder, and if he lacked the brilliance of some of those who surrounded him, he was a true professional, unflinching in nerve, consistent in form, always producing runs or wickets when they were most needed. He played an important part in Surrey's famous victory over Yorkshire at The Oval in 1889.

This was the match in which Yorkshire scored 138 and 141 and Surrey, having been bowled out for 114 in their first innings, were left to make 166 to win. They lost Shuter, Abel, W. W. Read and Lohmann for 43, and, with J. M. Read at number eleven because of an injured finger, their chances of victory looked slim. Henderson and Key added 34, and Henderson and Wood 31, but when the eighth wicket fell Surrey were still 30 runs short of their target. The time was now close to 6.15 pm when stumps should have been drawn, but it was agreed to play the extra half hour. Even then the game was not finished as Henderson and Beaumont fought to bring Surrey victory in gathering gloom. The gas lamps around The Oval were lit, and it was impossible for the spectators to see the ball. Henderson battled on with determination and shortly before 7.00 pm he cut Ulyett to the boundary to win what has become known as the 'Gaslight Match'. His own contribution was 59, the only plus 50 score of the match.

In 1889, Surrey shared the title of leading county with Lancashire and Nottinghamshire. They were still a force in the land, but their batting, without Roller and Montague Bowden, and with Walter Read not quite the power he had been in the previous season, was not what it had been in 1888. In that season, Read, in the game against Oxford University at The Oval, had hit 338, the second highest score ever recorded in first-class cricket at that time, in six-and-a-half hours of vigorous batting.

To share honours with others seemed something of a lapse for Surrey, yet the 1889 season was significant in that it saw two men of Nottinghamshire, now qualified for Surrey by residence, make their debuts for the County, John William Sharpe and William Henry Lockwood. For a few years, at least, they were to be among the best bowlers in the country as Surrey entered the first of the two great eras in her cricket history.

THE GOLDEN AGE

WISELY, THE SURREY COMMITTEE had not adopted an attitude of self-satisfaction since the successes of 1887. They had sought always to gather together a strong group of players as an insurance against injury or loss of form. For this reason, Lockwood and Sharpe were engaged and soon made their mark. Sharpe was a fast-medium pace bowler who, perhaps, burned himself out earlier than he need have done by trying to bowl too fast. Lockwood, played initially as a batsman, became a bowler of genuine pace who moved the ball into the batsman violently. His career was to be a chequered one, and he was never the easiest of men to handle, but Shuter and Key managed him.

Surrey began the 1889 season badly with two defeats, but they were beaten only once more against ten victories and claimed their share in the last unofficial Championship. On 10 December 1889, at Lord's, a private meeting was held between representatives of Surrey, Kent, Middlesex, Yorkshire, Nottinghamshire, Lancashire, Sussex and Gloucestershire. They decided a method of determining the County Championship so that only from 1890 is the title of Champion 'official', in that it is only from that year that the competition was officially constituted and the title awarded by the authority of the counties themselves.

Surrey's first-class season did not begin until the third week in May when they lost to the visiting Australians. More importantly, they were heavily beaten at Trent Bridge a few days later.

Gloucestershire came to The Oval on the last three days of May, and with Maurice Read hitting 135 and sharing a stand of 100 in an hour with Lohmann and Lockwood and Wood adding 100 for the eighth wicket, Surrey scored 464, averaging 80 runs an hour. Gloucestershire were then twice devastated by Sharpe, who took six for 60 and eight for 27 and heralded what was to be an outstanding season for him.

Surrey followed up the innings victory over Gloucestershire with a fine win at Old Trafford. Neither Lockwood nor Roller, who appeared in only a handful of matches, and those his last for Surrey, was able to play because of injury. Shuter won the toss and decided to bat even though the wicket had suffered heavily from rain on the Sunday. Only W. W. Read with 30 reached double figures, and Surrey were bowled out for 69. It proved enough to give them a first-innings lead of eight, and by the end of the day, Surrey were 92 for nine in their second innings. The first day had seen 29 wickets fall while 222 runs were scored.

Wood and Bowley took the score to 103 the next morning before

Bowley was bowled by Briggs. Harry Wood, ever a fighter, was unbeaten on 24. Lancashire needed 112 to win, but they never looked like getting them. In 90 minutes they were all out for 50, every man clean bowled.

For the third time in his career, Lohmann bowled unchanged throughout the match, and on this occasion he was joined by Sharpe. Their figures were:

Lohmann 20.2-8-33-6
         20.1-12-21-7
Sharpe   20-9-27-4
         20-10-23-3

A year later the pair were to bowl unchanged in the match against Somerset at The Oval.

Gloucestershire were beaten in the return match, and Lohmann and Sharpe routed Middlesex so that Surrey won by an innings even though they scored only 199. Rain prevented any play until 4.30 pm on the second day at Sheffield where Surrey had the better of the draw. At Hove, Sussex were trounced by an innings, eight wickets for Lohmann, ten for Sharpe; and in the return match, Sharpe took eight and Lohmann twelve as Sussex were again beaten by an innings.

It was Lohmann and Sharpe again to the fore as Nottinghamshire were brushed aside at The Oval, but, although they took 17 wickets between them against Kent at Canterbury, it was only Lohmann's batting which saved the day for Surrey:

> Surrey had a difficult chance before them when they went in just after half past one o'clock with 191 to win and little under four hours to play. On such a wicket, too, against bowlers like Martin and Wright, runs took a lot of getting, and though Lockwood made 40, when the fifth wicket fell the total was only 76. Lohmann, though, as he has often before, came to the rescue of the side with some very judicious batting, and, as it proved, he saved the game. Ten minutes still remained when Sharpe, the last man, came in, but he managed to play out time, and thus, after a most exciting finish, the game ended in a draw, Surrey wanting 42 to win with one wicket to fall. Lohmann's pluck unmistakably preserved Surrey from defeat, and too much praise can hardly be given him for a very fine performance.

One quotes this account from *Cricket, a Weekly Record of the Game* because it emphasises the tenacity of Surrey cricket at the time. Their success was founded on the consistent solidity of their batting. Every man was capable of contributing valuable runs, and did. At Lord's, against Middlesex, Bobby Abel carried his bat for 151 and Surrey made 425 in 350 minutes. Surrey won by an innings. This was followed by another innings victory, over Lancashire at The Oval, and this time Abel hit 147.

This win confirmed Surrey as the champions although their season was to end with two defeats, at The Oval by Yorkshire and by Kent. There were mitigating circumstances. Against Yorkshire, Key and Lockwood put on 189 for the sixth wicket. Key made 98, and Lockwood 102, the first century of his career. Their stand occupied just two-and-a-half hours. Lohmann and Streatfeild bowled Yorkshire out for 137 so that they were forced to follow-on 156 runs in arrears. They fared better in their second innings and made 247. Surrey needed 92 to win, but overnight rain had made the wicket treacherous as it dried under the sun, and neither Wood nor Henderson was really fit to bat. Both suffered badly injured hands, and Henderson, indeed, came in at number seven and batted one-handed. Yorkshire bowled finely and won by 15 runs. In the last game of the season, against Kent, George Watts was brought in as wicket-keeper because the three main choice keepers were all injured. Surrey lost by eight wickets, but the defeat served only to lessen their lead at the top of the Championship table.

The method that the counties had decided upon to determine the Championship was a simple one. Drawn games were ignored, and losses were deducted from victories. The first official County Championship ended thus:

	P	W	L	D	Pts
Surrey	14	9	3	2	6
Lancashire	14	7	3	4	4
Kent	14	6	3	5	3
Yorkshire	14	6	3	5	3
Nottinghamshire	14	5	5	4	0
Gloucestershire	14	5	6	3	−1
Middlesex	12	3	8	1	−5
Sussex	12	1	11	0	−10

The consistency of the batting and the magnificence of the bowling of Lohmann and Sharpe, both of whom passed 100 wickets in county matches alone were, with Shuter's bold captaincy and good fielding, the ingredients for Surrey's triumph. How much the bowling depended upon Sharpe and Lohmann can be seen from the fact that they sent down 738 and 866.1 overs respectively while the next in line for work was E. C. Streatfeild who bowled 110.1 overs and took 16 wickets.

The Championship success was celebrated with a dinner in 'the new dining pavilion at Kennington Oval, which had been specially furnished and decorated for the occasion'. One of the most interesting comments in the speeches at the dinner came from the president, Viscount Oxenbridge, who said that other teams had fallen away because the men could not keep themselves fit; such a thing could not be said of Surrey. Shuter demanded, and got, the full co-operation of his team. They were fit and they were eager. He instilled into them that they must 'win with grace and lose with good humour', and they had a professional approach which others envied.

The envy turned to wonder in 1891 when Surrey won 11 of the first 12 county matches and had by far the better of the twelfth, against Sussex at The Oval, which was ruined by rain. It was anticipated that the County would go through the season unbeaten in a Championship match (Cambridge University had won at The Oval by 19 runs). But Surrey lost to Somerset, elevated to first-class status for the first time, and to Middlesex in August by which time they were already assured of the title.

Once again the same eleven appeared in almost every match, with Brockwell at last claiming a regular place in the side, and every man made a significant contribution. Lohmann was as potent a bowler as ever, claiming 132 wickets in county matches at under 11 runs each, and if Sharpe was a little less effective than in his marvellous year of 1890, then Lockwood showed a great advance as a bowler. Lohmann also batted with dash at the beginning of the summer, a dreadfully damp one, and finished third in the averages behind Bobby Abel and Maurice Read.

Bobby Abel had now reached his full flowering. He was the first man in England to 1,000 runs, topped the first-class averages, and hit 916 runs in Championship matches alone, a feat unapproached by any other batsman. He was now firmly installed as the most popular of players at The Oval, and for years to come men would offer him as the yardstick and remember with pride that they saw 'The Guv'nor'. What Abel achieved was done with practice and perseverance, and with the trust and belief of those like Shuter, Burbidge and Alcock, who knew from the start that here was a batsman of immense potential whatever other critics might say. He had learned his cricket in Southwark Park 'on wickets calculated to frighten rather than inspire confidence in a batsman'. Perhaps it was these wickets which sharpened his reflexes and made him such a brilliant slip fielder. C. B. Fry described his style:

He has a curious manner of standing at the wicket (wrapping, as it were, his left leg round the front of his right); he holds his bat close to his thigh, and he faces the bowler with all his body above his waist. He is a very steady and careful player, but is, unless he dislikes the bowling particularly, by no means a slow scorer. He can certainly make very good use of loose or bad length balls. He scores a great many runs by cutting, being especially skilful at strong strokes off slow bowling behind third-man. For his stature he gets well over the ball in cutting fast bowling, though naturally enough the quick rising ball is not his *forte*.

Abel gained a reputation for not being at his best against quick bowling, but this is severe on a man who opened the innings for most of his career and scored his 2,000 runs with regularity over the last years of the nineteenth century. He was 31 when he first played for England against Australia at Lord's in 1888, yet the best was still ahead of him. As Altham commented, he

> developed that inexhaustible talent for run-making which was to make him one of the most successful opening batsmen in the history of the game. Who that ever saw it could forget that curious little figure, surmounted by a somewhat faded and shrunken chocolate cap, the slow half-waddling gait that marked its progress to the wicket, and then the mastery of technique that could reduce all but the very greatest bowlers to frustration.

Over and above his ability as a cricketer, Abel had the capacity to win the warmth of all who saw him play and to allow those who saw him to identify him in their hearts as a personal friend. Few have been so blessed; none more loved.

As with Abel, Surrey had to be patient for Bill Brockwell to develop, and Brockwell had to wait his chance with patience, too. Jephson, later to captain Surrey, described Brockwell as 'the Admirable Crichton of his cricketing world . . . a bright, crisp player, standing with legs well apart and forcing many a ball on the leg stump, and sometimes from the middle stump full haste towards the on boundary'. He was also a useful medium-pace bowler and a good slip fielder. His style contrasted with Abel's, as Shuter's belligerent style did, so that they were to blend into an outstanding opening pair.

If the 1891 title had been won before August, the following year represented a sharp contrast, for it looked for most of the summer as if Surrey's reign was over and Nottinghamshire would be champions. When the two sides met at The Oval on August Bank Holiday Monday, they stood level with seven points each, but Surrey had played one game more and had suffered defeat at Trent Bridge at Whitsun. Nottinghamshire were unbeaten in nine matches. No game had aroused so much interest as this meeting of the giants.

Surrey won the toss, and the first day ended with Nottinghamshire on 123 for eight, facing Surrey's moderate 129. The crowds had swarmed to The Oval for the contest as the *Daily Graphic* reported:

For nearly six hours this assemblage of 30,000 people sat or stood, doggedly watching every ball that was bowled, every stroke that was made, stolidly smoking all the while and all together. The Oval is the Newmarket of cricket. At other grounds the turf is brightened by a bordering of pretty frocks, the applause relieved by feminine chatter; but at The Oval the crowd is black, black thickly peppered with the pink of faces; and the batsman who smites the bowler for four or the bowler who smites the wicket of the batsmen is applauded in a roar.

The Oval was never merely a county ground. Even in the 23 years of Surrey depression, it had been a popular place of entertainment, and 'if Lord's represents the aristocracy of the game, The Oval may justly claim to represent the Commons, the other estate of the cricket realm'.

Box, in *The English Game of Cricket*, published in 1877, had extended the idea that The Oval held a particular fascination for the 'non-aristocratic class':

Their conditions of enjoyment are not trammelled, and their native instincts are allowed fuller play than would be considered quite in keeping at some loftier institutions. Here a boisterous shout with its echo is not regarded as a breach of etiquette, and a little homely badinage is not construed into vulgarity.

Certainly the crowds at The Oval were noted for their fervour, and the humour of the game was never missed. The fielder who erred could expect no mercy. For most of 1 August 1892, there was little humorous diversion. Surrey scored at little more than a run an over, and if Nottinghamshire scored at a brisker rate, they lost wickets just as quickly. Shacklock took eight for 59 for Nottinghamshire, but Lockwood, bowling unchanged, responded for Surrey with eight for 67. Another massive crowd (29,370 paid for admission) packed into The Oval on the second day and saw Lockwood take the last two Nottinghamshire wickets for the addition of a single. Surrey had snatched a first innings lead of five runs, but they failed to build on this slight advantage. Shuter alone showed positive form with the bat, and the home side were bowled out for 159. Needing 164 to win, Nottinghamshire closed on 109 for three and duly won by four wickets on the third morning.

The defeat was a bitter disappointment to Surrey, and when Nottinghamshire beat Kent and Middlesex within the next week the Championship, it seemed, was decided. Surrey beat Middlesex, but, with each side having four matches to play, Nottinghamshire had ten victories and were unbeaten; Surrey had nine wins and two defeats.

On 15, 16 and 17 August, Notts were thwarted by the weather, and by the stubbornness of W. G. Grace at Cheltenham, while at Taunton, where rain also held up play, Lohmann and Lockwood exploited a drying wicket and bowled Somerset out for 49 in the second innings to give Surrey a 186-run victory. The fixture list then took Nottinghamshire to Taunton and Surrey to Cheltenham.

Again the weather was bad, but Nottinghamshire succumbed in two days to Somerset to the astonishment of all, and Surrey, with Walter Read hitting a brilliant 107 in 110 minutes and Lockwood taking 12 for 115, beat Gloucestershire by ten wickets.

Lockwood took twelve wickets in the next match as Lancashire were beaten at The Oval so that Surrey had now edged one point ahead in the Championship race, although they had played one game more than Nottinghamshire, and had only one game to play, against Kent at The Oval. Surrey won the toss and batted first. They made 211, with Shuter, now at number seven, hitting a resolute 42. Kent fell to Lohmann and Lockwood and followed-on 110 behind. They made 173 in their second innings, but Surrey won by ten wickets in two days.

Meanwhile, Lancashire entertained Nottinghamshire at Old Trafford. Nottinghamshire won the toss and batted first, but they gave a miserable display and lost by an innings. They also failed to win their last game, against Kent, and Surrey, who won ten of their last 11 matches, were again the Champions.

Never, perhaps, was the determination and resolution of Shuter and his side seen to better effect than in this season. If one man encapsulated that determination, it was George Lohmann. He was 'the very personification of cricket':

With his fair moustache and hair, his wide blue eyes set rather far apart, his broad shoulders, yet lithe and supple frame, he was a wellnigh perfect example of the Anglo-Saxon type; his whole heart was in the game, which, indeed, he loved not wisely but too well, crowding into thirteen years more work than even his magnificent physique could stand.

His main partner now was Lockwood, for Sharpe, having toured Australia in the winter of 1891–92 with Lord Sheffield's side, which also included Abel, Lohmann, and Maurice Read, totally lost his form. He had overcome the loss of an eye in his youth, but that loss of form he was never to overcome. He played a few matches in 1893, and then he returned to Nottinghamshire in 1894, but five games there proved only that his talent was gone for ever.

Sharpe's successor had already appeared in the wings and in 1892, before his 22nd birthday, strode out as a Surrey player for the first time. His name was Tom Richardson, and he made his first-class debut against Cambridge University on 9 June, having bowled impressively in minor matches. In all matches, he took 29 wickets in his first season. Within a year, he was to be the foremost fast bowler in England.

As new faces appeared on the scene, others disappeared. Roller, Beaumont, Bowley and now Sharpe played their last for the County, and, in the early months of 1894, John Shuter decided that he must resign the captaincy and concentrate on business. It would have been pleasant had his last season been attended by success, but it was not to be, and for the first time since 1886, Surrey failed to finish as the top county. It was a season of transition. Lohmann's health broke down, and he was unable to play at all. Richardson and Lockwood bore the brunt of the attack and were well supported by Brockwell. The Reads batted well, as did Key, Brockwell was consistent, but Abel and, in particular, Henderson had poor seasons. Charles Baldwin, who had first appeared in the side the previous year, showed an advance as a stocky, solid, stylish batsman, but most interesting was the arrival of a 22-year-old all-rounder by the name of Tom Hayward.

Born in Cambridge, he belonged to a family which lived for many generations in Mitcham and was well connected with cricket. Both his father and grandfather played for Surrey, and his uncle, Thomas, was a leading professional batsman with Cambridgeshire. Tom Hayward's first first-class game for Surrey was in the opening county match of the 1893 season, the Whitsuntide match at Trent Bridge. He had hit a century against Leicestershire in a non-first-class game a few weeks earlier.

The Surrey side in the game against Nottinghamshire was weakened by the absence of Lohmann, Maurice Read and Wood. At the end of the 1892 season, Lohmann had shown symptoms of a chest complaint. He had undergone treatment in Torquay and then, on Christmas Eve, had sailed for South Africa with Maurice Read as a companion. Lohmann was taken to Matjesfontein in the Orange Free State where the altitude, the absence of dampness and the clarity of the air brought about a slow but steady improvement in his health. His career was not yet over, but Surrey would see nothing of him for another two years. Read returned to England in early April, but he did not return to the Surrey side until after the match with Nottinghamshire, by which time Wood had also recovered from one of his inevitable knocks. Although he did play against Nottinghamshire, Bobby Abel was far from fit, for he was troubled by problems with his eyesight, and it was his poor eyesight which was to account for his moderate form throughout the season and for his missing several matches.

In spite of being without three of their leading players, Surrey beat Nottinghamshire in fine style and raised hopes that they would retain the Championship. They recovered from the loss of their first five wickets for 65 to reach 238 through some fine hitting by Lockwood and a sound innings by Key. Nottinghamshire were shot out for 114 and 196, and Surrey won by seven wickets. The outstanding achievement of the match came from Tom Richardson, who took seven for 60 and seven for 85. It was not a performance without controversy, however, for half the Nottinghamshire side maintained that his delivery was not legitimate and that he threw his very fast ball. In his debut season, Richardson's delivery had been criticised by Billy Murdoch, the former Australian captain and Sussex cricketer, but Richardson learned to straighten his arm, and criticism was silenced. He finished the season with 174 first-class wickets at little more than 15 runs each, but he could not retain the title for Surrey who, for the first time for many years, lost more matches than they won. Yet there were moments when the quality of their greatest days reasserted itself.

They took on Yorkshire, the eventual champions, at The Oval at the end of June and were without Richardson who had a damaged finger. Shuter won the toss, and he and Abel gave Surrey a good start with a stand of 62, but it was Key's 100 in two hours that gave the Surrey innings substance. Then came a glorious display of vigorous hitting by Lockwood who came in at 273 for seven and hit 61 of the last 83 runs scored in 75 minutes. Having finished unbeaten, he took the ball and bowled Wardall with the first ball of the Yorkshire innings. Yorkshire closed at 9 for three and next day lost 17 wickets for a further 254 runs, and Surrey won by ten wickets.

Two months later, also at The Oval, Kent were Surrey's opponents. Surrey were without Lockwood, Maurice Read and Wood, who cried off late and was replaced by Marshall, who himself arrived late and did not take the field until 1.00 pm. Kent made 276, and Surrey ended the first day with 9 for the loss of Abel and Baldwin. Hayward had opened with Abel, and the next day, shortened two hours by a thunderstorm, he took his score to 112 in 300 minutes. The game was ruined by rain with the odds in favour of Surrey. Hayward

> watched the ball carefully throughout, and towards the end made full use of every loose ball he had, sending one on to the roof of the West Stand. Altogether it was a very fine performance, considering that the wicket was never really in favour of run-getting, and that his innings was so much interrupted.

It was spread over three days, in fact.

Tom Hayward's talent was recognised by *Wisden* who said that they would be 'greatly disappointed if he does not in the immediate future obtain a very high position', but none could have realised that the maiden century against Kent announced the start of one of the greatest of batting careers. The win over Yorkshire, Hayward's first century, Richardson's bowling and two victories over the Australians, the first for seven years, could not compensate the faithful for the loss of the Championship, and a lament appeared in *Cricket* which ended:

> The good old county, pray cheer up!
> Dame Fortune's favour curry,
> And once again the championship
> Bring back to brave old Surrey.

The lament grew louder in the winter when Shuter announced his retirement. It was as if a great blank had occurred in Surrey cricket. Shuter had the magnetic personality which cannot be won by experience. He was the best of captains; good humoured, brave and steadfast, tolerant of human error and able to bring the best out of men.

The loss of such a leader is not easily borne, but Surrey had the ready replacement in Kingsmill Key. As we have noted, Key was a fine, powerful batsman with many creditable performances to his credit. He was a short, stocky man who tended to put on weight, particularly late in his career, but he had been a fine all-round sportsman, getting his blue at Oxford for both cricket and rugby. He later became Sir Kingsmill Key, Bart, and in all his life he remained a clear and independent thinker. It was a quality he brought to his captaincy which was original, philosophic and imperturbable as befitted one who was always at his best in a crisis. He was 30 when he became captain of Surrey, established, proven and well respected in the side.

His first venture as official captain of the Club did not meet with success. Derbyshire, Essex, Leicestershire and Warwickshire were elevated to first-class status in 1894 although they did not compete in the Championship until the following year, when Hampshire also came back into the fold. Surrey's opening fixture was with Warwickshire, who had just beaten Nottinghamshire and who now proceeded to beat Surrey by seven wickets.

Two days later, Surrey met Derbyshire at The Oval. Lockwood was absent with a throat infection 'which gave the executive a chance of trying Mr Jephson, the old Cantab, who was very successful with the bat as well as with lobs, for the Crystal Palace and Wanderers Club last summer'. Surrey won by an innings, and Jephson's five overs of lobs in the second innings brought him two wickets, but it was Richardson, ten for 53, and Smith, seven for 64, who took the eye. Frank Smith had played in one county match the previous season. He had been recommended to Surrey by Baldwin, for, like Baldwin, he was Suffolk born. He qualified by residence and brought to the Surrey attack, briefly, the dimension it had been lacking since the departure of

Barrattt, a left-arm slow bowler to complement the speed of Richardson and Lockwood and the medium pace of Brockwell.

It was the custom in the later part of the nineteenth century to offer contrast in a pair of opening bowlers, and Smith blended well with Richardson. Richardson took 13 wickets as Nottinghamshire were brushed aside, and the pair bowled unchanged throughout the match when Gloucestershire were crushed at The Oval in two days in mid-May.

Gloucestershire won the toss and batted first, but W.G. was run out and the rest of the side collapsed to be all out for 82. Surrey took the lead with only three wickets down, and Key and Walter Read put on 105 for the fifth wicket. Good as this partnership was, it was the stand between Lockwood and Brockwell which caught the imagination:

No less than 166 were added while they were together, and of these, Lockwood, who played with more than ordinary care, only made 54, an innings without a mistake. Still, the best display on the side was that of Brockwell. It was the first hundred he has yet made for Surrey, as well as, at the same time, the best innings he has so far played. His 107 only occupied two hours and twenty minutes, and his hitting all round was marked by great power as well as judgement. Moreover, nothing like a chance could be urged in disparagement of an exceptionally good performance.

It was to be Brockwell's year. He had worked hard to become a serviceable all-round cricketer; now his batting blossomed to the extent that he scored more runs at a higher average than any other batsman in England. His five centuries were also the most in the land. Bobby Abel was a close second to him in runs and average.

Richardson and Smith completed the work they had started in the first innings and Gloucestershire were bowled out for 104 in their second knock. W.G. was caught by Brockwell without a run on the board. The final figures of the two bowlers were:

Richardson 20.2-5-45-4
18-6-54-5
F. E. Smith 20-7-27-5
17.4-2-44-5

When these two tired or could not complete the job there was Lockwood, and it was his ten wickets and Abel's 136 that were instrumental in beating Middlesex.

Then came a phenomenal period of bowling by Richardson. He took 12 for 59 against Cambridge University at The Oval, and 12 for 108 in the return at Cambridge. A large crowd flocked to Bramall Lane to see Yorkshire take on Surrey, for both sides were unbeaten in

W. H. Lockwood, one of Surrey's great fast bowlers, who played over 300 games between 1889 and 1904, and in two seasons performed the 'double'.

the Championship. Richardson took ten for 70, and Surrey won by 88 runs. At Old Trafford, he took twelve for 114, and Surrey won in spite of the rain. The next match was against Essex at The Oval.

Although not yet part of the Championship, Essex were a first-class side and had some fine players. They were led by A. P. Lucas who had won his spurs with Surrey. Lucas won the toss and Essex batted first on

William Brockwell, the stylish opening batsman of the 1890s, whose bowling was good enough to allow him to complete the 'double' in 1899. (Allsport)

a slow wicket on a rain-interrupted day. The wicket afforded the bowlers no help, but Richardson produced a performance which no other Surrey bowler had yet accomplished when he took all ten wickets for 45 runs in an unchanged spell of 15.3 overs. Seven of his victims were clean bowled, an eighth, Russell, played on, Burns was caught at the wicket, and Kortright offered a catch to Hayward.

Surrey had left out Key, Walter Read and Lockwood in view of the heavy programme ahead, but they still scored heavily, and at a rate of 73 an hour. Brockwell and Jephson added 120 in 95 minutes, and Jephson, although twice hit on the head, played 'by far the best thing he has ever done in first-class cricket'. Richardson struck again in the second innings, and Surrey claimed an innings victory.

In the space of 16 days, Tom Richardson had taken 61 wickets at 7.31 runs each. It was mighty bowling, and it underlines the fact that, in spite of the great batsmen that have worn the chocolate coloured cap, Surrey's fortunes have only been at their highest when they have had bowlers to whom one could apply the term 'great' without any sense of exaggeration or fear of contradiction.

Caught on a damp wicket at Lord's, Surrey were beaten by six wickets, but they bounced back in magnificent manner with a resounding victory over title-challengers Yorkshire at The Oval. Indeed, Surrey, Yorkshire and Middlesex were now level at the top of the table. A crowd of more than 20,000 crammed The Oval on the first day and were shocked by the news that not only were Richardson and Marshall out of the Surrey side through injury, but Maurice Read, too, had had to withdraw. Yorkshire were without Peel, but this hardly balanced Surrey's loss. Marshall had temporarily displaced Wood as wicket-keeper, but Wood, with his quality of indestructibility, was to return.

Key won the toss, but at 89 for three, Surrey were not well placed. Walter Read had not been in his best form, but his inspiration suddenly returned, and he and Brockwell began to savage the bowling so that, at lunch, after two hours batting, the score was 172 for three. They continued to score at a great rate in the afternoon until Brockwell was caught behind. The stand had realised 172 in under two hours. Both batsmen reached centuries. Read went on to make 161, and Surrey hit 401 in five-and-a-half hours. By the close of the first day, Yorkshire were 43 for five. Lockwood was their main destroyer, and he finished with seven for 94 as he and Smith bowled unchanged. Yorkshire fared better in the second innings, but they were beaten by ten wickets inside two days.

With Middlesex beaten by Kent, Surrey now took a firm grip on the Championship. There was a defeat by Kent, but two victories over Somerset and wins over Nottinghamshire and Gloucestershire were followed by an amazing performance against Lancashire which showed the remarkable resilience of the Surrey side.

Play could not begin until Friday morning because of heavy rain, and Surrey found runs hard to get on a wicket which gave the bowlers considerable help. In spite of a confident knock from Street, they were all out in two-and-a-half hours for 97. Lancashire were 46 for six in reply, but, with the wicket easing, their last four wickets realised 101 runs. Surrey ended the day on 41 for four and looked well beaten. Ayres, Street and especially Walter Read, who was unbeaten for 33, batted purposefully on the last morning, but Lancashire were left needing only 75 to win. If they believed this would prove easy, they were soon shaken from any complacency as Lockwood and Richardson tore into them. Five men were out for 9, seven for 26. Tinsley and Smith added 36 and halted Surrey's progress. Hayward took over from Richardson and had Smith caught at cover by Frank Smith. Bardswell joined Tinsley and eleven runs were added in quick

SURREY *v* ESSEX

Played at The Oval, Kennington, 18, 19 and 20 June 1894

SURREY WON BY AN INNINGS AND 261 RUNS

ESSEX	FIRST INNINGS		SECOND INNINGS	
J. A. Burns	c Marshall b Richardson	9	(2) b Smith	6
H. A. Carpenter	b Richardson	0	(1) Richardson	25
H. G. P. Owen	b Richardson	5	st Marshall b Smith	4
H. Hailey	b Richardson	3	absent ill	–
R. J. Burrell	b Richardson	31	b Richardson	1
†T. M. Russell	b Richardson	0	(7) run out	12
C. P. McGahey	b Richardson	1	(8) b Jephson	16
*A. P. Lucas	b Richardson	5	(6) b Richardson	3
C. J. Kortright	c Hayward b Richardson	5	(9) c J. M. Read b Richardson	34
W.Mead	b Richardson	11	(4) b Richardson	1
H. Pickett	not out	1	(10) not out	0
Extras	lb 1	1	b 3	3
Total		72		105

1st inns: 1-0, 2-13, 3-14, 4-27, 5-33, 6-47, 7-54, 8-55, 9-67
2nd inns: 1-14, 2-20, 3-25, 4-29, 5-37, 6-46, 7-53, 8-105, 9-105

BOWLING	O	M	R	W	O	M	R	W
Richardson	15.3	3	45	10	16.3	5	50	5
Smith	13	4	22	0	14	4	27	2
Street	2	0	4	0				
Jephson					5	1	17	1
Brockwell					3	1	8	0

SURREY	FIRST INNINGS	
R. Abel	c Pickett b Mead	65
J. M. Read	b Burns	59
T. W. Hayward	b Owen	35
W. Brockwell	hit wkt b Burns	108
*D. L. A. Jephson	not out	94
R. Henderson	c Burns b Mead	1
A. Street	b Mead	10
G. W. Ayres	b Kortright	16
F. E. Smith	c Lucas b Kortright	4
†C.Marshall	b Owen	22
T. Richardson	c and b Mead	6
Extras	b 13, lb 4, nb 1	18
Total		438

1st inns: 1-92, 2-136, 3-202, 4-322, 5-323, 6-341, 7-372, 8-376, 9-425

BOWLING	O	M	R	W
Kortright	38	10	96	2
Mead	48.3	11	139	4
Burns	47	12	104	2
Pickett	14	2	28	0
Owen	13	2	37	0
Carpenter	4	0	16	0

Umpires: R. Thoms and James Lillywhite, jnr

Richardson was the first bowler to claim ten wickets in an innings for Surrey in a first-class match.

*Captain; †Wicket-keeper

time before the former was caught at the wicket off Richardson, who had been brought back by Key as soon as Hayward had broken the eighth-wicket stand. Mold came to the wicket with one run needed to level the score. Tinsley slashed a ball to Brockwell at slip which was a very hard chance. It was not accepted, but the fielder did prevent a boundary and only one was run. Mold was then caught behind by Wood off Lockwood, and the match was tied. At this juncture, Wood was standing back to Lockwood, which was unusual, although it was his custom to stand back to Richardson.

Surrey followed this exciting match with innings victories over Kent and Sussex, and the title was once again back at The Oval. If Smith was not the power he had been the year before – his number of wickets dropped to 95 – Richardson and Lockwood were irresistible. Cardus suggested that they were 'the two most beautiful fast bowlers ever seen in action at the same time, but Lockwood's long, bounding run and elastic action could not match Richardson's high, rhythmical and majestic approach'.

'There was no frankness about Lockwood's attack,' wrote Cardus. 'His bolts seemed to come catastrophically out of the sullen air bred about the field wherever Lockwood moved. Temper was required to stir Lockwood to greatness.'

Tom Richardson, prince of fast bowlers, who three times topped 200 wickets in a season, establishing a long-standing record of 290 in 1895.

It was this unexpected venom that was Lockwood's most potent weapon. When the demon possessed him neither Ranji nor Fry could keep him at bay. There was a vicious sophistication in his bowling. He took 150 wickets in 1894. Richardson took 196 and this was the first of his four great seasons.

From 1894 to 1897, Tom Richardson was a Colossus among bowlers. Cardus said simply that he was 'the greatest cricketer who ever took to fast bowling'. He continued:

> His action moved one like music because it was so rhythmical. He ran to the wicket a long distance, and at the bowling crease his terminating leap made you catch breath. His break-back most cricketers of his day counted among the seven wonders of the game. He could pitch a ball outside the wicket on the hardest turf and hit the leg stump. The break was, of course, an action break; at the moment of 'release' his fingers swept across the ball and the body was flung towards the left.

He was possessed of a fine physique, inexhaustible energy and honesty of endeavour. He was 'perhaps', said *Wisden*, 'the greatest of all fast bowlers'. He was a 'simple-hearted giant whose energy passed naturally into fast bowling'. Honest, straightforward speed was his deadliest weapon, unrelenting and unremitting, yet if he had a weakness, it was that he could be too kind, considerate and gentle to the enemy.

It would have been hard to have convinced the 'enemies' of his weakness, for his successes of 1894 were as nothing compared to the triumph he enjoyed the following year.

In 1894, Surrey had won the Championship by a single point, and had not Yorkshire's game with Kent at Bradford been abandoned, they may well have had to share the title. For 1895, Surrey's jubilee year, the competition was extended to embrace 14 counties and a new system of deciding the title introduced. Defeats were still deducted from victories to give a number of points, but the points gained were then expressed as a percentage of the number of matches completed. It was a highly satisfactory system when there were few drawn matches, but as, in the Edwardian period, the bat dominated and draws proliferated, another system was introduced.

In spite of a shock defeat at the hands of Leicestershire in the opening match of the season, Surrey swept all before them in the first three months of the Championship. After losing to Leicestershire they won 14 of their next 18 Championship matches and did not suffer a reverse. The run was ended when Yorkshire beat them by an innings in Bobby Abel's benefit match on 12 to 14 August.

Abel had set the pattern for the triumphant run with the first of his eight scores of 200 or more. Essex made 251 at The Oval and reduced Surrey to 59 for three, but Fred Holland, a stylish batsman in only his second season, joined Abel in a stand of 215 in under three hours. Holland hit 123, and Abel made 217 in 300 minutes.

The next visitors to The Oval, Warwickshire, fell foul of Brockwell and Lockwood. Brockwell returned the best bowling figures of his career, eight for 22, and Lockwood hit 158 to lead Surrey to a massive 520 and an innings victory. Another big partnership between Abel, 165, and Holland, 171, the highest score of his career, of 306 for the third wicket was the highlight of the win at Cambridge.

At The Oval, on 27, 28 and 29 May, Surrey celebrated their jubilee with a match against England. The fixture had last been played 19 years earlier, and the sole survivor from that match was W. G. Grace. In spite of admission prices being doubled, a large crowd attended; and in spite of Richardson's six wickets, Surrey were beaten by an innings.

This was an interlude in the Championship race, and Richardson was now moving into his best form. He took 14 wickets at Edgbaston where Surrey were thwarted by rain and eight at Trent Bridge where Nottinghamshire were routed. Key hit 127 at more than a run a minute, and he and Richardson put on 79 in 25 minutes for the last wicket.

In his twelfth match of the season for Surrey, Richardson passed 100 wickets, and while he was taking wickets there were always batsmen to score runs. Abel and Hayward were in top form, and in the match in which Richardson reached his 100 wickets for Surrey, against Leicestershire at Grace Road, 20 and 21 June, Alf Street hit a remarkable 161 not out, the only century of his career.

Surrey were 94 for six when Alf Street came in, and Abel, the only one of the earlier batsmen to play with confidence, was out at 123. Wood and Street added 89, and Smith joined Street in a ninth wicket stand of 156 to which Smith contributed 45. Surrey were eventually all out for 385, Street having batted for 221 minutes and hit 25 fours.

He was always, perhaps, a fringe player, but he was one of those invaluable men who would come into the side, bat with resolution and bowl a few overs of medium pace when needed and give the side that strength and depth of reserve without which no team can ever aspire to greatness. 'Jim' Street was to win renown as an umpire, standing in a Test match and, at Taunton in 1919, giving out the Sussex last man Heygate for failing to reach the wicket in two minutes when the scores were level. Heygate was suffering from rheumatism, and the decision caused much controversy, but MCC supported Street.

In mid-July, The Oval staged its annual encounter between the Gentlemen and the Players. Surrey were well represented. W. W. Read, Leveson-Gower and Jephson, who played in only three first-class matches in 1895, were in the Gentlemen's side while Abel captained the Players Eleven which included Maurice Read, Hayward, Richardson and Lohmann.

Lohmann had returned from South Africa, and his appearance for the Players marked his reappearance in first-class cricket in England since his breakdown in health in 1892. He was to finish the season with 64 first-class wickets, but it was apparent that something of the old spark had gone.

When, in the autumn of 1892, it had been learned that Lohmann was threatened with consumption and ordered to go south it had come as the greatest of shocks, for the 'Hope of Surrey' was only a few months past his 27th birthday and at the height of his powers. In 1895, he was not the man he had been. He played frequently in 1896, but he drove hard terms with the Surrey committee which was unfortuante considering how generously he had been treated by the Club. He returned to South Africa and was in England in 1901 as assistant manager of the South African touring side. He died later the same year. He was not always the easiest of men, but there have been few finer cricketers.

Lohmann did not return to the Surrey side until 22 July when Kent were beaten by ten wickets at Catford Bridge. He was much needed. Neither Lockwood nor Smith had been as effective as in previous seasons, and a tremendous amount of work had fallen on Richardson, not that that worried the fast bowler who would have relished overs consisting of ten balls rather than the five of the time.

Lohmann marked his return in characteristic fashion. He and Richardson bowled unchanged throughout Kent's first innings, taking four for 23 and five for 16 respectively, and the home side were out for 43. In the second innings they took five for 67 and five for 50.

Sussex were also beaten by ten wickets at The Oval. The match had two curiosities in that Street strained a muscle while fielding and Holland was allowed to replace him and to bat, and when Surrey batting a second time needing one to win Brann deliberately bowled the ball towards point to register the winning wide. Tom Richardson devastated Sussex's first innings with nine for 49, and he and Lohmann bowled unchanged throughout the match at Derby to give Surrey an innings victory. Once more, one should honour outstanding bowling in a summer when the sun shone and batsmen prospered, for this was the year that MacLaren hit his 424 at Taunton:

Richardson 18-7-27-5
          19-8-33-6
Lohmann. 17.4-6-35-4
          18.1-7-24-4

They were again in fine form when a huge crowd gathered for the Nottinghamshire game at The Oval, but rain saved the visitors, and at Leyton, against Essex, it was Smith who paired with Lohmann for the Surrey success. Now came three reverses in four matches, Yorkshire and Lancashire winning at The Oval in spite of more fine bowling by Lohmann and Richardson, and Somerset beating a weakened Surrey side at Taunton where Richardson took 13 wickets and Somerset's Tyler took all ten Surrey first innings wickets for 49. These defeats were punctuated by a win over Kent at The Oval in a high-scoring match. Abel hit 106 and shared a second wicket stand of 144 with Hayward.

Another defeat at this stage would have severely threatened Surrey's hopes of taking the title. They were bitterly frustrated at Clifton. They trailed Gloucestershire by 61 on the first innings even though Richardson took eight for 91, but Key declared Surrey's second innings at 193 for nine, setting the home county to make what seemed a meagre 133. The match had been mutilated by rain which now came to Gloucestershire's aid, for they finished on 37 for seven. It was not to matter.

At Hove, Abel batted with supreme judgement and care for 139, Walter Read hit an enterprising 111, Tom Richardson took 12 wickets and Surrey won by an innings. The outcome of the Championship now hinged on the last match of the season at The Oval. All other counties had finished their fixtures. Surrey stood ahead of Lancashire who had 55.55 per cent, but if Hampshire beat Surrey, Surrey would drop to 52.38 per cent and Lancashire would be champions.

To the disappointment of a large crowd, but to the delight of those in the north, Hampshire won the toss and batted. Surrey were not at full strength. Key, Lohmann and Wood were all missing, and one of the replacements was all-rounder Ernest Nice, a player of very limited experience.

Richardson was at his best, bristling with endeavour, anxious to bowl from both ends if he were allowed. It was Lockwood, however, who took the first wicket. Apart from Hill, who hit a brisk 59 in an hour, no Hampshire batsman was able to stay long, and seven wickets were down for 116. An innings of 43 from Richards bolstered the later order, and the last three wickets added 66.

Abel and Maurice Read gave Surrey a steady start, and at the end of the first day the home county were 163 for two with Read unbeaten on 87. Brockwell offered the solidity while Maurice Read attacked the bowling. There were always times when Read offered the bowler encouragement, for he was never afraid to hit in the air. His 131

Maurice Read, Surrey and England batsman in the 1880s and early 1890s, who went on four tours of Australia.

Walter Read, who played for Surrey for 24 years, was one of the best batsmen in England in the 1880s, and saved a Test match at The Oval in 1884 by scoring 117 at number ten (still a record for a number ten in Tests).

occupied 145 minutes. It was his first 100 of the season, and it had come at exactly the right time.

Surrey moved into the lead shortly before the dismissal of Brockwell, and Walter Read and Street took the home county to a commanding position with a seventh wicket stand of 88. Hampshire began their second innings 192 runs in arrears, and the Championship was within Surrey's grasp. There was frustration when, after Richardson had dismissed Wynyard, Ward and Barton held up Surrey with a partnership of 76. Brockwell broke it, and the rest belonged to Richardson. When he bowled Wootton to end the match and give Surrey the title his figures for the innings were nine for 70. Wootton's was his 268th wicket of the season. Twenty-two more were to follow in the next week, 11 for the South and 11 for A. E. Stoddart's Eleven. His 290 wickets was to stand as a record for 38 years before 'Tich' Freeman took 304, and Freeman took 298 in 1933 so that Richardson remains third on the list, a position from which he is never likely to be displaced in view of the changes that have come over the game. One would also suggest, for the same reason, that his 252 wickets at 13.94 runs each in the season for Surrey will remain the County record for the foreseeable future.

Alongside Richardson's mighty achievement must be put Abel's 2,000 runs, the all-round cricket of Tom Hayward and contributions of immense value from Holland and Wood. Holland's 832 runs, average 33.28, showed the value of Surrey's second eleven and of the policy of strength in depth, but the resources had been sorely tested.

Richardson had taken 252 wickets, but no one else had taken more than 60. The strength of Surrey's bowling had been the major factor in a period of success which had seen them win the title seven times and share it once in the space of nine consecutive seasons, but that strength had begun to dwindle. A great and glorious era in Surrey cricket was at an end.

SURREY _v_ HAMPSHIRE

Played at The Oval, Kennington, 2 and 3 September 1895

SURREY WON BY AN INNINGS AND 20 RUNS

HAMPSHIRE	FIRST INNINGS		SECOND INNINGS	
H. F. Ward	b Lockwood	4	c Marshall b Brockwell	34
V. A. Barton	c J. M. Read b Richardson	23	(3) c sub b Richardson	57
*Capt. E. G. Wynyard	c J. M. Read b Richardson	21	(2) c Street, b Richardson	1
Capt. F. W. D. Quinton	b Richardson	1	c Marshall b Richardson	11
A. J. L. Hill	b Nice	59	b Richardson	9
F. H. Bacon	b Richardson	0	(7) b Richardson	6
C. J. Richards	b Richardson	43	(6) b Richardson	5
†C. Robson	b Nice	0	b Richardson	1
T. Soar	b Nice	6	c Marshall b Richardson	4
H. Baldwin	b Richardson	8	(11) not out	6
J. Wootton	not out	4	(10) b Richardson	37
Extras	b 5, lb 7, nb 1	13	b 1	1
Total		182		172

1st inns: 1-14, 2-28, 3-31, 4-85, 5-86, 6-116, 7-116, 8-140, 9-157
2nd inns: 1-6, 2-82, 3-106, 4- , 5- , 6- , 7- , 8- , 9-129

BOWLING	O	M	R	W		O	M	R	W
Richardson	34.2	9	85	6		29.2	7	70	9
Lockwood	15	3	38	1					
Nice	19	5	46	3		10	4	17	0
Hayward						6	0	34	0
Abel						4	0	11	0
Brockwell						16	6	39	1

SURREY	FIRST INNINGS	
R. Abel	c Quinton b Baldwin	24
J. M. Read	b Hill	131
T. W. Hayward	c and b Wootton	19
W. Brockwell	b Baldwin	28
F. C. Holland	c Quinton b Hill	25
W. H. Lockwood	b Hill	13
*W. W. Read	run out	43
A. E. Street	c Hill b Wootton	46
E. H. L. Nice	not out	1
†C. Marshall	c Hill b Baldwin	9
T. Richardson	b Wootton	3
Extras	b 16, lb 7, w 1, nb 8	32
Total		374

1st inns: 1-40, 2-95, 3-188, 4-239, 5-265, 6-266, 7-354, 8-359, 9-370

BOWLING	O	M	R	W
Baldwin	39	10	83	3
Soar	26	4	80	0
Wootton	29.1	8	74	3
Hill	22	6	77	3
Wynyard	2	0	6	0
Ward	6	1	22	0

Umpires: R. Thoms and James Lillywhite, jnr

Surrey's win clinched their eighth title in nine seasons.

*Captain; †Wicket-keeper

DOWNS AND UPS

SURREY WERE TO WIN THE Championship twice more before the First World War, but not for another 57 years would they produce another side of near invincibility which would sustain a standard of cricket out of the reach of other counties for year after year and which, like the team of the late 1880s and early 1890s, could be spoken of in terms of greatness.

There was nothing in the early weeks of 1896 to suggest decline. There were some brilliant achievements. Braund made his debut for Surrey in the opening match of the season, against Warwickshire, Abel and Walter Read hit centuries, the County won by an innings and all seemed right with the world.

Abel followed his 138 against Warwickshire with 231 against Essex when Richardson took 11 wickets, and again Surrey won by an innings. At Derby came the third innings victory, and Tom Hayward scored 229 not out. Holland hit 153 at Edgbaston where Surrey had to bat for a second time for the first time in the season, but still won by ten wickets. Hayward hit 153 not out and took seven for 83 as Gloucestershire were also beaten by ten wickets at The Oval, and there was victory in the Whitsuntide match at Trent Bridge and over Somerset at The Oval.

Another century for Abel, another innings win over Derbyshire, and Surrey seemed to be moving unstoppably towards yet another Championship. The draw at Bradford caused little concern, for Hampshire and Leicestershire were beaten in successive matches.

At Old Trafford, in mid-June, Surrey suffered their first Championship reverse of the season, and this was followed by humiliation at the hands of Middlesex at The Oval. J. T. Hearne and Rawlin bowled unchanged throughout the match, and Surrey were out for 45 and 126. It was, indeed, defeats at the hands of the southern counties, Sussex, Kent, Essex and Somerset which were to be Surrey's undoing. Even brilliant innings victories in successive matches over Yorkshire and Nottinghamshire could not compensate for these lapses, and defeat by Lancashire condemned Surrey to fourth place.

The County Ground at Taunton, where batsmen generally flourished, proved an uncertain place for Surrey at this period, and very few were their successes there.

Of the bowlers, only Lohmann, in his last season with the County, did better than he had done in 1895 although Richardson's 246 wickets, 202 of them for Surrey, could hardly be described as failure. But Richardson, like his batting colleagues, was at his best on hard, firm grounds. Never was this more in evidence than in the first Test match against Australia at Lord's where, on a true wicket, he and Lohmann bowled Australia out in 22.3 overs for 53 on the first morning. Richardson had six for 39, Lohmann three for 13. It was to be Lohmann's last Test match.

In 18 Tests, he took 112 wickets at 10.75 runs each. Not only is this the most inexpensive 100 wickets in Test history, but his strike rate of one wicket every 34 balls also remains a record. Lohmann was invited to play in the third and final Test at The Oval, but he declined, as, initially, did four other professionals. Alcock gave the Surrey version of this famous cricket strike, and none has disagreed with it:

> Hitherto, it may be premised, the payment to professional players who had represented England had been £10 per man. A very few days before the match a communication was received by the Surrey executive to the effect that Lohmann, Gunn, Hayward, Richardson and Abel would not play unless each received a fee of £20. The Surrey Club Committee very naturally felt that such an ultimatum ought not to have been hurled at them on the very eve of the match, and by their own men, in the last of the three Test matches. It subsequently transpired that some such suggestion had been mooted at Manchester, if not at Lord's, but without success. The manner in which the application was made to the Surrey Committee left them no alternative but to refuse. As a consequence, arrangements were made to fill up the places of the five irreconcilables. At the same time opportunity was given to the four Surrey men to withdraw the letter they had written. Abel, Hayward and Richardson wisely decided to take the course, and were after all included in the eleven. Lohmann intimated that he must consult his colleagues, and was left out of the eleven.

The reason for the players' move was that they believed that several of the leading amateurs, W. G. Grace and A. E. Stoddart, in particular, were receiving larger amounts in expenses than they, the professionals, were being paid. Both Grace and Stoddart were attacked in the press, and Stoddart withdrew from the side. Grace played and issued a statement relevant to payments made to him which won him public support.

The breach with the Surrey Club over this Test was part of a running battle that Lohmann was conducting at the time. As we said earlier, he was a hard bargainer and knew his own worth, but he asked too much, and on 2 September, at Hove, he took five for 67 and left the field as a Surrey player for the last time. Five years later, at the age of 36, he was dead. The sadness of the end and the rift with Surrey can in no way diminish what the County owed him, and he remains revered as among the very greatest of cricketers the world has known.

Surrey's tendency to be considered a fair-weather good-wicket side stemmed, in part, from the excellence of the wickets at The Oval. George Street had looked after the ground until his death in 1880, after which the pitch had got into rather bad condition for a time. He was succeeded by John Newton who had won an excellent reputation for producing good wickets at the South Essex Club at Upton Park.

In 1887, Sam Apted, a former Surrey Colt, friend of William Caffyn, and recently groundsman at the Bickley Park Club, was chosen from a number of well-qualified candidates to succeed Newton. Apted became a legend among groundsmen, and the wicket at The Oval had no superior. It was so good as to drive even the best bowlers to despair. Apted was meticulous in his preparation and would apply a liquid mixture to the pitch some three days before its use. The result was, as Fred Root, the Derbyshire and Worcestershire bowler noted, that it transformed 'a natural stretch of turf into the most perfect of cricket wickets'. Apted remained in charge at The Oval until 1911 when he was forced to retire through ill-health.

If Surrey's invincibility had gone, they were still a very fine side, and in 1897, they ran Lancashire close for the Championship. Indeed, it seemed within their grasp as the season drew to its close. Notts had been early pace-makers, but their tendency to draw rather than win was followed by five defeats in their last six matches. Yorkshire, too,

Surrey at the end of the nineteenth century. Back row: Wood, H. B. Richardson, Brockwell, T. Richardson, Lees, Hayes. Front row: Ayres, Jephson, Key (capt.), Hayward, Abel.

lost four matches in the closing weeks when Essex's challenge also faded. In contrast, Lancashire came with a rush as the season matured, but Surrey beat them at The Oval, and the County had only to win their last two matches, at Taunton and Hove, and the title was theirs. Once again, Taunton proved to be the bogey ground, and Surrey were beaten by 66 runs. They also had the worst of a draw with Sussex so that Lancashire were the Champions. Surrey's consolation was that their 17 victories were more than any other county.

Bobby Abel was the only batsman in the country to score 2,000 runs or more, and his six centuries again made him the leading century-maker. Against Hampshire, at The Oval, he and Brockwell, now established as an opener, put on 379 for the first wicket, which, at the time, was a record, beating by one run the record set up a month earlier by Brown and Tunnicliffe of Yorkshire. Abel hit 173, and Brockwell 225, which was to remain the highest score of his career.

Tom Hayward was one of four players in the country to complete the 'double', but the 1897 season saw the last of the great Walter Read. He played in only a few matches and hit 291 runs, average 24.25. He was now nearing his 42nd birthday, and his powers had shown something of a decline over the past four seasons, but he could still be a most entertaining batsman. Sadly, he was to enjoy only ten years of retirement.

As one passes, another takes the stage, and Walter Lees, who had made his debut in 1896, performed the hat-trick against Hampshire at Southampton. A little above medium pace and very accurate, Lees was to give splendid service. He took 78 economical wickets in 1897 and also showed that he was a more than useful batsman, but his best days were to come after the turn of the century.

However promising Lees, and however useful Hayward, Tom Richardson remained head and shoulders above all others. For Surrey, he took 238 wickets. In all matches, his total was 273. He sent down more overs than Lees and Hayward put together. It was the culmination of four mighty seasons, for, between 1894 and 1897, he took 1,005 first-class wickets in England plus another 69 in Australia in 1894–95. *Wisden* was to write afterwards that, after four years of constant endeavour it would have been better for him to have had a rest, but he set out for Australia and another Test series in the winter of 1897–98:

One remembers that when Mr Stoddart's team sailed from Tilbury, Maurice Read was full of forebodings as to the effect the tour might have on Richardson's future, thinking that a winter's rest after his strenuous labours would have been far better for him than Test matches on Australian wickets. After Richardson came home his falling off was plain for everyone to see. He took 161 wickets in first-class matches in 1898, but his bowling had lost its superlative quality, and only in two or three matches at the end of the season – notably against Warwickshire at The Oval – was he the old Richardson of the previous year.

By today's standards, a haul of 161 wickets in a season would seem miraculous, but by the standards that Richardson had set, a drop of more than 100 wickets and an increase in cost was near failure. His days were not yet done, but he was never again to be the force he had been over those four wonderful years between 1894 and 1897.

One of Richardson's problems was his tendency to put on weight, and with Lockwood having to be nursed because of injury, the dynamic pairing was a shadow of what it once had been. It was not without its moments of glory.

On 4 August 1898, Yorkshire came to The Oval. They had been beaten only once in the season and were well ahead in the Championship race. Indeed, they were to win the title by a comfortable margin. Key won the toss, and Abel and Brockwell began Surrey's innings with a stand of 143 of which Brockwell made 93. Lockwood joined Abel in a third-wicket stand of 109 in 50 minutes before Abel was out for 114. Key blasted 85, and Surrey reached 536. The following day, on a wicket which was unaltered in character and still offered comfort to the batsman, Richardson and Lockwood bowled Yorkshire out twice. Yorkshire's first innings lasted only an hour as Richardson, four for 43, and Lockwood, five for 30, bowled them out for 78. The visitors were handicapped by the fact that F. S. Jackson was unable to bat, but this was hardly an excuse for such a display. They slumped to 90 for five in their second innings before Milligan hit a lusty 63 to lift them to 186. Richardson took three for 57, Lockwood six for 96.

Lockwood was something like his old self with 134 wickets in all matches, but it was the batting which was Surrey's strength. Once more, Abel was the only batsman in the country to reach 2,000 runs, and against Lancashire at The Oval, Tom Hayward hit 315 not out. Brockwell and Jephson, who had now returned to cricket on a regular basis, also plundered runs merrily. Only once at The Oval did Surrey fail to reach 300 runs, and they went through the season unbeaten at home. When Hayward hit his triple century against Lancashire he and Braund put on 204 for the eighth wicket, and this remains a County record. Yet, in spite of their obvious enjoyment of run-getting at The Oval, Surrey failed to score easily on other grounds, and their lack of adaptability cost them dearly. They dropped to fourth in the Championship.

More than anything, of course, it was the bowling which was now a weakness, and it is bowling which wins titles. One can think of only one side – the Middlesex side of 1947 – which has won the County Championship almost exclusively because of its batting. For this reason, Surrey's success in 1899 was all the more remarkable.

For the first time since his debut year, 1892, Tom Richardson failed to take 100 wickets, and the 98 wickets he did get cost him more dearly than any wickets he had taken in England. Lockwood was much as he had been in the previous season, and his 106 wickets for the County were supplemented by 11 elsewhere, seven of them for England at The Oval in the first Australian innings. Lockwood did the 'double' in all matches as did Brockwell, and both played in one Test match. Hayward played in all five – 1899 was the first time five Tests were played in a summer – and was outstandingly successful.

Ranjitsinhji scored 3,159 runs in 1899, the first batsman to pass 3,000 runs in a season, but Abel, 2,685, and Hayward, 2,647, were also in prime form. It was a batsman's summer.

When Surrey met Yorkshire at The Oval the visitors hit 704, with Wainwright making 228 and Hirst 186, and Surrey replied with 551 for seven, Hayward 273, Abel 193. The two Surrey faithfuls put on 448 for the fourth wicket which remains the highest partnership for the County for any wicket.

Abel was not picked for any of the Tests against Australia which caused much debate. Howell, the Australian medium-pacer, did not play in the first two matches of the tour so that his debut in England came against Surrey at The Oval. It was sensational. He bowled 'The Guv'nor' first ball, and took all ten Surrey wickets for 28 runs. He also had Abel for nought in the second innings. The Surrey man also did badly for the South of England against the Australians, and there was a suggestion that he was temperamentally unsound, too nervous of the big occasion. He answered his critics in emphatic fashion.

When Somerset visited The Oval at the end of May they were handicapped by the absence of their slow bowler Tyler, and Sammy Woods was not 100 per cent fit. Nevertheless, they were not a bad side and had always given Surrey a certain amount of trouble. Key won the toss, and although Brockwell went early, runs began to flow. Abel and Hayward added 334 for the fourth wicket, and Vivian Crawford hit a maiden century full of clean, flowing drives, straight and true. At the end of the first day, Surrey were 495 for five, and altogether their innings lasted for over eight-and-a-half hours. Abel was at the wicket all this time for 357 not out.

One report suggested that he had started cautiously, continued cautiously and was playing cautiously when the innings came to an end. *Cricket, a Weekly Record of the Game* was kinder:

Abel did not show a sign of weakness; he hardly gave a chance: he never tired: and he never hurried. It may be that the bowling was not brilliant, but it takes a great batsman to make nearly 400 runs when it is not absolutely feeble, which it never was.

He hit a six, seven fives, 38 fours, 11 threes, 23 twos and 85 singles. He offered two chances, both stumping chances, one when he was 224, the other when he had added another 13 runs.

Abel's 357 not out is the highest score ever made for Surrey, and the third highest, behind MacLaren and Hick, ever made in a county match. It is the highest score ever made by a player carrying his bat through a completed innings. Abel carried his bat through an innings on eight occasions while his great predecessor, Harry Jupp, accomplished the feat on 12 occasions. Jupp was the first man ever to carry his bat through both innings of a match – against Yorkshire in 1874 when he hit 43 out of 95 and 109 out of 193.

Surrey's 811 remains the highest score they have ever made, and it has been bettered only once in a county match. At The Oval, it stood as a record until England hit 903 for seven in 1938.

That Surrey should make their highest score in 1899 was appropriate, for their Championship success was founded entirely upon the strength of their batting. Against Derbyshire at The Oval, Brockwell hit 102 before lunch. It was the third time in four years that he had scored a century before lunch on the first day of a match.

The change in the character of the Surrey side and the emphasis on the batting can be seen from the fact that whereas in three of the previous four seasons they had won more matches than any other side in the country, they now counted a high proportion of draws in their encounters. In 1899, Yorkshire and Lancashire won 14 and 12 matches respectively while, by the time the last game of the season was reached, Surrey had won ten games and suffered two defeats, and Middlesex, the other contenders for the title, had won eleven games and lost three, two of them by very close margins. This meant that Surrey had only to avoid defeat in their last match, against Warwickshire at The Oval, to win the Championship.

Batting first, Warwickshire were plunged to 78 for nine. Santall and Hargreave added 77 for the last wicket, but Surrey batted throughout the second day and left Warwickshire the task of scoring 307 to avoid an innings defeat. A heavy thunderstorm on the last morning brought the match to an end, and Surrey were Champions.

It was a creditable achievement, but none claimed that the side bore comparison with those which had won the title a few years earlier. Fred Holland had scored 1,000 runs in 1898, but had missed most of the Championship season through illness and injury and would not quite

SURREY *v* SOMERSET

Played at The Oval, Kennington, 29, 30 and 31 May 1899

SURREY WON BY AN INNINGS AND 379 RUNS

SURREY	FIRST INNINGS	
R. Abel	not out	357
W. Brockwell	c Newton b Gill	11
E. G. Hayes	c Daniell b Hedley	56
D. L. A. Jephson	b Hedley	18
T. W. Hayward	c Hedley b Cranfield	158
H. B. Richardson	c Daniell b Cranfield	1
V. F. S. Crawford	c Daniell b Stanley	129
*K. J. Key	c Cranfield b Hedley	43
W. Lees	c and b Gill	20
†C. Marshall	c Gill	2
T. Richardson	b Gill	0
Extras	b 8, lb 6, nb 2	16
Total		811

BOWLING	O	M	R	W
Gill	43.2	6	170	4
Cranfield	56	5	180	2
Robson	23	6	87	0
Hedley	48	16	105	3
Woods	16	1	73	0
Daniell	4	1	20	0
Nichols	14	1	76	0
Trask	6	0	24	0
Stanley	12	0	60	1

SOMERSET	FIRST INNINGS		SECOND INNINGS	
H. T. Stanley	b T. Richardson	8	c Marshall b T. Richardson	33
Capt W. C. Hedley	b Lees	1	c Crawford b Brockwell	7
E. Robson	b T. Richardson	5	c Marshall b T. Richardson	23
W. Trask	c Brockwell b Lees	70	lbw b T. Richardson	0
*S. M. J. Woods	b Hayward	49	b Brockwell	53
G. B. Nichols	b Hayward	0	b T. Richardson	9
G. Gill	b Brockwell	3	b Jephson	36
J. Daniell	c H. B. Richardson b Brockwell	50	c Crawford b Brockwell	0
Lt. C. S. Hickley	b T. Richardson	4	b Brockwell	8
†A. E. Newton	c Brockwell b T. Richardson	0	not out	20
B. Cranfield	not out	27	b Brockwell	0
Extras	b 12, lb 5	17	b 5, lb 4	9
Total		234		198

BOWLING	O	M	R	W	O	M	R	W
T. Richardson	28	5	77	4	21	3	59	4
Lees	23	6	52	2	9	2	33	0
Hayward	19	6	47	2				
Brockwell	12.4	6	25	2	24.3	7	76	5
Abel	7	1	14	0				
Jephson	3	1	2	0	7	2	21	1

Umpires: R. Thoms and A. A. White

Abel's score is the highest ever made for Surrey, and Surrey's score is the County record.

*Captain; †Wicket-keeper

reach the heights of 1898 again. Maurice Read had retired at the end of the 1895 season, Charles Baldwin in 1898, and 1900 was to see the last of Harry Wood. At the end of the 1899 season, the Championship won, Kingsmill Key resigned the captaincy. He had put on weight and, more importantly, he had a business career to follow. He was 35 years old and had much honour in other fields ahead of him.

Key had proved a most able successor to Shuter. He was devoted to the Surrey cause, immensely popular, sound in judgement, unselfish and loyal to his men. His resignation left Surrey with the problem of captaincy, but it was a problem of their own making.

In fairness, the Surrey executive was following a trend of the time. There was a feeling abroad that all was not well with the game. Cricket seems prone to excite the meddling of administrators, yet somehow it survives. The sickness, it was believed, was caused by wickets which, artificially prepared, were paradise for batsmen and on which professional batsmen indulged themselves by staying too long at the crease. Certainly, as we have noted, the number of draws increased significantly.

There were those who sought to purify the game, and they believed that this purification could only be brought about by encouraging more amateurs to play regularly. *The Times* had noted with regard to Surrey that 'the regret was often expressed among the general body of members that some of the leading amateurs of the day should have been allowed to drift away from the county'. One doubts that this represented the general view of those who followed the County for whom Abel, Brockwell, Hayward, Wood, Lockwood and the rest were consistently firm favourites whose professional expertise and attitude was admired.

Key certainly admired them and was loyal to them and resented a committee policy which demanded that as many amateurs as possible be included at all times. In 1899, two amateurs, Neville Miller and Harold Pretty, both hit 124 on their debut, Miller against Sussex at Hove and Pretty against Nottinghamshire at The Oval. Not all were as successful as these two, and even Miller and Pretty faded from the game after a few years and a few matches.

The invitations to amateurs to play for the County placed Key in the most difficult position. Edward Dowson, still at Harrow, was asked to play although, in fact, he did not appear until 1900. An invitation to Hugh Dolbey to appear against Kent caused the greatest stir, for Key was told to leave out one of the six professionals – Abel, Brockwell, Hayward, Lockwood, Lees or Hayes – to accommodate him. All six men were or were to become Test cricketers; Dolbey's first-class career extended to three matches with a highest score of 18 not out and seven wickets for 235 runs.

Such a policy was hardly likely to make for team harmony. The young amateurs drafted in were resented, particularly as those professionals who were asked to stand down received only half the normal match fee. Key became increasingly unhappy with the situation and into the position in which he, ever mindful and considerate of the professionals, had been placed. He decided to challenge the committee and wrote a forceful condemnation of the policy, offering his resignation. He also decided to holiday early so that Digby Jephson led the side in the closing weeks of 1899. No concession to Key's protest was forthcoming, and his resignation was confirmed in February 1900. He was, however, to continue to play for the County occasionally over the next few seasons.

The leader of the policy of purification was the Surrey President, Sir Richard Webster, Viscount Alverstone. He was not a noted cricketer, but he was a strongly influential man, President of MCC in 1903 and later a trustee. He was Attorney General and, from 1900 to 1913, Lord Chief Justice. He presided over Surrey from 1895 until his death in 1915, and he, with C. W. Alcock, was responsible for editing the first great history of the Club, *Surrey Cricket: its History and Associations*, which was published in 1902 and which remains an indispensable work for anyone interested not only in Surrey cricket but in cricket in general.

Viscount Alverstone was firm in his beliefs, and it was apparent that he viewed with suspicion the obvious successor to Key, Digby Jephson. There were two contenders for the Surrey captaincy once Key had resigned, H. D. G. 'Shrimp' Leveson-Gower and Digby Jephson. Leveson-Gower was a hard-hitting batsman and leg-break bowler who had captained both Winchester and Oxford with success. Jephson was an aggressive batsman with a wide range of shots and a bowler who had forsaken the fast over-arm of his early years for lobs. In this, he and Simpson-Hayward of Worcestershire represented an eccentric anachronism, but one which was often highly successful. Jephson had been Key's lieutenant and had led the side frequently, and Alverstone knew that he shared Key's views and was familiar with the professionals. Leveson-Gower was offered the captaincy, but tactfully he declined, pleading pressure of work. Jephson succeeded Key as captain of Surrey.

Alverstone, however, was determined that the preferential treatment for amateurs should continue, and he summoned the Surrey match committee to the House of Commons and gave them a firm directive:

Desirable as it is that the county should always be at the front in county cricket, I certainly do not consider that the championship should be the only object. I should like, if possible, to arrange matters in the future so that at least three places in the eleven in all ordinary county matches should be filled by amateurs.

He also stated that other amateurs should be used two or three times in the season and that there should be more changes in the eleven. He suggested that leading amateurs be approached in advance to see when they would be available and when they would like to play during the season. He also commented, much to the chagrin of the paying customer one feels, that while he wanted Surrey to win, he would be sorry if the Championship were to remain with the County for a long period. He was not to be sorry. Having won the title nine times in 13 years, Surrey would win only once more in the next 50.

If Alverstone may now appear to be something of a villain, it must be emphasised that he was only responding to the prevailing mood of those in authority in the game that something was wrong which had to be righted. He was standing against the tide of history, but he was neither the first nor will he be the last to do that, and what he did, he believed he was doing for the good of the game.

The departure of Key was much lamented, and most recognised that a golden age was finally at an end and that Jephson's task would be a difficult one. W. A. Bettesworth, with deference to Tennyson, mourned the *Passing of Key*:

Then spake Key-Arthur to Sir Bobby dear;
'My action of today unsolders all
The goodliest county team of famous bats
Who oft have made a record. Such a team!
They weep – the men I loved. I think that we
Shall never more, upon The Oval field,
Delight the crowds with scores of mighty length,
Knocking about the bowlers and the balls
At Kennington, as in the days that were.
I vanish, though my county may repine,
Tho' critics swear that I shall come again
To rule the team; but let what will be, be,
I am so greatly broadened i' the beam
That without rest I scarce could last the day.'

The poem was published in *Cricket, a Weekly Record of the Game* on 29 March 1900. By the next issue, 12 April, only four days before Surrey's opening match of the season against London County, Jephson had been confirmed as captain and the magazine appreciated his problems:

There is no reason why Mr Jephson should not be a distinguished successor to the other famous Surrey captains of recent years – Mr

John Shuter and Mr K. J. Key. He has a difficult task, but he is just the sort of man to face difficulties with a stout heart and to overcome them.

Jephson's difficulties were not restricted to the vice-like grip of Alverstone and the match committee in which he found himself beginning his reign as captain, for he was also inheriting a team that was ageing.

Wood, now 46, gave way to Fred Stedman behind the stumps, but a young man named Herbert Strudwick appeared on the scene for the first time. Abel was now 43, Brockwell 35, Lockwood 32, Richardson 30, and Hayward 29. Although still only 24, Holland was never to fulfil the earlier promise, and two players of his own age, Hayes and Lees, were to achieve more.

Ernest Hayes first played for Surrey in 1896 before his 20th birthday. An attractive batsman, particularly strong in driving, he was

Ernie Hayes played 500 times for Surrey between 1896 and 1919, and returned to coach in 1929.

107

also a fine leg-break bowler. He batted with great consistency and, like Tom Hayward, was recognised as a model professional.

In spite of Alverstone's decree and wishes, the only amateur, other than Jephson, to play with any regularity in 1900 was V. F. S. Crawford. A knee injury at Chesterfield the previous year had curtailed his season. He was a gloriously exciting batsman, noted for landing the ball on or over pavilion roofs with his clean, hard driving. He added great panache to the Surrey batting, but in 1903, he became secretary of Leicestershire and played for that county for whom he had a birth qualification.

Crawford had been assistant secretary at The Oval, and he had been a close friend and ally of Jephson's, so that his departure was doubly felt by the captain, who needed all the support he could get. Journalist, stockbroker and poet, Digby Jephson was never sure enough of himself to be an ideal captain. Although he had got his blue at Cambridge, it was his prodigious feats in club cricket for Wanderers and Crystal Palace which won him a place in the Surrey side. He became popular at The Oval because he hit the ball hard and often, and because of the peculiarity of his bowling; 'the Lobster' sent the ball spinning after a few crouched steps and the low under-arm delivery. He was, perhaps, too sensitive, too nice a man to cope with the impossible situation in which he found himself, and he suffered much unfair criticism in his three years as Surrey captain.

The albatross which hung permanently around Jephson's neck was that he did not enjoy the confidence of the committee, and the match committee of which the highly respected and successful Shuter was a prominent member would have the final say in all decisions. It was Jephson's duty simply to carry out their instructions and if he acted in a way contradictory to their wishes, they would counteract his decision, as they did when he had agreed to an MCC ruling that he would not put Lockwood on to bowl in 1901 because he was one who had a doubtful action.

Anthony Meredith, in his delightful study of Jephson and Kortright, the Essex bowler, *The Demon and the Lobster*, suggests that the committee were prejudiced against Jephson because of his lack of the right social credentials and his artistic leanings, his delight in music and poetry, which made him an unusual character, but Key, too, impeccable as were his social connections, had artistic leanings. C. B. Fry, who considered Key 'quite the most silent and the most original county captain ever', drew attention to the fact that Key's wife, Helen, was the sister of the poet Lascelles Abercrombie and was 'one of the most fascinating ladies I ever met. She, too, was a poet, and she was my first adoration. She was divinely charming, and I can still see the subtle perfume of her presence'. The gallant Fry, incidentally, was rejected by Surrey and moved off to his native Sussex.

Initially, things did not go badly for Jephson. Abel was in fine form, and he and Jephson put on 364 in four hours for the first wicket against Derbyshire at The Oval. Jephson hit 215 in about five hours and played 'one of the very best innings of his career'. *Cricket* had used the same description of his innings at Sheffield a month earlier when he hit 109 in two hours against an attack which included Rhodes, Hirst and Haigh. He hit a century against Yorkshire in the return match and took another off the Lancashire attack. In Championship matches, he took 40 wickets at just over 22 runs each, and there was justification for *Wisden's* complaint that he should have bowled more for he had bowled uncommonly well.

Lockwood and Richardson, in spite of his increasing girth, both took more than 100 wickets, and Abel scored twelve centuries in all matches while Hayward scored ten. This was excellent work, but it would be idle to pretend that all was well. The fielding was poor, and the zest had gone from the side. Surrey finished seventh in the table. Jephson, the friend of the professionals, was not always well served by them, for, not unnaturally, much of their attitude to the game was now cast in gloom and uncertainty. Although, in 1901, Surrey advanced one place to sixth, the position of the Club and its captain deteriorated.

Holland could not recapture form, and Brockwell, too, now suffered a reverse. Then there was Lockwood. 'A good fellow in himself', said *Cricket*, 'Lockwood has a host of friends. One can only hope that the weather will be on its best behaviour, and that the match itself will make for the substantial benefit he has so thoroughly earned.' The match was due to be played at The Oval on 25, 26 and 27 July. Lockwood had chosen Yorkshire as the opponents. It was a wise choice in that they were the reigning Champions and had not lost a match the previous season. Unfortunately, the game was abandoned without a ball being bowled.

Made miserable by the loss of a hard-earned benefit and by the criticism of his action that was emanating from some quarters, Lockwood took to drinking more heavily than usual and lost his place in the side for the second part of the season. To their credit, the Surrey Club handled Lockwood firmly and fairly. Years later, Home Gordon, not always the best judge of a man, was to write in his *Background of Cricket* that Lockwood 'was never likeable, and there was in his bowling a viciousness somewhat characteristic of the bad-tempered fellow he always showed himself'. Home Gordon also complained that 'his grim prowess made cricket history during a great period, but few anecdotes are attached to his name'.

Certainly, Lockwood did not make life easier for Jephson, but the Surrey Club were mindful of the service he had given and the greatness of the man as a cricketer. They arranged for Yorkshire to come to The Oval after the Championship matches were over and to play a special benefit match for Lockwood to compensate for the one that had been lost. They also invested part of the proceeds for him so that he had an assured income for the rest of his life. This contrasted sharply with the fate of poor Bill Brockwell, who had enjoyed a benefit in 1900 and was to spend all his money and die destitute.

The committee also acted on Lockwood's drinking, and he was informed that he would only be offered a contract for 1902 if he signed the pledge, and if it were broken, he would be instantly dismissed.

It would be felt that Jephson had enough to contend with in dealing with the loss of form of professionals and their wayward habits, but there was also the continued emphasis on the amateur quota, and, in 1901, as many as five places in the side were often filled by amateurs. When Harold McDonell, the Winchester captain, was suddenly known to be available for the match against Hampshire at Southampton on 1 August, Jephson was informed that he would have to leave someone out for him. The Winchester connection always seemed important to Surrey at this time.

Remarkably, in spite of all these vicissitudes, Jephson enjoyed a fine season, scoring 1,436 runs and taking 77 wickets in all matches. Even more remarkably, Hayward hit more than 2,500 runs, and Abel scored 3,309 at an average of 55.15.

Abel's 12 centuries in 1900 had established a record which had lasted only a year, for Fry hit 13 in 1901. His 3,309 runs beat the record that Ranjitsinhji set up in 1899 and was to last five years until 1906 when Tom Hayward had his *annus mirabilis*.

Ranji had made 3,159 in 1899 and when Surrey entertained Middlesex at The Oval at the end of August 1901, Bobby Abel was still 57 runs short of his third 1,000 of the season. Surrey batted second and Abel was at number four. He reached 3,000 shortly after lunch on the second day, and by the end of the day he was 155 not out. Jephson declared before 1.00 pm on the Saturday with Abel unbeaten on 205. He had batted five-and-a-quarter hours, and his cricket 'was always attractive and full of resource'. Unfortunately, the declaration had left him still 12 runs short of Ranji's record, and Abel wrote later, 'Mr Jephson was unaware of this at the time, and I do not know whether he regretted the closing of our innings more than I did when the circumstance was brought to his notice'.

The disappointment became greater when, in the next match, against Leicestershire, Abel was restored to his number one position and made 2 and nought while Jephson, 174, and Hayes, 108, put on 168 in 110 minutes for the second wicket in the first innings. At Hastings, Abel opened for an England Eleven against Yorkshire and made five, but in the second innings he hit 69 not out in carefree fashion, and the record was his. He added to his aggregate in the Players *v* Gentlemen match at Hastings and in the extra match against Yorkshire for Lockwood's benefit.

Apart from Abel's astonishing performance, there was optimism for Surrey in the batting of Leveson-Gower and E. M. Dowson. Edward Dowson, whose father had played for Surrey in the 1860s, was something of an infant prodigy. He first played for Harrow against Eton at Lord's in 1895 at the age of 15 and bowled finely with his slow left-arm spin. He was in the Eleven five years, and then in the side for four years at Cambridge, captaining the side in his last year, 1903. This was also the last year in which he appeared for Surrey. He was a graceful right-handed batsman, but, like so many talented amateurs, he was not able to give his life to cricket.

Whatever the success of Abel, Jephson, Dowson and Hayward, the committee were less than pleased and, in April 1902, the Annual Report contained the sentiment: 'The committee regret that they are unable to congratulate the members of the club upon the result of last season's Surrey cricket.' They were, however, glad to record that an unusually large number of amateurs played for the County. They seemed unable to link the two factors of lack of success and a predominance of amateurs, several of whom were not up to first-class standard but were keeping better cricketers out of the side.

For Jephson, nothing would go right. He seemed beset by problems on all sides, and his own form fell apart. He and the match committee were still at odds, and he received a cruel slight in June when the Committee selected the sides for the Gentlemen and Players match at The Oval and chose Dowson and Leveson-Gower, but omitted Jephson, their own captain. In fact, both Dowson and Leveson-Gower withdrew, and Jephson was the only Surrey player in the Gentlemen's side.

Surrey won their first match in 1902 in early June, but that was nearly a year since their last victory. Jephson could not find his form and was under severe criticism from disgruntled members and his colleagues in the press. In contrast, Lockwood was a reformed character, took 124 wickets and was recalled to the England side, taking 11 wickets in the Old Trafford Test. Richardson, too, although irreversibly overweight, claimed more than 100 wickets.

Bobby Abel again scored more runs than any other English batsman and played Test cricket for the last time. Hayward had a poorer season and showed an increasing reluctance to bowl, and Brockwell was in his last season with his great years now but a memory. In spite of this, Surrey won eight matches and finished fourth in the table. It failed to satisfy anybody. For Jephson, what measure of success there was came too late. He became more and more depressed as the season went on, fought off rumours in the press that there was a rift between himself and the committee and finally dropped himself in August so that Leveson-Gower led the side in the final matches.

In February 1903, Jephson tendered his resignation on account of business commitments. It was accepted. He had said that he would like to continue to play for Surrey if he could refind his form. In effect, he was to play three more games of first-class cricket in the next two years, and then his career was at an end. He had not been treated well.

Leveson-Gower was the natural successor, but again he declined to take on the job. Dowson, still at Cambridge, was invited to take over the leadership after the Varsity match of 1903. He replied: 'Cannot possibly accept captaincy.' The mantle fell on Livingstone Walker, a right-handed batsman and off-break bowler who had played for London County and for Surrey since 1900. He was 24 years old, a delightful man, but no more than a club and second-eleven cricketer.

Walker had very little experience of county cricket and none at all of leadership. It was not surprising, therefore, that Surrey floundered. These were difficult times, and when Walker left the County at the end of his one season of captaincy something close to chaos took over.

Walker's one year of leadership had seen the County drop to 11th in the Championship. In 33 first-class matches, they used 33 players. To add to the loss of Jephson and V. F. S. Crawford was the early failure of Brockwell and the illness of Bobby Abel. In the winter of 1902–03, his eyes again began to trouble him. The problem failed to go away, and, in March 1903, the Surrey Committee sent him to Ventnor, Isle of Wight, where, over a six-week period, he showed an improvement. He could not return to the Surrey side, however, until the end of May, and even then only when pressured to do so, for he considered himself far from fit. With Abel top scoring with 34, Surrey beat Gloucestershire by six wickets, their first Championship win of the season. Abel's return was rapturously received, and it was believed that the bad times were over. It was not the case. He played in only ten first-class matches and hit 314 runs. It was thought that the Club had dropped him, but a statement was issued which said that Abel himself had not felt equal to playing.

There were hopes that he would be fully restored to fitness in 1904. His sight was said to be clearer, and he began the season wearing glasses and batting with some success in the early matches. His form did not last, and he could not hold a place in the side. He was recalled as the team struggled painfully, but he played his last game at The Oval when Surrey drew with Sussex and he made 8 and 14. Against Somerset at Taunton, in August, he went to the wicket as a Surrey player for the last time. Somerset won by seven wickets, and Abel made 9 in the first innings and was lbw to Robson for nought in the second.

No more would the crowd gather in front of the players' dressing room and chant for 'Bobby!' The career of 'The Guv'nor', than whom The Oval has known no more popular player, was at an end. For some years, Abel had a sports shop close to The Oval. He had started in partnership with J. Lane at 310 Kennington Road, but then moved 'against The Oval' after dissolving the partnership. He was also to do some coaching, at The Oval and at Dulwich College, to write his memoirs and help to bring out a collection of Craig's rhymes.

Albert Craig, 'The Surrey Poet', was a familiar figure at The Oval in the last years of the nineteenth century. A Yorkshireman who had his early career in the Post Office, he discovered that he had a capacity for versifying and decided to earn his bread by the compilation of instant verses which celebrated the deeds of cricketers and footballers. He was a witty, good-natured and humorous man, a favourite with spectators when things were going well or when there were idle hours to kill, but not always welcomed by the authorities, so that eventually he was banned from the ground. He sold his verses and essays at a penny a sheet, and they were very popular if of no great literary merit as the following will testify:

For three long and tedious hours
Abel shows great batting powers:
'Tis no bed of rosy bowers,
'Twas a hard day's working.
Still the valiant little chap
Works away without mishap,
Never seems to care a rap,
Duty never shirking.

Abel retired in 1904. Craig died in 1909. Lockwood and Richardson played their last full seasons in 1903. Richardson lived for a time at Bath and played once for Somerset, but his bulk was now too great for a fast bowler. His unquenchable spirit and his eagerness to bowl every day all the time were, in a sense, his own undoing. *Wisden* was unequivocal in its judgement. From 1893 to 1897, the editor averred, it was 'quite safe to say that his work during those five years has never been surpassed'. But: 'Too much was exacted from him, but he ought not to have gone off as soon as he did.' He died of a heart attack on a walking holiday in France in 1912. He was 42.

As these great players dropped out of the game new stars began to arise. Wood had been succeeded as wicket-keeper by Frederick Stedman in 1900, by which time Stedman was already 28. Stedman was a good keeper, but he was desperately unlucky that he had just two years in the side when a great wicket-keeper came along. In the miserable year of 1903, 'the one particularly bright feature of Surrey cricket . . . was the development of Strudwick into one of the smartest wicket-keepers of the day'. Strudwick had 80 dismissals in the season and went to Australia in the winter as Lilley's understudy. In fact, he was to wait another six years for his Test debut. Stedman used to protect his chest with a copy of the South Western Railway timetable when he was keeping wicket. It was a prophetic gesture. He left Surrey to work for ten years on the Woodbrook Ground in Ireland and was killed in an accident on the railway at Wicklow in 1919.

Herbert Strudwick was to be associated with the Surrey Club for more than 60 years. He was born in Mitcham in January 1880, had his first trial for the County in 1896, kept wicket for them until 1927 and was the County scorer until his retirement in 1958. He owed his career as a wicket-keeper to Miss Wilson, the daughter of the vicar of Mitcham. He would watch the Mitcham Club play during his lunch hour when he was very young and was always fascinated by the game. He played cricket with the other choirboys of the parish church, and their games were supervised by Miss Wilson. It was she who suggested that Strudwick should keep wicket. He was about 10-years-old at the time and was in the habit of running in from cover to the wicket to take returns from the field. It was this that prompted Miss Wilson to suggest that Strudwick should become a wicket-keeper. He graduated from Mitcham Boys to South London Schoolboys and played in a few games at The Oval. When he was 16 he received a postcard from the Surrey Club inviting him for a trial. He was told to go into the nets and keep to the brisk leg-break bowling of Len Braund, who was to move to Somerset in 1899. He was doing well until he was hit on the head by a quicker ball down the leg side from Braund, at which the Surrey officials told him that he was, as yet, too young and that they would offer him another trial when he was older.

In 1898, he was offered another trial, and this time he was engaged, but not before he had the joint of the first finger of his right hand split by another ball from Len Braund. This was the first of a series of injuries which were to mutilate his hands over the next 30 years. Protection was scanty, and eventually he sought extra protection by having solid leather tips inserted in his gloves for thumbs and fingers. His method of protecting the palms was less orthodox, and he used dampened inner gloves. Offering advice to A. G. Pawson, the young Oxford University wicket-keeper, he said: 'You must rinse your hands in the chamber pot every day. The urine hardens them wonderfully.'

Initially, Strudwick played for Surrey Colts who were led by W. T. Graburn who had been his employer. He played for the second eleven in 1899 and had an outing for the first team against the West Indians in 1900, but he did not play again until 1902 when he kept against London County, the two universities and Warwickshire, the last match of the season. He deposed Stedman at the beginning of the 1903 season and beat the record which his predecessor had set up in 1901. He was established for the next 24 years.

A great wicket-keeper does not make a great side, and a rudderless Surrey limped through 1904 with one more defeat and one fewer victory than in 1903. On the resignation of Walker, no captain could be appointed, and, in 1904, Surrey were led by a plethora of amateurs. Harry Chinnery, who had not played since 1897 and was to play in only 30 matches for the County, captained the side in May, but he could not be induced to continue. In the following weeks, Leveson-Gower, Kingsmill Key, returning to the side at the age of 40, Lord Dalmeny, later Lord Rosebery, and John Raphael, still up at Oxford, 22 years old and with only one match for Surrey, in 1903, behind him, all captained Surrey. Forty players appeared for the County in first-class matches. It was a bizarre situation, and Surrey's fortunes were at their lowest ebb. Hayward and Hayes carried the batting; Lees, Nice and 'Razor' Smith the bowling. Help was at hand.

For 1905, the Surrey committee invited John Raphael to become captain of the eleven once his term at Oxford was complete. Until that time Lord Dalmeny was asked to lead the side. Dalmeny was the son of a former Prime Minister and became Sixth Earl of Rosebery on the death of his father in 1929. He was a famous figure in the world of horse racing, but none should underestimate his contribution to Surrey cricket. His influence on the side was immediate. He proved to be an energetic and capable captain, and his fairness, humour and authority earned him instant admiration and respect. Once again Surrey had enthusiasm in the field and a zest and spirit for playing the game which had all but disappeared in the previous few years. Where there had been a gathering of ill-disciplined individuals, there was now a team. Where 40 players had been fielded in 1904, there was now a nucleus of 15. So quickly was Dalmeny successful that, with Raphael's approval and wholehearted agreement, he was asked to continue to lead the side for the rest of the season, and, indeed, he captained Surrey until the end of 1907 when business pressures and public commitments forced him to step down.

Fortunately, Dalmeny also showed a considerable advance as a batsman. He hit centuries against Warwickshire and Leicestershire in 1905, when he reached 1,000 runs, and he also hit 1,000 runs in his last season as captain. Moreover, off the field, he used his considerable influence to Surrey's advantage. In 1905, he approached the Prince of Wales, later George V, the Club's Patron, for permission to use the Prince's feathers as the County's badge. The permission was granted. Yet the gesture concerning Surrey cricket of which Lord Dalmeny was most proud was related to a young batsman.

John Berry Hobbs was born in Cambridge, on 16 December 1882. He received no coaching, nor any form of formal instruction, but he forged his technique on Parker's Piece, which was tended by Dan Hayward, the father of Tom, who was idolised in Cambridge because of his doings for Surrey. A friend persuaded Tom Hayward to have a look at Hobbs and to recommend him to Surrey for a trial, which Hayward did, but, in the meantime, Essex had been approached and told that they should sign Hobbs. They declined even to offer him a trial. Jack Hobbs arrived at The Oval with a few other young men on 23 April 1903. He spent some 20 minutes in the nets and was then told that he was to play in a trial match later the same day. He played for J. N. Crawford's Eleven against N. A. Knox's Eleven and hit 37. He was informed that he must stay in London that night in order to play in another game the following day. One of those whom he met at the trial was Philip Mead, who was on the staff but was released by Surrey and joined Hampshire. In the second match, Hobbs scored only 13 before being bowled by Mead, but he was summoned to Alcock's office and offered an engagement to qualify for Surrey at 30 shillings a week. In his first game, for Surrey Colts against Battersea, he was out for nought, but by the end of his second year of qualification, it had been realised that here was a batsman of extraordinary talent: calm and composed with a technical authority which belied his lack of years and experience.

Hobbs was qualified for Surrey by the start of Lord Dalmeny's reign as captain, and he was included in the side for the first match of the season, against Gentlemen of England, led by W. G. Grace, at The Oval. He hit 18 and 88. The first Championship match was against Essex at The Oval. Surrey were bowled out for 138 of which Hobbs made 28 before being caught by Young off Tremlin. In the second innings, he made 155 before falling to McGahey. The match was played on 4, 5 and 6 May. The career of 'The Master' had been launched. Dalmeny was delighted and took a step of which he was proud for the rest of his life, he awarded Hobbs his County cap on the evidence of two first-class matches.

Although Hobbs finished the season with 1,317 runs, average 25.82, he did not maintain the form of the first two matches and was dropped down the order, having initially been used as Hayward's opening partner. However, he hit a second century against Essex, at Leyton, and *Wisden* said of him: 'He may fairly be regarded as the best professional batsman Surrey have brought forward in recent years', but they held the reservation that 'he should endeavour to brighten up his fielding'. This reads strangely to-day when Hobbs is recognised as one of the greatest cover fielders the game has known, but he was not a fielder in the covers at that time. He resented the criticism, feeling that the complaint was unfair, and that at the most he had fumbled two or three balls in the long field on a hot day. Dalmeny used to field him in the deep or at third man, customary places for a young man to pass an apprenticeship in those days. It was only after Lord Dalmeny retired that: 'I somehow got to cover point. I was very keen and quickly made that position my own particular play. I was never a long thrower, but was very quick and accurate for short distances'.

It was not just the advent of Hobbs nor the assumption to the leadership of Lord Dalmeny that brought about the resurgence in Surrey cricket, but the arrival of other fresh blood and the development of some of the established players. J. N. Crawford, younger brother of Vivian, made his debut in 1904 as did, briefly, Neville Knox, while Hayes was a model of consistency as a batsman and Lees reached his peak as a bowler with 193 first-class wickets in 1905 and 168 in 1906.

The rise of Knox was dramatic and sudden. Born in 1884, he was the mainstay of the Dulwich College attack for three years. He bowled impressively against Lancashire and Oxford University in 1904 and the following year was considered the best fast bowler in the country. He stood well over six feet and was loose-limbed with a long and angular run which started somewhere in the region of long off. He used his physique to great advantage and generated a considerable pace with 'an undeniable off-break'. Hobbs said of him later that Knox was probably the best fast bowler he ever saw.

In 1906, his second full season, Knox was a sensation. *Wisden*, who named him, along with Hayes and Crawford, among the 'Five Cricketers of the Year', was unrestrained in its assessment of Knox:

When Knox was sound he and Lees could bear favourable comparison with any pair of bowlers in the country, being certainly more difficult on fast wickets than Hirst and Haigh. It is necessary to insist in the strongest way on what Knox's presence meant in the eleven. Faster than any English bowler since Kortright, and always likely, even on the truest pitch, to get up to a very awkward height, he was literally a terror to the majority of batsmen. When he was at his best only a few men played him with real confidence. He was far from depending entirely upon the pace and ugly rise of the ball as at times he broke back almost as much as Richardson used to do in his prime.

For Surrey, Knox had become what Lockwood and Richardson had been in their finest seasons, but there was a disturbing shadow over his achievements:

Knox's terrific bowling was beyond everything the match-winning factor, but unhappily the fast bowler was scarcely ever sound for a

week together. Troubled for about half the season by an acute form
of shin soreness he got through his work under great disadvantages,
and from time to time he was compelled to stand out of the eleven.

This acute shin soreness was more than a passing annoyance. Knox
was forced to struggle against chronic lameness, and often he played
when he should have stood down. 'Only sheer pluck and resolution
enabled him to get through the work he did.' In 1907, when he played
in his only two Test matches, against South Africa, injury was already
beginning to take its toll of him, and he dropped out of the game in
1910.

If the bowling of Knox and Lees was a match-winning factor for
Surrey in 1906, the year belonged to Tom Hayward above all others.
In his 14th season for Surrey, at the age of 35, he hit 2,814
Championship runs. In all matches for Surrey, he scored 3,246 runs,
average 72.13, which remains a record for the County, and his
aggregate in all matches was 3,518 runs, average 66.37. That aggregate
has only been beaten twice in the history of the game, by Compton
and Edrich in 1947, although, as one Surrey historian pointed out, it is
doubtful if the two great Middlesex batsmen had to contend with
bowling of the quality of Haigh, Hirst, Blythe, Tarrant, Brearley and
Mead.

Hayward was a man of dignity, jealously proud of his profession
which he did nothing to sully. For him, cricket was not merely a skilful
and tenacious game, it was a thing of beauty that he would not
profane. His bat was straight; his off-drive classical in execution. He
drove and cut with freedom and brillance, but he never scorned or
jeopardised defence. For ten years he and Hobbs were to form one of
the greatest opening partnerships the game has known.

In Dalmeny's first year of leadership, Surrey had risen to fourth in
the Championship; in his second, 1906, they finished third and came
close to winning the title. The Oval was revitalised. It was a season of
'brilliant success' and the interest in matches was 'almost as keen as in
the great days when John Shuter was captain'.

For three months, Surrey had the most exciting team in the
country, and it was only in August that they fell behind Kent and
Yorkshire. Having said this, it must be admitted that the crucial defeat
came in the match against Kent at The Oval on 14 and 15 June. Surrey
were all out in under an hour-and-a-half on the first morning. Frank
Woolley, who was making his first appearance against Surrey, took
three of the first four wickets, but it was Fielder, six for 30, who did
most of the damage. In reply, Kent were 61 for five, but Woolley hit
72 in 65 minutes, and the visitors took a first innings lead of 127.

Batting again, Surrey lost Hayward for 15 and closed at 47 for one.

Tom Hayward, the prolific opening batsman who was the first professional to score 100 hundreds and whose run aggregate in 1906 was not exceeded until Compton and Edrich beat it in 1947.

Next morning, however, Hobbs, Hayes, Goatly and Spring nearly brought about a revival. 'Gar' Goatly was a stolid player who assisted the County throughout the Edwardian period, but was a little too cumbersome in the field to command a regular place. He was dressing room attendant at The Oval in the years between the wars. 'Mossy' Spring was an all-rounder who, like Goatly, could never hold a regular place, but Ernest Hayes, an England player, was, as we have said, one of the most attractive and reliable of players who was second only to Hayward among Surrey batsmen in 1906. These four attempted to revive Surrey's fortunes against Kent on that June day, but, eventually, Kent were left to make a meagre 128 to win.

Walter Lees breathed life into the Surrey cause with a magnificent spell of bowling, and although Dillon and James Seymour put on 54 for the second wicket, Kent were 66 for five. The eighth wicket fell at 99, and when the last man, Fielder, joined Woolley, the score was 109, 19 runs still needed for victory. Woolley had been missed on one, but as the runs came the tension mounted. With four needed, Fielder was stranded yards out of his ground, but, in the excitement, the throw was wild and wide of Strudwick and went for overthrows so that Kent won by one wicket. The name of the fielder has been clothed in anonymity, but the significance of the defeat can never be hidden.

In late July, Surrey beat Yorkshire at The Oval and then lost to Kent at Blackheath, and eventually Kent had only to draw their last game to win the title. Yet, none of this would have been relevant had Fielder been run out at The Oval as he should have been. It is worth considering the final positions:

	P	W	L	D	Pts	%
Kent	22	16	2	4	14	77.77
Yorkshire	28	17	3	8	14	70.00
Surrey	28	18	4	6	14	63.33

Had Surrey beaten Kent at The Oval, they would have finished with 16 points, 72.72 per cent, while Kent would have ended with 66.66 per cent. On such a slender thread as a throw can a Championship hang.

We have dwelt on the achievements of Hayward, Hayes, Hobbs, Knox, Dalmeny and Lees, but there was one other cricketer who made a rich and thrilling contribution to Surrey cricket at this time, John Neville Crawford. He did not celebrate his 20th birthday until 1 December 1906, by which time he had played the first five of his 12 Test matches and, in his first full season, had taken 118 wickets and scored 1,174 runs to become the youngest player to achieve the 'double'. He was to repeat the feat in 1907.

J. N. Crawford was from a cricketing family. His father and uncle played for Kent. His brothers played for Leicestershire; Vivian, of course, had first made a great impression with Surrey. John Crawford made his debut for Surrey in August 1904, when he still had a year at Repton School ahead of him. By the end of that first season, he had taken 44 wickets at under 17 runs each with his medium-pace off-breaks. He left school in 1905 and was in the MCC side that went to South Africa the following winter. He played in all five Tests.

Always playing in spectacles, he was an upright, orthodox batsman who relished the straight drive and hit hard and often. No schoolboy cricketer has found the transition to the highest level as easy as Crawford did, and his achievement of being the youngest ever to complete the 'double' was unapproached until Brian Close's performance in 1949. In his first season, 1904, Crawford bowled unchanged throughout the match against Gloucestershire at Cheltenham in harness with H. C. McDonell. He took ten for 78, and Surrey won by 119 runs. Two years later he hit a ball on to the top balcony at Lord's, and he also despatched several into the pavilion at The Oval. In the first decade of this century, he seemed to be the most exciting all-round talent to have emerged for many years. 'Few men', said *Wisden*, 'except W. G. Grace and A. G. Steel, have won a bigger position in the cricket world at the same age.'

With Hayward at the pinnacle of his form, Hobbs on the threshold of the greatest of international careers, Hayes a player of exciting consistency, Knox the most devastating fast bowler in England, Strudwick one of the very best of wicket-keepers, Lees a threatening leader of the attack, and Crawford an all-rounder of flair and genius, it seemed that Surrey were on the verge of great things. In 1907, they were also able to add the considerable talents of Alan Marshal, an Australian all-rounder.

Marshal qualified for Surrey by residence, but the way in which that qualification was brought about caused controversy and animosity in the cricket world. He was born in Queensland and learned his cricket when his family moved to Brisbane. He gained further experience playing for the Paddington Club in Sydney, but returned to Queensland and was selected for the state side, 1903–04. At that time, Queensland were not in the Sheffield Shield so that Marshal's opportunities were limited. Passionately devoted to the game and eager to earn his living by playing it, he set sail for England to qualify for Surrey.

The importation of an Australian player was not new. Middlesex had earned yeoman service from Albert Trott and Frank Tarrant. Worcestershire employed Cuffe, and Derbyshire signed the West Indian batsman Ollivierre, but these importations had strong critics and opponents. Essex put forward a motion that the period of qualification for an overseas cricketer should be extended from two to five years, but the motion was defeated by eight votes to seven. Shuter was the Surrey representative who cast his vote against the motion, and his voice would have had a strong influence. Essex were at that time, 1906, not among the most influential of counties, but their chairman, C. E. Green, who had been President of MCC in 1905, was a powerful man, and he was violently opposed to the importation of players. He regretted the defeat of the Essex proposal and felt that both the Australian states and the English counties would lose by the export-import of cricketers which, he believed, was reducing the high level of sport of which cricket had always been proud. At the Annual General Meeting of the Essex Club in April 1907, he waged a particular attack on Surrey who, 'with all its splendid traditions, should at least have been above descending to importations. It was not cricket.'

The anger over the importation of Marshal was stronger than it had been over any other player. He was undoubtedly a magnificent prospect, a splendid hitter of the ball, an outstanding fielder and a bowler of great variety, though Surrey were late to discover this. His ability was not questioned. What was at issue was Surrey's method of obtaining his services. He fulfilled the necessary two years' residential qualification, but while he was doing this it became common knowledge that Surrey were paying him a winter allowance. Many saw this as a form of poaching, of bribing an overseas player to come to England. The worry was that the residential and birth qualifications which had brought stability and quality to English cricket for a quarter of a century would be undermined by wealthy and powerful counties, Surrey and Lancashire in particular.

During his period of qualification, Marshal played for W. G. Grace's London County Eleven, although by 1905 the side no longer played first-class matches, and he excited by his tremendous hitting. In 1906, in minor matches, he is reported to have scored 4,350 runs with 14 centuries. The following year, he was in the County side, but he was something of a disappointment. He failed to play his natural game and was obviously affected by some personal abuse to which he was subjected and by the argument over his eligibility. Nevertheless, he scored more than 1,000 runs and:

> All through the summer he fielded splendidly, being by far the surest catch in the eleven, and in August a tardy discovery was made of his ability as a bowler. Right hand, medium pace, he got a fair amount of spin, and his great height made the flight of the ball rather difficult to follow.

Marshal was not the main disappointment of 1907. Hayward, Hobbs, Crawford, Lees and, eventually, Hayes, all did splendidly in what was a wet summer, but Knox, of whom so much had been

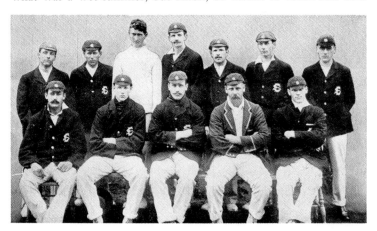

Surrey, 1907. Standing: Strudwick, Baker, Marshal, Holland, Nice, Hobbs, J. N. Crawford. Seated: Hayes, N. A. Knox, Lord Dalmeny (capt.), Hayward and Lees.

expected lost all his devil. He announced late in the season that he was done with first-class cricket and intended to take up singing as a profession. In fact, he did play a little in 1908 and 1910, but his career, which had flashed across the cricket firmament like the brightest of meteors, to all intents and purposes, was over.

In spite of the failure of Knox, and of Marshal to fulfil his potential, Surrey enjoyed a good season. They were one of the two counties to beat a strong South African touring side and they finished fourth in the County Championship. It was said that the only dimension that the County lacked to make them a great side was a left-arm bowler, but others would suggest that they were not, perhaps, making the best use of the resources at their disposal.

W. C. 'Razor' Smith had been on the staff since 1900. Against Hampshire in 1904, he had taken nine for 31, and he was to do the hat-trick against the same county in 1908. He regularly took 50 wickets a season and bowled well on all types of wicket, but it was believed that he was a wet wicket bowler and for this strange reason, he could not command a regular place in the side. Rushby first played in 1903 and had proved himself a most capable fast-medium bowler, but his opportunities were few until 1909. 'Bill' Hitch was a little luckier and his great promise as a quick bowler in 1907, his debut season, was to be rewarded with a regular first team place within a couple of seasons.

Lord Dalmeny announced in August 1907 that he would have to relinquish the captaincy. His reign had been short but highly successful, and he had done much to re-invigorate the Club after an unhappy period. Sadly, 1907 saw the death of C. W. Alcock, who had been the County secretary for 35 years. He was a man of calm, quiet intelligence, immense energy and great vision. No man before or since has done more to further the cause of Surrey cricket. So much that is good and is now taken for granted was brought about by his administration. He was succeeded by William Findlay, whose appointment caused some controversy as he was a Lancastrian. He was destined for a major role in cricket government and was later to become secretary of MCC.

The resignation of Lord Dalmeny left Surrey with a problem of captaincy akin to the one that had existed before Dalmeny had accepted the post. H. D. G. Leveson-Gower was named as Dalmeny's successor, but he was unable to play for most of May, and the side was led by Capt Bush, Crawford and by Lord Dalmeny in those opening weeks. It was not a happy situation, but the County transcended it. They were never really in the hunt for the title, but they finished fourth and enjoyed a good season in spite of the damp weather which was not conducive to their style or temperament. It may have been better had Surrey kept a more stable side, but 26 players represented the County during the course of the season. Thirteen of these men played in fewer than half the matches, and such chopping and changing could not have helped the side.

The season of 1908 began chilly and cold. Surrey opened their fixtures with a match against the Gentlemen of England. The first day, Easter Monday, 20 April, saw The Oval covered in snow, and further snow falls interrrupted the play. Surrey won by an innings and 41 runs, but the match is famous in that it marked the last appearance in first-class cricket of W. G. Grace. The grand old man, he was in his 60th year, hit 15 and 25. It is good to think that The Oval, which saw 'The Champion's' century in the first Test match played in England 28 years earlier, should also see the last of that astonishing career.

If Marshal had been something of a disappointment in his first season with Surrey, in 1908 he was an overwhelming success. He hit 1,884 runs, took 56 cheap wickets and was named as one of the 'Five Cricketers of the Year'. The first, and highest, of his five centuries came at Worcester. Surrey trailed by 28 on the first innings and lost Hayward, Hobbs and Hayes before those arrears were cleared, but Marshal and Crawford attacked the bowling and turned the game in Surrey's favour so that they eventually won by 14 runs. Marshal hit 176 in 200 minutes.

In August, within the space of ten days, he played two sensational innings. With Andy Ducat, who made a most favourable impression this season, he added 123 in 65 minutes against Middlesex, and his 108 came in under two hours. In the next match Surrey went down to Yorkshire, their first defeat at The Oval for two years, but Kent, the next visitors, paid the price for this indignity. Hitch had match figures of 13 for 111, and Kent were bowled out for 111 and 103. Surrey were 154 for two when Marshal joined Hobbs, and in 70 minutes before the close of play, they added 124. They added another 115 in an hour the following morning, and Marshal, whose 167 occupied less than three hours, outshone his more illustrious partner.

Hobbs showed that he was now a batsman of remarkable maturity and a master of all wickets, however spiteful, while Hayward proved as durable as ever. Lees lost form a little, and again the splendid Smith deserved more chances than he received. Ernest Kirk showed promise as the left-arm bowler for whom Surrey had been searching, but it was a promise that was to remain generally unfulfilled.

J. N. Crawford was again in masterly form, but he faded a little towards the end of the season, and this, allied to the fact that he missed six matches, cost him the 'double' for the third year in succession, for he finished two wickets short. He failed to take a wicket in the final game, against Leicestershire at The Oval, which was completely ruined by rain, but which was a match of interest in that J.N. captained

Surrey and V. F. S. Crawford captained Leicestershire. It was in this game that Harry Altham, still at Repton and later to win fame with Hampshire and, more significantly, as an historian and champion of cricket, first appeared for Surrey.

Three months before this, at the beginning of June, John Crawford hit the highest score of his career in a memorable display against Somerset at The Oval. The two counties had not met for three years, and Surrey went into the match without Hobbs, who was injured. Leveson-Gower won the toss and Surrey quickly lost Marshal who opened with Hayward. Hayes hit 56 in 70 minutes, and when Holland, who was in his last season, joined Crawford the score was 149 for four. At the end of the day, they were still together, and the total was 403. They advanced it to 457 the next morning before Holland fell to Lewis for 87. Holland had proved an admirable foil for Crawford, for their fifth wicket partnership of 308, which is still a County record, had lasted only three-and-a-half hours. Crawford's 232 was made in under four hours and included two fives and 28 fours. The brilliance of his driving in power and beauty sent waves of excitement through the crowd. Having hit 232, he bowled unchanged with Smith and took four for 64 as Somerset were all out for 111. When the visitors batted again he took four for 58, and Surrey won by an innings and 204 runs. None then could have had an inkling of the unhappy events of the following season which, after a gap of 80 years, still seem among the saddest in the history of a great club.

The 1909 season began so well. A fine all-round performance by Crawford was instrumental in victory over Northamptonshire. In the next match, against Hampshire at The Oval, Hobbs and Hayes shared a second wicket stand of 371 in two-and-three-quarter hours (a rate of more than two runs a minute, 135 runs an hour), after Hayward had fallen to Newman at 59. Despite this phenomenal rate of scoring, Hobbs's innings did not contain a blemish nor did he offer a chance. Hobbs was 'The Master', the one who could execute all the shots and accumulate runs with a speed and serenity that never profaned the text book. He made 205, and Hayes went on to reach 276, the highest score of his career, in four-and-a-half hours. His display was not quite without fault, but it was a stunning achievement and contained three fives and 33 fours. His first 200 came in five minutes over three hours. The stand is the fourth highest in the County's history, and it remains a record for the second wicket. Surrey hit 742, the highest score of the season, and won by an innings and 468 runs.

The brilliance of the batting against Hampshire was sustained in the next match when Warwickshire were the visitors to The Oval. At lunch on the first day, Surrey were 195 for five. They were all out for 242, but took a first innings lead of 87. At the start of the second innings, Hayward and Hobbs put on 352 in three-and-three-quarter hours. Hayward made 204 not out, Hobbs 159, and Surrey won by 171 runs.

Such form excited interest for the visit of the all-conquering Australians to The Oval. At 176 for three, Surrey looked set for a big score, but they collapsed before Whitty and were out for 191. Some quite magnificent bowling by Rushby gave Surrey the edge. He dismissed Noble, Ransford and Armstrong in the space of three overs, and, in spite of a late rally, Australia were bowled out for 157, Rushby taking six for 38. Hayward carried his bat through Surrey's second innings for 96, but he received scant support, and the Australians were left with the task of scoring 213 to win. This seemed a simple task, and the tourists approached it in a somewhat lethargic manner. At 174 for four, the match appeared to be over, but Marshal broke a stand, and Rushby, Hitch and Crawford bowled finely before Lees was recalled by Crawford, who was leading the side, to dismiss McAlister and give Surrey victory by five runs. It was a momentous achievement, and the hero of the hour was Tom Rushby, with match figures of ten for 88.

The match with Essex was ruined by rain after Hobbs had hit 99 and Hayes 106, but Derbyshire were crushed by 283 runs. Rushby took ten for 56; 'Razor' Smith ten for 51. Crawford was again leading the side in the absence of Leveson-Gower who played in only 11 matches during the season.

So far all had been triumph, but, although there were many more successes to come, it was at this point that things began to go wrong. Surrey lost at Trent Bridge, but Tom Hayward scored a century of outstanding quality in the second innings. Unfortunately, by the time he had completed his 100 he was limping badly, and the lameness, said to be caused by water on the knee, haunted him for the rest of the season. He missed several matches, could not play in the Test series and often appeared in the Surrey side against the advice of the doctor. He was absent when Surrey lost to Lancashire at The Oval in June in a match in which the home side lost the services of both Lees and Leveson-Gower through injury.

For reasons it is now difficult to comprehend, Surrey had arranged to meet Oxford University at Reigate on the same days that they were entertaining Lancashire at The Oval and therefore engaged in two first-class matches at one and the same time. Both matches were lost, and although the side at Reigate was obviously a very weak one, it contained some interesting names, notably John Shuter, who came out of retirement at the age of 54 to lead the side. M. C. Bird, soon to be captain, and William Abel, son of the famous Bobby, also appeared.

There was now a sequence of events which continue to amaze even at this distance of time. There was a rain-ruined game with

Gloucestershire followed by defeat on a spiteful pitch at Sheffield. Derbyshire were beaten at Chesterfield where Smith and Rushby bowled well, but, at Old Trafford, Surrey not only lost by an innings, but were deprived of the services of Hobbs with a torn finger nail which was to keep him out for ten matches. Crawford was also injured at Old Trafford, damaging a shoulder, but he was to recover quickly enough to be asked to captain Surrey in their next match, the return game with the Australians on 15, 16 and 17 July. Before this match took place momentous things happened.

Without offering an explanation, the Surrey committee suspended Alan Marshal until the end of July. No reasons have ever been given for this astonishing action at the height of the season, but perhaps Jack Hobbs offered a clue in his ghosted autobiography, published in 1935. Hobbs's ghost for this book and for much else that he offered under his name was Jimmy Bolton, a most distinguished and experienced writer on cricket and soccer for a long period. Hobbs quotes an incident at which he was not present. He says that after the game at Sheffield 'Razor' Smith bought a child's ball, which the team headed to each other on their way to the station. Hobbs left them at the station and did not travel to Chesterfield for the next match as he was playing for England at Leeds:

> It appears that, at Chesterfield, they 'headed' and kicked the ball again on the way to their hotel with the result that a constable asked Alan Marshal for his name. As he wouldn't give it, he was taken to the police station, and then the others who followed him had their names and addresses taken. They also gave the name of Walter Lees, who had not gone with them at all.

Hobbs suggests that when the matter was brought before the Chief Constable he dismissed it because he was 'a true sport' and the case did not reach court. Trivial as the incident appeared to be, if it reached the ears of Lord Alverstone, we can be assured he would not have been amused. *Wisden* could offer no light on the subject, but hinted at dark business with terms like 'gross irregularities' and 'insubordination'. Worse was to follow.

When Crawford was given the side for the match against the Australians he noted that not only were Hobbs and Marshal not in the eleven, but Davis who had hit 112 at Chesterfield, and Rushby, the hero of the earlier victory over the Australians, were also missing. Rushby was the County's leading bowler, and his omission made it apparent that a rift existed between the committee and some of the leading professionals. Crawford made a stand, and he refused to lead the side on the grounds that the committee had left out essential players, notably Rushby. Crawford's stand in defence of the professionals had no precedent, and the Surrey committee was incensed. A resolution was passed that Crawford should never again be asked to play for the County. With that resolution was committed one of the most wicked wastes in English cricket history, certainly in the history of Surrey.

It is possible that there were faults on both sides and that a little more tact and restraint would have solved the matter. As it was, bitter feelings were aroused and Crawford left England in October 1909, to take up a post as an assistant master at St Peter's College, Adelaide.

At the Annual General Meeting the following spring, J. N. Crawford's father, Rev J. C. Crawford, put a motion on the agenda 'that the Committee of the Surrey County Cricket Club be asked to rescind the resolution passed with regard to Mr J. N. Crawford'. Lord Alverstone said that the motion could not be moved as it involved a question of confidence in the committee. He said, however, that if Crawford came forward in a sportsmanlike way, he would be happy to give his personal support to the proposition. This meant, of course, that an apology was expected. There was to be a reconciliation, but by then Alverstone was no longer President and the cruellest of wars had been fought.

John Crawford played for South Australia for ten seasons with consistent success. He toured New Zealand with an Australian side in 1914 and, at Temuka, against a South Canterbury Fifteen, he and Victor Trumper put on 198 in 69 minutes. He then added 50 in nine minutes with Noble and ended by making 354, 254 of them in sixes and fours, in 330 minutes. Surrey supporters could only sigh with regret and wonder. He was still short of his 24th birthday when he went into his self-chosen exile.

Rushby decided that he, too, had had enough. As the result of the friction between the professionals and the committee, he signed for Accrington in the Lancashire League, although his exile was to be a short one.

Marshal returned from his suspension and played with his customary panache. Sam Apted had said that The Oval would not be big enough for Marshal once he found his feet, and the Australian gave demonstration of that when he drove his way to a glorious 100 in two hours against Yorkshire at the end of August. Needing 113 to win, Yorkshire were bowled out for 26 by Rushby (8.1-4-9-5) and Smith (8-3-12-5). It was the lowest score in their history until Hampshire bowled them out for 23 at Middlesbrough in 1965.

Marshal's 110 against Yorkshire at The Oval in August 1909, was his swansong. After five matches the following season in which he made a top score of 12 and took three wickets, the Surrey committee terminated his contract. *Wisden* maintained that Surrey would not have taken such action without good reason. There was talk again of irregularities, and it was always suggested that Marshal was not good with money. One story told how he was called to task for being overdrawn at the bank. He is alleged to have said that he could not be, for he still had some cheques left in his cheque-book. He returned to Queensland, but he was never given the opportunity to display his talent at the highest level. He had it in him to be a great cricketer, but he was not the first nor the last to be diminished by a fatal flaw in his character. When the First World War broke out he joined the Australian Imperial Forces, fought at Gallipoli, and died of enteric fever in a military hospital in Malta in July 1915.

To the trauma with the professionals and the departure of Crawford was added the fact that Leveson-Gower, the captain of the side, found it possible to play in only five Championship matches in 1910, yet Surrey finished second in the table. They benefited greatly from a new system which was introduced for that season whereby the number of wins was expressed simply as a percentage of the number of games played. Surrey won 16 of their 28 games, and their seven defeats no longer told against them. Had the scheme that had been in operation for the 14 years prior to 1910 still been effective, Surrey would have finished some way down the table.

There are those who argue that the system adopted for 1910 was the correct one, that it encouraged positive cricket and that captains had to strive for a victory from the first ball of the match. This was much to Surrey's liking, for even in their poorest days, they were a side who went all out for victory. In the absence of Leveson-Gower, Surrey were led by Morice Bird. Bird had won fame at Harrow by scoring a century in each innings against Eton in 1907. He played occasionally for his native Lancashire, but most of his county cricket was played for Surrey whom he captained until 1913.

M. C. Bird was a fine forcing bat who went with Leveson-Gower's side to South Africa in 1909–10 and with Johnny Douglas's side to the same country four years later. He appeared in all five Tests in both series which is, perhaps, a little flattering to his ability. He was a tall and strong man and a dominant personality although he was not the most capable of captains. He was certainly a very useful county player, a hard-hitting bat and a medium-pace bowler. In his first full season, 1910, he hit 904 Championship runs, and this was in a summer when runs were hard to come by. That Surrey did as well as they did was due to some quite remarkable bowling by W. C. 'Razor' Smith.

William Charles Smith was nicknamed 'Razor' because he was very thin. Born in Oxford in 1877, he had come to London to play for the Crystal Palace club which was to form the basis of W. G. Grace's London County. Grace was impressed with Smith's off-break bowling, played him in a match against Surrey and recommended him to the County. Smith joined Surrey in 1900, but for ten years he laboured under the reputation that he was a wet-wicket bowler and he could not command a regular place in the side. When one considers that Surrey had had no slow bowler of quality at their disposal since the days of Southerton and had to rely exclusively on a seam attack, this is quite astonishing.

None doubted the ability of Smith to turn his off-breaks sharply, but in 1910, it appears that he added another weapon to his armoury. This was the ball that went with the arm. It was generally pitched on leg stump and would often rear awkwardly so that many batsmen were caught at short square leg in fending off the delivery.

For such a form of attack, the bowler needs the aid of an expert fielder, and in this respect Smith was wonderfully supported by 'Bill' Hitch, ever cheerful, who took some dazzling catches in positions close to the bat on the leg side. Hitch himself was developing into a fine fast bowler, but it was Smith who carried all before him in 1910. He had given notice of his quality the previous season when, given more opportuinity, he had taken 95 wickets at 12.43 runs each in Surrey's troubled season. He quickly showed that that had been no one-year wonder when he began the 1910 campaign with 12 for 85 in the win over Warwickshire and followed this with eight for 35 in the first innings of the match with Derbyshire which was, in fact, restricted to one day. No play had been possible on the first day, and the game was abandoned on the Saturday due to the death of King Edward VII. A week later, the match with Essex at The Oval was restricted to two days because of the king's funeral.

Knox made fleeting appearances and did enough to show what might have been, but Surrey were frequently handicapped by the absence of Hayes, with injury, and Hayward, because of the death of his father. Hobbs batted with customary calm authority, and there were some exciting excursions from the belligerent Capt Bush who scorned to wear batting gloves. For the first time for some years, however, it was the fielding, inspired by the ebullient Hitch, and the bowling, in the person of Smith, which were Surrey's strengths.

Twenty-five times in the course of the season Smith took five or more wickets in an innings; eight times he had ten wickets in a match. The most remarkable of his achievements came at The Oval in July in a match against Northamptonshire which is still commemorated in the pavilion, where the score-card is preserved. The game could not begin until after lunch on the Monday, but it was all over shortly after 3.00 pm on the Tuesday. Surrey batted first and lost Hobbs, Hayes and Hayward for 33. Ducat, a model professional, neat and tidy in all he did, batted in exemplary manner, hitting 67 out of 124 in an hour-and-a-half. Bush, Bird and William Abel gave him adequate assistance, but nine wickets were down for 161. At this point, Strudwick was dropped by Knight at long-off, and, relishing his escape, the wicket-keeper helped Smith to add 72 for the last wicket. Smith's 31 not out proved to be the second highest score of the match, and the stand with Strudwick occupied only half-an-hour.

Northamptonshire were 15 for nought at the close, but on the Tuesday, they lost 20 wickets for 87 runs. Smith bowled unchanged throughout the match. He took 14 wickets for 29 runs, which remains the best analysis ever recorded for a 14-wicket haul, although Derek Shackleton of Hampshire equalled it in 1955. Smith finished the match with a hat-trick when he dismissed East, Wells and Haywood, and he should have had a hat-trick in the first innings had Hayes held on to a chance at slip. In defence of Hayes, it should be pointed out that his hands had been considerably damaged by fielding in the slips to Richardson and Lockwood in their prime. The third and little finger of his right hand curled up because of nerves damaged by frequent bruising. Indeed, it was damaged hands which were to cause his eventual retirement, for he was finding it increasingly difficult to grip the bat.

That the wicket gave Smith some assistance in the victory over Northamptonshire is undeniable, but he appeared to have the ability to make the ball do everything that he wanted it to do. In Championship matches alone, he took 215 wickets at 12.56 runs each. In all matches, he took 247 wickets at 13.05 runs each. He was far and away the most successful bowler in the country. Only J. T. Hearne had a better average, 12.79; Blythe was the second highest wicket-taker with 175.

Smith was never to play for England. He was chosen for a match against South Africa in the Triangular Tournament of 1912, but he was injured and the chance did not come again. He had a frail physique and a weak heart, and he left the game in 1914, but he continued the Surrey connection by working for the sports manufacturers, Surridge, until his death in 1946.

It could not be hoped that Smith would do as well in 1911 as he had done in his most memorable of seasons, yet his performances by no means paled in comparison. With 160 wickets he was the second leading wicket-taker in the country, and, as *Wisden* pointed out: 'Any man who has to do half his bowling at The Oval in fine weather is deserving of sympathy.' The same could be applied to Rushby, who had returned from his one year in the Lancashire League and accepted new terms with Surrey, and to Hitch, both of whom took more than 100 wickets in Championship matches alone.

Surprisingly, in such a hot, dry summer, some of the batsmen did

SURREY *v* NORTHAMPTONSHIRE

Played at The Oval, Kennington, 25 and 26 July 1910

SURREY WON BY AN INNINGS AND 131 RUNS

SURREY	**FIRST INNINGS**	
T. W. Hayward	c Smith b Thompson	8
J. B. Hobbs	c East b Smith	17
E. G. Hayes	c Ellis b Thompson	0
Capt. H. S. Bush	c Wells b Thompson	19
A. Ducat	st Ellis b Seymour	67
*M. C. Bird	b Thompson	19
W. J. Abel	b Seymour	9
G. J. W. Platt	b Thompson	1
W. C. Smith	not out	31
J. W. Hitch	st Ellis b Thompson	3
†H. Strudwick	b Smith	31
Extras	b 19, lb 2, w 4, nb 3	28
Total		233

BOWLING	**O**	**M**	**R**	**W**
Thompson	26	4	62	6
Smith	14	1	69	2
East	8	1	40	0
Seymour	8	0	34	2

NORTHAMPTON-SHIRE	**FIRST INNINGS**		**SECOND INNINGS**	
R. F. Knight	b Platt	4	c Abel b Smith	6
J. Seymour	c Bird b Platt	8	c Hayes b Platt	1
*G. A. T. Vials	b Smith	5	c Hayes b Smith	4
S. G. Smith	st Strudwick b Smith	12	b Smith	2
G. J. Thompson	b Platt	7	b Platt	18
W. East	b Smith	2	c Hayes b Smith	5
A. P. R. Hawtin	lbw b Smith	0	b Smith	7
E. M. Crosse	c Bird b Platt	2	c Platt b Smith	2
R. A. Haywood	c Bird b Smith	0	c Ducat b Smith	2
W. Wells	st Strudwick b Smith	0	b Smith	0
†H. Ellis	not out	0	not out	0
Extras	b 10, nb 1	11	b 6	6
Total		51		51

BOWLING	**O**	**M**	**R**	**W**	**O**	**M**	**R**	**W**
Smith	19	9	16	6	9.1	3	13	8
Platt	17.5	7	24	4	9	1	32	2
Hitch	1	1	0	0				

Umpires: F. G. Roberts and W. Flowers

Smith's 14 for 29 is the best analysis of a bowler taking 14 wickets in first-class cricket.

*Captain; †Wicket-keeper

not do as well as may have been expected, only Hayward and Bush playing to their true form, and Surrey dropped to fifth in the table. This was mainly due to some rather bizarre performances in a season when first innings points came into being for the first time.

All began well and not a defeat was suffered until the game at Trent Bridge at the beginning of June, but it was quite typical of the County that, having beaten Notts in the return match over the August Bank Holiday, a match in which Bush scored a thrilling century, they should then collapse in the next game against Middlesex and lose by an innings.

The year was notable, however, for a number of things. It marked the first appearance of D. J. Knight, an attractive batsman from Malvern College, and of Andy Sandham. Sandham hit 53 against Cambridge University in June, and he later took 60 off the Lancashire attack in a high-scoring game at The Oval. It was noted that he played particularly well on the leg side. Sandham had been batting well for the second eleven, but Surrey were reluctant to offer him a contract because of the wealth of batting they had and because Sandham held a good business position with excellent prospects. The Surrey coach, E. H. D. Sewell, a far-travelled and multi-talented man, persuaded them otherwise, and so began the career of the young man from Mitcham who was destined to do great things and become an immense favourite.

As Knight and Sandham arrived so Lees and Davis departed. William Davis was a desperately unlucky player. He never let Surrey down when he was given the opportunity, all too rarely, and he was a batsman who often found himself omitted after he had just hit 100 or 50 runs. Another to leave The Oval was Sam Apted of whom the public showed their appreciation in a generous benefit the previous season. He had made the wickets at The Oval supreme in the country. Tom Martin, his chief assistant, succeeded him, but it was another Martin, Austin Walter – 'Bosser' – who was to carry on the great tradition of Apted when he tended the wickets at The Oval from 1924 to 1940.

In the latter part of the twentieth century we have come to accept that counties lose their leading players for several matches in the season because of the abundance of Test matches and one-day internationals. The season of 1912 gave some inkling of what was to come when the Triangular Test Tournament between England, Australia and South Africa, two Test trial matches and the usual Gentlemen and Players fixtures were all scheduled. Surrey lost Hobbs for all these matches, and the rest of the summer seemed filled by rain. On top of the bad weather and the intrusions of the representative matches, there was injury and ill-health for 'Razor' Smith. In the first three months of the season, absent with a finger injury sustained in a Test trial and with a bout of illness for many matches, he took 59 wickets. In the last three weeks of the season, six matches, he took 50 wickets at 9.80 runs each. His final figures for the season were 112 wickets at 16.96 runs each. It was to be the last season in which he was to take 100 wickets. Rushby had 93 wickets and Hitch 119, and Hayes had a fine all-round season, but it was a soggy year, poor for revenue and showing Surrey to no great advantage.

Had Smith maintained form and fitness, it is likely that Surrey would have challenged strongly for the title in 1913, for they finished third and were again a side to be reckoned with. Hobbs was now without equal in England, and Hitch was the fastest and hardest working bowler in the country, as well as a fielder in a class by himself. He could also clout the ball very hard and far on occasions, as he proved in the Scarborough Festival when he played two astonishing innings for the Players against the Gentlemen. He made 53 not out in the first innings and hit 68 not out in the second, when he and Booth of Yorkshire put on 96 in 35 minutes. He had also taken seven for 59 in the Gentlemen's second innings so that he was well deserving of the souvenir of the occasion presented to him by Lord Londesborough.

Although often referred to as a cheerful cockney, Bill Hitch was born in Lancashire. His family moved to Newmarket when he was very young, and Hitch learned his cricket at Cheveley. He was brought to the notice of Surrey by Tom Hayward who had been bowled by him when Hitch played for Eighteen of Cambridge against Hayward's Eleven. He came to London in the spring of 1905 and began his two-year qualification period. His greatest quality was his undying zest for the game, but he had pace, accuracy and tireless endeavour.

Rushby, too, bowled well that season, and Harry Harrison, so long in the shadows, hit 1,000 runs for the first and only time. He had been a bricklayer before becoming a cricketer and had massive hands which, many believed, enabled him to take so many fine catches. Against Sussex at The Oval on 30 June and 1 July 1913, he and Sandham put on a record 298 for Surrey's sixth wicket. Sandham made 198 and Harrison 138 not out, one of the two centuries he made in his career. The partnership lasted ten minutes under four hours.

Aided by nine not outs, Harrison finished second to Hobbs in the averages, but the man who deserved the greatest of accolades was Tom Hayward. On Thursday, Friday and Saturday, 26, 27 and 28 June, Surrey entertained Lancashire at The Oval. With J. T. Tyldesley making 210 and E. Tyldesley 110, Lancashire scored 558. Hayward and Hobbs opened the Surrey innings on the Friday afternoon, and Hayward, battling against great odds and suffering several blows on the body and one on the face, batted for four hours and fifty minutes and hit 139. When he reached three figures he became the first man after W. G. Grace to have scored 100 first-class centuries. He was warmly applauded by a crowd of approximately 5,000, but the feat failed to gain the respect and acclaim which had gone to Grace 18 years earlier. However, there were warm tributes, and Archie MacLaren wrote:

> I doubt if any professional has been more careful in his living or more painstaking in his methods to attain success for the captains for whom and the sides for which he has played.

Hayward set the tone for the professionals at The Oval. He was the senior professional in all aspects, setting down standards of behaviour which others violated at their peril. He led by bearing and by example. In June 1906, he hit four centuries in a week which is a record, and the following year, he and Hobbs created another record when they shared four first-wicket century partnerships in a week. When he hit his hundredth 100 Hayward was 42, and he had one more season of first-class cricket left to him, 1914.

It was a strange season, haunted by the advance of war. Bird had resigned the captaincy and was succeeded by Cyril Wilkinson. Wilkinson was a good all-round sportsman. He was a hockey international and a capable batsman, good enough to hold his own in the County side. He led the side with tact and discipline, but he could play little after the end of June, and in the closing weeks of the season the team was captained by Tom Hayward whose judgement and control was very highly praised.

The batting was strengthened by the return of Andy Ducat, who had missed the previous season because he had broken a leg playing soccer, and the team as a whole was fortified by the arrival of Percy Fender. Fender was born in Balham in August 1892. However, he had played for Sussex from 1910 to 1913 doing well enough as an aggressive batsman to be picked for the Gentlemen against the Players. He worked in a wholsesale stationery firm of which his father was managing director, and it seemed logical for him to move to London and to play for the county of his birth.

Fender's effect on the Surrey side was immediate, not simply in the runs he scored or the number of wickets he took, but in the vitality he brought to the side and in the magnificence of his fielding. His catching at slip was a tremendous boost to Hitch. Rushby and Hitch were the mainspring of the attack, but with 'Razor' Smith playing few matches, Fender was their vital support with his brisk leg-breaks which brought him 82 Championship wickets. His batting was always highly entertaining, but, as *Wisden* remarked in naming him one of the 'Five Cricketers of the Year':

> It would be flattery to describe Mr Fender as a sound batsman, the temptation of the pull too often leading him astray, but he is such a fine and daring hitter that he must always be very dangerous, more especially in the latter part of an innings when bowlers are getting tired.

Fender could not have had a better start with Surrey. He hit 44 not out in the opening match against Northamptonshire to help his side to a draw in a match in which they had been outplayed for much of the time, and in the second game, against Somerset at The Oval, he brought the visitors' first innings to a close with a hat-trick, Daniell, Bridges and Chidgey being his victims, all bowled.

Thanks to a century by Hayes, Surrey won that match by 241 runs, and victories over Worcestershire and Somerset again, at Bath, followed. At Bradford, Hobbs, who was in majestic form throughout his benefit year, and Hayes hit centuries on a soft wicket which gave help to Hirst and Rhodes. Hobbs made 151 runs, with his century coming in 75 minutes and including five sixes and eleven fours. Surrey led by 33 on the first innings, but were bowled out by Drake and Rhodes for 189 in their second innings, Hobbs making another delightful 74 out of 107 in 75 minutes. Rushby, five for 63, and Fender, four for 39, bowled Surrey to victory by 28 runs.

Returning to The Oval, Surrey entertained Warwickshire and were greatly indebted to Hitch, who took six for 74, including the hat-trick, for dismissing the visitors for 226. Hobbs hit his second century in a week. It was another masterly performance, 183 out of 224 from the bat in 170 minutes. Fender then plundered 140 in two hours and he and William Abel put on 87 in 60 minutes. The pair then took four for 21 and five for 38 respectively, and Surrey won by an innings.

A draw at Trent Bridge was followed by defeat at the hands of Essex at The Oval, but this was the only reverse suffered until Warwickshire won at Edgbaston in the penultimate game of the season. A Hobbs double century and fine bowling by Hitch and Rushby gained revenge over Essex at Leyton. A succession of draws was ended by two victories over Lancashire and by wins over Hampshire and Sussex. In the last days of July, Surrey met Kent at Blackheath – they had not beaten Kent in Kent for 17 years. Kent were a powerful side, and Surrey were not to lay the bogey for some years to come, but, in 1914, they pressed Kent hard. The home side made 349, and in reply, Surrey hit 509. Hayward and Hobbs began with a stand of 234 in 175 minutes. Each batsman scored 122, 'their play throughout being as masterly as it was brilliant'. Their centuries were followed by 105 from Donald

John Knight, a graceful young batsman who was prominent in the eleven in Oxford. It was Knight's first century for the County. The match was drawn.

On Bank Holiday Monday at The Oval, 15,000 people paid for admission to see the match against Nottinghamshire. Hobbs rewarded them with his highest innings of the season, and Surrey reached 542, the third time in the season that they had passed 500 runs. On the second day, George Gunn and Hardstaff batted dourly, and 'so bad was the barracking, at times, that several of the offenders were removed by the police'. It mattered little. Rain restricted play to 45 minutes on the last day. By then the world had changed.

Before the game against Nottinghamshire had begun Germany had declared war on Russia and her troops had violated Luxembourg. Crowds thronged Whitehall as German cavalry moved inexorably towards the Belgian border. On Monday, 3 August, the first day of the Nottinghamshire match, Germany invaded Belgium, and Great Britain declared war the following day.

The army immediately requisitioned The Oval, and Hobbs, whose benefit match against Kent was due to be played on the ground the following week, was given the option by the Surrey Committee of postponing his benefit until after the war or of having his benefit match transferred to Lord's where Surrey were to play the matches against Kent and Yorkshire originally scheduled for The Oval. Hobbs chose to have his benefit match at Lord's, but it was something of a disaster as Kent were beaten in two days. The takings were poor, and a restricted collection brought in much less than it would have done at The Oval. Surrey offered to discount it as a benefit, retaining the gate-money, keeping the subscription list open and re-staging the match after the war. Hobbs accepted this generous offer.

The second game at Lord's was against Yorkshire. Yorkshire arrived in London with eight successive victories to their credit, but they were savaged by Hobbs and Hayward. In three hours and forty minutes the great pair put on 290 for the first wicket. Tom Hayward played faultlessly until reaching his century after which he hit out wildly. It was the 104th and last century of his career. It was also the last time that Hobbs and Hayward ever shared a century partnership for the first wicket.

Hobbs was out at 349, and Hayes then took up the assault. Surrey closed at 434 for three. Hayward declared after 115 had been added the next morning, the declaration coming when Fender was out. Hitch bowled finely, as he did all season. When Yorkshire followed-on he was given splendid support by the other 100-wicket-taker of the year, Tom Rushby.

A win at Cheltenham, a draw against Middlesex at Lord's and a defeat at Edgbaston preluded the last game against Gloucestershire at The Oval, which had now been returned to the Club by the military authorities. Gloucestershire, owing to enlistments, could field only ten men. Hobbs, who was possibly at the peak of his aggressive form in 1914, hit 141, and Surrey won by an innings. D. J. Knight scored 102, and Fender took nine for 155 in the match which was over in two days.

The Surrey committee, at a special meeting, decided to cancel the last two matches of the season, against Sussex at Hove and Leicestershire at The Oval. Popular feeling against continuing first-class cricket while a war was raging was beginning to run high. In an impassioned recruiting speech, Lord Roberts had made a pointed reference to people who went on playing cricket at such a time and W. G. Grace had implored cricketers to rally to the colours.

Having beaten Gloucestershire in the last days of August, Surrey held a clear lead over Middlesex at the top of the table, and they needed only a first innings lead over Sussex or Leicestershire to win the Championship. As Surrey cancelled those two matches, some people argued that they had forfeited the right to be Champions and that the title should remain in abeyance for a year. This view received no official support, and at a meeting of the MCC Committee on 9 November 1914, a motion was raised saying that Surrey should be declared Champions. Pelham Warner, representing Middlesex, stated that his county had no objection to make against this decision, and, belatedly, Surrey were named as County Champions.

By November, it had little significance compared to what else was happening in the world where the slaughter of twelve million people, 'half the seed of Europe', was well under way.

SURREY *v* YORKSHIRE

Played at Lord's, 13, 14 and 15 August 1914

SURREY WON BY AN INNINGS AND 30 RUNS

SURREY	**FIRST INNINGS**	
†T. W. Hayward	c Wilson b Rhodes	116
J. B. Hobbs	st Dolphin b Drake	202
E. G. Hayes	c Dolphin b Kilner	134
D. J. Knight	c and b Oldroyd	21
J. W. Hitch	run out	16
A. Ducat	not out	34
P. G. H. Fender	b Rhodes	5
H. S. Harrison		
W. J. Abel		
†H. Strudwick		
T. Rushby		
Extras	b 10, lb 9, nb 2	21
Total	(for 6 wkts dec)	549

BOWLING	**O**	**M**	**R**	**W**
Booth	32	3	118	0
Drake	32	2	119	1
Hirst	18	1	61	0
Rhodes	38.5	6	134	2
Kilner	19	3	59	1
Oldroyd	7	0	37	1

YORKSHIRE	**FIRST INNINGS**		**SECOND INNINGS**	
B. B. Wilson	c Strudwick b Hitch	4	c and b Rushby	95
E. Oldroyd	b Hitch	25	b Rushby	16
D. Denton	c Harrison b Hitch	44	c Hayward b Fender	52
R. Kilner	c Abel b Rushby	5	b Hitch	54
W. Rhodes	b Fender	29	b Hitch	2
G. H. Hirst	c Ducat b Hitch	39	b Fender	13
P. Holmes	lbw b Abel	5	b Hitch	27
A. Drake	st Strudwick b Abel	10	c Fender b Rushby	28
T. J. Birtles	not out	22	b Hitch	3
M. W. Booth	b Hitch	2	c Ducat b Rushby	1
†A. Dolphin	b Abel	12	not out	1
Extras	b 4, nb 3	7	b 14, lb 3, w 2, nb 4	23
Total		204		315

BOWLING	**O**	**M**	**R**	**W**	**O**	**M**	**R**	**W**
Hitch	26	9	64	5	26	8	66	4
Rushby	21	6	56	1	20	6	30	4
Fender	13	5	30	1	27	10	94	2
Abel	12	1	47	3	14	1	61	0
Hayes					10	2	35	0
Hobbs					3	1	6	0

Umpires: E. Parris and H. R. Butt

★Captain; †Wicket-keeper

THE FENDER YEARS

THE FIRST WORLD WAR WITH ITS pain and suffering separates us from the Golden Age of cricket like some impenetrable barrier. There was military cricket and schools cricket at The Oval in the years between 1914 and 1918, and the Surrey Club itself undertook three or four matches a year against schools like Merchant Taylor's, Westminster and City of London. On the Western Front, Sassoon saw men

> . . . in foul dug-outs, gnawed by rats,
> And in the ruined trenches, lashed by rain,
> Dreaming of things they did with balls and bats.

Of men who had played for Surrey, Blacklidge, Curwen, Lewis, Raphael and Marshal never returned. At home, the Committee struggled to keep the Club alive and make possible a return to cricket when hostilities ceased. Financially, it was difficult, but they managed it. Lord Alverstone died and was succeeded as president by Sir Jeremiah Colman who had been a most able treasurer, but a motion was passed restricting the president's term of office to three years. Never again was a man to dominate the Club for such a period of time as Alverstone had done.

Surrey players appeared from time to time in what matches were played during the war. Lance-Corporal Sandham and Lieutenant Miller were in the United Services' side. E. C. Kirk and D. J. Knight were highly successful for the Artists' Rifles side. Spring and Hitch played in the Bradford League, and Fender and Knox, both of whom had taken commissions, appeared for the Army against the Australian Army and for a combined Army and Navy side.

Fender had enlisted in the Inns of Court Regiment and became a lieutenant in the Royal Fusiliers. In 1915, he transferred to the Royal Flying Corps. He later served in India where he suffered from a series of illnesses, and when he returned to England he was still in a poor state of health. A few games of cricket seemed to speed his recovery, but he sustained a badly broken leg when playing soccer in the autumn of 1918, and he was unable to play for Surrey in the first post-war season, 1919. This was a grievous blow as it left the Surrey attack almost exclusively in the hands of two men, Hitch and Rushby, who toiled manfully, both capturing more than 100 wickets in all matches and sending down nearly 2,000 overs between them, while William Abel, the next hardest worker, bowled 303. It was not a season that cricket administrators can look back on with any pride, for 1919 was the year that they decided to limit county matches to two days. It was not a system that was to the liking of anybody; to those who played on the splendidly prepared wickets at The Oval it was a disaster.

Wilkinson led the side as he had done in 1914 although, again, he dropped out towards the end of the season and D. J. Knight took over. Hayward had retired, but Hayes returned for one season to play as an amateur. He hit the last of his 45 centuries for Surrey in the match at Southampton in July. Hampshire made 315, and Hayes joined Ducat after Hobbs and Harrison had been dismissed for 182. They put on 353, which is still a Surrey record for the third wicket. Hayes made 153 and Ducat 271. Wilkinson declared at 579 for four, but, although Hampshire were bowled out for 289 in their second innings, there was no time left for Surrey to get the 26 runs they needed to win the match, an all too familiar situation in the two-day fiasco of 1919.

Andrew Ducat had a fine season, for, as well as his 271 against Hampshire, he hit centuries against Sussex and Middlesex and made 306 not out against Oxford University at The Oval. Ducat's runs came in four hours and forty minutes. It took him nearly two hours to reach his first 100 after which he battered the bowling to all parts of the field. He hit three fives and an astounding 47 fours. 'On taking out his bat he was lifted shoulder high by the spectators before he could reach the pavilion.'

Born in Brixton, Ducat played his cricket for Southend Cricket Club before joining the staff at The Oval in 1906. A tall, strong-shouldered athlete, Ducat played soccer for Woolwich Arsenal in their Plumstead days and won the first of his international soccer caps in 1910. He moved to Aston Villa and captained them when they won the FA Cup by beating Huddersfield Town 1-0 at Stamford Bridge in 1920. He won his last England soccer cap in 1921, which was the year he played his one Test match, against Australia at Headingley. An aggressively entertaining and aesthetically pleasing batsman and excellent fielder, as one would expect in such a fine all-round sportsman, Ducat was a man of great dignity and charm. He was immensely popular among his colleagues to whom he was known as 'Mac', and in a side that was studded with batsmen of high quality, this quiet, unassuming, careful-living and vigorously fit man bore comparison with the best, as more than 23,000 runs and 52 first-class centuries would testify.

Like Ducat, D. J. Knight showed that, if anything, the war years had seen him come to full maturity in his batting. Knight was in his last year at Oxford, but he did not find his best form until joining Surrey after he had come down. He hit five centuries and was an admirable opening partner for Hobbs. Knight was an elegant, stylish batsman, a product of Malvern and the Golden Age. In 1920, he became a master at Westminster School, suffered a severe blow on the head while

Andy Ducat, an excellent batsman, played for England at both cricket and soccer, and died while batting at Lord's in 1942.

fielding at short-leg after which, many said, he was never again the same batsman, and began to play less. He won two Test caps in 1921, but he gradually drifted from the game until, surprisingly, he reappeared for Surrey in 1937 at the age of 43.

The most significant return in 1919 was that of Crawford. He had returned to England and his differences with Surrey had been settled, but he was now 33 and was to play only a few games before his retirement in 1921. Nevertheless, he topped the Surrey batting averages in all matches in 1919 and took 19 wickets to finish fourth in the bowling. His most memorable achievement in 1919 was in the match against the Australian Imperial Forces in their second appearance against Surrey at The Oval. Hobbs had hit a double century in the first match, which was drawn, and the return fixture marked the reappearance of Crawford in the Surrey Eleven after an absence of ten years.

Facing the visitors' total of 436, Surrey were 44 for six when Crawford joined Wilkinson. They put on 146, Wilkinson hitting 103, but when Rushby, the last man, joined Crawford 45 were still needed to save the follow-on. Rushby stayed put, and Crawford launched a magnificent attack upon fast bowler Jack Gregory so that 80 runs were added in 35 minutes, and Rushby scored just two of them before he was stumped. Crawford ended with 144 not out which included two sixes, a five and eighteen fours. It was a wonderful return, but it was also the 15th and last century of his career. He took part in one other notable match that season, and that was the last game of the year at The Oval. Kent were the opponents, and Jack Hobbs had selected the fixture for his delayed benefit. The match was, of course, restricted to two days, with the finish at 7.30 pm. Surrey had led by 90 on the first innings, but, with only an hour-and-a-half of the match remaining, Kent still had three second innings wickets standing and were forging ahead, and even though Hitch brought an abrupt end to the innings, Surrey were left with what most considered an impossible task of scoring 95 to win in 44 minutes.

Hobbs and Crawford opened the Surrey innings, and Crawford at once hit out at the bowling. Hobbs was more circumspect, but once he felt assured, he scored as briskly as Crawford. Of the first 35, scored in 14 minutes, Crawford made 27. Twenty-five runs came in the next seven minutes, and after 29 minutes, at a rate of eight runs an over, the target was reached when Hobbs drove Freeman for the winning boundary. Hobbs made 47, Crawford 48, and there was one bye. The crowd stood cheering in front of the pavilion for a considerable time. 'The Master' could not have wished for a more fitting climax to his benefit match.

Hobbs's benefit raised £1,671, a considerable sum in 1919, and he used the money to start his famous sports' outfitters and that lovely shop in Fleet Street which, for so many years, was a Mecca for lovers of the game and for schoolboys whose deeds had earned them the award of a bat presented by the now much missed Star, the London evening newspaper.

Surrey finished fourth in 1919 at the end of which season Findlay resigned as secretary to take up his appointment with MCC. He was succeeded by John Shuter. Shuter was 65 years old and, although he seemed in excellent health, was too old to take on such a strenuous job. That he agreed to do so was in loyalty to the Club which had been his life. Sadly, his tenure of office was brief, for he collapsed and died at his home in Blackheath on 5 July 1920.

Shuter's death came as a great shock to the cricket world, and although his great achievements are now a century in the past, the debt that the Surrey Club owes to him should never be forgotten. He, more than any other man, established Surrey as the leading county cricket club. In their appreciation of him, the committee said:

> . . . his name will be handed down as an inspiring leader, a great cricketer, and one who exercised a wide influence in upholding the best traditions of the game, and the true spirit in which it should be played.

A. M. Latham carried out the secretarial duties until the end of the 1920 season when, from a large number of applicants, Richard Palairet was appointed to succeed Shuter. Palairet was an all-round sportsman from a famous cricketing family, and he was to serve Surrey with the majesty one associates with his batting for Oxford University and Somerset. He held the post until 1932.

On the playing field, Surrey enjoyed another successful season in 1920 and looked for a time as if they would win the Championship. Three successive victories were followed by a surprise defeat by Somerset. Then came eight wins and two draws in ten Championship matches before Surrey travelled to play Kent at Blackheath on Saturday, 24 July. At this time, Surrey were top of the table and in a very strong position, but Kent, although not the force they had been before the war, were still a good side.

Matches had now reverted to three days, and the Saturday start, which Surrey had pioneered in 1913, was now in operation. The game at Blackheath could not start until 2.30 pm on the first day because of the damp state of the pitch, but it was all over by 4.30 pm on the Monday. Surrey were bowled out for 61 and 73, and Kent won by an innings and 32 runs. It was the ninth time in eleven matches that Surrey had lost to Kent at Rectory Field, Blackheath, which was a very popular venue for the meetings between the two counties. For Surrey, Blackheath was unquestionably a bogey ground, and when all else was going well the spectre of Blackheath always loomed.

Two more defeats and a draw in the next three games ended Surrey's Championship aspirations, but they were to participate in the grand climax of the season when they visited Lord's for the final fixture. Middlesex had won eight games in a row and victory over Surrey would give them the title, with Lancashire close on their heels.

A crowd of 25,000 saw the first day's play, and there were almost as many present on the Monday. Andy Sandham played a superb innings of 167 not out, and Surrey led by 73 on the first innings, but, set to make 244 to win in just over three hours, they reached 100 for two before collapsing to 188 all out. The victory was the crowning of

Pelham Warner's career; the defeat made little difference to Surrey who had still finished in third place.

Sandham had at last established himself as Hobbs's opening partner, and Peach had won a regular place in the side. Having recovered from his injury and illnesses, Fender reclaimed his place in the Surrey team and, as the season drew to its close and Wilkinson dropped out of the side, Fender began to show those qualities of exciting leadership which were to shape Surrey cricket for the next decade. Fender's return gave the untiring Hitch and Rushby some much needed support, and, indeed, Fender was the only one of the trio to take 100 wickets in Championship matches, yet it was as a batsman that he was to astound the world that season.

On the Wednesday, Thursday and Friday, 25, 26 and 27 August, before the final showdown at Lord's, Surrey played Northamptonshire at Northampton. The home side won the toss and, thanks to a fine century from 'Fanny' Walden, better known as an outstanding footballer for Tottenham Hotspur and England, they made 306. The first day ended early through bad light with Surrey having scored 12 for the loss of Hobbs's valuable wicket.

Woolley (brother of Frank) accounted for Sandham, Wilkinson and Shepherd the next morning, but runs had come at a fairly brisk pace, and, half-an-hour before lunch, Surrey were 160 for four. Either side of lunch, Peach and Ducat put on 288 in approximately two-and-a-quarter hours. Ducat was out for 149 at which point Fender joined Peach. In 42 minutes, they added 171 before Wilkinson declared shortly after tea.

As Richard Streeton has pointed out in his admirable biography of Fender, Fender's innings was 'carnage among the dead and dying', for Peach and Ducat had already demoralised the Northamptonshire bowling, and a number of catches were dropped. Nevertheless, Fender's innings was an astounding piece of batting, and although his record of 100 in 35 minutes has since been equalled by Steve O'Shaughnessy when playing for Lancashire against Leicestershire in 1983, it was equalled only when runs were being offered freely in pantomime fashion.

Surprisingly, Fender's world record attracted only minimal notice at the time, although it was recognised, as was the fact that the 1,475 runs scored in the match was a record aggregate for the County Championship. Perhaps the statistic that gives the clearest indication of the magnitude of the achievement is Streeton's observation that the stand of 171 in 42 minutes between Peach and Fender translates into a scoring rate of 244 runs an hour, a rate unapproached before or since over such a period as a half-an-hour or more.

Ducat's innings became almost forgotten, as did that of poor Alan

Peach. Peach was a wonderful bits and pieces player, and this was the first and the highest of his four first-class centuries. He was always a big hitter of the ball and a very useful medium-pace bowler who could spin the ball appreciably. He became coach of the County in the years immediately before the Second World War, and left Surrey a great legacy by introducing the Bedser twins to The Oval. Fender later said that his intention had been to stay quiet and allow Peach to reach his hundred before a tea-time declaration.

In the winter of 1920–21, Fender, Hitch, Hobbs and Strudwick were all members of the England party that toured Australia where all five Tests were lost. Fender was the only one of the four without Test experience, and he won his first caps on that tour. While he was winning those caps he was appointed captain of Surrey.

Wilkinson had been unable to play regularly in 1919, nor in 1920 when, on top of his business commitments, a leg injury had kept him out of the side. The man originally marked down to succeed to the Surrey captaincy was Miles Howell, who had led Oxford University at both cricket and soccer and whose father and brother had both played for the County, but, as it transpired, he was unable to play with any regularity. Indeed, he played only 36 times for Surrey between 1919 and 1925, assisting the County, as *Wisden* noted, 'whenever they could get him, though it usually meant that some pro whom other counties would have welcomed with open arms had to stand down for him'. After 1925, Howell played mainly for the Free Foresters.

The inability of Howell to play had allowed the job of captaincy to fall on Fender – initially because he was the only amateur in the side but after Wilkinson's resignation because he had displayed such enterprise and imagination when he had led the side. It is well over half a century since Percy Fender last captained Surrey, yet his name continues to excite controversy and debate. 'He remained to the end of his career,' wrote Louis Palgrave, 'the best county captain in England.' The fact that he was the best captain never to lead England has become common coinage; and Robertson-Glasgow wished 'he could have captained England; for he surely earned it.' E. M. Wellings, who played under Fender, and against him, balanced this view in his *Vintage Cricketers*:

> That Fender never captained England was a matter of much discussion and controversy. Fleet Street, I remember, often called for his appointment, but in this case the pen was not mighty enough. If Fender could have taken most of the Surrey side into the England team, he would have been the right choice. As that was impossible I think the selectors were right to look beyond him to Arthur Gilligan, Frank Mann, Arthur Carr and Percy Chapman during the time he was at his peak.

NORTHAMPTONSHIRE *v* SURREY

Played at Northampton, 25, 26 and 27 August 1920

SURREY WON BY 8 WICKETS

NORTHAMPTON-SHIRE	FIRST INNINGS		SECOND INNINGS	
W. Adams	b Rushby	3	c Hobbs b Fender	31
A. P. R. Hawtin	c and b Fender	34	b Rushby	5
R. A. Haywood	c sub b Hitch	15	c Peach b Fender	96
C. N. Woolley	c Wilkinson b Fender	58	lbw b Hitch	42
F. I. Walden	c Hitch b Lockton	128	b Rushby	63
S. H. G. Humfrey	b Ducat	24	b Hitch	31
W. Wells	c Strudwick b Hitch	4	c Rushby b Shepherd	71
*R. O. Raven	b Ducat	4	lbw b Shepherd	28
J. V. Murdin	b Shepherd	15	c Strudwick b Shepherd	4
A. E. Thomas	not out	8	c Ducat b Hitch	30
†B. Bellamy	c Hitch b Fender	11	not out	13
Extras	lb 2	2	b 9, lb 6, nb 1	16
Total		306		430

1st inns: 1-3, 2-24, 3-105, 4-115, 5-171, 6-188, 7-203, 8-278, 9-288
2nd inns: 1-12, 2-54, 3-161, 4-209, 5-264, 6-288, 7-365, 8-376, 9-393

BOWLING	O	M	R	W	O	M	R	W
Hitch	24	6	90	2	28.2	2	137	3
Rushby	25	10	66	1	27	5	68	2
Lockton	20	5	53	1	10	0	34	0
Shepherd	6	1	17	1	13	5	27	3
Fender	21.5	1	69	3	29	1	118	2
Ducat	9	4	9	2	8	1	23	0
Peach					4	2	7	0

SURREY	FIRST INNINGS		SECOND INNINGS	
J. B. Hobbs	c Bellamy b Murdin	3	b Walden	54
A. Sandham	c Hawtin b Woolley	92	b Thomas	6
*C. T. A. Wilkinson	b Woolley	43		
T. F. Shepherd	c Bellamy b Woolley	9	(3) not out	42
H. A. Peach	not out	200		
A. Ducat	c Bellamy b Thomas	149	(4) not out	11
P. G. H. Fender	not out	113		
J. W. Hitch				
J. H. Lockton				
†H. Strudwick				
T. Rushby				
Extras	b 9, lb 1	10	b 2, lb 5	7
Total	(for 5 wkts dec)	619	(for 2 wkts)	120

1st inns: 1-5, 2-97, 3-127, 4-160, 5-448
2nd inns: 1-24, 2-93

BOWLING	O	M	R	W	O	M	R	W
Wells	31	6	133	0				
Murdin	22.4	0	162	1	9	1	37	0
Thomas	23	0	142	1	14	3	24	1
Woolley	26	3	116	3	9.3	2	26	0
Humfrey	4	0	36	0				
Haywood	4	0	20	0				
Walden					4	0	26	1

Umpires: J. Moss and T. M. Russell

Fender's century in 35 minutes remains the fastest in first-class cricket.

*Captain; †Wicket-keeper

Surrey

P.G.H.Fender

Percy Fender, popular with cartoonists, columnists and all who loved cricket.

Fender's record in the 13 Tests in which he appeared, the last against South Africa in 1929, was, in fact, moderate, but nothing will dissuade those who saw him at The Oval, and many who did not, from 'the opinion that here was the man who should have captained England for a long period and here was the man who has had no superior as captain of Surrey. Said Robertson-Glasgow:

> He hated the dull finish, the formal declaration, the expected stroke, the workaday over. He rescued treasures of cricket from dust and oblivion, snatched off the covering and showed them to an astonished and delighted public. He would assail a famous batsman

148

with a sequence of dropping full-pitchers. I have seen him, and him alone, cut a ball square for six. He would declare an innings closed with an abruptness which threatened committeemen with heart-failure.

Moreover, in a world where most people live mundane lives and follow jobs which offer them little pleasure, interest or excitement, Fender was admired as something of an eccentric, a sort of civilised Groucho Marx. Beloved of cartoonists, he was at one and the same time cricketer, writer, billiard player, bridge player, wine merchant, broadcaster, club man and socialite. He kept goal for Casuals when they won the AFA Cup, 1913, for the Belgian Leopold Club and, in non-league matches, for Fulham. He was ever in the public eye and so were Surrey.

Richard Streeton's appreciation of him as a captain is that:

> He had a deep knowledge of cricket, its history, laws and technique, and the judgement to interpret pitches and match situations. He kept dossiers on players and had a knack for recalling a batsman's weaknesses in matters of bowling and strokes and, equally important, his preferences. Fender had the insight to utilize these things at the right moment, and harnessed to this were the craft and knowing instincts of a successful gambler. His ability was all slightly tinged, too, with gamesmanship, though always within the laws.

It was Fender's use of gamesmanship which roused some of his opponents to ire and which, Wellings felt, would have made it difficult for him to have won the following of an England side, most of whom would have suffered at his hands. Certainly Wellings himself recalls bowling Fender middle stump when playing for Oxford University against Surrey at The Oval in 1929. Fender had made 18 at the time, but stayed to get 74, the umpires, deferring to Fender, saying that they had not seen whether he was bowled or whether the wicket-keeper had disturbed a middle stump which was leaning backwards.

One thing is sure: for the best part of a decade when Surrey's bowling resources were limited, Fender led the County with a verve, enthusiasm and intelligence that made them always strong contenders for the Championship. Such leadership assured Surrey of an eager and faithful following and made Fender himself one of the most discussed cricketers in England. He could not have begun his period of captaincy in more difficult circumstances. England were in the middle of a sequence when they lost eight Test matches in succession to Australia, and Jack Hobbs tore a thigh muscle when scoring 85 for Lionel Robinson's XI against the Australians at the beginning of May. This injury kept him out of the game for two months. He returned at the end of June and appeared against Oxford University at The Oval. At

Headingley, he hit 172 not out against Yorkshire in what was to be the only County match in which he appeared during the season. He played for the Players against the Gentlemen at The Oval and was chosen for England against Australia at Headingley, but he was taken ill with appendicitis and was unable to bat or to play again for the rest of the season.

In the absence of Hobbs, other batsmen grasped the opportunity to show their quality. Sandham and Ducat scored heavily and, like D. J. Knight, made their first appearance for England. On being told he was selected for the Headingley Test, Ducat refused to believe it, thinking that his team-mates were playing a trick on him. Fender, Hitch and Strudwick also played in this unhappy series. Andrew Jeacocke had hit over 1,000 runs and was particularly strong in driving. He was also a fine slip fielder. He now opened the innings in the absence of Hobbs and formed an admirable partnership with Sandham. An amateur, Jeacocke was born in Islington, but played for Surrey under a residential qualification. In 1922, however, his cricket came to an abrupt end in August after friction and controversy. Kent, or Lord Harris, had challenged his qualification for Surrey, saying that it was not valid. In fact, the house in which he lived was in Kent, but the other side of the road was in Surrey. For the last years of his career Jeacocke played mainly for Free Foresters.

Another to come to the fore in 1921 was Tom Shepherd. He had forced his way into the side with some startling performances in the second eleven in 1920, when he scored 709 runs, average 101.28 and took 38 wickets at 15.50 runs each. He bowled medium pace, and his batting was founded on good technique and temperament. He was one of those happy players able to adjust to the needs of the game and of the team. He eagerly took the opportunity to command a regular place in the Surrey side and hit 1,907 runs at 52.97 which left only Hobbs, from his four innings, above him in the averages.

Shepherd's season included six centuries, the most welcome of which came at Blackheath, so long 'the Surrey graveyard'. Kent made 464 for nine declared, and Surrey were 183 for six when Bill Hitch joined Shepherd. Hitch had broken down when bowling on the Saturday, but he threw off his injury worries to hit 106 in two hours as he and Shepherd added 200. Shepherd was not out for 210, and Surrey were all out for 448. Inevitably, the match was drawn.

The game at Blackheath was played for Fairservice's benefit, and Hitch had chosen the return match at The Oval ten days later for his benefit, for the rivalry between Surrey and Kent was so intense as always to draw big crowds. In fact, 58,000 people paid for admission on 6, 8 and 9 August, and they were well rewarded. Sandham hit 123. Howell was run out for 99, the highest score he ever made for Surrey although he hit eight centuries elsewhere, and Hitch hit 71. Surrey made 339 and took a first innings lead of 85. When they batted again Sandham made 95 and Ducat 97. Fender declared and set Kent to make 412 in five-and-a-quarter hours. They failed gloriously, and Surrey won by 75 runs shortly before 6.30 pm.

Sandham was in brilliant form at this time and the two knocks against Kent brought him to 604 runs in three completed innings while in June he had hit 292 not out, his highest score for Surrey, against Northamptonshire at The Oval. This followed the match against Essex at Leyton where he had been unwell on the Saturday and dropped down to number eleven. He joined Ducat at 307 for nine on the Monday and hit 58 before being run out by Perrin. In 100 minutes the pair added 173 which remains a record for Surrey's last wicket, but then it is not often that one finds a batsman of Sandham's calibre going in at number eleven. Ducat hit 290 not out in four hours and forty minutes.

Another record to fall in 1921 was for bowling. At Taunton, Surrey made 236, thanks mainly to a late flurry by Billy Abel who hit 72. Somerset were all out for 110 in 35.5 overs. Bowling unchanged, Tom Rushby returned figures which remain a record for the County: 17.5-4-43-10.

W. J. D. Hunt, a staunch follower of the Surrey Club, points out that of the five bowlers who have taken all ten wickets in an innings for Surrey (Richardson, Watts, Laker and Lock were the others) three were in Cape Town during the second Test between England and South Africa in January 1957. Laker and Lock were in the MCC party, and Eddie Watts was coaching in schools in the area.

In spite of Rushby's record, bowling was not Surrey's strong point. Fender took 111 wickets for the County, and Rushby, Hitch and Peach all got into the seventies, but the size of Fender's achievement as a leader can be gauged from the high placings that Surrey reached in the early 1920s when their bowling was so thin. It was fitting for Tom Rushby that he should establish a Surrey record in 1921 for it was his last season with the Club. He dropped out of the game through illness the following year. In 17 seasons for Surrey he may have had his differences with the administration, but he never lost his enthusiasm for bowling his medium pace for however often and however long it was required. There were many, many times when he and Hitch were the Surrey bowling. There was no one else.

Fifteen victories, one defeat, and seven draws, in three of which first innings points were gained, took Surrey to the last match of the season at Lord's in the knowledge that victory would give them the Championship. The game was played on 27, 29 and 30 August, and more than 50,000 people watched the three days play. Fender won the toss, but the advantage of batting first was quickly discounted when

Knight, Sandham and Ducat were out for 56. Douglas Jardine, who first appeared for Surrey this season, and Shepherd added 144 in as many minutes. Shepherd finished with 128 not out, but Surrey were out for a rather disappointing 269.

In the absence of Rushby, the Surrey attack was opened by Hitch and Gilbert Reay, a tall, well built, fast-medium amateur bowler who captained the Beddington Club for many years, but whose appearances for Surrey were limited after a promising debut in 1920. Reay took four for 44, and Middlesex were all out for 132. With Knight at his majestic best, Surrey were 115 for two in their second innings, but they collapsed before Nigel Haig and were bowled out for 184. Nevertheless, Middlesex had to make the highest score of the match, 322, in order to win.

Lee and Twining negotiated a difficult quarter-of-an-hour at the end of the second day and scored 19. Harry Lee was lbw to Reay at 48, but 'Young' Jack Hearne joined Twining in a stand of 277 in four hours and ten minutes. Both batsmen scored centuries and both were out, as was Bruce, but Middlesex won by six wickets and took the Championship for the second year in succession. In his first season as captain, Fender had led Surrey to second place. He was never able to take them that one place higher.

It was not for lack of effort on Fender's part that Surrey failed to bring the Championship back to The Oval. In 1922, he did the 'double' in matches for Surrey alone, and, under his inspiring leadership, the County won 13 and lost only one of their 24 games, but the points and percentage system told against them and they finished third. That they should finish so high with an attack which now relied almost exclusively on Fender himself was remarkable. Had they possessed a first-rate strike bowler, Surrey would have won the title without question. They sighed for another Lockwood, Lohmann or Richardson, but Rushby's career was at an end and even the indomitable Hitch was beginning to show signs of wear. He dropped out of the side through injury in the last month of the season. For Fender, *Wisden* could find no praise too high:

Essentially a change bowler – the best in England, as he has been aptly described – he became by force of circumstances the chief attacking force, and had to get through an enormous amount of work, bowling 959 overs. He had often to keep himself on a little too long, but for all that the 143 wickets he took did not cost him quite $19\frac{1}{2}$ runs each. As he played half his cricket at The Oval and was not in the least helped by the bad weather – he is far more formidable on fast wickets than on slow ones – his figures are in reality much better than they look on paper. Despite all his labours as a bowler he did bigger things as a batsman than he had ever done before, and was still about the most brilliant of slip fieldsmen. Over and above all this he was, by general consent, by far the best of the county captains, never losing his grip of the game and managing his side with a judgement that was seldom at fault.

Fender had his men behind him and got the last ounce out of them. It was never dull when playing under Fender, for he was always producing the unexpected, and not only with his leg-breaks. The Surrey fielding was exhilarating, and the delight in the batting and in the general exuberance of the cricket drew very large and enthusiastic crowds to The Oval so that the finances, as well as the cricket, were in good order. The crowds were well rewarded with what they saw. Hobbs, although still convalescing at the beginning of the season and having to miss several matches in order to rest, reasserted himself as the greatest batsman in the world and now moved towards one of the most memorable periods of his most memorable career. Sandham, too, had now established himself as one of the finest of opening batsmen, but it was Fender who excited most when the mood gripped him.

Against Hampshire at The Oval in May, he produced a display of hitting that none had seen since Jessop was at his height. He hit 185 in 130 minutes. Three weeks later, at Leicester, he played another amazing innings. With Hobbs hitting 145, Surrey had made 501 for eight in their first innings. Fender took six wickets and Leicestershire were bowled out for 334 so that they had to follow-on. They saved the innings defeat easily, but to the astonishment of all, Fowke, the Leicestershire skipper, declared at tea time on the last day and left Surrey to make 150 in 80 minutes. *Wisden* suggested that he acted very rashly; others began a legend which indicated that the inexperienced Leicestershire skipper had been led astray by Fender who had pleaded that several of his players had strains, that they faced a long journey to Bradford and could do with a rest from fielding in a match which had become meaningless. Fowke took pity and paid the price. Surrey were 42 for three, but Fender hit 91, and Surrey reached their target in 63 minutes:

Fender finished the match with a straight drive into the pavilion, his audacious punishment of good length bowling that had proved fatal to other men bringing about the astounding result. Fender scored 28 of the last 29 runs in eight minutes.

At the end of July, he hit 137 out of 217 in 90 minutes against Kent at The Oval in a match in which nearly 48,000 people passed through the turnstiles in the first two days. His grandeur continued into 1923 when he again did the 'double'. If Surrey slipped to fourth, it was no fault of his:

> Mr Fender must be spoken of separately. He was the great all-round force on the side – bowler, batsman, slip fieldsman, and an unequalled captain. He was no doubt disappointed that Surrey did not win more matches but personally he had a glorious season. The amount of work he got through was astonishing, but he kept fresh to the end. From force of circumstances, the support at his command being so moderate, he bowled 1,000 overs in county matches but his batting did not suffer. Indeed he had never combined such sound defence with his brilliant hitting. There was a time when he seemed to think every ball could be sent to the boundary, but the years have brought restraint. In bowling he stood out by himself with 136 wickets. As always, with his pronounced spin and variety of device, he was in proportion much better on hard wickets than on soft ones. He is too experimental to keep runs down to the requisite level on a pitch spoilt by rain.

Sadler, Peach and Hitch gave him the most support, and for Hitch, nearing the end of his career, there was one great day when, for the first time since 1897, Surrey beat Kent in Kent and laid the bogey of Blackheath. Hitch made it possible with a first innings haul of seven for 33, and Surrey went on to win by 222 runs.

Hobbs had a moderate season by his own standards, 2,087 runs, average 37.94, in a damp year, and there were suggestions that his reflexes were slowing, that he had not come to terms with the fact and was losing his wicket through impetuosity. Whatever faults he may have developed, he quickly righted them. It was generally accepted that Hobbs had reached his peak in 1914, yet, in the 16 seasons he played after the First World War, only once did he fail to average 50 (1923) until his last, limited season in 1934. He had hit ten centuries in 1922, which brought his total to 99, so that all attention was focused on him at the beginning of the 1923 season. He was held in the greatest affection by all the sporting public, and they did not have to wait long to celebrate his 100th hundred.

Surrey's second match of the season was against Somerset at Bath. Hobbs was out for nought in the first innings as Surrey were bowled out for 91. Somerset took a first innings lead of 59. Only three overs had been possible on the Saturday, the first day, and Hobbs was batting again by the end of the second. He began the last morning with 19 to his credit, but Sandham, Ducat and Shepherd had all gone cheaply – indeed, Hobbs had participated in the running out of the last two. Feeling somewhat upset at his lapses, Hobbs was partnered by the uninhibited Hitch whose response to a crisis was bludgeoningly simple. Such an approach must have eased Hobbs, and the pair added 121. With his score on 97, Hobbs pushed the ball to cover and went through for a single. He turned to see the return to the keeper reckless and wide, and he happily accepted the two overthrows. There was national rejoicing. Hobbs was approaching his 41st birthday, and it was felt that this was the pinnacle of a great career, for he now stood level with Grace and Hayward in having scored 100 hundreds. None could have imagined that Hobbs was little over halfway to what he would achieve in his distinguished career and that even greater glories lay ahead.

He added four more centuries to his total before the end of the season, and by the end of the 1924 season his total had risen to 110 and three more were scored on the tour of Australia in 1924–25. The 1924 season had seen Surrey climb to third again in the Championship, and, in the wettest of summers, lose only to Hampshire at Southampton. It was a match Surrey should have won, for Hampshire needed 43 to win when their last pair, Boyes and Livsey, came together. Boyes survived a strong appeal for a catch behind, and then Livsey, on eight (he went on to make 35), was missed off a simple chance in the slips, and Hampshire won the match.

Fender's bowling was less effective than in previous seasons, and the medium-paced Sadler, Peach and Fenley all shared the honours with him. Stanley Fenley was a slow leg-break bowler who was born in Kingston and was home on leave from Africa. Surrey had had no genuine slow bowler since 'Razor' Smith and were delighted with Fenley's success. He had played as an amateur in 1924, but they offered him a professional contract, and he appeared for the County until 1929, never quite repeating the promise of that first year. He appeared three times for Hampshire in 1935.

Peach took 73 wickets for Surrey in 1924, and his great moment came against Sussex at The Oval in June when he took a career best eight for 60 and became the first Surrey player to take four wickets in four balls. Sadler also had a good match, against Yorkshire at The Oval, when he took ten wickets and brought about a Surrey victory, but it was the batting, inevitably, that was the Surrey strength. Jardine played a full season and batted solidly and successfully, and Sandham and Hobbs were a wonderful opening pair, finishing first and second in the national averages. That the batting remained so strong was remarkable when one considers that Ducat missed the entire season because of a football injury and later was appointed manager of Fulham. Surrey still had an option on his services, and he played in seven Championship matches in 1925, but that was the year that Shepherd, Sandham and, in particular, Jack Hobbs dominated the batting. For Hobbs, this was to be a 'golden summer'.

'The dashing young batsman of pre-war years had become a little more restrained,' said Louis Palgrave, 'a little less impetuous, but the sparkle remained, the technique was unimpaired, the inimitable footwork and timing as perfect as before.' Surrey beat Hampshire in thrilling style in the opening match of the season and then trounced Gloucestershire with Hobbs hitting 104. Another century followed, against Glamorgan, and Surrey gained their third win in as many matches.

A fourth successive win followed when Hobbs and Sandham began the match against Warwickshire at The Oval with a partnership of 232 in two-and-a-half hours. Hobbs hit 120, Sandham 181, and the pair added 216 against Essex at Leyton in the next match. Here, Hobbs hit his fourth 100 in successive matches, but he damaged a heel and the match was drawn. Peach had hit 109 and Sandham 90 in this game, but it was becoming clear that, as ever, the bowling was a poor support for the batting, and this was underlined when Sussex drew at The Oval and at Trent Bridge where Hobbs returned to the side and hit his fifth century in consecutive matches. *The Times'* cricket correspondent was quick to note the weakness:

> The chief impression left on my mind by recent cricket is that Mr Fender must be feeling very uneasy about Surrey's bowling. He is bowling as well himself as at any time in his career, but he is in danger of having too heavy a burden imposed upon him. Except now and then from Peach he is not getting half the support he needs. The weakness of the bowling, suggested at Leyton and by the failure to force a win against Sussex at The Oval, was made quite apparent during the closing part of Saturday's play at Trent Bridge, in the first of the really significant matches. By reason of their wealth of batting Surrey can go into the field this season with little fear of being beaten on a hard wicket, but the problem of how to get the other side out in fine weather will, from the present appearances, require a lot of solving.

Indeed, the solving was still a quarter of a century in the future. Hitch played in only ten matches in what was his last season. Fenley was disappointing. Supporters were asking why Bill Abel could find no place in the side, and only the observant Peach, ever ready to practise and to learn, could match Fender in work or success. A narrow win at Leicester and a first defeat of the season, at Old Trafford, left Surrey at third place in the table in the first week in June. When Essex came to The Oval on 13 June, Fender won the toss, and although Sandham and Jeacocke went quickly and Hobbs began sketchily, runs soon began to flow. Shepherd scored briskly, and Jardine hit with more power than usual and began to overtake Hobbs.

At lunch, Hobbs had made 60 and after the break,

> as he gradually approached his hundred the atmosphere all round
> the game became electric. After remaining at 99 for some time, he
> scored the necessary single, and a roar went up which might have
> been heard at Leyton. As if to answer the last question and to relieve
> the spectators of any further anxiety, he promptly hit a ball to the
> boundary and reached his 1,000 runs.

Hobbs was the first to 1,000 runs in 1925, and his sixth century of the
season in the win over Essex started excited talk about W. G. Grace's
record of 126 centuries. It must be remembered that Grace had set a
standard which lingered in the minds of many as being invincible.
Hobbs hit 87 runs in the second innings against Essex and followed that
with a century in each innings against Cambridge University later in
the week. Should any think that the Light Blues were as meagre
opposition then as they often are today, they should note that Surrey
lost the fixture at The Oval in June 1925. Hobbs hit his two hundreds,
and Ducat, returning to the side after a long absence, scored 91, but
Cambridge, set to make 426, won by six wickets.

Back to the serious business of the Championship, Surrey
entertained Somerset at The Oval. The visitors were bowled out for
206 on a perfect pitch, and Surrey ended the first day on 134 for the loss
of Sandham. Hobbs was 80 not out. On the Monday,

> chief interest in the early part of the day's play naturally centred on
> Hobbs. It is an accepted fact that this great batsman will soon set up a
> new record that may stand for all time, and the achievement of
> adding yet another three-figure innings to his ever lengthening
> series is now greeted almost with a sense of relief.

Hobbs duly reached the 122nd century of his career, and Ducat and
Shepherd also hit centuries and added 180. Surrey went on to win by
an innings.

In three-and-a-quarter hours at Edgbaston on 24 June, Hobbs hit
215 with two sixes and 22 fours. His runs were made out of 311, 18 of
which were extras. Fenley took seven wickets in Warwickshire's first
innings, but when the home side followed on, they scored 407, and
eventually Surrey won a thrilling match by five wickets with eight
minutes to spare and rain beginning to fall.

Yorkshire inflicted the second Championship defeat of the season
on Surrey at Bradford. Surrey's only consolation was that when
Fender had Leyland caught by Jardine it was his thousandth first-class
wicket. At Portsmouth, Hobbs rested, Sandham hit a century, Bert
Geary took six for 52 with his medium pace and Surrey won.

In spite of Hobbs failing in both innings, Lancashire were beaten at

The Oval. Any fears that 'The Master' was running into a lean spell were dispersed when he captained the Players at Lord's and scored 140. Surrey's next match was against Kent at Blackheath, and now the ghost that had haunted them throughout the Edwardian Age and beyond was well and truly laid.

A vast crowd saw Fender and Shepherd take four wickets apiece and Kent bowled out for 281 on the Saturday. Hobbs and Sandham had put on 121 before the close. On the Monday morning, having been at the wicket for two-and-a-half hours in all, Hobbs hit Woolley to the square-leg boundary to complete his 12th century of the season. So excited were the crowd that the game was held up for several minutes. Hobbs was out with the score at 199, having scored 105, and Sandham, 88, was out two runs later. Shepherd took over and hit a devastating 207 in the rest of the day's play. Surrey made 547 for five, and Kent collapsed before Fender and Fenley on the last day.

During the course of his century, Hobbs had become the first batsman in the country to reach 2,000 runs for the season. Having reached the mark on 20 July, he was still short of Mead's feat of having reached 2,000 runs on 12 July in 1921, but had equalled Hayward's mark of 1904. Hobbs now stood one century short of Grace's record, and crowds, cameras and newsmen flocked after him wherever he went. 'Will he make the century today?' was the constant question. But he was out for one at Hove where Surrey won by an innings. They had now clambered into second place and were not to lose another Championship match, but Yorkshire were unbeaten and were to remain so, and they never looked likely to surrender their lead.

Fender incurred the wrath of The Oval crowd on 25 July. He won the toss and asked Kent to bat first when more than 25,000 people, the biggest crowd for three years, had arrived in hope of seeing Hobbs equal Grace's record. Kent batted all day, and rain ruined the match after Sandham, not Hobbs, had made 100. Victory at Gloucester, a draw against Nottinghamshire, and rain-ruined matches with Leicestershire and Middlesex all left the thousands of people who had seen the matches frustrated, for the record-equalling century did not come. On Saturday, 15 August, Surrey began their match against Somerset at Taunton. Again a huge crowd arrived to see if Hobbs could equal Grace's record.

Somerset batted first, and were bowled out for 167 by 4.00 pm. They were not a strong side in 1925, and only Worcestershire and Glamorgan finished below them in the table. With a tea interval at 5.00 pm insisted upon, much to the annoyance of some spectators and journalists, Surrey had two-and-a-quarter hours batting on the first evening. At 6.00 pm, with 45 minutes left, Hobbs had made 53: 'He had driven but little; most of his runs had come from neat placing shots to leg'. Suddenly, he changed his game and doubled his rate of scoring. The crowd grew more and more excited, but Hobbs just lost his race against the clock and finished on 91 not out.

He had had one piece of fortune.

He had scored 86 when he called his partner, D. J. Knight, for a risky run. Hobbs was almost down the pitch before Knight could start. It seemed certain that Hobbs would be run out; but Knight deliberately crossed him, thus throwing away his own wicket in order that Hobbs might go on batting. It was a fine piece of self-sacrifice.

Six thousand people, a vast crowd for Taunton in 1925, were present on the Monday. Hobbs played with the greatest care. Three singles took him to 94, and then a no-ball from Robertson-Glasgow was swung high to the leg side boundary. Another single followed, and then a single to leg brought Hobbs his 100. The cheers, it was said, could be heard at Taunton station, and crowds gathered outside Hobbs's shop in Fleet Street and clapped and cheered. Fender came on to the field with a champagne glass, although whether it contained champagne or ginger ale for Hobbs, the teetotaller, none would say. Congratulations poured upon the Surrey batsman.

The hundredth run had come off the bowling of Bridges, and, after one more run, it was Bridges who captured the wicket of Jack Hobbs. The news of Hobbs's performance dominated all the newspapers, but few were prepared for what was to come, so intent had they been to capture the moment when Hobbs equalled Grace's record. MacBryan played a fine innings for Somerset, and at 2.15 pm on the Tuesday, Hobbs and Sandham went out to open the Surrey second innings with 183 needed to win. There were only a few hundred people present. At 4.38 pm, Hobbs pushed a ball from Young past short leg to complete his second 100 of the match and to establish a new record in first-class cricket which he was to build upon in the next nine years and which looks unassailable for many years to come. Sandham completed a ten-wicket victory six minutes later.

The batting of Jack Hobbs dwarfed all else in cricket in 1925. It captured the imagination as few sporting achievements had ever done before or have done since. He was given a standing ovation when he next appeared at The Oval, against Yorkshire, and he ended the season with a record 16 centuries. His last was 106 for the Rest of England against Yorkshire, the Champion County, at The Oval and that was preceded by 266 not out for the Players against the Gentlemen at Scarborough. He finished top of the national averages with this record: 48 innings, 5 not outs, 3,024 runs, 266 not out highest score, average 70.32. He hit 16 hundreds and five fifties.

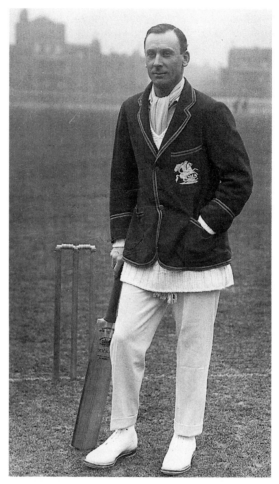

Jack Hobbs, 'The Master', for many the greatest batsman in the history of the game, and the scorer of more runs and more centuries than anybody else in first-class cricket.

That season saw, too, the pinnacle of Fender's achievement in leading Surrey to second place for the second time. Thereafter came decline. Hobbs missed many matches in 1926 as England took priority in the fight to regain the 'Ashes'. That they were successful in their struggle was due in no small measure to Hobbs who shared a wonderful opening partnership with Sutcliffe in the deciding Test at The Oval. Strudwick also played in the series, and Sandham and Shepherd were called up for trial matches. Fender, too, played in a Test trial, but Surrey dropped to fifth, their lowest position since 1912.

SOMERSET *v* SURREY

Played at the County Ground, Taunton, 15, 17 and 18 August 1925

SURREY WON BY 10 WICKETS

SOMERSET	FIRST INNINGS		SECOND INNINGS	
J. C. W. MacBryan	b Holmes	6	b Fender	109
A. Young	c Sadler b Lockton	58	c Strudwick b Sadler	71
T. E. S. Francis	b Sadler	0	c Strudwick b Lockton	12
*J. C. White	b Sadler	1	c Strudwick b Sadler	30
P. R. Johnson	c and b Lockton	30	c Peach b Fender	16
E. F. Longrigg	b Sadler	5	run out	4
R. A. Ingle	b Fender	22	c Shepherd b Peach	23
G. Hunt	b Lockton	4	b Fender	59
R. C. Robertson-Glasgow	c Jardine b Lockton	4	c Sadler b Fender	5
J. J. Bridges	c and b Shepherd	25	b Fender	26
†M. L. Hill	not out	0	not out	1
Extras	lb 8, w 4	12	b 9, lb 5, nb 4	18
Total		167		374

BOWLING	O	M	R	W		O	M	R	W
Sadler	16	4	28	3		21	2	59	2
Holmes	6	2	12	1		17	0	56	0
Fender	13	3	39	1		35.5	8	120	5
Lockton	16	4	36	4		9	2	15	1
Peach	9	2	21	0		20	7	46	1
Shepherd	6.3	1	19	1		21	5	60	0

SURREY	FIRST INNINGS		SECOND INNINGS	
Hobbs, J. B.	c Hill b Bridges	101	not out	101
A. Sandham	c Longrigg b Bridges	13	not out	74
D. J. Knight	run out	34		
T. F. Shepherd	b White	0		
D. R. Jardine	run out	47		
E. R. T. Holmes	c Hill b Robertson-Glasgow	24		
*P. G. H. Fender	st Hill b Young	59		
H. A. Peach	b Young	20		
W. C. H. Sadler	c Johnson b Young	25		
†H. Strudwick	not out	10		
J. H. Lockton	absent	—		
Extras	b 15, lb 8, nb 3	26	b 6, lb 1, nb 1	8
Total		359	(for no wkt)	183

BOWLING	O	M	R	W		O	M	R	W
Robertson-Glasgow	26	1	144	1		6	0	42	0
Bridges	37	5	115	2		11	3	27	0
White	29	13	51	1		14	6	34	0
Hunt	4	1	14	0		8	4	15	0
Young	5.3	1	9	3		15.5	1	39	0
Longrigg						3	0	18	0

Umpires: H. Draper and H. Young

Hobbs equalled and beat W. G. Grace's career record aggregate of 126 centuries by scoring two in the same match.

*Captain; †Wicket-keeper

It was not the absence of batsmen, however, which caused the drop, but the fact that the bowling was now thinner than ever.

The good years immediately after the First World War and the huge crowds that attended matches at The Oval had made the Club's financial position a healthy one, and the big mound at the Vauxhall end of the ground and extensions to the east wing of the pavilion were constructed in 1926, but the results did not match the new accommodation. There were moments of glory however. Ducat, 235, and Shepherd, 121, put on 261 in three hours for the third wicket against Leicestershire, and Shepherd followed this with 101 not out in the second innings. Surrey won by 119 runs with ten minutes to spare.

At Southampton, Hobbs, 200, and Gregory, 134 not out, put on 276 in two hours and ten minutes for the second wicket against Hampshire. Gregory had made his debut the previous season when he played three matches, and this was his first 100. In the penultimate match of the season, at Lord's, Hobbs hit the highest score of his career, 316 not out, which is also the highest score hit at Lord's, and at The Oval, on 24 June, he and Sandham put on 428 for Surrey's first wicket. This is a record opening partnership for the County and is the second highest stand for any wicket, the highest being the 448 that Bobby Abel and Hayward put on against Yorkshire at The Oval in 1899 in their fourth wicket record partnership. Hobbs hit 261 and Sandham 183.

Andy Sandham lived perpetually in the shadow of Hobbs and Sutcliffe. In another generation, he would have been England's number one. He first played for Surrey in 1911 and his career was to last until 1937. During that time, he hit more than 33,000 runs for Surrey and averaged 43.89. He played 14 times for England, only three of them in England, and averaged 38.21. His last Test innings was 325 against West Indies in Kingston, Jamaica. This was, at the time, 1930, the highest score ever made in a Test match.

Self-effacing, quiet, courteous and polite, Sandham was the perfect foil for Hobbs. They had no need to call nor even sometimes to look at each other. The ball would be dropped at the batsman's feet, and they would cross for a single before any in the field had realised that they had moved, yet Hobbs and Sandham never opened together for England. Sandham was short and sturdy. He excelled in hooking and cutting, for he relished fast bowling, and he had a fine square drive. It is not always appreciated how much Hobbs owed to him in the closing years of his career, for Sandham sensed when 'The Master' wanted the bowling and when he needed a rest and adapted accordingly. No county has had a more loyal servant.

Sandham hit 230 against Esssex at The Oval in 1927; ten days earlier on the same ground, Shepherd had hit 277 not out and Ducat 142

One of the most popular servants of the County, Andy Sandham was player for 26 years, coach for 12 and scorer for 12.

against Gloucestershire. They added 289 in two-and-three-quarter hours. These were heady days for batsmen in spite of the absence of Hobbs for five weeks with illness, and until the rains came in July, Surrey were challenging strongly. In the absence of Hobbs, Tom Barling, who had done well in second eleven cricket, was given an extended run and took his chance well, hitting centuries against Kent and Warwickshire.

Another interesting debutant was the 37-year-old Joe O'Gorman. He first appeared in the Surrey side in May 1927, scoring 31 not out and 20 not out against Glamorgan. More importantly, he had Bates caught by Sandham with the first ball that he bowled in first-class cricket. He played in the next game, which was the match against Essex in which Sandham hit 230. He and Sandham put on 119 in 65 minutes for the eighth wicket; O'Gorman finished with 42 not out. In Essex's second innings, his slow bowling accounted for Hubert Ashton and Morris. At Leicester, he scored 13, and that was the extent of his first-class career which left him with an average of 106. Joe O'Gorman was better known as a music hall comedy act in partnership with his brother Dave. Both brothers played for Richmond, and Joe took more than 1,500 wickets in club cricket. His grandson has recently played for Derbyshire.

Joe O'Gorman was not to be the answer to Surrey's bowling

problem. Nor was Geary, who had played intermittently since 1922 and took 79 wickets in 1927. He bowled medium pace, but he did not command a regular place after 1927, the season in which his 79 wickets at 25.06 placed him at the top of the Surrey bowling averages. No Surrey bowler could win a place in the top 50 of the national averages, excepting M. J. C. Allom and E. R. T. Holmes, both of whom did most of their bowling at university. Holmes was captain of Oxford, and Allom was up at Cambridge.

Fender was more expensive and less successful, but he finished the season in a blaze of glory. Surrey's last game of the season was at Lord's, and Middlesex were struggling at 37 for three from 23 overs when Fender put himself on at the Nursery End. Hendren hit him for four in his first over, and both Hendren and Enthoven took singles in the next. With the third ball of his third over, Fender bowled Enthoven with a quicker ball of full length. Mann opened his account with a single, and Hendren hit a two before the over ended. Bowling a brisker medium pace to Hendren, Fender bowled the great Middlesex batsman with a ball that broke back sharply so that his fourth over was a wicket maiden. His fifth produced four wickets. Horton was bowled by a googly off the first ball, and A. P. Powell was bowled by the next. Lunch punctuated the over. Durston kept out the first ball after the break and played on to the second. J. A. Powell was lbw first ball. Mann hit a four off Allom, and Price was dropped by Holmes at backward short-leg off the first ball of Fender's sixth over. The batsmen ran a single. Mann blocked the next ball and then was yorked.

Middlesex were all out for 54. Fender had taken six wickets in eleven balls at a personal cost of one run. His final figures were: 5.3-2-10-7. Only one of his seven victims, J. A. Powell, who was lbw, was not bowled. Fender's seven wickets had actually come in a space of 19 balls at a cost of four runs. He took four for 71 in the second innings, hit 42 and 20 not out, and made the winning hit to take Surrey to victory by five wickets.

This was, in fact, the last match in which Herbert Strudwick appeared for Surrey. He had stood down on several occasions during the season, and, at the age of 47, had decided to retire. The last of his 28 Test matches had been played the previous summer when he had kept in all five Tests against Australia which ended with triumph at The Oval. Surrey's faithful scorer of more than 40 years, Fred Boyington, had died in May 1927, and the Club appointed Strudwick as his successor.

Strudwick was one of the world's great wicket-keepers. When he retired it was with 1,235 catches and 258 stumpings to his credit. It was a record that was to remain intact for 40 years. Gnarled and twisted fingers were the legacy of the battering he had taken over the years. He

*One of the leading wicket-keepers of his day,
Herbert Strudwick played over 550 games in
25 years for Surrey, and set a career record for
most dismissals behind the stumps which lasted for
over 40 years.*

was a man of energy and humour, and he based his wicket-keeping on
the philosophy that if you had the patience and concentration to
expect a catch every ball, a stumping would come easily and naturally.
'In all my career,' he wrote, 'I have done nothing startling, except
when I broke the wicket-keepers' record; but I have tried to play the
game, have never appealed unless I felt confident and I am more proud
of this than any other performance of merit.'

This man of modesty and charm had a right to be proud. 'He was
first of all a gentlemen and a sportsman', said Herbert Sutcliffe, and no
more genuine sportsman ever took the field for Surrey than
Strudwick who was a teetotaller and a non-smoker.

The retirement of Strudwick emphasised the changing character of
the Surrey side. Ted Brooks had established himself in the team as
wicket-keeper although he had arrived at The Oval as a medium-pace
bowler from Cheam. He quickly became popular with his acrobatic
keeping and his great sense of comedy on and off the field. Gregory
and Barling, too, were forcing their way into the side, and Jardine was

already a considerable cricketer, while Allom and Holmes hovered in the wings at university.

Little was seen of Holmes in 1928, and if Surrey had found it hard to bowl sides out when conditions were to the advantage of bowlers, they could hardly be expected to prosper in a summer when the sun shone endlessly and wickets were hard and fast. Peach and Fender toiled ceaselessly and took 93 and 99 wickets respectively for Surrey in all matches – indeed Fender completed the 'double' when his games outside the County were taken into account, but apart from Shepherd, they had little in the way of support, and wickets were bought at very great expense. It was a batsman's summer, and Surrey managed only five Championship victories.

One of these was at Trent Bridge where Peach, four for 21, and Fender, six for 24, bowled out Nottinghamshire, third in the table, for 50 to set up a Surrey victory by seven wickets after Nottinghamshire had led by 169 on the first innings. The other win of significance was over runners–up Kent at The Oval by 14 runs when Fender and Peach bowled out the visitors for 116 on the last day.

The win over Essex at Leyton was highlighted by a third wicket stand of 317 in 200 minutes between Ducat, 208, and Shepherd, 145 not out. This was Ducat's fourth century in as many matches. The first in the sequence had come at Old Trafford when Surrey had hit 567 and Lancashire 588 for four. Andrew Sandham and Ducat put on 299 for the second wicket, and Sandham had been forced to retire with severe stomach pains when his score was 282.

One dwells on these batting feats to underline the strength of Surrey at this time, and, by implication, the weakness of their bowling. The first four in the order, Hobbs, Sandham, Ducat and Shepherd, all averaged more than 50, and the youngest of them, Sandham, was 38. On top of these four, Gregory, Barling and Fender scored 1,000 runs in all matches for Surrey, and Jardine, who could play in only six matches for the County, topped the national averages with 1,133 runs, average 87.15. Hobbs was just behind him, and these two were members of the MCC side that toured Australia in the winter.

Still Surrey searched for a bowler. They had enlisted a fast bowler who had been born in Epsom, but had been on the Essex ground staff. As with Hobbs, Essex missed their chance with him and Surrey signed him. His name was Alf Gover, and he played his first game for Surrey against Sussex at Horsham on 13, 14 and 15 June 1928. He was 20 years old, and his debut coincided with Surrey's first defeat of the season, by an innings. He was out for nought and 2, and he bowled Wensley for 97. Gover's wicket cost him 55 runs, and he bowled 24 overs. He finished the season with 37 wickets, but they cost him 35.21 runs each. For the second eleven he had 12 wickets at more than 22 runs each.

Wisden called him 'a young fast bowler with a long run', and said he 'achieved nothing striking'.

The same could be said of him in 1929 when Surrey slipped lower down the table to tenth, and even their batting became suspect. Again Hobbs, though in fine form, missed several matches through illness, and *Wisden* drew attention to the fact that he had missed 42 of Surrey's 108 competition fixtures in four seasons. Jardine was rarely available, and Garland-Wells, who had bowled promisingly and hit lustily the previous season, appeared in only five matches. Maurice Allom, down from Cambridge, bowled his fast-medium pace to good effect, but, in truth, Surrey were sinking into mediocrity. There were sparks, like the appearances of Stan Squires, an amateur good enough to be offered a professional contract, but they were few in a period of gathering gloom.

In 1930, Hobbs played his last Test match, and, at the age of 47, still topped the Surrey batting averages and passed 2,000 runs in all matches. Sandham, Ducat and Shepherd were still close behind him, and Gregory could now be classed as an all-rounder. Allom showed moments of high quality, and he made his Test debut at Christchurch in January 1930, when New Zealand entered Test cricket. His debut was remarkable. In his eighth over in Test cricket, he took four wickets in five balls, including the hat-trick, and finished with five for 38. A tall, burly, genial fast-medium bowler, he was never to reach those heights again, and business began to eat into his availability for Surrey and for cricket in general.

Allom was Surrey's leading bowler in 1930, but Gover was now pressing him hard with 69 wickets at an average of 24.15 in all matches. The untiring, wholehearted Peach was now nearing the end of his career.

Alan Peach was a cricketer whose worth could not be measured by figures. He launched himself at the game with a zest, and the crowd loved him for it. There were chuckles round the ground and a stirring in the crowd when he and Fender were at the wicket together. No man worked at the game harder nor enjoyed it more. His last season with the Club was 1931, for at the end of that season it was announced that both he and Ducat were not to be re-engaged. Peach was to return to The Oval as coach and held the post until 1939. Ducat made the last of his 52 centuries against Warwickshire at The Oval in June 1931 when he and Hobbs added 248 in three-and-three-quarter hours. Ducat was 45, but, like Hobbs, he was timing the ball as sweetly as ever, even if his scoring powers were beginning to show signs of diminishing. He was much missed when he left The Oval, for he was the most likeable of men. He was later to become coach at Eton, and he died suddenly in 1942. He was playing for Surrey Home Guard against

Surrey, 1930. Back row: Gregory, Squires, Brooks, Gover, Lock, Wilson and Barling. Front row: Peach, Ducat, M. J. C. Allom, Sandham and Shepherd.

Sussex Home Guard at Lord's on 23 July, and began his innings shortly before lunch. On the resumption, he took his score to 29. He played a ball from Eaton to mid-on and prepared to receive the next delivery, but he suddenly fell forward, and it was discovered that he had collapsed and died of heart failure. The sporting world was saddened and shocked even at a time when there was so much about which to grieve.

The 1931 season, when only Hobbs and Sandham were really at their best among the batsmen and Gover and Fender carried the bowling, saw the last of R. C. N. Palairet as secretary. He retired and was succeeded by A. F. Davey, who had been secretary of Somerset. The 1931 season was also to be Fender's last as captain. It was a season which saw him engaged in even more controversial events than usual. He upset Lancashire by getting his fielders to tread down the wicket at The Oval when it was damp so that it would not dry hard and ridged. When Lancashire protested he asked them to show him any law that he was breaking. At Bournemouth, he bowled lobs to Giles Baring because he thought a declaration had been too long delayed, and so altered his field that it took 12 minutes to complete an over. Against

Yorkshire at The Oval, he had appealed to the umpires and been allowed to lead his side off the field because it was too wet underfoot. The crowd had become incensed, and the Surrey committee asked the captains to resume playing. They did, but Fender and the umpires issued a statement saying that they considered the ground unfit for play.

There was nothing new in these incidents. Legend and controversy abounded when Fender was playing. Life was never dull. He was eager and sharp, and he played to win. Gover said of him:

> He had the finest cricket brain I have ever come across in over 50 years in cricket. Everything I have done I owe to Percy George; he taught me so much. A fine player and the greatest of captains, of course, but pitches, people's technique, the lot: he knew it all.

Fender had been captain of Surrey for 11 years, and had led the County for much of the season before 1921 when he took over officially. He had offered to stand down as captain early in the 1931 season when it became obvious to him and to several others that Jardine was most likely to lead England in Australia in 1932–33 and needed experience. Fender's offer was rejected, but as the season progressed and results failed to improve, there were murmurings that a change of leadership was needed. More importantly, economies were now in force at The Oval, and the professional staff was being trimmed, which is why Peach and Ducat had left at the first sign that their powers were waning. Fender was not of the school that felt that amateurs should be played at the expense of professionals for the sake of economy whether they were good enough cricketers or not. In this respect, he was at variance with some of his committee.

In January 1932 Fender was contacted at his office and asked if he would go to The Oval after work. There he met two members of the committee who told him that it was felt that it was time for a change of captaincy and that Jardine would lead the side in 1932. Fender was neither surprised nor totally aggrieved, for he felt that Jardine was the best possible choice, and he stated that he would willingly continue to play for Surrey under Jardine's captaincy. Unfortunately, the matter did not end there. The news of his dismissal was leaked to the press, together with the information that no successor had yet been appointed.

This caused a tremendous rumpus, for Fender was widely accepted as the best captain in England and was still immensely popular. A furious debate raged in the press, and, at the end of February, in an attempt to settle the situation, the Club issued a statement in which they said that nothing had been finally decided except that a change of captaincy was thought to be desirable. They hinted that a suitable successor had not yet been found, but in March Jardine was confirmed as captain with Allom as vice-captain.

Fender never captained England, and he never led Surrey to the title, yet his reputation is as firm today as it was during his wonderful reign. Jardine, his successor, was 'a very good captain' according to Garland-Wells, 'but Fender was a genius'. He was ever-probing, a restless, exciting intelligence that was willing to grasp the nettle of danger without a moment's hesitation. He was a glorious original who made the world a better place for his presence, and there have not been too many like him that we should forget him too easily or too soon.

CLOSE OF PLAY

FENDER CONTINUED TO PLAY for Surrey even though he had been deprived of the captaincy, and if he was not quite the all-round force he had been in his younger days, he was still a very useful cricketer and a great help to Jardine and to all the young cricketers. But Percy George was essentially a leader, and, as Ronald Mason expressed in a delightful homage to this man who gave perpetual delight and excitement:

> Loyally as he always served other captains, particularly Surrey captains under whom he played when at last he was superseded, he was at his best and most valuable when in control. Reduced to subordinate rank, he looked lost and fettered, a great prince in prison lying.

His successor was to reign for two short years and was to leave the game abruptly, all too soon and, one feels, a little embittered and disillusioned by the treatment he had received at the hands of some of his countrymen.

Douglas Jardine was 31 when he became captain of Surrey. He had been playing first-class cricket for ten years, although rarely had he been able to give himself regularly to the game. He was supremely orthodox in style, without a hint of profanity. His fluency of style gave him an impregnable defence, but he was also a batsman capable of a wide range of aggressive shots when the occasion demanded. He tended to be somewhat withdrawn in manner, but the ascetic picture, the cold man, that emerges from the numerous accounts of the

Douglas Jardine earned his fame on the international field, particularly in the 1932–33 bodyline tour of Australia, but was an excellent captain of Surrey in the seasons on each side of that tour.

bodyline series is only a half-truth. He may have been a private person, but he had warmth and a deep appreciation of and respect for the great cricketers about him. In 1933, he wrote:

> The ablest, the quickest, and the most enterprising cricket brain with which it has been my fortune to come into contact is that of my old captain, Mr P. G. H. Fender. For many years Mr Fender was called upon to take wickets without bowlers. His manner of making bricks without straw was a liberal education. He could at any time produce three entirely different plans of campaign. Though we occasionally differed – generally, I think, because I was too conservative – we always agreed that in nearly every game there comes a crisis when gambling is necessary. True, we used to differ over the precise moment of crisis. I take this opportunity of saying that he was nearly always right.

It is not simply what Jardine says about Fender here that is of interest, but what he says about himself. The passage comes from the second chapter of Jardine's book on the bodyline tour, *In Quest of the Ashes*, and the tribute to Fender is a generous interpolation. Certainly Jardine was more conservative in his approach than Fender – all other county captains were – but he was a thoughtful captain with a great deal of cunning about him, and he was positive in all he did.

Jardine was not helped by the weather in the early stages of his first season as Surrey's captain. Nine of the first ten matches in 1932 were drawn and the other abandoned without a ball being bowled. Eventually, nine Championship matches were won and two lost, and Surrey made a welcome climb to fifth place. Hobbs and Sandham were still the backbone of the batting – Robertson-Glasgow said that bowling to them at The Oval was like bowling to God on concrete – and Jardine and Shepherd enjoyed good seasons.

It was Shepherd's last season with the County. This full-blooded batsman and useful bowler accepted a job as coach and groundsman to the Wandsworth Gas Company, and another Oval favourite was gone, but new favourites were emerging. Gregory, Barling, Squires and Parker, who made his debut this season, suggested the nucleus of a new, young, talented side, and of the amateurs, Allom bowled finely and gave great hope for the future while Freddie Brown, who had made a few appearances the previous season, was nothing short of sensational.

Brown was born in Lima, Peru, and educated at The Leys School, Cambridge, where his cricketing prowess won great attention. He went up to Cambridge and won his blue as a freshman in 1930. He played for England against New Zealand in 1931 and qualified for Surrey by residence. In 1932, he appeared for the County regularly and, in all first-class cricket, he did the 'double'. In many ways, his leg-break and googly bowling was something of a disappointment, for his length was erratic and he bowled, perhaps, a little too quickly, but on his day he was capable of running through a side. His batting was thrilling, and, at 21 years of age, he was a cricketer of exciting potential. He began the season with four for 50 against MCC and five for 76 against Somerset, and his Championship record at the end of the year was 95 wickets at 15.98 runs each. As Allom took 67 at 18.70, and Gover had days when he gave glimpses of the greatness that was to come, it seemed that Surrey at last had an attack that could lead them to the top of the table again.

Brown had the added quality of his batting. It was a ferocious innings at Blackheath that first drew attention:

Despite a stand of 110 by Squires and Shepherd, Surrey had seven men out for 171, but the last three wickets added 174 in ninety-five minutes. Brown brought about this change. Going in fourth wicket down at 139, he got 53 out of 78 in an hour, reached 101 thirty-five minutes later, put on 50 more in twenty minutes and, when caught near the sight screen, had scored 168 in two hours ten minutes with four 6's and twenty-one 4's as his chief hits. Brown drove and pulled with splendid power, and cut finely besides placing many strokes with skill. Parker batted in good style while Brown made 91 runs out of 104.

Parker, it should be noted, was at number eleven.

The match at Blackheath was drawn, but a month later, Brown's all-round ability was prominent in a stunning victory over Middlesex at The Oval. He and Parker bowled Middlesex out for 141. Hobbs made 92, but Surrey were 195 for five when Brown joined Jardine. They added 143 in 85 minutes. Brown reached his 100 in as many minutes and quite overshadowed Jardine, who made a majestic 126.

At 385 for eight, the Surrey innings looked to be near its end, but Allom, 57 not out, helped Brown to add 155 in 65 minutes. Brown was finally caught off Haig. He had given a glorious display of hitting, scoring 212 out of 345 made while he was at the wicket in 200 minutes. He hit seven sixes, two of them out of the ground, and 15 fours.

Surrey led by 399 on the first innings, but Middlesex fought doggedly. Hendren hit 145, Jim Sims 103, and an innings defeat was avoided. Brown took five for 81 to give him match figures of eight for 119. Surrey were left with the task of scoring 57 in 20 minutes. They hit seven and were credited with a wide off the first over, but Brown, who had opened with Shepherd, was caught off the last ball. Fender fell to the second ball of the second over so that Surrey were 9 for two in five minutes. Block and Shepherd hit 36 before both were run out, and when Jardine joined Ratcliffe 11 were needed from the last over. Ratcliffe took a single from the first ball, but Jardine was unable to pierce the field from Durston's next two deliveries. The fourth ball he hit high to mid-off, but Enthoven missed the chance and the batsmen ran two. The next ball was wide of the off stump and short, and Jardine chopped it for four, and the last ball of the match he drove to the pavilion rails to bring Surrey an exciting victory.

Spencer Block, who was mentioned above, had been an outstanding cricketer at Marlborough and had won his blue at Cambridge. He first played for Surrey in 1928 and hit 117 against Leicestershire in 1931. He was one who was regarded as a possible successor to Fender, but 1933 was his last season for Surrey and in six seasons for them he appeared in only 30 matches.

Alan Ratcliffe's career with Surrey extended to seven matches, the last of them in 1933. In 1931, he hit 201 for Cambridge against Oxford, which was a record for the Varsity match, but it was a record which stood for only one day as the Nawab of Pataudi hit 238 not out for Oxford, who went on to win by eight wickets.

These were but two of the talented amateurs of the 1930s who were unable to realise their cricketing potential because of the economic necessity of following a career. Brown and Allom were to become victims of this necessity.

Brown went with Jardine's team to Australia in 1932–33 although he did not play in the series. He and Jardine returned to a Surrey side in 1933 that was full of hope and expectation even if Hobbs had decided to play only when he felt up to it and when the weather was warm. Surely a side that could field Sandham, Hobbs, Barling, Squires, Gregory, Jardine, Parker, Brown, Fender, Allom, Brooks and Gover, and had Whitfield, Fishlock and now Watts pressing for inclusion would be as strong as any in the country. Certainly it would have been had those 12 or 15 always been available, but Jardine did not appear in the side until the end of May, when he hit 75 and 105 against Sussex. He then played intermittently until injury ended his season in August. He led Surrey in seven matches.

The vice-captain, Allom, played in only five so that, at various times, Surrey were led by seven different players: Jardine and Allom, and Fender, Block, Brown, Hobbs and W. T. Cook, the second eleven skipper, who captained against Oxford and Cambridge. This was, as it had been in 1904, a recipe for disaster. *Wisden* was emphatic on the point:

> There was no settled policy, and with the batting order changed in match after match it was only natural that some of the men failed in consistency while the bowlers also found themselves handicapped.

The ideas of Jardine and Fender – two captains of vastly differing methods, especially in their placing of the field – seldom met in common line of practice, and the result of it all was that Surrey, while these changes in leadership were going on, rarely played the same sort of cricket twice in consecutive matches.

If Hobbs could turn the clock back by hitting 221, his last double century, in his first match of the season, against the West Indian tourists, and Fender, too, with 88 wickets, could hint at former triumphs, it was not possible to recapture the verve that had been associated with Fender's tenure of office. Too much had changed. The old skipper still had a remarkable eye for the game, however, and Alf Gover recalls the victory over Essex at The Oval in 1933 when Jardine was leading the side. Surrey, thanks to an opening stand of 153 between Hobbs and Sandham, made 268. Gover had a fine spell of bowling, taking six for 17, and Essex were all out for 66 and had to follow on. Between the innings, Fender asked Gover to ask Jardine if he could switch ends. Fender had spotted a worn patch on the rain affected wicket that he thought he would be able to exploit. Gover says that he would not have done it for anyone else, and Fender did not explain what he had in mind, but he made the request and although Jardine was surprised, it was granted. Fender took eight for 29 in 25 overs.

Brown played in fewer games than he had done in 1932 and could not recapture the same form, but Gover's advance was most marked and he took 116 wickets. Occasionally, he was paired with Eddie Watts, a 21-year-old fast-medium bowler who was playing as an amateur and looked full of promise.

Parker did not develop with quite the speed that was expected, but he did begin to climb the batting order on occasions, while Gregory did enough as an all-rounder, a bits and pieces player in the Peach mould, to earn a trip to India with Jardine's team. It was to be the closest that he ever got to Test cricket.

In a season unsettled and uncertain, Tom Barling and Stan Squires gave the greatest encouragement. They were the leading run-scorers, with 1,776 and 1,504 respectively in Championship matches, and on occasions they batted with panache. Barling was a naturally aggressive player, but, on forcing his way into the first team, he had played with a caution which was foreign to him, no doubt over-anxious to establish himself. Suddenly, he found it possible to throw off his inhibitions, and his batting began to flourish. At Southampton, in the opening county match of the season, he hit the highest score of his career, 269, and he batted with a glorious sense of freedom. At The Oval, in August, he hit 112 against Yorkshire. Sandham and Squires put on 291 for Surrey's second wicket. Sandham was out for 98, but Squires hit a brisk 178. Fender dominated a stand of 82 with Barling, who then put on 177 with Winlaw. Allom declared at 560 for six, the highest score against Yorkshire for 32 years and Surrey's highest against the northern county. Verity, three for 115 in 57 overs, was not amused and, without warning, suddenly bowled a lob which was promptly no-balled by umpire Chester.

Allom was outmanoeuvred by Sellers as the Yorkshiremen batted tardily in an attempt to stop Surrey taking the new ball, which was then offered after a side had scored 200 runs, and although Yorkshire had to follow on, the match was drawn.

These were brief joys in what was a difficult and confusing season, and the confusion deepened when, while still in India, Jardine informed the committee that he wished to resign the captaincy. He had run into some trouble in India, especially with regard to the umpiring of Frank Tarrant, who was replaced for the third Test, but he knew well that there was a faction in England, led mainly by Warner, who were opposed to him. Warner did not want him as captain of England and wrote to Sir Alexander Hore-Ruthven in South Australia to the effect that an Australian green cap had the same effect on Jardine that a red rag had on a bull:

> It is hoped he may retire at the end of the Indian tour, but in many quarters here – where they do not know the truth – he is a bit of a hero.

History has treated Jardine badly. He led England in Australia and regained the 'Ashes' in overwhelming fashion. He employed a method of attack which his opponents considered unfair, but which did not violate the laws and could be countered by sensible batting as Jardine himself showed when he batted against the West Indians. Pelham Warner was one of the managers on the tour, and Jardine believed that Warner was one of those who had let him down with his ambivalent, not to say two-faced, attitude. The outcome of it all was that Jardine had had enough of cricket, and with the pressures of business crowding upon him he said that he would not be able to play regularly and therefore could not consider captaining the side. In fact, he never played for Surrey again.

In the history of the County, he will always remain a somewhat hazy figure. His reign was so short, and the focus on him was always at international level. These things have tended to obscure the fact that he was respected and that men were loyal to him. He could be severe, and his captaincy had neither the spark nor the sense of fun that Fender's had, but he was held in affection. What else has been obscured is that at the time that he retired, when he was 33 years old, he had no superior as a number five batsman anywhere in the world. In 33 Test innings, he averaged 48. His average for Surrey was nearly 45.

The problem that confronted the Surrey committee was who should succeed Jardine. Speculation was rife. Allom had virtually dropped out of first-class cricket, and Brown was playing less and less. There was considerable surprise when Errol Holmes, who had captained Oxford University in 1927 but of whom little had been seen since, was named as captain. He had not played for Surrey for five years, nor had much been seen of his vice-captain, H. M. Garland-Wells.

Errol Holmes was not a master tactician. He was a most graceful cricketer, a product of the Malvern tradition which placed much emphasis on style and joy. Holmes was a character of great charm and sweetness. He had returned from the stock exchange to cricket, and the *News Chronicle* dubbed him the 'laughing philosopher'. Dashing and debonair, he was also known as the 'last of the dandies', and certainly he was something of an anachronism. He bravely announced a new approach when he arrived to take over the side. He believed that county cricket was becoming dull and stagnating. The real spirit of the game was being lost because there was a tendency to play safe and because batsmen were concentrating on preserving their wickets rather than on scoring runs. His own approach, as he wrote, was simple: 'What success I had can, I think, be attributed to my natural desire to hit the ball. I hated being kept quiet.' He wanted his bowlers to bowl a full length and at the stumps. He believed that county cricket would benefit from the spirit of life and enjoyment that pervaded country house cricket. He was, in truth, an amateur in a game that was becoming increasingly professional and, at Test level, attritional. In fairness, it should be said that the Club was at a difficult time, and a fresh approach was very much needed after a period of intrigue and uncertainty. Holmes brought with him no great insight into the game, his manipulation of his bowlers and the timing of his declarations left something to be desired, but he did bring a breath of welcome fresh air. His own play exemplified his attitude to the game, free and attacking batting and, initially, tear-away bowling, although he later moderated his run.

Holmes had rather an unfortunate start in his term of office in that Glamorgan beat Surrey inside two days at The Oval, the first time the Welsh county had won there, and, in both 1934 and 1935, Surrey finished in eleventh place. These were transitional times, for 1934 saw the last of the great Jack Hobbs. He was approaching his 52nd birthday and appeared in only eight county matches. At Old Trafford, on 26, 28 and 29 May, he turned out in George Duckworth's benefit. Lancashire made 263, and Hobbs and Sandham began Surrey's reply with a stand

A dashing batsman, Errol Holmes was a pre-war captain who returned in 1947 to lead the side for two more seasons.

of 184. Sandham made 78, and Hobbs was second out, at 210. He had hit 116. It was his 199th and last first-class century. His final appearance for Surrey was in the County's last match of the season, against Glamorgan, at Cardiff, at the end of August. He was lbw to J. C. Clay for nought. Hobbs had two more matches, in the Folkestone Festival. In the second of them, Players against Gentlemen, he scored 24 and 18. He was bowled by Allom in the first innings and caught by Garland-Wells in the second. So ended the most illustrious career of one of the most dignified men that the game has known. Altham, who played with him, against him and knew him well, wrote the most accurate of appreciations:

As the years moved on he had inevitably to forgo some of his early brilliance, but he never lost stature in the process, never became a mere technician, but remained, as Neville Cardus said, a great artist. He was never much concerned with the mere amassing of runs but rather with the art of batsmanship and the challenge of a situation. Given that challenge, whether in the form of a great occasion, a difficult wicket, formidable bowling or, as it may be, a combination of all three, and his stature stood revealed beyond question as that of the greatest English batsman since W.G., great in technical resource of course, and in ease and beauty of style, but above all, I feel, in that serenity which was the reflection of the man himself.

Fender was to play his last game a year after Hobbs. In 1934, he appeared in 15 county matches and finished top of the bowling averages with 72 wickets at 26.52 runs each; technically, perhaps, Fishlock was top, but he took only seven wickets.

In 1935, Fender played in 13 county matches, hit 371 runs and took 55 wickets, a number bettered only by Gover and Watts. Shortly before the start of the 1936 season he was practising in the nets at Lord's and was later joined in the dressing room by Errol Holmes, who asked him which two or three matches he thought he might like to play in during the coming season. Fender was surprised and asked Holmes if he really meant that he only wanted him to play in a couple of games. Holmes said that he thought that was the case, at which Fender said that he could see no point in playing at all if that was really the policy. He later wrote to Surrey confirming this view, and he received a letter of thanks in reply. Both letters were published.

Surrey could have still done with Fender's services, but he was 44, and there comes a time for everyone to depart. It was a sad farewell, and an element of controversy haunted him to the end. There were times when he was his own worst enemy, for, conservative as he was in many respects, he was a rebel to the end of his very long life. A light went out at The Oval when Percy George Fender ceased to play there.

The Oval itself had undergone changes in appearance as well as in personnel. During the winter of 1933–34, the fence which had surrounded the ground was removed and replaced by a brick wall. The wall was completed at the main entrance by a pair of wrought-iron gates which had been subscribed for by members of the Club and which were erected in honour of Jack Hobbs.

In personnel, *Wisden* claimed that more amateurs were able to play regularly in 1934, but this is hard to justify. Holmes, Garland-Wells and Fender appeared with some regularity as we have noted, but Brown and Winlaw appeared in nine games each, and there were no other amateurs in the side. Roger de W. K. Winlaw would not play

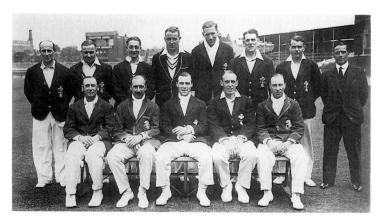

Surrey, 1934. Back row: Gregory, Barling, Squires, Watts, Gover, Brooks, Wilson and Strudwick. Front row: Hobbs, P. G. H. Fender, E. R. T. Holmes (capt.), H. M. Garland-Wells and Sandham.

for the County after this season. He was yet another amateur to be claimed by business. He enjoyed a splendid season for Cambridge in 1934 and assisted Surrey when he came down. He batted impressively and played a significant and heroic part in the victory over Middlesex at The Oval. Middlesex were bowled out for 184, but Surrey lost Sandham and Squires cheaply. Winlaw hit 61 and Gregory 121, and Surrey took a first innings lead of 175.

The visitors battled back bravely, and Surrey were left to make 118 to win. They lost six men for 43, and Winlaw had retired hurt after being struck over the eye by a ball from fast bowler Jim Smith. Garland-Wells hit a lusty 45, but when the ninth wicket fell Surrey were still 14 short of their target. Courageously, Winlaw came out to bat again. The runs mounted slowly, and as a ball from Allen went through to wicket-keeper Price standing back, the batsmen ran a bye so that Brooks could keep the bowling. He was felled by Smith's next delivery, but he got up to hit two fours and win the match. It was the sort of situation that Ted Brooks relished.

Winlaw returned to Bedfordshire at the end of 1934 and took over the captaincy of the side. He was killed on active service in 1942 in a flying accident which also took the life of C. T. Ashton. The only new amateur to appear in 1935 was Hugh Bartlett. He had played once in 1933 and played twice in 1935, but thereafter he played with great success for Sussex. Bob Gregory had taken over from Hobbs as Sandham's opening partner, and he batted magnificently in 1934, only to fall back the following season, losing his aggression and seemingly troubled by the new lbw law. As a fielder, he remained in a class of his own, good enough to be asked to act as England's twelfth man. The

Winlaw and Brooks shake hands after sharing a last wicket partnership of 14 which brought Surrey victory over Middlesex, August 1934. Winlaw had been forced to retire hurt having been hit by a ball from Jim Smith, but he bravely returned to help win the match.

Surrey fielding was not now as good as it had been in its golden days, nor as good as it was to be in years to come, and one man who suffered more than most was Alf Gover.

Gover had now taken on the mantle worn at other times by Lockwood and Fender and Rushby in that he carried the bowling on his shoulders. In 1935, he was the only bowler to take 100 wickets for Surrey in Championship matches, and his main assistance came from Watts who bowled half the amount of overs that Gover sent down.

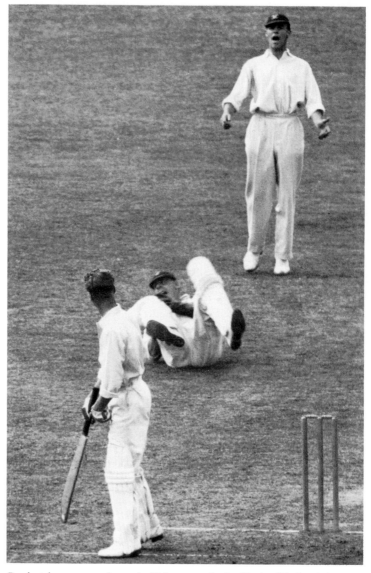

Brooks takes a spectacular catch. Holmes appeals. Joe Hardstaff is the victim.

There were strong criticisms of how Gover was used, for at times he was kept on for an hour-and-a-half at a stretch. He had been asked to shorten his run in order to maintain longer spells, but Norman Preston was violent in his condemnation of Surrey's tactics and in the obsession with pace bowling:

A few years ago Surrey possessed such attractive personalities as Hobbs, Sandham, Ducat, Shepherd, P. G. H. Fender, Hitch, Strudwick and Peach. Those times have gone and Surrey seemed to dwell in the past. They still remembered the days when those great fast bowlers, Lockwood and Richardson, carried everything before them. Indeed, Surrey have continued to put their faith on speed all down the years.

This was rather harsh on Gregory who, according to Fender, rolled the ball rather than spun it, but still captured wickets with his occasional leg-breaks. The truth was, however, that Surrey had been unable to unearth any spin bowlers of quality. There were suggestions that Fishlock should have bowled more, but his bowling days in first-class cricket were practically over after 1934, and now, winning a regular place in the side for the first time since his debut in 1931, he was giving the Surrey batting the substance that it needed. Against Warwickshire at The Oval on 22 May, Fishlock, batting at number six, and coming in at a desperate time, hit five sixes and 14 fours in an innings of 113 not out. It was his first century and the first by a Surrey left-hander for 68 years, and it was the start of a rapid rise to the top level.

The other memorable batting achievement in 1935 was Sandham's century at Basingstoke on 26 June. It was the first first-class match to be played at Basingstoke for 21 years. Hampshire were bowled out for 79, and Sandham and Gregory put on 84 for Surrey's first wicket. Sandham went on to make 103, the 100th hundred of his career. It is an amazing record that of the 23 batsmen who have hit 100 hundreds, four have been Surrey players.

While the batsmen enjoyed themselves, the outstanding bowling performance was at New Road, Worcester. Having conceded 22 runs before taking a wicket, including 14 runs in one over, Alf Gover took eight for 34, the best figures of his career. In completing this spell, Gover emulated Richardson, Lockwood and Peach by taking four wickets in four balls. He had Thorp lbw and bowled Perks and J. Horton with the last three balls of one over and bowled Jackson with the first ball of the next. In the second innings, he took four for 58, and Surrey won by ten wickets.

How many wickets Gover would have captured had he been better supported in the field one cannot imagine, but in 1936 he carried all before him, with or without the support of his fielders, and, in all matches, he took exactly 200 wickets at 17.73 runs each. This was the first time that an English fast bowler had taken 200 wickets in a season since Tom Richardson in 1897.

Gover received neither the honours nor the praise that his bowling earned in the years immediately before the Second World War. He was criticised because his run up was ungainly, because he did not have the classical action of a Larwood or an Allen, yet these criticisms were countered by *Wisden* when they named him one of the 'Five Cricketers of the Year' in 1937:

> . . . considering he stands 6 foot $2\frac{1}{2}$ inches, weighs 13 stone 10 pounds and puts every ounce of energy into each delivery, it is not really surprising that a man of his build should appear awkward. The important fact is that at the vital instant of releasing the ball his action is quite correct with the left shoulder pointing down the pitch towards the opposing batsman.

Even more important was the fact that Gover consistently got batsmen out on all types of wicket. He would have got many more out had many of the catches he induced batsmen to offer to slip been taken. In county matches alone in 1936 he took 171 wickets at 15.42, having, wisely, been allowed or encouraged to return to his full run. His form could not be ignored, and in the rain-ruined Test trial at Lord's, he took five for 93, the best bowling performance of the match. For the Players against the Gentlemen, he took six for 41 in the first innings. He was given a chance in the England side for the second Test against India at Old Trafford and must have felt it was like being back at The Oval as both Merchant and Mushtaq Ali were dropped off him at slip in the opening overs. He did not take a wicket and, incredibly, he was not selected for the England party that G. O. Allen took to Australia, although it was something of a hotch-potch side that could very much have done with his presence.

Two matches against New Zealand in 1937 and one against India in the first post-war season were to be the extent of his Test career after that unlucky debut at Old Trafford. He deserved more. He may have run to the wicket with arms pumping like a piston, but few men have thought more about the game and none had had more enthusiasm for it or worked harder at it.

If Gover was unlucky not to be chosen for the tour of Australia, Laurie Fishlock was more fortunate, although a broken bone in Australia was to cost him any chance of playing in a Test. In 1936, he scored heavily as a middle-order batsman, played two Tests against India and, although he did not do well, was picked for the tour. For Surrey, he was a tower of strength, playing straight and firm and being particularly strong in front of the wicket. He was also an excellent fielder in the deep as befits a professional footballer. Somewhat uncertain at the start of an innings, Fishlock was, however, essentially sound in technique. His misfortune was that he had been a late starter, and he was 29 before he produced his best form and gained Test recognition in 1936.

Errol Holmes, who had led an MCC side to Australia and New Zealand in 1935–36, was also asked to go with Allen's side in the winter of 1936–37, but, for business reasons, he had to decline. Although he was now bowling less, Holmes enjoyed another excellent season with the bat, ever eager for runs. He hit two centuries for Surrey at The Oval, against Hampshire and Yorkshire, and although neither of them could bring victory, both innings were of high quality.

Gover, six for 61, had helped to bowl Hampshire out for 267, and Surrey built up a big score in reply, with Barling, Fishlock and Holmes scoring heavily. Holmes completed his 100 in two-and-a-half hours and was joined by Ted Brooks. In 75 minutes, the pair added 168, a Surrey record for the ninth wicket. Holmes finished on 171 not out, and Brooks was bowled for 70, which was the highest score he made in first-class cricket. He was not a good batsman, but he loved a challenge, was proud of his work as night-watchman and was no mean performer. Whatever lapses the Surrey slips made, Brooks made few. He was one of the most exuberant of wicket-keepers and maintained a very high standard. If he had been a better batsman, he might well have forced his way into the England side in 1938 when Ames was injured. Fifty years later, he might well have earned a living as a professional darts player, for he had a great passion for the game.

Holmes made another century at The Oval, in the last game of the

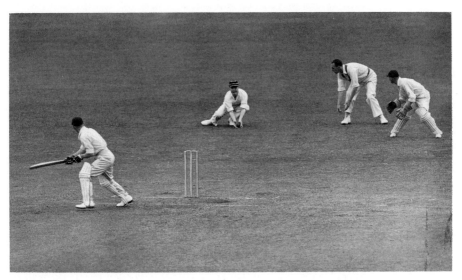

Gover suffers again. Dickinson puts down a slip catch offered by Barber of Yorkshire, July 1939.

season, and it, too, involved a notable stand. Yorkshire had made 315, and Surrey were 162 for five in reply when F. R. Brown joined Holmes in a partnership of 222. Holmes hit 172, and Brown 109.

Brown was available for 18 matches which gave a great boost to the attack. The Surrey bowling was also enhanced by the arrival of two slow bowlers, Daley, a leg-spinner, and King, slow left-arm. Unfortunately, Daley injured a finger the following season and did not repeat his initial success while King, too, failed to live up to the early promise.

One man who gave Gover good support was his brother-in-law, Eddie Watts. A strongly built fast-medium bowler who could move the ball both ways, Watts was a tireless worker, and he and Gover formed a most determined opening attack. At full strength Surrey were a formidable proposition for any side in the country, but Squires was bowling little, and Parker was troubled by injury which, with representative calls, tended to reduce their effectiveness. The County had, nevertheless, climbed to sixth in the table, membership had increased dramatically and the crowds were flocking back to The Oval in expectation of lively cricket again. What seemed to be lacking to make Surrey Championship contenders was, inevitably, a good spin bowler, and strength in depth. When hit by representative calls and injuries they had tried, without success, to persuade Hobbs and Hitch back to first-class cricket so thin were they in reserves.

The Club did manage to lure D. J. Knight back to the county game in 1937. It was ten years since he had last played for Surrey and even then he had played but little. He was now 43, and the idea that he would solve Surrey's opening bat problem was not a sound one. At the end of May, he hit 105 in under two hours against Hampshire, displaying the wristy power that had made him one of the most exciting and stylish batsmen in England 16 years earlier when he had last hit a first-class century, but it was apparent that, artist with the bat that he still was, he could no longer stand the strain of long days in the field, and he quietly dropped out of the side.

His place as opener was taken by Fishlock, who had had a poor time in Australia and returned to England seemingly lacking in all confidence and quite unable to score runs. Then, when Sandham stood down from the game with Oxford University at The Oval, on 23 June, he opened with Knight and scored 143. Six more centuries followed, and he ended the season a better player than ever.

An equally happy story was that of Bob Gregory who recaptured the form which had eluded him for a couple of seasons. He finished top of the Surrey averages. On 12 June, against Glamorgan at The Oval, he and Sandham put on 344 in five hours for the second wicket. Gregory hit 154, one of his seven centuries of the season, and Sandham

Two of a long line of footballers who have played for Surrey. Bob Gregory (left), a stalwart of over 400 matches from 1925 to 1947, played for Fulham and Norwich, while Tom McMurray (right), who appeared occasionally in the 1930s, turned out for Tranmere Rovers, Millwall and Rochdale.

hit 239, the last double century of his career. In the final match of the season, the same pair added 167 against Sussex at Hove. Again both batsmen made hundreds. It was the 107th and last of Sandham's career in what was his last game for Surrey. He had been told a month earlier that the County would not be renewing his contract, but he left it to Surrey to announce his retirement without fuss or bother. He was 47, and he had maintained his high standard as a player and as a gentleman until the last. After the Second World War he was to return to Surrey, first as coach, then as scorer.

Stan Squires, now settled at number four after a period as an opener, not only continued to bat with great consistency, but his off-breaks were employed to give the attack greater variety, and he took 40 wickets in Championship matches. Allom reappeared very briefly, but once again the bowling was predominantly in the hands of Gover and Watts, with Parker's medium pace giving able support and making him a most valuable all-rounder.

For the second season in succession, Gover, his away swinger and vicious break-back taxing the best of batsmen, captured 200 wickets, again reaching the mark when playing for Leveson-Gower's Eleven in the Scarborough Festival. Leveson-Gower was both president and chairman of the Surrey Club and was the organiser of the Scarborough Festival, a great benefactor to the game, receiving a knighthood for his services.

They shall not pass. Stan Squires batting against Kent. Bob Gregory at the non-striker's end.

Gover proved his point with regard to his exclusion from the party that had gone to Australia when, in the MCC's 150th Anniversary Match at Lord's, playing for the Rest of England against the MCC Australian Eleven, he took three for 76 and seven for 44. At one time, he took five for 5 in 14 balls. He was also one of the most significant contributors to Surrey's first win of the season. This did not come until the second week in June when Somerset were the visitors to The Oval. Gregory and Squires hit centuries, Surrey reached 406 and took a first innings lead of 142. Batting again on the last day when the pitch was affected by rain, Surrey were bowled out for 35, their lowest score for 44 years. Their tormentor was the genial Bill Andrews, who took eight for 12, including a hat-trick of Fishlock, Parker and Brooks. Of the twelve runs he conceded, six came in one hit by Barling.

Needing 178 to win, Somerset lost seven wickets for 43 runs, Gover having torn into them with typical aggression, never believing that there was such a thing as a lost cause. Wellard was dropped twice, and then hit fiercely to bring Somerset within 12 runs of victory with one wicket to fall. Then, in an over-eagerness to keep the bowling, Wellard attempted to steal a single as the ball went through to Brooks, but the wicket-keeper hit the stumps with his throw and Molyneux was run out.

In assessing Gover's achievements, one must consider two things.

The first was emphasised by *Wisden*, who said of Brooks: 'He was Gover's only reliable supporter behind the stumps, for slip fieldsmen constantly dropped vital catches.' The second was that he did half his bowling at The Oval where the wickets were the best in England.

The pitch at The Oval was tended by 'Bosser' Martin, and his expertise was acknowledged, not only in that he was called to Lord's in 1935 to rid the ground of 'leather-jackets', but that, in 1938, he provided a wicket at The Oval on which Len Hutton scored 364 and England made 903 for seven against Australia. Not surprisingly, being asked to bowl on The Oval wicket for half of his matches took its toll of Gover.

Early in 1938, he toured India with Lord Tennyson's side. He was highly successful in the early part of the tour, but a knee injury kept him out of all but two of the last nine matches. The injury did not clear and not only did it reduce Gover's effectiveness in the 1938 season, but it meant that he had to miss several matches. Indeed, Surrey sent him on holiday for a period in hope that he would recover full fitness. He ended the season with 84 wickets at 23.88 runs each, disappointing by his standards, but by no means a poor showing in the circumstances.

Gover's poorer form thrust more responsibility on Watts, and he responded to the task admirably, taking 114 wickets in Championship matches at under 18 runs apiece. He was also a very useful hard-hitting batsman.

More work was also given to Jack Parker, and he claimed 60 wickets in county matches. He was ever experimenting, perhaps too much, but 1938 saw him in better health than he had been before, and his form began to excite. A tall man who used his height to good advantage, Parker was primarily an attacking batsman who was good in a crisis. Against Warwickshire at Edgbaston in August, he hit his first century for the County, and one of the Surrey officials was quoted in the *News Chronicle* as saying that within a few years he would be 'number five on the card for England'. Following another outstanding season in 1939, he was selected for the England party to tour India, but the tour never took place because of the outbreak of war, and when first-class cricket resumed in 1946 he was 33, and his chance of an England cap had gone.

Parker was a fine slip fielder, and Surrey's fielding improved considerably in 1938. The team as a whole seemed to have gained in confidence, and, although they were never real challengers for the title, they moved to third place in the table, their highest position for 13 years. It was the advance of the younger players more than anything else which was responsible for the climb up the table. Gregory hit 243, the highest score of his career, against Somerset in the opening match of the season at The Oval, and he lost none of his form when he was again asked to become Fishlock's opening partner later in the season.

Fishlock continued to delight and played an astonishing innings of protest against the Australians in May. The tourists had batted until lunchtime on the second day and scored 528. They bowled Surrey out for 271, but did not enforce the follow-on, nor make any attempt to win the match, and the crowd demonstrated noisily and angrily. Surrey were left 75 minutes in which to make 490. Fishlock showed his contempt for the way in which the match had been conducted by hitting 93 out of 104, unleashing some stunning drives.

The problem of finding him an opening partner became acute, and both McMurray and Whitfield were tried without much success. Ted Whitfield had been at The Oval for ten years, but he had never been able to reproduce in the first team the outstanding success he had

Surrey's leading batsman at the time of the Second World War, Laurie Fishlock's Test career was from 1936 to 1946–47, yet because of the war comprised only four Tests.

enjoyed in the second eleven. In 1938, he was told that he would be given an extended run in the County side, and although he did not settle happily into the role of opener, he began to score freely once he dropped down the order.

In mid-July, Surrey entertained another county away from The Oval for the first time when they played Hampshire at Guildford. In fact, as we have noted, Surrey had played home matches at Lord's in 1914, but this was due to circumstances beyond their control, and the venture at Guildford in 1938 was the first time that they had voluntarily gone outside The Oval for a county match. The bowlers reviewed the prospect with more pleasure than the batsmen who were quite happy to enjoy the wicket 'Bosser' Martin provided at The Oval, but, when Errol Holmes won the toss, they were to find Guildford very much to their liking.

There was an uncertain start, but Fishlock played positively, and the substance of the innings came from a fifth wicket stand of 155 between Parker and Whitfield. Parker batted very correctly, and he was particularly strong in his driving and in his leg-side play. Whitfield's batting was a revelation as he at last produced the form which had made him so exciting a prospect in the second eleven. He showed a wide range of strokes and, with 15 fours, reached his first Championship century six years after his only other century in first-class cricket, 101 not out against the Indian tourists at The Oval in 1932. Monty Garland-Wells in characteristic cavalier style hit 53 in an hour, and Surrey made 433.

In the absence of Gover, Watts was able to choose his end, and he dismissed McCorkell with the first ball of the innings. Blake fell to Berry shortly after, and Hampshire, in spite of some vigorous blows from Creese, never made an effective recovery and followed on 215 runs in arrears.

The match had been played before a large crowd in fine weather, but Hampshire's second innings was on a damp pitch, and the Surrey attack relished the assistance it gave them to take their side to an innings victory.

It was a great festive occasion with the drums of the Second Battalion of the Queen's Royal Regiment playing during the lunch and tea intervals of the first day and a dance being held in the pavilion on the second evening. It was a happy decision to take a first-class game to Guildford, and the Guildford week has long been established as a most successful part of the Surrey calendar. There are many who would like to see more games played at Guildford, but one must remember that, under the agreement with the Duchy of Cornwall, 50 days of cricket must be played at The Oval each year, and this does not leave room for manoeuvre.

Fred Berry, who deputised for Gover at Guildford, was a medium-pace inswing bowler whose opportunities were limited. He had joined Surrey from Windhill in the Bradford League, and, in 1938, took 44 wickets and clouted 104 not out against Cambridge University at The Oval in June. In the same match Whitfield hit 198, the highest score of his career. Undoubtedly Whitfield's best performance was against Yorkshire at The Oval, ten days after the match at Guildford. He hit 77 and 174 not out, a most fluent and exciting innings, which helped Surrey to beat Yorkshire by 262 runs. It was one of only two defeats that Yorkshire, the Champions, suffered during the season.

Unhappily Whitfield could not sustain this sort of form into 1939 when Surrey were captained by Monty Garland-Wells who had been vice-captain under Holmes but whose appearances had been irregular. Holmes himself had found it increasingly difficult to play regularly due to the demands of the stock exchange. He had once compared his Surrey side to the New York exchange: 'First up to great heights and then down to the depths.'

Garland-Wells was a cricketer in the Holmes mould, always eager for bright cricket and a result. He was a fine all-round sportsman, an ebullient character who kept goal for England in an amateur soccer international in 1930, and later for Clapton Orient. He was a medium-pace bowler and a batsman who believed that every ball should be hit. His tenure of office began sensationally as Surrey won seven of their first ten county matches, but they lost their way in June and finished in eighth place. Gover recovered form and fitness, and both he and Watts took over 100 wickets in all matches. Parker had a splendid all-round season, and Freddie Brown appeared more often than he had done for several years. He took 74 Championship wickets and had eight for 94 in the first match against the West Indian tourists. He still hit the ball hard, and he took 119 in 105 minutes off the Yorkshire bowlers at Headingley, but this innings still failed to save Surrey from defeat.

Gregory, in his benefit year, Fishlock, Squires and, until he injured a knee, Barling, all batted with energy, consistency and success, but a young man named McIntyre failed to do himself justice when given an extended run as a batsman, for he was not yet considered as a wicket-keeper. He had played one match in 1938 and taken a wicket.

Brooks gave way as wicket-keeper in mid-season to Mobey, who had been on the staff since 1926 and was now 35 years old, six years junior to Brooks. Mobey won his place as a result of two fine displays of keeping for Minor Counties against the West Indians at Lord's, always a ground at which it paid to do well, and against Oxford University in The Parks. The match at Oxford also saw the first-class debut of a medium-pace bowler named W. S. Surridge who took five for 41 and three for 59 and hit a couple of vigorous shots.

SURREY *v* HAMPSHIRE

Played at Guildford, 13, 14 and 15 July 1938

SURREY WON BY AN INNINGS AND 71 RUNS

SURREY	FIRST INNINGS	
L. B. Fishlock	c McCorkell b Court	59
R. J. Gregory	lbw b Court	15
H. S. Squires	b Boyes	16
T. H. Barling	b Heath	25
J. F. Parker	lbw b Boyes	85
E. W. Whitfield	b Court	138
H. M. Garland-Wells	c Paris b Boyes	53
*E. R. T. Holmes	c Herman b Court	11
E. A. Watts	b Heath	0
F. Berry	c McCorkell b Heath	2
†E. W. J. Brooks	not out	12
Extras	b 5, lb 9, nb 3	17
Total		433

1st inns: 1-46, 2-82, 3-114, 4-126, 5-281, 6-359, 7-402, 8-415, 9-433

BOWLING	O	M	R	W
Herman	32	4	72	0
Heath	31.5	0	113	3
Court	29	4	85	4
Hill	11	1	42	0
Boyes	28	5	86	3
Creese	6	2	18	0

HAMPSHIRE	FIRST INNINGS		SECOND INNINGS	
†N. T. McCorkell	c Barling b Watts	0	b Berry	8
J. P. Blake	c Parker b Berry	8	b Parker	8
G. Hill	lbw b Watts	26	b Gregory	9
W. L. C. Creese	c Fishlock b Parker	54	c Squires b Watts	11
J. Arnold	b Watts	14	c Fishlock b Parker	21
A. E. Pothecary	c Berry b Gregory	41	c Watts b Parker	20
*C. G. A. Paris	b Watts	43	c Berry b Watts	39
G. S. Boyes	b Garland-Wells	3	c Gregory b Parker	2
O. W. Herman	c Berry b Gregory	1	c Whitfield b Gregory	13
R. C. Court	c Parker b Gregory	11	c Garland-Wells b Gregory	0
G. E. M. Heath	not out	10	not out	9
Extras	b 3, lb 2, w 1, nb 1	7	lb 3, nb 1	4
Total		218		144

1st inns: 1-0, 2-11, 3-65, 4-85, 5-118, 6-163, 7-172, 8-173, 9-192
2nd inns: 1-23, 2-40, 3-65, 4-70, 5-105, 6-110, 7-114, 8-133, 9-133

BOWLING	O	M	R	W	O	M	R	W
Watts	16.1	2	50	4	14	4	39	2
Berry	13	0	36	1	14	3	15	1
Parker	14	4	30	1	16	1	52	4
Squires	11	3	33	0				
Gregory	17	3	48	3	15.2	4	34	3
Garland-Wells	5	0	14	1				

Umpires: H. W. Lee and E. Robinson

The first County Championship match played at Guildford.

*Captain; †Wicket-keeper

Monty Garland-Wells, captain in 1939, has one swipe too many and loses his middle stump.

So impressive was Mobey's wicket-keeping that, like Parker, he was chosen for the MCC side to tour India under the captaincy of A. J. Holmes, but the tour was cancelled, and, like others in that party, notably John Langridge and Emrys Davies, Mobey was not to have the chance again.

On 21 June, Surrey were due to begin a three-day match with Oxford University at The Oval, but not a ball was bowled that day, nor was one to be bowled on the scheduled last day. There were two newcomers in the Surrey side, 6 ft 3 in twins by the name of Bedser. E.A. opened the innings and scored 14. A.V. was bowled for nought. Both bowled, eight-ball overs in 1939, and neither took a wicket. They were in the side for the next match, against Cambridge

Eddie Watts puts one through the slips. Lilley (wicket-keeper) and Voce of Notts are the fielders.

University, when E.A. scored 1 and A.V. 12 not out. Eric Bedser had George Mann lbw; Alec was to have to wait another seven years for his first first-class wicket.

The outstanding performance of the season came from Eddie Watts. At Edgbaston, on 19, 21 and 22 August, Surrey hit 336, and Warwickshire were bowled out for 115, Freddie Brown taking six for

195

46. Following on, Warwickshire were bowled out for 220, and all ten wickets fell to Eddie Watts. At one time, he had a spell of six for 4, and his final analysis was: 24.1 overs, 8 maidens, 67 runs, 10 wickets. He was only the third Surrey bowler to have accomplished the feat.

From Birmingham, Surrey went to Swansea where they beat Glamorgan by six wickets, and then on to Lord's where they drew with Middlesex and Stan Squires hit 142, the last century for Surrey before first-class cricket was brought to an end by war. The last match of the season should have been played at The Oval against Lancashire, but in the worsening international situation, The Oval was requisitioned by the authorities, as it had been in 1914, and the game was transferred to Old Trafford. Surrey hit 350 for eight declared. Bernard Constable, who had made his first-class debut against the West Indian tourists in July, was playing his first Championship match. He was played for his bowling and batted number ten.

Lancashire were bowled out for 211. Watts finished the innings by bowling Wilkinson. The wicket gave him figures of five for 60. Surrey made 212 in their second innings, Parker 77 not out, and the game was abandoned because of the international crisis. Surrey travelled back to London on Friday, 1 September, which should have been the last day of the match, and on the Sunday, Neville Chamberlain made that sombre announcement that Britain was at war with Germany. Once more the world was plunged into chaos and horror.

'For myself,' wrote Monty Garland-Wells whose first-class career ended with the war, 'I loved every moment of 1939 and other years when I played for Surrey . . . I don't think anyone could have had a more cheerful or willing set of players than those who comprised the XI that year.'

Cheerful as the players may have been, the entire summer's cricket in 1939 had been played in an air of impending doom and in a sense of unreality. When first-class cricket returned the world was to be a very different place.

REHABILITATION

TRAVELLING TO MANCHESTER FOR the last county match before the outbreak of war, the Surrey side had encountered a delay of three hours at Crewe as the railway system was choked with the movement of troops and evacuees. The Oval was requisitioned before war was declared, as it had been in 1914, but this time it was not returned after a fortnight. It stayed impounded throughout the war. First it was used as a searchlight site and then prepared as a giant prisoner-of-war camp for parachutists, but they never came, and the great old ground spent the duration of the war in a state of frustrating neglect and maltreatment. Seven high-explosive bombs and countless incendaries fell close to the ground, but, like St Paul's Cathedral on the north side of the Thames, The Oval survived.

In 1940, the County undertook a programme of nine matches against Surrey club sides on Saturdays. Few first-team players were available, but some young players were seen to good advantage. The following season, it was Surrey Colts who undertook a programme of matches, and Bernard Constable and Alec Bedser were well to the fore. The Colts' side was to carry the Surrey colours in club cricket throughout the war, and David Fletcher of the Banstead Club was one who showed great promise in these matches.

The more noted Surrey players were seen in the matches at Lord's and elsewhere which involved such sides as the Army, the RAF, London Counties and British Empire XI. One of the most popular matches at Lord's in the last years of the war was the game between Middlesex and Essex and Kent and Surrey. Holmes, Garland-Wells, Brown, Dickinson, who played ten games in 1939 when down from Cambridge, Allom, Gover and Watts were all in the army. Barling, Gregory, Parker, Squires and Whitfield were in the RAF, which Fender had rejoined, while Fishlock and Berry were engaged in munitions work. Fishlock, being a trained engineer, found his expertise in making aircraft parts was much needed. Whittaker, a promising young batsman, was also in the army, and, with Brown, he was taken prisoner during Rommel's push into Egypt in 1942 and interned in Italy.

Throughout the war, Surrey was kept solvent by the endeavours of the committee and the generosity of members who continued to pay their subscriptions. In the early years of the war, it was realised that a considerable amount of damage had already been done to the pavilion and other buildings at The Oval and that a large sum of money would be needed to restore the ground.

On 21 August 1945, the Club celebrated its centenary, but, owing to the war, there could be no match to mark the occasion. The prisoner-of-war camp that was never used had not been dismantled until the spring of 1945, and the pavilion and the ground were in a chaotic state. The Duchy of Cornwall had extended the lease on the ground until 1984 and had expressed a wish that the ground should be used for other recreations and not remain closed for half the year. This was in line with the Club's thinking, but they rejected an approach from the Greyhound syndicates to establish a greyhound racing track at The Oval. The Club noted its centenary by launching an appeal for £100,000 in order to carry out the necessary reconstruction of the ground, and the Club's patron, HM King George VI, made one of the first donations, £100.

There were changes in personnel at The Oval when cricket resumed in 1946. B. A. Glanvill was now president and chairman, and Brian Castor was to take over from Davey as secretary at the end of 1946. 'Bosser' Martin had retired, and his place was taken by Bert Lock, who, like Apted and Martin, was to win fame as a groundsman. Lock had played for the County as a medium-pace bowler in the early 1930s so he was no stranger to The Oval. He was demobilised from the RAF on 5 October 1945, and started work at The Oval three days later, foregoing any thought of holiday or leave. He had six months in which to make the ground ready for first-class cricket, and the task which confronted him was enormous. He describes the scene that met him at The Oval:

> The square (i.e. the long strip of playing pitch) had not been touched for six years, and was covered with long coarse grass full of weeds. The outfield had been used for a searchlight, gun-site, and a prisoner-of-war camp, with miles of barbed wire supported by nearly 1,000 poles all in concrete two feet deep. There were four huts erected on one foot thick concrete bases, with a number of drains in between. At the Vauxhall end were large pits. Weeds grown to a great height covered the whole area (I even found a bramble bush). There was also an 'assault course' at the Vauxhall end which had to be removed, and thousands of bricks from the bomb-blasted West wall. Fences and stands were in a shocking state of repair, and hundreds of seats calling for a new coat of paint.

The general opinion was that there would be no cricket at The Oval for two or three years, but Lock and his crew believed otherwise. He sought the permission of the committee to turf rather than seed the ground. He walked for miles over the marshes at Gravesend until he found areas of weed-free turf. Some 11,000 square yards of The Oval were levelled, and 35,000 turves were laid. On 27 and 29 April 1946, a trial match took place at the ground, and on Saturday, 18 May, the

After playing for Surrey since 1927, Tom Barling enjoyed his best season in 1946, when he topped 2,000 runs.

first county game for seven years at The Oval began. There have been many great achievements by Surrey cricketers, but none of them has been greater than the achievement of Bert Lock and his crew in making The Oval ready for first-class cricket in six months after the ravages it had received during the war.

With the ground ready, the County now looked to its players. The nucleus of the 1939 side had returned unscathed from the war, but it is worth considering their ages and the years that they had lost. Of the side that played regularly in 1939, Gover (38), Fishlock (39), Barling (40), Gregory (44), Squires (37), Parker (33), Mobey (42) and Watts (35) were to reappear regularly in 1947. To them were added the Bedser twins (28) and McIntyre (28). Bennett, the captain, was 34. This meant that the average age of the Surrey side in 1946 was nearly 36, yet five of the side were comparatively inexperienced cricketers, and there was no strength in depth. Outside the players mentioned above, Whittaker, Constable, Pierpoint and, for one match, Lock and Yeatman were the only others to appear in the Championship.

The greatest problem that the County faced, however, was that of captaincy. Holmes, Brown and Garland-Wells were all unavailable so that there were no amateurs to call upon. What happened has become the subject of much speculation and apocryphal story, but the man who was asked to lead the side was N. H. Bennett. How little was known of him can be seen from Norman Preston's comment in the Spring Annual of *The Cricketer*, 1946:

> Several of the Surrey professionals met for the first time their new captain, N. H. Bennett, at the opening of the East Hill Cricket School, run by A. Sandham and A. R. Gover. Born on September 23, 1912, at Walton-on-Thames, Bennett has never figured in first-class cricket but he is known in London club circles as a hard-hitting batsman. In 1930, he headed the Stowe batting, while in 1936 he appeared in the county second team. During the war he has served in the Far East, rising to the rank of Major in the Royal Engineers. I am told he has a pleasing personality and when he settles down he should make plenty of runs.

Bennett had played five innings for Surrey second eleven in 1936, and although, at various times, he appeared for Brondesbury and the Maoris, he could hardly be described as being well known in London club circles as he had been in New Zealand on business in the years immediately before the Second World War. The folk tale is that the appointment of Nigel Harvie Bennett was a clerical error and that the man destined for the job was A. C. L. 'Leo' Bennett, a famous club cricketer with the BBC, who had been educated at Dulwich and lived in Surrey. Leo Bennett played for, and captained, Northamptonshire on several occasions. It had been decided to ask Leo Bennett to lead Surrey when N. H. Bennett walked into the offices and asked if he could be offered some second team matches as he was now back in England. A case of mistaken identity followed, and he was offered the captaincy, which was accepted. The tale may be fiction, but the fact that N. H. Bennett was appointed captain remains one of the great mysteries of Surrey cricket.

One can only admire his courage in accepting the post although he cannot have anticipated how difficult the task would be. His one year in first-class cricket was not to be a happy one, but he scored some useful runs towards the end of the season.

The Club had lost its complete stock of towels and other equipment during the military occupation of The Oval, and extra clothing coupons were needed to replace these and to kit out the players. Each player was provided 15 extra coupons, but these were hardly sufficient for the purpose of buying flannels, shirts, blazers, towels and socks. Bennett was instantly capped and was noted as wearing a 'real pre-war Surrey blazer'. It had belonged to R. de W. K. Winlaw whose relatives had returned it to the Club after his death, intending it no doubt as an item for exhibit in the pavilion. It was an innocent enough act for the new captain to wear the blazer, but it was one that was hardly likely to go down well with a group of hardened professionals who were struggling to assemble kit themselves and, if not hostile to the new skipper, were at least a little sceptical of him.

It was soon apparent that Bennett had little knowledge of the county game, which was not surprising, and that he had little control over the senior professionals. At times it seemed that there were orders and counter-orders being barked from every corner of the field. One must sympathise with Bennett to a certain extent, but, as Michael Barton, one of his successors, has commented, he neither sought nor took advice from those more experienced in the game and who initially were eager and willing to help, and he suffered in consequence.

Wisden wrote of Bennett that his

> want of knowledge of county cricket on the field presented an unconquerable hindrance to the satisfactory accomplishment of arduous duties. This prejudiced the general work of the side, and several bad spells culminated in consecutive defeats in the last six Championship matches. From eighth in the 1939 table Surrey fell to twelfth.

This was obviously highly unsatisfactory for a side which had enough talent to be challenging in the top three, yet the season was by no means one of unending gloom. Of the pre-war players, only Watts and Squires failed to reproduce their old form. Gover passed 100 wickets and played in The Oval Test against India. Fishlock, too, played in this Test and was in the MCC side that went to Australia, but, although he played in one Test, the last, at Sydney, it was not a happy tour for him.

Parker, though frequently indisposed, had an excellent all-round season, and, like Fishlock, Barling and Gregory scored heavily. Barling and Gregory shared a third-wicket partnership of 267 in under three-and-a-half hours against Nottinghamshire at The Oval on the Saturday of the August Bank Holiday. Gregory hit 154 and Barling 233 not out. About 13,000 saw the play on Saturday, and 17,000 on the Monday. Among them was Field Marshal Montgomery, who had been born in the local vicarage. At Guildford, Tom Barling hit 172 against Oxford University, which remains the highest score hit by a Surrey batsman at that ground.

Jack Parker scored over 14,000 runs and took over 500 wickets in a first-class career lasting from 1932 to 1952. He was selected for the tour of India which was abandoned on the outbreak of war.

It was not only Surrey batsmen who thrived, and one of the most remarkable events of the season came on 11 May, the day that first-class cricket returned to The Oval. The visitors were the Indian tourists, and with Alec Bedser in good form, they were reduced to 205 for 9. The Indian numbers ten and eleven were Sarwate and Banerjee. They added 249, the highest last-wicket partnership to be recorded in England, and both batsmen hit centuries, unique in the history of the game for the last two batsmen in the order to do this. Sarwate hit 124 not out, and Banerjee finally fell to Parker for 121. Gregory hit a second-innings century for Surrey, but the tourists won by nine wickets.

Alec Bedser was the outstanding bowler of the year and began his Test career with seven for 49 and four for 96 at Lord's. The twins had been through much since their initial brush with first-class cricket in 1939. They had lived in Woking for all but the first six months of their lives until the war took them to foreign lands. They were called up with the Militia in September 1939, and served with the RAF Police until being transferred to the Investigation Branch. They went to France in January 1940, and were among the force evacuated from Dunkirk later the same year. From 1943, they served in North Africa, Italy and Austria. They were demobilised in May 1946, and then they began their first-class careers in earnest.

On 4 and 6 May, they were in the Surrey side that beat MCC at Lord's. Jack Parker hit the County's first post-war century, and Alec Bedser, wicketless in the first innings, when Alf Gover had taken six for 52, returned figures of six for 14 in 9.1 overs in the second. His first six victims in first-class cricket were Denis Compton, J. G. W. Davies, R. W. V. Robins, N. S. Mitchell-Innes, A. W. H. Mallett and Jack Young. He bowled above medium pace, but Mobey stood up to him as he always liked his wicket-keepers to do. Alec finished the season with 128 wickets at 20.13 runs each, won his first Test caps and was chosen to go to Australia. A great career in the game was born.

Eric was less successful, but he hit a maiden century, 101 against Hampshire at Kingston, where a week's cricket was arranged to augment the appeal fund. The game was outside the County Championship, but had first-class status. He took 25 wickets in all matches and showed signs of becoming a very useful all-rounder.

The appeal did not raise as much money as the Club had hoped although it was enthusiastically organised by Errol Holmes and later by Louis Palgrave. The problem was that it was a time of great austerity, and £100,000 was too optimistic a target. Nevertheless, the Centenary Appeal produced some exciting and entertaining moments, the most memorable of which was the celebration match at The Oval on 23 May 1946. The King and 15,000 people saw Surrey play an Old England XII (Freeman bowled and fielded, but would not have batted) and if ever an event convinced cricket fans that the war was over, it was this game. Sandham, Fender, Jardine, Knight, Allom, Brooks and Holmes were all back at The Oval, and Hobbs and Strudwick umpired. Sutcliffe, Woolley, Hendren, Tate and 'Tich' Freeman brought a great sense of history and dignity to the occasion, and few clubs can have celebrated their centenary in such a magnificent manner, albeit a year late. A similar match was staged in 1947, but without quite the same impact.

In celebrating the old, there was cause also to welcome the new. Arthur McIntyre, a fine outfielder at this time, and Geoff Whittaker added 201 in two-and-a-half hours for Surrey's fifth wicket against Kent, and both men hit maiden first-class centuries.

In the following match, against Combined Universities, at The Oval, Jim Laker and David Fletcher made their first-class debuts. Laker took three for 78 and three for 43, and Barling hit 134 not out,

*The Surrey Centenary was celebrated in 1946, a year late. King George VI is shaking hands with
'Tich' Freeman of the Old England XII, 23 May. A great occasion.*

but the hero of the match was Bernard Constable who, batting at
number eight in a strong Services' side, hit 107 before becoming one of
Laker's victims.

Laker was given two more games in the Kingston Festival at the end
of the season. Squires took eight for 52 in the first match, against
Hampshire, the match in which Eric Bedser hit 100, and Laker
captured his first county wicket in bizarre fashion. Exton was the
batsman, and he hit the ball hard to Gover at short-leg who put his
sweater up over his head in self-protection, but the ball stuck between
his legs, and Exton was out.

Both Laker and Fletcher were to gain regular places in the side in
1947 when Holmes, at the age of 41, made a reluctant, but successful
return to lead the side. The year was to see the last of Bob Gregory and
Alf Gover. Gregory hit 73 in a friendly match against Essex and 104
against MCC at Lord's. It was his 38th and last first-class century.
Injury brought an early end to his season, and this great club man,
prepared to do anything for his side, announced his retirement.

Gover worked as tirelessly as ever and captured 109 wickets in
Championship matches alone. Stuart Surridge tells how in one of the

early county matches in which he played he fielded at slip to Gover and took a catch one-handed, high above his head. Gover came out with an expletive which caused a reprimand from Errol Holmes, but Alf's excitement was caused by his astonishment that there was somebody fielding at slip who held a catch off him. No one will ever be able to estimate the number of wickets he *should* have had. Yet he took all with a smile, and still he pumped and pounded in for more. He became one of those cricketers who was loved because there was something in the soul of those who watched which could identify with his ceaseless endeavour and perpetual good humour. He had learned the game in a hard school. He told a joke against himself as to how, in his early days, he was conned by a seemingly nervous Patsy Hendren who led Gover to believe that he was frightened of fast short-pitched bowling. Only after three fours and a word from Jack Hobbs did he realise that Hendren had been leading him on to serve up the type of bowling he relished most.

Gover tells also how Hobbs called him to one side in the dressing room when, as a young man, he came off the field cursing and swearing about the catches that had been dropped off him. Hobbs told him plainly to behave himself, and thereafter, for a long time, Alf Gover called Jack Hobbs 'Sir'. He took from Hobbs and Sandham the tradition that they had taken from Hayward, who had inherited it from Abel who had learned from Jupp. Moreover, Gover understood the meaning and the value of that tradition, and he has carried it with dignity, intelligence and mirth. More than any other man he links the Surrey past to the present and the hopes for the future, and the County's debt to him is a very great one.

The injury and ultimate retirement of Gregory gave an early chance to Fletcher, who hit three centuries in the course of the season and won rapturous applause from the press and a place in the Players' side against the Gentlemen. He was never quite to live up to the role in which the press would have cast him, but he was a fine player of sound judgement, common sense and a delightful range of shots, particularly on the off. Perhaps his best performance in 1947 was at Bradford when he carried his bat through the innings for 127 out of 271. With Alec Bedser taking seven, and Eric Bedser taking eight, wickets. Surrey went on to beat Yorkshire by five wickets.

Fletcher's highest score of the season, and, as it transpired, of his career, came at Trent Bridge when Surrey, replying to Nottingham-shire's 401, hit the highest score ever made against that county and the highest score that Surrey have made away from The Oval. It is worth noting the details of this remarkable performance in what was a rather dull draw. Nottinghamshire reached 201 for four in their second innings. It is also worth noting that Fletcher was playing in only his

Alf Gover – a lifetime of service.

second county match. He batted five hours twenty minutes and hit a six and 22 fours.

Fletcher shared stands of 155 for the second wicket with Gregory and 263 with Squires for the third. On the last morning, Surrey added 263 in two hours, Parker and Holmes putting on 247 in 110 minutes. Holmes reached his century in 90 minutes; Parker took 100 minutes to reach three figures.

Even the loss of Fishlock with appendicitis brought no great reduction in Surrey's run-scoring powers. Squires and Parker were as good as ever they had been, and Eric Bedser, accepting whatever place he was asked to bat in the order without complaint, quietly reached 1,000 runs for the first time. Arthur McIntyre took over from Mobey

SURREY *v* NOTTINGHAMSHIRE

Played at Trent Bridge on 24, 26 and 27 May 1947

Nottinghamshire 401 (A. V. Bedser 4 for 79) and 201 for four

SURREY

E. A. Bedser	b Jepson	12
D. G. W. Fletcher	b Butler	194
R. J. Gregory	lbw b Voce	87
H. S. Squires	c Stocks b Butler	154
J. F. Parker	not out	108
★E. R. T. Holmes	not out	122
Extras	b 13, lb 16	29
Total	(for 4 wkts dec)	706

T. H. Barling, †A. J. W. McIntyre, E. A. Watts, A. V. Bedser and A. R. Gover did not bat.

★Captain; †Wicket-keeper

behind the stumps and not only proved himself a highly competent and exciting wicket-keeper, but gave a substance and panache to the lower middle order batting which was the envy of other counties.

For Surrey batting had never really been a problem, but at last a balanced attack began to take shape. Jim Laker grabbed the opportunity given to him and took 66 Championship wickets at 16.65 runs each. He took 79 wickets in all matches, was seventh in the national averages and was selected to go to West Indies with the MCC side led by G. O. Allen. There he began his Test career with the wicket of Clyde Walcott and first-innings figures of seven for 103. He was one of England's few successes in a series in which they were outclassed.

Alec Bedser showed no falling off in form after the rigours of the series in Australia, and Eric Bedser's off-breaks began to bring reward. Squires's mixture of off-breaks and leg-breaks were also used to advantage at times, and there was promise in the slow left-arm bowling of Australian-born John McMahon. Another slow left-arm bowler, Tony Lock, was having considerable success in the second eleven, but he had to go off and begin his national service.

In spite of these encouraging signs, there seemed to be a lack of determination in the side, and at the beginning of July 1947, Surrey stood perilously close to the bottom of the table. They rallied to climb to sixth in the table, but there was the over-all feeling that the side was not realising its full potential. The disappointment in this was sharpened by the success of arch-rivals Middlesex from north of the

Australian John McMahon enjoyed a brief success as a slow left-arm bowler in the late 1940s.

Thames. When the sides met at The Oval in August 47,000 paid for admission, and the gates were closed on a crowd of 30,000 on the Saturday.

Surrey suffered a setback at the beginning of 1948 when Tom Barling, after nine games, dropped out of the side and retired from first-class cricket. He initially took up a position as assistant coach at The Oval, but he later became coach at Harrow School. Matters were complicated further by illness to David Fletcher, which explained his loss of form, and by the inability of Errol Holmes to play in more than nine matches because of the calls of business. Watts, too, had virtually dropped out of the side following an operation. On top of these factors was injury to McIntyre which kept him out for five county matches and Test calls which deprived the side of Alec Bedser and Jim Laker for long periods. Yet, in spite of all these things, Surrey came very close to winning the Championship. In the opinion of many, Stuart Surridge included, they should have done so.

The season began with defeat at the hands of MCC at Lord's, but the game had encouraging signs for Surrey. Stuart Surridge formed an impressive opening attack with Alec Bedser. Arthur McIntyre hit a delightful century in the first innings; and Michael Barton scored an equally delightful 124 in the second. This was Barton's first game for Surrey. He had won his blue at Oxford in 1936 and 1937, but nothing had been seen of him since then. He was a tall, elegant forceful batsman who had done well at Winchester and had played for Norfolk with considerable success on a few occasions. His club cricket was played for The Mote at Maidstone. His exciting debut for Surrey was followed by 4 and 15 against the Australians, 132 and 29 against Nottinghamshire, and 103 and 15 against Leicestershire. Three centuries in his first four matches for the County naturally caused much excitement. It was not likely that Barton would be able to keep up such form, but he proved a valuable member of the side and reached his 1,000 runs for the season in all matches which was a considerable achievement considering that the burden of captaincy was also thrust upon him when Holmes was out of the side, which was very often.

Fishlock was a great strength in these early matches, when Surrey did not do well. He hit a masterly 81 not out against the all-conquering Australians, carrying his bat through an innings of 141. At Leicester, when Surrey gained their first victory of the season, he shared a fourth wicket partnership of 244 with Barton and went on to make 253 in six hours and twenty minutes. It was the highest score of his career.

Surrey's first real run of success did not come until the beginning of June. Rain restricted the match against Gloucestershire at The Oval to one day, and on that day only five hours play was possible. Surrey fell to the combined wiles of Cook and Goddard for 133. Crapp hit splendidly for Gloucestershire, and when he was sixth out at 98 there were still 33 minutes remaining. The target was reduced to three runs in the last over with two wickets standing, but Laker bowled both Lambert and Cook as they attempted to make the winning hit, and Surrey won by two runs with one ball to spare. Laker finished with eight for 55.

There was victory at Ilford by four wickets, and then Lancashire came to The Oval. Surrey batted rather laboriously to reach 300, and, on a rain-affected pitch against McMahon and Eric Bedser, the visitors only just avoided the follow-on. Cranston, seven for 43, bowled Surrey out for 123 in their second innings so that Lancashire were left to make 248 to win. They were 119 for five, but Winston Place was batting with complete composure, and he was now joined by Wharton in a stand of 97. With five wickets in hand, Lancashire needed only 32 to win. Eric Bedser then bowled Wharton and dismissed Nigel Howard and Cranston with the score on 232. Squires

Eric Bedser, a selfless all-rounder for Surrey from 1939 to 1962, an off-break bowler and steady batsman.

captured Roberts, and with Lancashire needing two to win, Hilton hit Eric Bedser high to long-off where Fishlock held a magnificent running catch. Eric Bedser had taken five for 75, and Surrey had won by one run.

Eric Bedser's advance as a bowler was a tremendous boost to Surrey, particularly as his brother and Laker were missing for so many matches, but it was McMahon with 85 Championship wickets who made the greatest advance of any of the Surrey players during the season. If, at times, his length was a little erratic, he spun the ball appreciably and was always testing batsmen. Like Surridge, whose batting excited the crowd in the way that Peach's had done in past years, McMahon was awarded his county cap. Surrey had discovered him playing club cricket for Southgate, and there were high hopes of him, but he could not repeat the form of 1948 and later moved to Somerset.

The County could not string together a consistent run of success, but, in August, the Championship was very open. Most people would point to the innings defeat at Cardiff as being the reason that Surrey did not take the title, for Glamorgan were the eventual Champions, finishing four points ahead of Surrey. One more victory would have taken Surrey well clear, and Stuart Surridge maintains that one more win should have come in Stan Squires's benefit match against Middlesex.

It was Surrey's penultimate match at The Oval, and the pitch was affected by rain. Surrey fell to Jack Young for 156, but they still gained a first innings lead of 38. Young took seven wickets for the second time in the match as Surrey were bowled out for 103, although they were handicapped by the absence of Eric Bedser who had been taken ill and could not bat. Middlesex needed 142 to win in as many minutes, but they lost half their side for 39 and looked beaten. Mann and Robins added an enterprising 62, and then Jim Sims came in at number eight and hit 36 of the last 41 runs. He was twice dropped, and he and Laurie Gray, not noted for his batting, were allowed to score the last ten runs. Surridge is still frustrated by memory of the occasion:

> I didn't bowl a ball at them. I stood fuming at mid-off while Errol ignored me, and it was too late when Alec was brought back. We should have won that game and the Championship. Surrey should have won the Championship every year after the war. They had the players. It was the close-to-the-wicket fielding that was the problem. It needs good fielding to turn good bowlers into great bowlers.

So Surrey just failed to win the title, and Holmes retired for the second and last time and was succeeded by M. R. Barton, who had held the reins for much of 1948.

Barton inherited a side that was changing in character. Of the pre-war stalwarts only Fishlock, Squires, Parker and Watts were left. Watts played but five games in 1949 before retiring, and the season was also to be the last for Stan Squires.

Michael Barton was, indeed is, a quiet, gentle and elegant man. He has been described by some close to the Club as 'the last of the amateur gentlemen'. One hopes not, but it is not an inappropriate description. He had much to commend him as captain of Surrey. His natural charm and courteousness won him many friends; his willingness to seek and listen to advice from senior professionals won him many more. In one of his first games as captain in 1948, he had been confronted by Sellers and Yorkshire at The Oval and had not announced his team before the toss because there was a doubt about McIntyre's fitness to keep wicket. McIntyre had to play, but he could not bat in either innings, and Sellers generously allowed Kirby, the substitute, to keep wicket in Yorkshire's second innings. It was all part of a learning process.

*Michael Barton captained Surrey from 1949 to 1951,
handing over to Stuart Surridge just before the great run in
the 1950s.*

Barton's achievement was remarkable when one considers that his
first-class experience before 1948 had been restricted to two seasons
with Oxford more than ten years earlier, yet he settled into the
captaincy and carried out the job with ease, dignity and considerable
success. He acknowledges the immense debt that he owed to Stan
Squires in his first season, for Squires was a patient and kindly man
who was so delighted that he had been able to earn his living by
playing the game for which he had the greatest passion that he set
himself never to sully nor demean his profession. He was liked and
respected by all who played with or against him, and for young
players he was a model in style and attitude. His father had wanted him
to follow a career in a City stockbrokers, but Squires leapt at the
chance that Surrey offered him to leave the office for the cricket field.
As a batsman he never appeared to have to hit the ball with any
ferocity, for his technique was founded on the sureness of his timing
and the suppleness of his wrists. With the exception of one post-war
season he was a most consistent scorer, and a useful wicket-taker with
his variety of spin. In 1949, he hit more than 1,700 runs, including five
centuries, one of them, against Derbyshire, an innings of 210.

Squires was a familiar and popular figure at The Oval, and

elsewhere, with his thick glasses (which for a period he forsook for contact lenses) making him instantly recognisable. There were those who believed that it was only the weakness of his eyesight which prevented him from becoming an England player, but his eyesight did not prevent him from scoring over 19,000 runs and hitting 37 centuries, nor from being a fine golfer and squash player. That he should be such a help to Barton and play so well in 1949 was a comfort to all who knew him, for, in January 1950, he died of leukaemia at the age of 41. His death was much lamented, and he was much missed, but he is still remembered at The Oval with the greatest affection.

Like Squires, Fishlock was a model of consistency. He topped 2,000 runs in Championship matches alone, hit seven centuries, including two in the match against Nottinghamshire at Trent Bridge, and was the leading left-handed batsman in the country. When he was going well and Squires was in form Surrey looked the best side in the Championship, for Laker was gaining in maturity and was on the threshold of becoming the greatest off-break bowler the world has known and Lock was showing exciting promise while, according to *Wisden*, 'Surrey owed much to Surridge, an amateur brimful with enthusiasm'. If one man leapt ahead more than any other, however, it was Eric Bedser. He had developed into one of the best off-spin bowlers in the country, with 88 wickets to prove it, and he hit 1,740 runs in all matches. This was all-round cricket of a quality that Surrey had not known since the days of Fender.

Another all-round cricketer of the highest quality was Arthur McIntyre. Restored to full fitness, he hit more than 1,000 runs, and with 94 dismissals, 71 caught and 23 stumped, he came close to the very elusive and rarely performed wicket-keeper's 'double'. Only Yarnold of Worcestershire had more victims, and, as Barton points out, McIntyre was still learning his trade in 1949.

In spite of the consistency of Fishlock, Squires and Parker, the exciting advance of Eric Bedser, Lock, McIntyre and Surridge, and the obvious brilliance of Laker, Surrey dropped to fifth in the table, and, with so much praise lavished upon them, it was hard to see why. One reason was that they were handicapped by an injury to Alec Bedser, who strained a hip joint but still managed to take 110 wickets. Another handicap was the lumbago that troubled Parker and made him, as Barton discovered, a reluctant bowler. Worst of all was the falling away of Fletcher and an injury to Whittaker.

Stuart Surridge believes that David Fletcher was one of those natural cricketers who failed to follow his own instincts and became a lesser player because of his slavish adherence to the coaching manual. The glories of 1947 were never to come in such plenitude again, and one wonders if, in 1949, he had quite recovered from the effects of the pneumonia that had laid him low the previous season. Poor Geoff Whittaker was destined always to be something of a fringe player dogged by wretched luck.

Whittaker was not an automatic choice at the beginning of the season, but he replaced Fletcher for the game at Northampton on 18 to 20 May. Eric Bedser and Fishlock were out cheaply, but Whittaker launched a violent assault on the bowling. His innings of 148 included nine sixes, three off successive balls from Broderick, and eight fours, and in the second innings, when he hit another two sixes, he scored 89 not out. He had no success against Warwickshire or Derbyshire when Squires hit 210 and Alec Bedser and Jack Parker bowled unchanged through Derbyshire's first innings and shot the visitors out for 52, but then, just as he was running into top form again, a knee injury kept him out of the side for what was the best part of half a season.

This gave Bernard Constable a belated chance for a run in the County side. He hit his first 100 for Surrey in Watts's benefit match against Middlesex. Constable and Squires added 191 for the third wicket, and with Surridge taking six for 49 in the first Middlesex innings, Surrey gained their first victory over their close rivals since the war. It ended a run of six defeats. Squires's 115 proved to be his last century in first-class cricket.

Squires was sorely missed in 1950 when his steadiness at number three would have been invaluable, for the Surrey batting was probably the weakest that it had been for the best part of a century. Fishlock began in poor form, but soon found his touch and yet again passed 2,000 runs and topped the County averages. Parker, too, was forceful and the ever-reliable all-rounder. Constable held a regular place in the side and played some useful innings while McIntyre was good enough behind the stumps – he again finished second to Yarnold with 78 dismissals – and with the bat to win a Test cap and a trip to Australia. But Whittaker, Fletcher, Eric Bedser, whose bowling deserted him totally, and Barton found it hard to muster runs.

The weakness of the batting is most clearly seen when it is remembered that in 12 Championship innings the side failed to reach 200. Yet, in spite of these obvious flaws in the batting, Surrey finished level at the top of the Championship table. It was the first time for 36 years that they had found themselves at the top. Whatever criticisms could be levelled against the batting, none could be aimed at an admirably varied attack. Alec Bedser and Surridge were potent with the new ball, and Parker did excellent work as first change. Laker, not yet fully recognised by the England selectors for the great bowler he was, and Lock, an exciting emerging talent, were a formidable spin attack, beautifully contrasted, the quicker left-arm spin of Lock complementing the off-breaks of Laker.

In the Test Trial at Bradford, playing for England against the Rest, Laker returned the amazing figures of 14 overs, 12 maidens, 2 runs, 8 wickets – and he still played in only one Test match against West Indies and was not picked to go with Freddie Brown's side to Australia. Brown had played in only a handful of matches since the war, and none for Surrey since 1948, but he suddenly emerged from retirement to captain Northamptonshire, where he had taken up a business appointment, and later England.

Two of Laker's victims in the Test Trial were Eric Bedser and Peter May. Eric Bedser, as we have indicated, had a poor season, taking only 13 very expensive wickets in all matches and scoring only 731 Championship runs, but two centuries outside the Championship took him past the 1,000 runs mark and lifted his average. Peter May was in his first year at Cambridge and an innings of 227 not out against Hampshire and several other stylish knocks had quickly earned him a high reputation. He had been educated at Charterhouse and, although born in Berkshire, had a residential qualification for Surrey. Barton was aware of this and invited May to play for the County after the Varsity match. He was still short of his 21st birthday.

Two victories and two draws in the first wet weeks of the season gave little indication of what was to come, and defeat at The Oval by

The spin twins. Jim Laker and Tony Lock gaze out from The Oval dressing room.

Essex seemed to hint at a familiar pattern. Alec Bedser and Surridge bowled Essex out for 232, and in the second innings, Alec Bedser and Laker bowled out the visitors for 108, but Fishlock, 27 and 57, Parker 93 and nought, Constable 25 and 16, and Whittaker 9 and 29, were the only Surrey batsmen to reach double figures and the match was lost by 17 runs.

Surrey suffered another defeat at the beginning of July when they lost to Yorkshire at Sheffield by five runs. Their defeats, like many of their victories, tended to be by the narrowest of margins, and the game at Sheffield underlined Surrey's perversity. Yorkshire made 271 in their first innings. They had been 67 for four, but they were rallied by a Yardley century. Surrey struggled for runs in reply, and only a tenacious 60 not out by Constable and 41 from Barton helped them to get within 73 of the Yorkshire score. Rain had marred the match, but the home side went for quick runs, and Yardley declared, setting Surrey the task of scoring 221 in 170 minutes. There were some spirited knocks, and Surrey showed much more fight than they had done in the first innings, but, when Surridge and Lock, the last pair, came together, 33 runs were needed in 25 minutes. Surridge treated the bowling with disdain, and both batsmen scored freely until, with six runs needed and five minutes remaining, Lock essayed a mighty heave at Wardle and was lbw.

This win took Yorkshire to the top of the table above Lancashire and Warwickshire with Surrey, who had played one game less, in fourth place. Victories over Warwickshire, Kent, Gloucestershire twice, and Worcestershire maintained Surrey's challenge, but they also suffered two more defeats, by Kent at Blackheath, remembrance of things past, and Yorkshire at The Oval. Then came victory over Middlesex at The Oval in Fishlock's benefit match, and Surrey were joint second with Yorkshire, 20 points behind Lancashire, although Surrey had now played one game more than their rivals.

The victory over Middlesex had been a wonderful benefit for the faithful and consistent Fishlock. The beneficiary himself hit 111, McIntyre hit 85, and Surrey made 401. The match had added interest because it marked the return of Denis Compton to first-class cricket after an absence of two months because of a knee injury. He did not disappoint and made 115 not out, but Middlesex were all out for 229 and had to follow on. In their second innings, with Laker taking eight for 57, they were out for 199, and Surrey won by ten wickets. Appropriately, Fishlock made the winning hit.

A crowd of 48,530 people watched the three days cricket, and the previous year at The Oval more than 50,000 had paid for admission over the three days. These were still heady days, but for many counties they were drawing to a close.

Peter May had first joined the Surrey side for the match at Bristol. Fishlock and Constable were the batting heroes, and Laker, eight for 45 in the first innings, the bowling hero, as Surrey won by five wickets. May scored 1 and 1, but his presence in the next few weeks was to be decisive in bringing a share of the Championship to The Oval. At Worcester, he hit 118, and it was this game which started Surrey's late burst of success, for the win over Middlesex followed, and then came successive victories over Nottinghamshire, Sussex, Essex, Middlesex (at Lord's) and Worcester (at The Oval).

Lancashire arrived at The Oval on 26 August needing only to lead on the first innings and claim the four points to win the title. It should have been an exciting encounter, but it turned out to be a dour affair, often negative. Lancashire won the toss, and Place and Washbrook opened. Alec Bedser bowled the first over, and the second was bowled by Surridge. With his second ball he bowled Washbrook and with his fourth ball he bowled Place. This was not the start for which Lancashire had been looking, and the loss of those two quick wickets determined their policy for the rest of the day, even the rest of the match. The Red Rose county ground their way to 221 at less than two runs an over. They would have scored much less had Surrey not put down five catches. Ikin, who was badly dropped on nine, scored 52 in four hours and ten minutes.

Fishlock, Fletcher and Constable were out with the score on 39, but May and Parker added 93. Barton went cheaply before McIntyre joined May in a stand of 71, and the Lancashire score was passed. Surrey took a first innings lead of 66 and four vital points. Their hero was unquestionably the young Peter May, and his innings of 92 in five hours was rewarded with a county cap. To be awarded one's cap after only eleven matches was quite unusual, but May's was a mature talent, and the part that he played in the successful closing matches of the season was recognised by all. He himself has said how much he owed to Laurie Fishlock and Jack Parker. They were professional in their approach to all that they did. They advised him and guided him through partnerships and were a constant source of help and inspiration.

To their shame, Lancashire made no attempt to win the match. They concentrated solely on preventing Surrey from winning, and, ultimately, they paid the price. They had adopted a surprisingly negative approach before the start, omitting their left-arm England spinner Bob Berry and playing a young amateur seamer from Manchester University, Dickinson, who had played only once before and had not taken a wicket. In 119 overs, Lancashire scored 203 for four, and the match was drawn. Even Bernard Constable was allowed to bowl 30 overs of his occasional leg-breaks and take one for 58.

Lancashire had now completed their programme, and Surrey needed to beat Leicestershire at The Oval in their last game to earn a share of the title. The great fear was the weather, and it was a fear that was justified. The opening day saw two interruptions for rain and play ended 80 minutes early. The start was delayed for three-and-a-half hours on the second day so that it was necessary for Surrey to waste no time in the field or at the crease. Alec Bedser bowled magnificently. At a little above medium pace, he bowled inswingers to a leg trap and the Leicestershire batsmen floundered. Nine wickets were down for 68. Walsh adopted the bold approach and hit 41, and the last wicket realised 45.

Fishlock was quickly on the offensive, and although Walsh accounted for Fletcher and May, Surrey took the lead with only two wickets down. Fishlock and Constable put on 101, and Fishlock hit 11 fours in his 108 which was made in under three hours. With the weather always a threat, the later batsmen went for quick runs and lost their wickets in the fray.

On a worn wicket, made more difficult by rain, Leicestershire had little hope of survival against a Surrey attack which was capable of exploiting any conditions. Les Berry and the Australian Victor Jackson battled bravely, Jackson for two-and-a-quarter hours, but, in spite of dropping four catches, Surrey were not to be denied. The last Leicestershire pair saved their side from the indignity of an innings defeat, and Surrey had to bat again to score two runs. Barton opened with Fishlock and faced the bowling of Charles Palmer who obligingly sent down a full toss which the Surrey captain hit to the boundary to give his side a share of the County Championship.

There was a large and enthusiastic crowd, and there were scenes of much delight at the end of the game. As Peter May said many years later:

> To a county which had not known such success for 36 years, half a Championship was glory indeed. For most of the next decade a halved Championship would have been something of a disappointment but none of us in 1950 could have guessed what was to follow and we were far from blasé then.

Surrey fielded practically the same side in 1951 that they had done the previous season, but the frailties in batting cost them more dearly. A poor start to the season could not be rectified, and the County were never in contention for the title. *The Cricketer* reported:

> At the beginning of the season Surrey beat a good MCC side by an innings, Laker having a match analysis of 10 for 34. After losing on the first innings to Lancashire they went to Nottingham and won by ten wickets – and then came a slump, three matches being lost in

SURREY *v* LEICESTERSHIRE

Played at The Oval, Kennington, 30, 31 August and 1 September 1950

SURREY WON BY 10 WICKETS

LEICESTERSHIRE	FIRST INNINGS		SECOND INNINGS	
L. G. Berry	c Fletcher b Bedser	13	b Lock	49
F. T. Prentice	c Barton b Surridge	13	c McIntyre b Bedser	13
M. Tompkin	c Fletcher b Bedser	3	c McIntyre b Bedser	0
*C. H. Palmer	c Laker b Bedser	7	c Laker b Lock	4
V. E. Jackson	c Fletcher b Bedser	0	c Lock b Laker	49
G. Lester	c McIntyre b Bedser	4	b Surridge	5
W. R. Parkins	c Clark b Surridge	2	c and b Bedser	2
C. R. D. Wooler	c McIntyre b Bedser	7	c Lock b Laker	21
J. E. Walsh	c Laker b Bedser	41	not out	6
†P. Corrall	b Bedser	1	c McIntyre b Bedser	0
T. J. Goodwin	not out	18	c Bedser b Laker	1
Extras	lb 2, nb 1	4	b 4, lb 6	10
Total		113		160

BOWLING	O	M	R	W	O	M	R	W
A. V. Bedser	22	6	53	8	32	11	43	4
Surridge	19	4	51	2	17	5	49	1
Laker	3	1	5	0	33.4	16	43	3
Lock					17	10	15	2

SURREY	FIRST INNINGS		SECOND INNINGS	
L. B. Fishlock	c Goodwin b Walsh	108	(2) not out	0
D. G. W. Fletcher	st Corrall b Walsh	18		
P. B. H. May	lbw b Walsh	3		
B. Constable	c Walsh b Palmer	51		
*M. R. Barton	c Lester b Jackson	9	(1) not out	4
T. H. Clark	c Prentice b Palmer	27		
†A. J. W. McIntyre	c Wooler b Palmer	1		
J. C. Laker	c Walsh b Jackson	6		
A. V. Bedser	not out	18		
W. S. Surridge	b Palmer	0		
G. A. R. Lock	not out	20		
Extras	b 5, lb 5, nb 1	11		0
Total	(for 9 wkts dec)	272	(for no wkt)	4

BOWLING	O	M	R	W	O	M	R	W
Goodwin	16	2	40	0				
Wooler	8	1	27	0				
Palmer	23	7	62	4	0.1	0	4	0
Walsh	15	0	63	3				
Jackson	27	10	69	2				

Umpires: F. Chester and E. Robinson

This victory ensured a tie in the Championship with Lancashire.

*Captain; †Wicket-keeper

succession, at The Oval, to Glamorgan, Somerset and Essex. This set-back was too big a handicap to overcome and in the end the county dropped from equal first place to sixth. In that disastrous May spell at The Oval, A. V. Bedser was unable to play owing to ill health, and then the Test matches claimed him, so that he played in only 15 Championship games. As Bedser has probably never bowled better in his life than last season this was a tremendous handicap.

Laker, too, was absent for five Championship matches and played in two Tests. At The Oval, in the final match against South Africa, he took ten wickets for 119 and virtually won the game for England after they had trailed by eight on the first innings. Peter May, too, was in magnificent form, hitting 2,339 runs in all matches and topping the national averages as well as winning his first Test caps and hitting his first Test century, but his advance to the highest level meant that he could play in only seven Championship matches. The fact that he hit 614 runs in those games with a century in each innings against Essex at Southend and a century against Middlesex at Lord's emphasised how much his vital late season contributions were missed. He averaged 76.75 in ten innings for Surrey, and second to him was Whittaker with 37.27.

Whittaker regained a regular place in the side and became a renowned six-hitter. He hit 185 not out against Kent at The Oval, 'yet', as *Wisden* said, 'one felt, despite his thirty-two 6's, he could do better with only a little discretion and become one of the big personalities that modern cricket badly needs'.

Brazier, Clark and Fletcher could not command regular places in the side, but Eric Bedser refound his bowling form, taking 61 wickets and scoring over 1,000 runs. When one considers that he was rarely given the chance to bowl on a wicket that would have given him great assistance, for Laker, naturally, and the ever-improving Lock had first call, Eric Bedser's quality as an off-break bowler can be measured. He was also pressed into service as an opener, for Surrey struggled to find a regular pair as Fishlock, after the first weeks of the season, dropped to number four in the order.

Fishlock showed little loss of skill even if he did not score so prolifically as in the past, but Parker fell away a little and was more reluctant than ever to bowl. Perhaps one of the problems that beset Surrey and upset the rhythm of the side was the constant changes in the batting order. Constable was luckier than most, finding himself regularly at number three until he lost form late in the season. He responded well and scored consistently early on. Like Squires, he was to be a greatly under-rated cricketer.

There were moments of joy for Surrey. On 11 July, in spite of a period of inactivity caused by calluses forming on his spinning finger, Jim Laker became the first bowler to reach 100 wickets for the season. This was in the game against Worcester at Dudley which followed the match against Kent in which Whittaker had hit his 185 not out. Of Whittaker, *The Cricketer* wrote: 'What a pity it is that the spirit of adventure, typified by the forceful batting of G. J. Whittaker of Surrey, is not more widely in evidence. He used his bat as a weapon to bludgeon the bowlers. Against Kent at The Oval he roused the crowd time and again.' One of Whittaker's sixes was a straight drive into the seats at the Vauxhall end which caused a gasp of wonder, but such feats could not compensate for the general disappointment after the success of the previous year.

Michael Barton scored more than 1,000 runs in the season and always led the side with a quiet efficiency, but he decided that the time had come for him to stand down as captain. He could look back on his three-year term with pride and satisfaction. Untried, untested and little known, he had come out of retirement and taken on a difficult task at a difficult time, and he had led the side to a share in the title. He left Surrey a tidier and more efficient side than he found them, and he won many friends with his attitude to the game and to those who played under him.

The Surrey committee named Stuart Surridge as Barton's successor. When he was appointed he told the committee that Surrey would win the Championship five years in succession, but he was that kind of man, a tremendous enthusiast, and people just smiled.

THE GOLDEN AGE OF STUART SURRIDGE

SURREY HAD TWO OPTIONS IN choosing a successor to Barton; they could name Surridge or import a captain from another county. May was still up at Cambridge so that he was, for the time being, ruled out. The abolition of the distinction between amateurs and professionals was still a decade in the future, and although counties had had professional captains, indeed Warwickshire had won the title under one, Tom Dollery, it was not the custom to appoint a professional captain. Such an appointment at The Oval or at Lord's would not have been well received. When they had been short of amateur talent Leicestershire had imported Charles Palmer from Worcestershire to become captain/secretary, and Northants, for the same reason, had called upon Freddie Brown, but the number of amateurs who could give time to the game was growing fewer season by season. The only two professionals at The Oval who might have been considered for the job in 1952 were Fishlock and Parker, but both were at the veteran stage and nearing retirement. Surridge maintains that he had the field to himself, that there was no one else whom the committee could have chosen. That may be true, but one thing is certain and that is that he had the backing of Barton, who recommended to the committee that Surridge should succeed him.

Walter Stuart Surridge was born at Herne Hill on 3 September 1917. He was educated at Emanuel School, Wandsworth, where, in 1935, he was captain. Until his last two years at school he was a wicket-keeper, but the school needed a fast bowler so he took on the job. There was no cricket coach at Emanuel School, but, as a junior member of Surrey, Surridge attended the Easter nets at The Oval and was instructed by Alan Peach. In winter, he went to the famous Gover/Sandham Indoor School at East Hill, and, like so many other players, first-class and otherwise, he owes a great debt to the coaching he received from Alf Gover. Michael Barton remembers with affection how Gover, when coaching the amateurs, could make his point by where he placed the emphasis in his instruction: 'Turn your wrists over, *sir!*'

While still at Emanuel School Surridge played for the Young Surrey Players Eleven which was captained by Alan Peach and which included, among others, the Bedser twins, McIntyre, Whittaker and Constable. He has insisted that one of the factors that made his captaincy of Surrey such a success was that he had grown up with half the players and that they knew him. He played for Surrey Second

Stuart Surridge leads out his men at The Oval.

Eleven and made his first-class debut in 1939 for the Minor Counties, as we have seen.

He was a farmer during the war, and he made his debut for Surrey in 1947, appearing with more regularity as the seasons passed. Before he took over the captaincy of Surrey he had been well trained in leadership. In the nineteenth century, his grandfather had founded a business of sports good manufacturers. It has remained in the family ever since. His father insisted that if Stuart was to take over the business, he must learn the job from the bottom and fill every position in the firm. In order to learn how to give orders one must first learn how to take them. Stuart Surridge learned his job felling timber with the men in the days when hand-saws and axes were the only machinery. Many cricketers went with Surridge in the winter months to toughen up in preparation for the coming season, Bob Gregory, Alan Moss, Arthur McIntyre and Frank Tyson among them.

The willow trees for the bat-making were grown on the farms in Surrey and Berkshire while the firm was run from the offices in The Borough. Later it moved out to Witham in Essex. The interest in farming has continued, and one branch of the Surridge family farms, more expansively, in Australia.

Surridge asserts that he learned an early lesson from Brian Sellers when Surrey were playing against Yorkshire and had been on top for most of the match only to lose in the end. He spoke to Sellers after the match and said, with some despair and naivety: 'We were winning. You turned it round on us.' Sellers looked at him and replied: 'Remember one thing, lad. It's no bloody good being second.' It was a lesson he never forgot when he became captain, and he retained the greatest admiration for Sellers: 'He was tough. He was hard. He stood no nonsense, and he led by example. He wouldn't ask anybody to field closer to the bat than he was prepared to field himself.'

Fielding was the greatest attribute that Surridge brought to the side as a player. *Wisden* said of him after his first season in charge:

> His ability in this direction resulting in the acceptance of some catches which might be regarded by many cricketers as bordering upon the impossible, at times exerted an unnerving effect upon opposing batsmen and paved the way to more than one of the twenty victories.

But it was not just his own fielding which became supercharged, for he infected and demanded more of those around him. Critics had described the Surrey fielding in the early 1950s as efficient or satisfactory; Surridge thought it was awful, and that there was a lack of enthusiasm. He insisted on practice and concentration on this aspect of the game, and suddenly players found they were enjoying their cricket more. For the rest of the decade sides felt that they were being attacked by Surrey in the field, and many succumbed to the pressure, frightened almost to put bat to ball.

If there were any doubts about Surridge when he took over, it was that some of his players felt he had too little experience. Did he have any problems? 'Not after the first two matches,' he says. It did not take people long to know who was in charge at Surrey. He had undertaken the job only on the understanding that he had complete control of the team. Sandham was coach and dealt with the Second Eleven. Surridge respected Sandham's experience and perception. When he needed replacements in the first team he would simply say to Sandham that he wanted a batsman or a seam bowler and would know that Sandham would send the right men for the job.

In concentrating on his captaincy and his fielding, one runs the risk of neglecting Surridge's fine qualities as a player. He stood nearly 6ft 2in and used his height to great advantage in his fast-medium bowling. He took 78 wickets in 1952, and he would have taken more in the next four years had he been more selfish and had less concern for his professionals. He accepted the advice of his father because he knew it to be true that it was the professionals who needed encouragement because what they were doing was in order to earn a living. He kept the side happy by always giving his main bowlers a chance to bowl when the wickets were giving them help or there was a chance of easy victims. When the wicket was good and the going was hard Surridge would bowl and often deliberately throw up a few long hops or full tosses in an effort to break the stand. He never claimed anything cheap for himself.

As a batsman, his appearance coming down the pavilion steps always brought cheers of delight and anticipation. The highest score he ever made was 87 against Glamorgan in 1951, but he frightened a few bowlers and fielders over the years with the violence of his batting. He could turn the course of a game. When Surrey were making their challenge for the title in August 1950, they travelled to Hastings and faced a total of 404 which Sussex had made in good time. Surrey were 141 for eight and looking doomed for the follow-on when Surridge joined Constable. They added 86, of which Surridge made 55 with some ferocious hits. The follow-on was saved, and Surrey went on to win the match.

As a captain Surridge established a record which, one suspects, is likely to last for a very long time, even, one would hazard, for ever. In the five seasons in which he led Surrey they won the Championship five times. Lancashire had won the title during the three years in which Leonard Green had been captain in the 1920s, and Alfred Shaw led Nottinghamshire to four titles in his four years as captain in the 1880s, when the Championship was not on an official basis, but none has a record that challenges that of Stuart Surridge.

When Surrey took the title in 1952 the old *Playfair Cricket Annual* welcomed the event with a succinct judgement:

> By common consent, the best side won the championship. Surrey had probably the strongest and almost certainly the best balanced attack in the history of the club; the close fielding was brilliant; and the virile batting was equal to all demands. Apart from these things, there was that intangible factor, a true team spirit, which sprang from the inspiration and boisterous precept of Surridge in his first year of command.

The comment on the 'virile batting' is particularly interesting in that it was Surrey's batting which was to be most often criticised over the next four years. Roy Webber said that it was not possible to be kind about Surrey's batting 'as it was so remarkably fallible for a Championship side', yet it changed little in the five years of Surridge's leadership except that May was able to play more often and Barrington, Stewart and, for a time, Subba Row took over from

Fishlock, Parker and Whittaker, which hardly suggests a weakening. Surridge's attitude is straightforward:

> If you get 200, the other side has got to get 201. We didn't get a lot of runs. We didn't need to. We got enough. Besides, if we had got many more, I wouldn't have known when to declare.

The bowling was beyond reproach, and it is worth considering the figures of the leading bowlers over the five-year period:

	Overs	Maidens	Runs	Wickets	Average
G. A. R. Lock	3,703.5	1,457	7,164	550	13.02
A. V. Bedser	3,704.2	1,029	7,736	475	16.28
P. J. Loader	2,214.4	510	5,150	312	16.50
J. C. Laker	3,606.5	1,212	7,512	450	16.69
E. A. Bedser	1,992.4	640	4,129	189	21.84
W. S. Surridge	2,018.5	413	5,258	187	28.11

These are impressive figures. When one realises that they represent the work of six men playing in the same team at the same time they are breathtaking. Loader had appeared once as an amateur in 1951, was offered a professional contract and began to appear as Alec Bedser's deputy in 1952.

Surrey's record over the years of Surridge's reign should also be studied:

Year	P	W	L	D	Pts	Margin of winning title
1952	28	20	3	5	256	32 pts
1953	28	13	4	10	184	16 pts
1954	28	15	3	8	208	22 pts
1955	28	23	5	0	284	16 pts
1956	28	15	5	6	200	20 pts

The system of scoring during this period was 12 points for a win and four points for a first-innings lead in a match drawn or lost. Surrey had one match in 1953, two in 1954 and two in 1956 in which no result was reached because of bad weather.

Surridge's approach to a match was simple, and in the Fender tradition. He went for victory from the very first ball that was bowled. The side engaged in constant fielding practice before and during the season, and everyone adopted the attitude from the start of the season that every game was a vital one.

In 1952, the early season running was made by Middlesex, although Surrey quickly showed their promise by beating the Indian tourists and Gloucestershire in low-scoring matches. Then came a victory of quality against Sussex at The Oval. John Langridge and Jim Parks hit centuries, and Sussex declared at 365 for nine. Fletcher and Eric Bedser began Surrey's reply with a partnership of 169. Bedser made 73, and Fletcher hit 116 in two-and-three-quarter hours. Constable, McIntyre and Whittaker all hit briskly, and Surridge declared at 432 for seven. At lunch time on the last day, a draw looked certain, but in the afternoon, Lock had a spell of four for 8, the last six Sussex wickets fell for 18 runs, and, needing 70 to win, Surrey hit off the runs in under 20 overs.

These early season victories caused no great surprise, but what did draw attention was the quality of the Surrey fielding and catching. Leslie Smith in *The Cricketer* spoke of Surrey having found another Bill Hitch, one of the best short legs of his day, in the person of Tony Lock:

> In recent matches G. A. R. Lock has held a number of brilliant catches in that position. His three in succession off E. A. Bedser's off-breaks helped Surrey to beat the Indians and he also shone in the match with Gloucestershire. The short leg catch he held in dismissing Emmett was really remarkable, as the ball travelled with such force that it knocked Lock off his feet, while a little later he held one almost as good to get rid of Graveney.

A draw at Ilford was followed by victory at Rushden, an uncommon venue for a Northamptonshire home match. The victory was founded on another splendid opening partnership of 94 between Fletcher and Eric Bedser, after which the pitch crumbled. Clark, at number four, was left stranded on 26 not out, and Surrey were out for 182. Freddie Brown took six for 42 against his old county, but it proved to be insufficient. Alec Bedser took eight wickets and Laker nine in the match, and Surrey won by 132 runs. The outstanding batting performance came from Tom Clark who, on a wicket giving the bowlers every assistance, hit 92 in the second innings. He was a polished player, especially strong on the on-side, but by no means limited in his repertoire of shots. He had worked as a labourer in the winter in order to lose weight and to get himself fit for the season. He was broad-shouldered and dependable, and he epitomised the Surrey spirit and attitude. Surridge rated him very highly, and the pity was that Clark was so often hampered by hip trouble.

Wins over Warwickshire at The Oval, Nottinghamshire at Trent Bridge and a draw in a rain-marred match with Leicestershire at The Oval were followed by an innings victory over Gloucestershire inside two days at Bristol. This win brought Surrey's record to six wins and two draws in eight matches and took them eight points clear of Middlesex at the top of the table. Middlesex were now to fade from the scene, and the main challenge was to come from Yorkshire.

Tom Clark was a sound batsman of the Championship years, hampered by hip trouble. He was another Surrey footballer, who played for Walsall.

The win at Trent Bridge in the first days of June was significant in that Clark and Parker added 165 for the fifth wicket, and Parker hit his last century for the County. Equally significant was the fact that, in an effort to find the ideal preparation for the Trent Bridge pitch, the Nottinghamshire committee had ordered that the heavy roller should not be used on the strip for a week before the match. The result was that Alec Bedser was able to bowl, in the second innings, on a wicket which suited his fast medium pace to perfection, and he took six for 23 as Nottinghamshire were all out for 52 in 90 minutes, their last five wickets falling for the addition of two runs.

In the drawn game against Leicestershire, Eric Bedser and Laurie Fishlock both hit centuries in the second innings and added 186 in under three hours for the third wicket. It was Fishlock's 50th and last hundred for Surrey.

By 24 June, still unbeaten, Surrey had increased their lead to 20 points. They had beaten Essex at The Oval for the first time since 1938, drawn at Llanelli, and won at Blackheath as well as beating Cambridge University by an innings at The Oval.

In the match against Glamorgan, Surrey were bowled out for 248, and the home side made 257. This was the first time in the season that a side had taken any points off Surrey, and it was the only time in the season when a full strength Surrey side surrendered points to the opposition. Even without Laker and Alec Bedser, they overwhelmed Kent at Blackheath. Their close catching was exhilarating, and Jack Parker established a County record which was to last five years when he held seven catches at slip.

Clark and Fletcher hit centuries in the match against Cambridge, but in the absence of Laker and Alec Bedser, Dennis Cox, fast right-arm medium, took seven for 22, the best performance of his career. 'Cox,' says Surridge, 'was a fine cricketer, but we were so strong that he spent his time in the Second Eleven and grew old with the rest of the team.'

Success followed upon success, and by 22 July, Surrey had a 44-point lead over Yorkshire, who had played a game less, but Surrey had suffered a first defeat of the season, against Lancashire. Fletcher had played one of his finest innings when, trailing by 14 on the first innings, Surrey had been asked to make 275 to beat Hampshire at Guildford. They had five hours in which to get the runs, and they won with 35 minutes to spare and five wickets in hand, Fletcher hitting 123.

Against Somerset at The Oval at the beginning of July, Bernard Constable hit 205 not out, the highest of his 27 centuries in his first-class career, and Surrey won by an innings and 180 runs.

In talk of Surrey cricket, studded with great names like Hobbs, Hayward, Hitch, Sandham, Laker, Lock and May, the name of Bernard Constable is rarely mentioned, but for Stuart Surridge, and for many who watched those years of glory, he was the great unsung hero of Surrey cricket. He was a neat, compact, nimble batsman who could dance down the wicket to attack or defend. He was slightly built, and he moved so lightly on his feet as to suggest a dancer. It was this grace of movement that made his cover fielding a delight to watch. 'He knew,' says Surridge, 'exactly where to position himself. He had studied batsmen and knew their strokes so that he positioned himself at just the spot where he knew that they would hit the ball. He was a marvellous fielder.'

The match against Yorkshire at The Oval on 5, 7 and 8 July naturally drew much attention, and there was even some angry crowd reaction. Yorkshire made 137, Surrey 285. When Yorkshire batted again Len Hutton hit a century, but on the last morning, intent only on saving the game, they batted dourly, and there was some barracking from the crowd. Umpire Price reacted by sitting down and refusing to allow the match to continue until the barracking stopped. One wonders how he would have reacted to the one-day game, and the crowds that attend.

Eventually, Surrey were left to make 102 in 100 minutes, and

Bernard Constable, an unsung hero of Surrey cricket who, despite losing years to the war, achieved 1,000 runs for a season 12 times.

Fishlock and Eric Bedser gave the side a rollicking start, lashing the ball to all parts of the field. Gordon Ross told the story of how Fishlock had arrived late in the morning, believing the game started at 11.30 am and not 11.00 am. He batted splendidly as Surrey sought victory, but appeared to throw his wicket away unnecessarily. He came panting into the dressing-room, offering the view that Surrey could still get the runs even though there were only ten minutes left. There were, in fact, 40 minutes remaining. Again his timing was half-an-hour adrift. Surrey won in fine style.

There was a comfortable win at Kidderminster, and then a quite stunning victory over Kent at The Oval. Peter May was now in the side, and he hit 124 as Surrey took a first innings lead of 133. Godfrey Evans, in swashbuckling form, and a more sedate O'Linn brought Kent back into the game, and Murray-Wood's declaration left Surrey the task of scoring 188 to win in 92 minutes. It was a declaration which at least gave Kent an equal chance of victory if Surrey accepted the challenge. All knew by now, of course, that Surrey would accept any challenge. *Wisden* told how:

> Although wickets fell frequently, Surrey pursued their aggression to the end without regard to the risk of defeat. They required 128 in the last hour, 50 with seventeen minutes to go, and 26 when the eighth wicket went eight minutes from time. Surridge, the next man in, scored from eight of the nine balls bowled to him, but before he slashed Dovey over extra cover for the final stroke he and Clark were missed in the deep. With less than a minute left and the game still open, Kent raced into position and Dovey hurriedly bowled the first ball to ensure another over.
>
> So marked was the tension in the final minutes that the crowd rose to their feet and a burst of cheering broke out as Surridge made the winning hit with the clock pointing to a shade after half-past six.

Surridge remembers the game vividly because it showed all that he believed to be good in cricket, both captains going for a win all the time:

> Jack Hobbs was in the Committee Room, and he'd bet we wouldn't do it. I didn't see the first ball that Dovey bowled, but I got hold of the second.

This famous victory was followed by the first defeat of the season as Surrey, without May, Lock, Laker and Alec Bedser, went down to Lancashire. It seemed to matter little as the four returned from their Test duty, and Nottinghamshire were routed in poor weather. They were bowled out for 84 and 51, and Surrey made 215 for four. It was an historic match in that Alec Bedser took his 1,000th first-class wicket, and took eight for 18 in the second innings which was to remain the best bowling performance of his career.

After beating Middlesex at The Oval, Surrey lost twice in a week, to Warwickshire and to Yorkshire, and there were suddenly suspicions that they might crack although they still held a lead of 28 points. There was no loss of nerve. On 20, 21 and 22 August, Derbyshire visited The Oval. Rain delayed the start until 3.00 pm, and then Eric Bedser and Fletcher, a fine opening pair throughout the summer, began Surrey's innings with an invaluable partnership of 42. After that wickets began to tumble on the damp turf, and Surrey were out for 156. Then came Lock. He caught Hamer off Surridge before a run was scored, took two more stunning catches and produced a bowling spell which gave him six for 16 in 10.3 overs. Surrey made 258 for four in their second innings, and Surridge gave his bowlers the last day in which to bowl out Derbyshire. They needed only one session. When Alec Bedser bowled Smith to claim his fourth wicket Derbyshire were out for 95, and Surrey were Champions.

A large crowd gathered in front of the pavilion and called for Surridge and his team. Surridge's acceptance speech was typically modest and honest. He pointed to his team-mates below and said to the crowd: 'There are the boys. What more can I say?'

The season saw the end of the careers of Parker and Fishlock. Surridge tried to persuade them to stay on: 'They were wonderful pros. A1 men.' But they were both delighted and thrilled by what had happened and felt it was best to leave the game then and there. They were probably right to end on such a high note.

Surrey had amassed more points than any side since the war. For eight Championship matches they had been deprived of their leading players, yet they had gained 52 points from those matches, and they had not lost a match when they were at full strength. Moreover, at the beginning of the year, at a dinner given by the Cricket Writers' Club to the Indian tourists, Lord Cobham had urged people to remember that cricket was a game to be played for fun. He was depressed that he had seen some cricketers who did not look as if they liked the game. Surrey had answered him by bringing joy back into cricket. The Oval was an exciting and bubbling place to be.

Parker and Fishlock were missed at the start of 1953 when, on occasions, an old head would have been an advantage, for May, now regularly available, was slow to find his form. The Australians gave him a hard time when they beat Surrey at The Oval in two days at the beginning of May, and, unwisely, in the view of many, he was left out of the England side after the first Test. He reasserted himself later in the season and was recalled for the deciding Test at The Oval and played an important part in England regaining the 'Ashes' for the first time in 20 years.

There was no indication in the opening county game of the season that Surrey would find any difficulty in holding on to the title. On Saturday, 16 May, Warwickshire came to The Oval to begin the county programme. They had won the Championship in 1951 so that they were an attractive side. The match was all over in a day, and the Surrey members rose as one when the triumphant Surrey side walked off the field. It was the first time since 1857 that a first-class game at The Oval had been completed in one day.

In fairness the conditions were treacherous for batsmen, but Warwickshire were subjected to unrelentingly aggressive bowling of the highest quality supported by dynamic fielding. Alec Bedser bowled unchanged throughout the match, and his first innings return of eight for 18 equalled his best in first-class cricket. Intelligently adapting to the conditions because he could not gain a foothold on the damp turf, he reduced his pace and attacked the leg stump. The hawks in the leg trap did the rest. It was a wonderful way for Alec Bedser to start his benefit year.

Surrey lost only two wickets in passing Warwickshire's meagre score of 45, but they slipped to 81 for seven, and it was the aggression of Surridge, Laker and Lock that raised them to 146. Surridge's 19 included three sixes in four balls off Hollies, and Lock was hitting fiercely when he was hit over the eye by a ball from Grove and taken to hospital.

Laker joined Alec Bedser in the attack when Warwickshire batted again, and after tea he performed the hat-trick. It was the first of three hat-tricks to be performed by Surrey in 1953. The game had not started until mid-day, but with Warwickshire dismissed in 75 minutes and 70 minutes, it was over ten minutes into the extra half-hour. The day saw 29 wickets fall and 243 runs scored, and Surrey, out for 146, won by an innings and 49 runs.

For Alec Bedser, this match, as were so many others, was a triumph. He was a giant among bowlers, and for the first six or seven years after the Second World War, until the arrival of Statham, Trueman and Tyson, he was the beginning, middle and end of the England attack. A large and heavy man, yet quick and agile, he moved in smoothly off a run that was never exaggeratedly long and hustled the ball on to the batsman with an action which was precise and economic. He was in the great tradition of S. F. Barnes and Maurice Tate, fast-medium, relentlessly accurate with an ability to move the ball sharply both ways and with a capacity for work which would shame many who play the game today.

In all that he did, and has done, there is a workmanlike honesty. He is not a man of frills. He is blunt, straightforward, a jealous respector of tradition and conservative by habit and nature. He was never a man who needed encouragement or inducement to be loyal or to give of his best, for such qualities and characteristics were natural to him. His mind can grasp no reason for playing the game unless those attributes are part of one's make up. The problem is that because he gave of himself so naturally and unstintingly it was possible for spectators and commentators to take him for granted, for it appeared that he could go on bowling for ever. Sometimes he did. But to accept him as a bowling machine, grinding out over after over, smoothly and precisely, and amassing hundreds of wickets year after year is to miss the man's inventiveness, variety and subtle command of his art.

Bedser took nearly 2,000 wickets in first-class cricket, and he bowled for much of his time on wickets that were death to most bowlers. He troubled Bradman, and he troubled Compton and Hutton, and there are not too many who did that.

It was not likely that such form as was shown in the sensational one-day win over Warwickshire could be sustained, but Surrey led the table at the end of May in spite of injuries and representative calls. Reserves like wicket-keeper Kirby, who played in glasses, and left-arm spinner McMahon, who had lost his place to Lock, did well when given the chance, as did Ron Pratt, a left-handed batsman and off-break bowler, who was also a brilliant fielder in the Surrey mode of the time. Another to sparkle on a few occasions was Alan Brazier, a forceful right-handed batsman whom Sandham recommended to Surridge as worthy of a regular first-team place. He scored prolifically in the Second Eleven, but as a first-team player he never really found his touch, and he later moved to Kent. Luckier were two other reserves, Ken Barrington and Peter Loader.

Peter Loader, a Test match bowler, whose great work in the Championship years is sometimes a little overlooked in comparison with that of Bedser, Laker and Lock.

SURREY *v* WARWICKSHIRE

Played at The Oval, Kennington, 16 May 1953

SURREY WON BY AN INNINGS AND 49 RUNS

WARWICKSHIRE	FIRST INNINGS		SECOND INNINGS	
F. C. Gardner	c Laker b A. Bedser	7	c Laker b A. Bedser	7
T. W. Cartwright	lbw b A. Bedser	0	lbw b A. Laker	9
D. D. Taylor	c Fletcher b A. Bedser	0	lbw b A. Bedser	20
†R. T. Spooner	c Whittaker b A. Bedser	16	c and b Laker	0
*H. E. Dollery	c Lock b A. Bedser	8	c Surridge b Laker	0
R. E. Hitchcock	c Whittaker b Lock	3	c A. Bedser b Laker	0
A. Townsend	c McIntyre b Lock	7	run out	0
R. T. Weeks	not out	0	c Surridge b A. Bedser	0
C. W. Grove	c Fletcher b A. Bedser	3	c Constable b Laker	10
K. R. Dollery	c Brazier b A. Bedser	0	not out	0
W. E. Hollies	c Laker b A. Bedser	0	c sub b A. Bedser	0
Extras	lb 1	1	b 2, lb 3, nb 1	6
Total		45		52

1st inns: 1-3, 2-3, 3-8, 4-27, 5-30, 6-36, 7-42, 8-45, 9-45
2nd inns: 1-20, 2-22, 3-26, 4-26, 5-26, 6-32, 7-32, 8-49, 9-52

BOWLING	O	M	R	W	O	M	R	W
A. V. Bedser	13.5	4	18	8	13.4	7	17	4
Surridge	6	1	17	0				
Lock	7	2	9	2				
Laker					13	6	29	5

SURREY	FIRST INNINGS	
E. A. Bedser	b K. Dollery	5
D. G. W. Fletcher	c Townsend b Weeks	13
B. Constable	c Grove b K. Dollery	37
T. H. Clark	c K. Dollery b Hollies	2
A. F. Brazier	c Townsend b Hollies	6
G. J. Whittaker	b K. Dollery	0
†A. J. W. McIntyre	c and b K. Dollery	9
J. C. Laker	c H. Dollery b Hollies	18
*W. S. Surridge	b Grove	19
A. V. Bedser	not out	5
G. A. R. Lock	retired hurt	27
Extras	lb 4, nb 1	5
Total		146

1st inns: 1-5, 2-27, 3-50, 4-61, 5-65, 6-77, 7-81, 8-108, 9-119

BOWLING	O	M	R	W
Grove	10.1	3	29	1
K. Dollery	11	4	40	4
Weeks	8	1	24	1
Hollies	10	4	48	3

Umpires: L. H. Gray and E. Cooke

The first first-class match to be finished in one day at The Oval for 96 years.

*Captain; †Wicket-keeper

Barrington made a quietly impressive entry into first-class cricket, playing in nine matches, scoring over 200 runs and hitting 81 in the innings victory over Worcestershire at The Oval in mid-July. He was a young man very eager to hit the ball hard. Loader's appearances as understudy to Alec Bedser were of a more dramatic nature. At Edgbaston, he took eight for 72 and four for 45, but Surrey lost, and in the next match, at Blackheath, he took nine for 28 and four for 85, and the game was drawn. He bowled magnificently in these games, accuracy in length and direction complementing a lively pace. He was desperately unlucky not to take all ten wickets at Blackheath, for Doug Wright, the last man, ran himself out.

The defeat at Edgbaston was the third that Surrey had suffered in a period of three weeks, and, with Sussex in top form and leading the table convincingly, it seemed that Surrey were not to retain their title, particularly as Middlesex had run into fine form, too. Indeed, a fourth defeat, at the hands of Gloucestershire, at the end of July left Surrey 14 points behind Middlesex with Sussex, who had a terrible run, dropping to third place with the same number of points as Surrey in one more game.

The Surrey batting had been strengthened in late July by the arrival of Subba Row, who had had a highly successful season at Cambridge. May, too, was now in scintillating form, and as their nearest rivals wavered, Surrey prospered. Nottinghamshire and Hampshire were beaten at The Oval. May hit 159 at Lord's where Surrey had the better of a draw, and in the return match at The Oval, with Lock taking nine wickets, they won convincingly, and Middlesex's interest in affairs was over.

In the last match at The Oval, Fletcher and Clark hit centuries, and Surrey beat Glamorgan by 172 runs. Surrey now travelled to Hove for a decisive game. To retain any chance of winning the title, Sussex had to beat Surrey, and they began well by claiming Clark, May and Constable for 49 runs on a damp pitch after a delayed start. Fletcher batted 285 minutes for 81. In contrast, Surridge clouted 38, and Surrey reached 220. The Sussex batting was incomprehensibly subdued. Needing to score briskly, they managed a rate of less than two an over and lost eight wickets in taking first-innings points. The match was destined to be drawn. Surrey batted out time, May scoring 136 not out against some occasional bowling, and Surrey were Champions for the second year in succession.

They beat Hampshire at Bournemouth in the final match of the season to bring their total number of points to 184. Only Glamorgan in 1948 had won the title with fewer points since the war. Of the five Championships won under Surridge, this was probably the least satisfying in that it depended much upon the mistakes of others, but the County Championship tests the quality of a side because it is determined in all weathers throughout four months of the year, and none had the staying power nor the ability to cope with setbacks or absences in the way that Surrey had.

Their capacity to succeed when everyone about them doubted was never more in evidence than in the wet summer of 1954. Yorkshire won six of their first seven matches to set a furious pace in the Championship. Middlesex and Warwickshire also began well, and Derbyshire moved into menacing form in June. It seemed that Surrey were out of the hunt. When they began their game against Essex at The Oval on 28 July they stood eighth in the table, 46 points adrift of the leaders, Yorkshire. Surrey had ten matches to play and victory over Essex by ten wickets heralded the start of one of the most remarkable runs in the history of the County Championship. Surrey failed to win only one of those last ten matches, and, paradoxically, that 'failure' saw them at their finest.

Surrey, 1954. Back row: (unknown), H. Strudwick, R. C. E. Pratt, P. J. Loader, T. H. Clark, K. F. Barrington, D. F. Cox, M. J. Stewart, J. Tait, A. Sandham. Front row: A. F. Brazier, J. C. Laker, E. A. Bedser, P. B. H. May, W. S. Surridge, A. V. Bedser, A. J. W. McIntyre, G. A. R. Lock, B. Constable, D. G. W. Fletcher, R. Swetman.

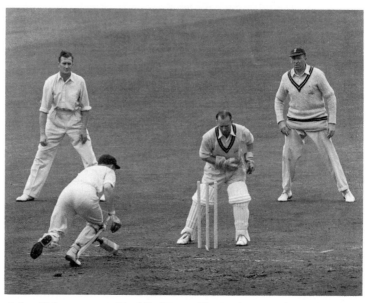

Arthur McIntyre stumps Horsfall of Essex, The Oval, 1954. Laker and Surridge at slip.

Nottinghamshire were crushed by ten wickets inside two days. The match against Northamptonshire at Kettering also ended in two days, but it was a much closer affair. Laker, six for 58, was prominent as the home side were bowled out for 125, but Surrey collapsed against Broderick and were all out for 121. Laker took five for 31 when Northants batted again and were out for 133. Needing 138 to win, Surrey were 119 for eight when Lock joined Laker. With Lock defending doggedly on a wicket which was treacherous, 12 were added. Loader came to the wicket with seven wanted. He hit two, and Laker clumped Starkie for four to win the match. His 33 not out on top of his 11 wickets showed the man's all-round value to the team. As well as being the best off-break bowler in the world, he averaged over 17 for Surrey and hit two centuries in the course of his career.

On 7, 9 and 10 August, Middlesex were the visitors to The Oval. This was the only match of the last ten that Surrey failed to win, but it was the one that showed them at their most dynamic. Norman Preston, the editor of *Wisden*, drew special attention to Surridge (who often did a couple of hours work at the business in The Borough before coming to The Oval) and to this match in particular in his appraisal of Surrey's achievement during the season:

> Above all the retention of the title came about through the supremacy of the attack, supported by fielding of uncommon

excllence, together with the initiative and imagination of the captain, Surridge, who so accurately assessed the tactical risks and possibilities of each situation. Of few players would it be more true to say that his batting and bowling averages completely misrepresented the full value of Surridge to the side. Surridge thought and acted in terms of attack from the first ball and once again the force of his own drive infected his men. A typical example of his initiative occurred in the match with Middlesex early in August. Surrey needed every point possible to keep alive what appeared to be a faint chance of winning the Championship and, when rain limited play to three-quarters of an hour on the first two days and prevented a start before lunch on the last, their hopes of taking any points from the match looked remote. Surridge was not prepared to regard the position as hopeless. Surrey responded to his call for aggressive batting and, following a declaration, they bowled out Middlesex for 51 in two hours ten minutes, with a quarter-of-an-hour of extra time remaining.

Leicestershire, Gloucestershire, Worcestershire and Middlesex, at Lord's, were all beaten within the next fortnight. No other county could match such form, and when Worcestershire came to The Oval on 25 August Surrey needed only to win the match to retain the title.

Rain had affected the wicket and play could not begin until 2.00 pm. Surridge won the toss and asked Worcestershire to bat. In 100 minutes, they were bowled out for 25, which was the lowest score in first-class cricket since 1947 and is the lowest score hit against Surrey this century. The last eight Worcestershire wickets went down for five runs, Lock taking five for 2 in 33 balls.

Surrey moved into a solid lead, and with May and Barrington going well, they seemed set for a good score. Peter May remembers the occasion:

Worcestershire were short of spin in those days, the pitch seemed easier and I was enjoying myself when to my astonishment I saw Stuart appear on the balcony and declare. It was not yet half past five on the first evening. Our score was 92 for three. In those days the amateurs still used the upstairs dressing room. Downstairs among the rest of the side the general verdict was that the captain must have gone mad. His explanation as he led us out was that it was going to rain, which did not entirely clear up the misgivings.

Most of the Surrey members and supporters were of the opinion, like the players, that the captain had gone mad, and the capture of two wickets for 13 runs before the close did little to dissuade them otherwise. The dismissal of Peter Richardson should have given some warning of what was to come, however, for Richardson offered no stroke at a ball from Laker and lifted his bat high above his shoulders, but the ball turned and rose so steeply that it still took the edge of the bat for him to be caught at the wicket.

Within an hour the next morning, Surrey had won. At one time, Worcestershire were 18 for six in their second innings, and it was only a few shots by Yarnold as the fielders clustered round the wicket that boosted the score to 40. Having scored only 92 themselves, Surrey had won by an innings and 27 runs in little more than five hours of cricket. The madman was looked upon in awe as one who saw further and deeper than other men.

Surrey were Champions for the third year in succession. They confirmed their superiority with victory over Lancashire in the last game which meant that from their last ten games they had taken 112 points out of a possible 120, and only rain, one suspects, had robbed them of the other eight. The 158-run aggregate of the Worcestershire game remains the lowest for a completed match in the County Championship. In the last month of the season, Laker took 48 wickets at 9.39 runs each, and Lock 43 at 9.45, yet neither of these two bowlers was in the side to tour Australia, a fact which still leaves people astonished. Both took more than 100 wickets in all matches as did Alec Bedser and Peter Loader, and the strength of the attack was, indeed, Surrey's chief reason for success. In many quarters, it was thought that Alec Bedser did not have a good season by his standards, but most bowlers would have been well pleased with 99 Championship wickets at 14.18 in a 'bad' season. Loader's advance was considerable, and he found his way into the MCC side that went to Australia, but of the three Surrey players in the party, only May played a significant part in the Test series.

Michael Stewart made an impressive start to his first-class career, hitting 134 against Essex at Colchester in his second match. He did not maintain that form and was criticised for his tendency to hook too early in an innings, but he opened with a certain flamboyance, and his fielding was of the highest quality in a team of outstanding fielders.

May was the outstanding batsman, and Subba Row contributed many valuable runs in the lower order, but, in a side in which everybody was invariably contributing something with the bat, it was the form of Ken Barrington in August which played a decisive part in that memorable surge on the Championship. The success of Barrington and the arrival of Stewart and Loader emphasised the strength in depth of the Surrey team. From the side that beat Worcestershire at The Oval, for example, Eric Bedser, Fletcher and Subba Row were all missing, yet all three made vital contributions and played in three-quarters of the matches during the season.

SURREY *v* WORCESTERSHIRE

Played at The Oval, Kennington, 25 and 26 August 1954

SURREY WON BY AN INNINGS AND 27 RUNS

WORCESTERSHIRE	FIRST INNINGS		SECOND INNINGS	
D. Kenyon	c Surridge b Bedser	8	c Stewart b Lock	0
P. E. Richardson	c May b Bedser	0	c McIntrye b Laker	9
L. Outschoorn	b Laker	9	c Lock b Laker	3
R. G. Broadbent	c Laker b Lock	3	c McIntyre b Laker	1
N. Hughes	run out	0	hit wkt b Bedser	2
L. N. Devereux	not out	2	retired hurt	1
R. O. Jenkins	c Stewart b Lock	1	c Laker b Bedser	1
†H. Yarnold	c Barrington b Lock	1	not out	14
★R. T. D. Perks	c Barrington b Laker	0	b Bedser	2
J. A. Flavell	c Constable b Lock	0	c Clark b Laker	3
J. R. Ashman	c and b Lock	0	c Bedser b Loader	2
Extras	lb 1	1	lb 1, nb 1	2
Total		25		40

1st inns: 1-1, 2-16, 3-30, 4-20, 5-21, 6-23, 7-25, 8-25, 9-25
2nd inns: 1-0, 2-5, 3-13, 4-16, 5-16, 6-18, 7-23, 8-26, 9-40

BOWLING	O	M	R	W	O	M	R	W
A. V. Bedser	9	4	12	2	6	3	7	3
Loader	6	3	5	0	2.4	1	3	1
Laker	8	3	5	2	17	9	25	4
Lock	5.3	4	2	5	10	7	3	1

SURREY	FIRST INNINGS	
T. H. Clark	c Richardson b Perks	10
M. J. Stewart	c Flavell b Perks	11
P. B. H. May	not out	31
B. Constable	c and b Ashman	29
K. Barrington	not out	10
†A. J. W. McIntyre		
J. C. Laker		
★W. S. Surridge		
A. V. Bedser		
G. A. R. Lock		
P. J. Loader		
Extras	w 1	1
Total	(for 3 wkts dec)	92

1st inns: 1-12, 2-31, 3-77

BOWLING	O	M	R	W
Perks	12	1	43	2
Flavell	3	1	17	0
Ashman	8	3	29	1
Devereux	1	0	2	0

Umpires: F. S. Lee and E. Cooke

Surrey's victory clinched the 1954 Championship. The aggregate of runs is the lowest for a completed match in the County Championship.

★Captain; †Wicket-keeper

Swetman, too, had deputised most ably for McIntyre on occasions and had been a member of the Second Eleven side which went through the season unbeaten and won the Minor Counties Championship to complete a Surrey double.

This quality of reserve strength became apparent in 1955 when, with Subba Row having moved to Northamptonshire and Clark troubled by injury, Surrey were still able to sweep all before them. The County played 34 first-class matches in 1955. They won 27 of them and lost the other seven. Draws did not interest them. Their number of Championship wins, 23, and points, 284, were records. If one must point to one season in the Surridge era which stands supreme above all others, it is the season of 1955.

It began with 12 wins in succession – nine of them were Championship matches. The most remarkable of these victories was at Leicester in the third week in May. Lock, Laker and Clark bowled Leicestershire out for 114, but Charles Palmer, the Leicestershire skipper, a medium-pace bowler of average ability, took eight wickets for 7 runs in 14 overs and Surrey were out for 77. It is generally accepted that Palmer brought himself on for one over as he wanted Munden and Jackson to change ends, but he bowled Peter May with his third ball. He had found a spot which he exploited to the full, and he took eight wickets before conceding a run, and it was Laker who broke the sequence when he hit Palmer for four. In spite of this debacle, Surrey won by seven wickets.

The only side which had in any way kept pace with Surrey at the start of the season was Yorkshire, and Arthur McIntyre had chosen the game with them at the beginning of June for his benefit. The excitement was great, and 45,000 people paid for admission on the first two days. Yardley won the toss for Yorkshire and asked Surrey to bat first on a pitch which had been saturated. It was a wise decision. With Appleyard's brisk off-breaks rearing awkwardly to give him seven for 29, Surrey were bowled out for 85 in two-and-a-half hours. By the close, Yorkshire were 108 for seven.

That Surrey were in such close contention was due mainly to Lock, who not only bowled magnificently, but took a memorable return catch to dismiss Lowson. He held the ball inches from the ground with his right hand as he flung himself across the pitch. The Yorkshire innings ended on 131 on the Monday morning, and, batting a second time, Surrey were indebted to Fletcher, who took four-and-a-half hours to score 84. May batted with more enterprise, and there were valuable contributions from Clark and Constable. More rain made the pitch difficult again, and play could not begin until a delay of half-an-hour on the last day.

Surridge declared and set Yorkshire the task of scoring 216 to win.

Loader bowled Hutton for 1, and Bedser had Lowson for nought. Billy Sutcliffe played what Surridge considers to be one of the finest innings he ever saw played on a bad wicket. He made 40 in two hours and twenty minutes before Alec Bedser took a brilliant left-handed catch off his own bowling to dismiss him. Surrey went on to win by 41 runs. They now had maximum points from eight games and led Yorkshire by 20 points.

They suffered their first defeat at Headingley on 21 June. More than 60,000 people saw the three days of this match, and the gates were closed on a crowd of 35,000 on the Saturday. 'The atmosphere resembled that of a Test match.' Surrey led by 102 on the first innings, but Trueman and Cowan bowled them out for 75 at the second attempt, and Yorkshire went on to win by six wickets. It was Surrey's first defeat for eleven months. They still led Yorkshire by 12 points and had a game in hand.

Briefly, in July, when Surrey surprisingly lost to lowly Kent, they surrendered the lead to Yorkshire, but even then they had games in hand. On 24–26 August, they entertained Sussex at The Oval and, recovering from 26 for four, they won by an innings. The victory assured them of the Championship.

They lost their next match, away to Hampshire, and Surridge admits now that it was the only time in his five-year reign that the team was not in the right frame of mind: 'We'd done well, and we had a little party and a few drinks before the Hampshire game. It showed.'

The superlatives had been exhausted. What more could people write about Surrey? Alec Bedser took more than 100 wickets, and Lock and Laker took over 300 between them in Championship matches alone. Seven Surrey men had played for England in the course of the season, and Peter May was now captain of his country. Ken Barrington had won his first two Test caps. Like May and the Bedsers, he was born in Reading. He was a genial man of great good humour who was to become immensely popular with all who met him. Initially a rather carefree attacking batsman, his early experiences in Test cricket – he made nought on his debut – and the competition for places in the Surrey side made him reassess his game. He decided to echew risky shots from his batting, to develop his powers of concentration and to become the sheet anchor of the side. The transformation was to make him the backbone of Surrey and England.

Michael Murray, the former Middlesex cricketer and now chairman of that club, recalls a story which reflects what the man achieved:

> In the mid 1950s I used to play golf with Ken in a foursome every Sunday and he was very good company as well as being a skilled golfer. On one occasion an incident occurred which I think

reflected Ken's enormous powers of concentration. He had taken his stance on the tee and was addressing the ball when the three other players saw a Mars Bar wrapper blowing towards him from his right. It was difficult to know whether to stop him and risk him fluffing his shot or to ignore it. We all chose to ignore it and the Mars Bar wrapper fluttered between his toes and the ball at the precise point Ken was swinging through his shot. The ball sailed away down the middle of the fairway and we all applauded this terrrific feat of ignoring the Mars Bar wrapper. Ken's response was 'What Mars Bar wrapper?' It is hardly surprising that such dedicated concentration should later have been so successfully reflected in his cricket career which regrettably was cut short all too soon.

The application that Barrington showed in shaping his career was, perhaps, no more than every member of the great Surrey side of the 1950s did in one way or another. Arthur McIntyre, born within a quarter of a mile of The Oval, had joined the staff as a leg-spin bowler and as the lad in charge of the bicycle shed. He played cricket in North Africa and Italy during the war, and it was on the suggestion of the Bedsers and of Errol Holmes that he turned to wicket-keeping, but he won his County cap purely as a batsman. Herbert Strudwick helped him enormously in his early days, and McIntyre was soon recognised as one of the two premier keepers in England. His aggressive batting and, above all, his keeping to an attack of such variety and vitality as Surrey's established him as one of the outstanding players of his time. Alec Bedser always maintained that McIntyre behind the stumps made him a better bowler.

In 1956, McIntyre was to miss more than half the season with a hand injury, and his presence was much missed, but Surrey still won the Championship for the fifth year in succession. Swetman was a capable deputy for McIntyre, although he was not in the same class as a batsman, but Stewart and Clark scored heavily and, as ever, there was always somebody who would produce the runs when needed.

Clark hit the two highest scores of his career in successive matches in July. The higher, 191, was made at Blackheath where Kent were beaten by 173 runs. This was a memorable match in that in Kent's second innings, Tony Lock took all ten wickets for 54 runs, and his figures for the match, 16 for 83, remain a record for the County. It was also the match in which Peter May hit his second century of the season.

The first had come at The Oval a few days earlier when Kent were also the opponents. May had been having a very lean time, and although he was captain of England and vice-captain of Surrey, Surridge said to him: 'Look, Peter, there's a lot of good players in the Second Eleven. I can't go on ignoring them.' May is a deceptively

Two great players for Surrey and England. A very young Peter May shaking hands with Jim Laker.

gentle man, for beneath the courtesy and the reticence there is a steely determination. He would not have been the great cricketer he was without it. His reply to his friend Surridge was 'Don't worry, skipper, I'll get you a hundred to-day!' And he did.

Lock's ten-wicket performance at Blackheath was the second time in the season that a Surrey bowler had taken all ten wickets. The first was against the Australian tourists in the middle of May.

Ian Johnson won the toss, and the Australians appeared to have gained considerable advantage from this as Burke and McDonald put on 62 in 95 minutes. McDonald batted freely to score 89, and when he was caught at the wicket the Australians were 151 for four. Laker now caused such devastation in the Australian batting that five wickets fell for 48 runs, and 12 of these were hit in one over by Davidson, Laker being the bowler. The last wicket added 42, but Wilson finally fell to Laker to give the off-spinner all ten wickets. It was the first time since 1878 that a bowler had taken all ten Australian wickets, and in 1878, the bowler had been a Surrey man, Barratt.

A patient innings by Constable, 'the great unsung hero of Surrey cricket', and some fierce hitting by Laker took Surrey into the lead, and Surridge and Loader plundered 34 for the last wicket. When they batted again the Australian vulnerability to the turning ball became

245

apparent, and a significant chapter in English cricket history was written. Surrey won by ten wickets, so becoming the first county for 44 years to triumph over an Australian team. Later in the year, Laker took 46 Test wickets in the series, including 19 at Old Trafford. It was the crowning achievement of the greatest off-spinner the world has known.

Laker was a Yorkshireman by birth, but his cricket was played for Surrey. He was a passive, phlegmatic player in that he would look the same whether he had just taken a wicket or been hit for six, but the passivity hid a burning passion. He was the master of his art. Line and length were under complete control all the time, and the control was founded on the perfection of his action. He bowled his off-breaks, not by rolling the ball out of his hand as some latter-day off-break bowlers have done, but by spinning the ball with his fingers, sometimes to the extent that fingers became raw and sore or that calluses formed. He was not, as has been asserted, a bad-wicket bowler. 'He could turn the ball on anything,' says Stuart Surridge. 'When I stood at short leg to him I could hear the ball zipping through the air. He needed a little cajoling at times, but he always gave his best, and he could spin them out whatever the wicket.'

Surridge's admiration for Laker did not prevent him from dropping the great man in his benefit year. Surrey had arrived at Lord's, and as Middlesex were one of the leading sides in the Championship, the game had an added importance. 'Jim was worried about his finger,' says Surridge, 'and I felt that if he went into the match worried about himself, he wouldn't give one hundred per cent, which was probably wrong of me because he always did. It was a spur of the moment decision, and I brought in Eric Bedser.'

Surrey were bowled out for 113, but they still won by 71 runs. Lock had 12 for 75, and Eric Bedser four for 49. Eric Bedser again proved his worth as an all-round cricketer in 1956, 804 runs and 92 wickets in all matches. He would bat anywhere, and there was a solid grandeur in his batting. If it had not been such a wretched summer, he might well have done the 'double', but rain robbed him. Surridge valued Eric Bedser's contribution highly and is adamant that if he had left Surrey for another county, Eric would have played for England. He was a very fine off-spinner, but his chances at The Oval were reduced because of the presence of Laker and Lock, and to the England selectors he was always in the shadow of Laker. Like his brother, Eric's cricket was founded not only on unquestionable ability and endeavour, but on the qualities of faith and loyalty. He had started out as a medium-pacer, but had changed to off-breaks so that he and Alec would not duplicate each other. They were, and are, inseparable, and when, in 1988, a lunch was held to celebrate their 50 years at The Oval the warmth of the affection in which they are held was obvious to all.

SURREY *v* THE AUSTRALIANS

Played at The Oval, Kennington, 16, 17 and 18 May 1956

SURREY WON BY 10 WICKETS

AUSTRALIANS	FIRST INNINGS		SECOND INNINGS	
J. W. Burke	lbw b Laker	28	c and b Lock	20
C. C. McDonald	c Swetman b Laker	89	c Laker b Lock	45
K. D. Mackay	c Surridge b Laker	4	lbw b Laker	4
R. N. Harvey	c Constable b Laker	13	c May b Lock	10
K. R. Miller	not out	57	c Swetman b Lock	2
†L. V. Maddocks	b Laker	12	c Laker b Lock	0
R. R. Lindwall	b Laker	0	c Constable b Lock	4
*I. W. Johnson	c Swetman b Laker	0	run out	5
A. K. Davidson	c May b Laker	21	c May b Laker	7
P. Crawford	b Laker	16	not out	5
J. W. Wilson	c Swetman b Laker	4	st Swetman b Lock	1
Extras	b 4, lb 8, nb 3	15	lb 4	4
Total		259		107

1st inns: 1-62, 2-93, 3-124, 4-141, 5-173, 6-173, 7-175, 8-199, 9-217
2nd inns: 1-56, 2-73, 3-83, 4-85, 5-85, 6-89, 7-92, 8-101, 9-104

BOWLING	O	M	R	W	O	M	R	W
Loader	15	4	30	0	2	2	0	0
Surridge	8	2	8	0	1	1	0	0
Laker	46	18	88	10	25	10	42	2
Lock	33	12	100	0	31.1	9	49	7
Cox	5	0	18	0				
Clark					8	4	12	0

SURREY	FIRST INNINGS		SECOND INNINGS	
D. G. W. Fletcher	c Maddocks b Johnson	29	not out	9
T. H. Clark	c Maddocks b Burke	58	not out	8
B. Constable	c and b Johnson	109		
P. B. H. May	st Maddocks b Johnson	27		
K. F. Barrington	c Miller b Johnson	4		
†R. Swetman	st Maddocks b Davidson	0		
D. F. Cox	b Davidson	13		
J. C. Laker	c McDonald b Johnson	43		
*W. S. Surridge	c Harvey b Johnson	38		
G. A. R. Lock	b Davidson	0		
P. J. Loader	not out	12		
Extras	b 10, lb 3, w 1	14	b 1, lb 1, nb 1	3
Total		347	(for no wkt)	20

1st inns: 1-53, 2-112, 3-147, 4-192, 5-195, 6-221, 7-278, 8-302, 9-313

BOWLING	O	M	R	W	O	M	R	W
Lindwall	2	1	10	0	8	4	8	0
Crawford	1	0	4	0	7	3	9	0
Johnson	60.3	12	168	6				
Davidson	44	14	101	3				
Wilson	19	9	34	0				
Burke	7	2	16	1				

Umpires: L. H. Gray and K. H. McCanlis

Surrey became the first county for 44 years to beat the Australians and Laker the first bowler for 78 years to take ten Australian wickets in an innings.

*Captain; †Wicket-keeper

Although Surrey were always in a challenging position in 1956, the County did not head the table until the first week of July, and then only briefly. It was two victories over Essex, two over Middlesex and one over Sussex that took them clear in August. Lancashire were the only county with a slender hope of overtaking them so that the meeting between the two counties at The Oval at the end of August was eagerly awaited. Lancashire had to win this match to retain any chance. They did well. Tattersall and Hilton bowled Surrey out for 96. Lancashire ended the day at 40 for two, and then it rained for two days, and Surrey were Champions for the fifth year in succession, a record which remains unapproached.

They had two matches to play, but the game at Worcester was badly affected by rain with Surrey leading on the first innings, and the match with Warwickshire at The Oval was abandoned without a ball being bowled.

Surrey lost to the Rest of England at The Oval,

and the only real moments of enthusiasm occurred when Surridge, the Surrey captain, appeared for his final innings. He was applauded all the way to the crease and again after Milton caught him superbly in the leg-trap where Surridge himself was such a fearless fielder during five successful years as leader.

In those five years, Surridge had held 220 catches lurking close to the wicket. Moreover, he had fulfilled his promise that Surrey would win the Championship five years in succession. He looks back in pride and pleasure: 'It was a most enjoyable experience. They were great men.'

Indeed they were. 'There were giants on the earth in those days.'

THE CHANGING FACE OF CRICKET

SURRIDGE STOOD DOWN FOR a number of reasons. He felt that the Second Eleven were growing old together without being given enough opportunities to display their talents at first-team level, and, above all, he felt that Peter May, as captain of England, must be allowed to lead his county. Surridge had achieved what he promised, and when he handed over to May he told him that he thought he was passing on a side that would win the Championship for another three years. He was one year out.

There are those who feel that May's task was an easy one, that all he had to do was carry on where Surridge had left off. In fact, he had the most difficult of tasks. Surrey had won the title five years in succession under his predecessor so that May was in the position where anything less than the Championship would be seen as failure.

May succeeded because he was his own man. His philosophy was that of Surridge, persistent aggression from the first ball to the last, but his way was his own. He had learned much from Surridge, but he had inherited much too from Hutton, his captain in the England side, and with these two influences he blended his own positive, intelligent and highly personal approach. He was a gentle man, but he had a very hard streak, and he was uncompromising in his demands. He was also ably served by his vice-captain, Alec Bedser.

Peter May was the best batsman that England had produced since the war, and, arguably, he had no superior anywhere in the world. He had been destined for greatness since his early days at Charterhouse. He was technically and temperamentally sound. He was tall, powerful and purposeful. He had command of all the shots, and he knew when to use them. His batting had the charm and elegance of the traditional amateur, yet it had, too, a ruthless professionalism. He demonstrated this in the first Test match against West Indies in 1957 when he and Colin Cowdrey destroyed the great spinner 'Sonny' Ramadhin.

It was feared that the pressures of captaining England and Surrey as well as being his country's leading batsman would affect him. In a sense, they did. He led both sides to triumph, topped the Surrey averages, the national averages and scored more runs than anybody else on either side in the Test series.

Surrey lost none of their dynamism. The tone was set in the first Championship match of the season when, with victories over Cambridge University and MCC behind them, Surrey hit 259 against Glamorgan at The Oval and bowled out their opponents for 62 and

31. Lock had match figures of 12 for 34. The only mishap in the first two months of the season came when Northants were victorious at The Oval at the end of May.

Northamptonshire were, in fact, Surrey's closest challengers, but they were emphatically beaten in the return game at Northampton five days later. This was a memorable match because it saw Micky Stewart establish a world record by taking seven catches in the second innings. Six of the catches were taken at backward short leg and one in the gully. Alec Bedser, Laker and Lock were the bowlers to benefit. Surprisingly, none of these catches was really difficult, but this could not be said of many of the 77 catches that Stewart held during that season.

Stewart's world record of seven catches at Northampton was equalled by Tony Brown of Gloucestershire in 1966, but it has never been beaten. His 77 in a season remains a Surrey record and is second only to the 78 that Wally Hammond held in 1928. Fielding was again a dominant feature of Surrey cricket, for Tony Lock made several stunning catches. He finished the season at The Oval with match figures of ten for 60 and four catches in each innings to establish another Surrey record. Warwickshire were the victims, and they were beaten in two days.

Alex Bannister drew attention to the quality of Surrey's fielding when he assessed their performance over the season:

> To stand at Stewart's 'pocket picking' distance at short leg needs more than a safe pair of hands, quick reflexes and a stout heart; it demands complete faith in his bowlers to maintain an accurate length. They never failed him. Barrington, in his first season at slip, shared with Stewart and Lock the outstanding performance of exceeding 60 catches. Surrey, by having their youngest players in the positions nearest the wicket, further prove this modern theory is the soundest.

Perhaps Bannister's comment needs a little explanation. In over-simplified terms, it had been customary for most counties to position their elder statesmen close to the wicket, particularly at slip, in order to save their legs and to leave the running in the outfield to the young men. The Surrey formula had been a complete reversal of that policy. The number of catches taken by Stewart, 77, Lock and Barrington, 64 each, places them among the top dozen leading catchers in the record books. They are likely to remain there, for since the reduction of County Championship matches in 1969, 49 by Chris Tavaré in 1979 is the most that a fielder has taken.

By mid-July, Surrey were 52 points clear in the Championship, and although they lost to Gloucestershire at the end of the month, there was never any likelihood that they would be caught. Nottinghamshire and Hampshire were brushed aside, and Fletcher's benefit match was ruined by rain when Surrey were within 15 runs of taking a first innings lead over Middlesex.

Stephenson, the Somerset wicket-keeper, had chosen the Surrey match at Weston-super-Mare for his benefit, for he was assured of a big crowd. Surrey, playing and looking like magnificent Champions, attracted a vast number of people wherever they went. Somerset made 250; Surrey 286. When the home side batted again Tremlett played a fine innings of 83 in an hour, and Wight batted solidly, but Laker took five for 19 in eight overs, and Surrey needed 153 to win.

The asking rate was close to four an over, and Surrey found themselves struggling against a determined attack and the clock. May played well, and Barrington hit briskly to ease the worries. The seventh wicket fell with the scores level, and when Laker hit Langford for the winning single there were just eight minutes of extra time remaining. The date was 16 August, and only Warwickshire, in 1951, had assured themselves of the Championship at such an early date. The final margin of Surrey's superiority was enormous:

	P	W	L	D	No result	Bonus points	Pts
Surrey	28	21	3	3	1	48	312
Northamptonshire	28	15	2	10	0	22	218

The batting had been exhilarating – May, Stewart and Barrington all passed 1,000 runs in Championship matches – while the bowling, with young Gibson impressive in his few outings, was of a class unapproached by any other county. The figures in Championship matches point to the reason for Surrey's dominance:

Lock	153 at	11.58
Laker	85 at	12.41
E. A. Bedser	60 at	13.40
Loader	101 at	14.73
A. V. Bedser	109 at	15.57

Alec Bedser had suffered an attack of shingles in Australia in 1954–55, and he had not seemed to recover his form fully after that illness. He played his last Test match in 1955 and ended with 236 Test wickets which was then a record. In 1957, although not regaining his England place, he was back to his best for Surrey. May had wanted him as his vice-captain, and it had proved a wise choice, for Bedser had had to lead the side in one third of the Championship matches: 'Bedser was a brilliant deputy. His wide experience, deep technical know-ledge, shrewdness and willingness to encourage the new members earned him a new stature in English cricket.'

Lock's performance was all the more praiseworthy in that he was troubled by an injured knee which was to need rest and treatment in the coming seasons, but nothing defeated Tony Lock. 'I used to egg him on,' says Stuart Surridge, 'but you never had to ask Tony Lock to produce the goods. I used to get after him, but he was a natural genius, and he had brain power as well as ability.'

None worked harder at the game than Lock. He started as a slow left-arm bowler who spun the ball little, and he practised hard until he could spin the ball on any surface. He also increased his speed so that he was often, like Derek Underwood, close to medium pace. His quicker ball, however, was to lead him into trouble and the legality of his action was questioned. Again he worked assiduously. He remodelled his action so that, in his final phase, which began around 1959, he was a slow left-arm bowler of the classical and orthodox style. The tigerish perseverance that he showed in these periods of transformation permeated all he did. After his time with Surrey, which ended in 1963, he gave noble service to Western Australia and Leicestershire.

A time of change was taking place at Surrey. At the end of 1957, Brian Castor retired as secretary and was succeeded by his assistant, B. O. Babb. Castor had seen Surrey through a difficult period in the years after the war (in which he had been a prisoner in Japanese hands) and the strength of any club rests firmly on the quality of its administration. He was firm but kind to staff and players and active and influential throughout the game. He was rather gruff in manner, but there was great humour in the man as evidenced by his public address announcements to the pigeons who had invaded the outfield. Booming over the loudspeaker would come the order: 'Go away, you pigeons. Go to Lord's!'

Other changes came with the retirement of Arthur McIntyre, a top-class wicket-keeper to the last, at the end of 1958. He succeeded Andy Sandham as coach, Sandham taking over as scorer from Strudwick, who thus went into retirement after serving the Club for 60 years.

Surrey won the Championship for the seventh season in succession in 1958. It is a record that is likely to stand for the foreseeable future. In a wet summer, they won more games, 14, and lost fewer, five, than their nearest challengers, Hampshire, who finished 26 points behind the Champions. If the triumph lacked the force of the previous season, it was achieved by overcoming many difficulties in the form of illness, injury and representative calls.

Alec Bedser went down with pneumonia on the eve of the season and could not play until July so that his ability and expertise were both missed. With May also absent on international duty, McIntyre led the side most capably on several occasions. Lock's knee and Laker's finger injuries meant that they missed occasional matches, but Gibson and Sydenham took their chances well.

David Gibson, fast-medium bowler and useful batsman, benefited from a fine physique as befitted a county rugby player and schoolboy international, and David Sydenham's left-arm fast-medium gave the attack an extra dimension on occasions.

Batting stuttered a little in the damp conditions, but May rose head and shoulders above everybody else in the country. Not only did he score more runs than any other batsman, but his average per innings, 63.74, was more than 17 runs better than his nearest rival, Willie Watson, 46.62. For Surrey, May averaged 64.23, scored his runs briskly, was the only man to reach 1,000 runs and by his inspiring and enterprising approach, he invariably put his side in a strong position.

Constable and Fletcher also gave consistent service, and they shared a fourth-wicket partnership of 137 in the opening Championship match when Gloucestershire were beaten by nine wickets. This was the first of five consecutive victories which culminated with Lancashire being outplayed at Old Trafford. In their second innings, with Gibson taking four for 8, Lancashire were bowled out for 27, their lowest score this century, and this on a wicket on which May had hit an imperious 174.

Such form was not sustained, and, at the end of July, having suffered four defeats, Surrey were 18 points behind Hampshire and in third place. At the beginning of August, they entertained Nottinghamshire at The Oval. Surrey led by 11 on the first innings, and, in a low-scoring match, needing 96 to win, they were 25 for two. May came to the wicket and hit the first ball he received from Jepson, who had just bowled Stewart, straight back over the bowler's head for six. It was an astonishing display of confidence and left Nottinghamshire stunned. The win over Nottinghamshire was followed by a draw at Leicester and a two-day win over Middlesex. So, on 12 August, Surrey stood in second place, four points behind Hampshire.

Wins over Middlesex and Worcestershire and a draw with Northamptonshire preceded Somerset's visit to The Oval on 27, 28 and 29 August. Consistent batting took Surrey to 313 for nine declared. Gibson took five for 21 as Somerset were bowled out for 66. Rain did not allow for any more play, but the first-innings lead had given Surrey sufficient points to assure them of the Championship.

They did not concede a point until 6 June when Northamptonshire took a first-innings lead at The Oval. Raman Subba Row hit 300 in this match, so equalling the highest score ever made against Surrey, but usually the outstanding performances were in favour of the

Champions. When Surrey were having their fine run at the beginning of the season Peter Loader took nine for 17 to end the match against Warwickshire at The Oval before lunch on the third day. These were the best figures of Loader's career.

Surridge described Loader as a 'superb bowler'. His 13 Test matches indicate how strong England were in fast bowlers at this period, for surely he would have commanded a regular place at an earlier or later time. As it was, against West Indies at Headingley in 1957, he performed the first hat-trick in Test cricket since the war. He had a long high-stepping run and was wiry and aggressive. He was also highly intelligent and versatile in that he could adapt his pace and control to exploit conditions or the age of the ball.

Loader was one of five Surrey players who went with the MCC side to Australia in 1958–59, May (captain), Laker, Lock and, rather surprisingly, Swetman being the others. It looked as if it was one of the strongest England sides to leave these shores, but things did not go well, and that tour was, perhaps, the point from which the fortunes of England and Surrey began to decline for a while.

Peter May did not make a full return to cricket in England after the tour. His recent marriage made him an absentee until the end of May, and then, in the third week in July, he had to undergo an operation which brought his season to a premature end. He played in only seven Championship matches, and Alec Bedser led the side for most of 1959. He did admirably, but May's brilliant batting was sorely missed.

Barrington, Constable, Stewart, Clark and Fletcher enjoyed good seasons, but the outstanding contribution came from John Edrich, a 22-year-old left-hander who had played in five first-class matches in the three previous seasons, one of them a Championship match in 1958. Injuries to Clark and Fletcher caused Edrich to be drafted into the Surrey side for the game at Trent Bridge on 16 May 1959. He was asked to open the innings and hit 112 and 124. He added five more centuries before the end of the season, in which he scored 1,799 runs, average 52.91, even though he twice broke a finger, being idle for four weeks in mid-season and having to retire in the last match.

This was a severe blow as, having won at Bath and Gloucester, Surrey needed victory in their last two matches to be sure of retaining the Championship. In fact, they won neither. Middlesex scored 308. Surrey replied with 219, and were eventually asked to make 265 in 143 minutes. They finished on 129 for nine with Loader and Alec Bedser batting out time. Meanwhile Yorkshire had won in sensational manner at Hove and were the new Champions.

In a dry summer, none of the Surrey bowlers was as successful as in previous seasons. Lock was in the process of remodelling his action, and Laker had lost the edge of his bowling. In truth, the great side was

Two young Surrey players at the Alf Gover School in 1959: John Edrich and Roy Swetman.

in the process of breaking up. Before the start of the 1960 season Laker had retired. Unfortunately, he left with some rancour and unwisely gave his name to a book which was highly critical of the County. Happily, a few years later all was forgiven on both sides, and Laker returned to The Oval to serve the Club well before his premature death. Surrey also played the 1960 season without Peter May, who was recuperating from his operation, and neither Clark nor Constable was able to appear. Constable had a knee cap removed, and Clark was troubled by arthritis, and, as it transpired, was never to play again.

Edrich confirmed the promise of the previous season, and Stewart, Barrington, Fletcher and Parsons scored consistently. Edrich and Stewart began the season with an opening partnership of 204 against Northamptonshire, but the match was drawn, as were four of the first five games, and Surrey were never in a position to challenge for the title.

Brian Parsons was a mature player before he claimed a regular place in the Surrey side, so strong had been the competition. Born in Guildford in September 1933, he gained his blue at Cambridge in 1954 and 1955, but national service had prevented him from joining the staff at The Oval until 1958. He was a cultured-looking right-handed batsman who, for a few seasons, was consistent rather than brilliant.

Willett, Tindall, Storey and Long were other younger players whose names began to appear on the team sheet. Arnold Long deputised for Swetman in three matches and made his first-class debut against Essex at Brentwood. He caught Savill off Lock to claim his first victim, and in the next match, against Hampshire, he stumped 'Butch' White. Swetman played in 11 Test matches for England between 1959 and 1960, without ever suggesting that he was the real successor to Evans or McIntyre. Neat and compact, he kept creditably for Surrey until 1961, and he later played for Nottinghamshire and Gloucestershire.

Gibson showed a considerable advance in 1960, but the attack, Lock apart, was a shadow of what it had been three or four years earlier. Lock, having remodelled his action, took 139 first-class wickets, and his Test career was far from over.

Alec Bedser captained in all but three Championship matches and took 67 first-class wickets. He led Surrey out against Glamorgan in the last three days in August, shared an unbroken eighth-wicket stand of 47 with Swetman and took five Glamorgan first-innings wickets for 25 runs. Surrey won by an innings. It was the 72nd time that he had taken five wickets in an innings for Surrey, and when he had Don Shepherd lbw it was his 1,459th and last wicket for the County. He announced his retirement from first-class cricket, and we had seen the last of one of the greatest of medium-pace bowlers.

The following season was the last for his brother and for Fletcher. Clark was not to reappear in what was his benefit year, and Swetman moved on. May returned in 1961, but England duty claimed much of his time, and Stewart, who had been appointed vice-captain in succession to Alec Bedser, led the side for much of the time. He did not have a happy season with the bat, but still managed 1,000 runs for Surrey as did Barrington, Edrich, Willett, Parsons and Constable, who made a wonderful return to the side after his knee operation.

Willett and Tindall brought fresh aggression to the middle order, but it was the attack, so long the strength of the side, that began to look thinner and thinner and found it harder and harder to bowl out sides at The Oval where batsmen began to dominate again. Fifteenth in the table was a shattering drop and confirmation that the golden days

Alec Bedser, great bowler and great administrator. (Allsport)

were finally at an end. Not even the resurgence in 1962 could really hide that fact. Surrey climbed back to fifth in the table and, beaten only three times, they were outside contenders for the Championship until the last weeks of the season, and were still pleased to finish fifth. May had retired from Test cricket and played in 21 Championship matches, the most that he had played in for five years, and with Stewart and Edrich opening, Barrington at number three, May at four and Constable at five, and Parsons, Willett and Tindall also scoring well, Surrey possessed a batting side as strong as any in the country.

The main problem remained in attack because Gibson, in whom so many hopes were rested, again broke down with injury. Sydenham responded magnificently, and both he and Loader took more than 100 wickets while Lock, back in the England side for three Tests against Pakistan, was 'his true self and a grand team-man'. Ron Tindall, like Willett a soccer player of note, was encouraged with his off-breaks, and he performed nobly, although it was apparent that he would never become a spinner in the top flight. Richard Jefferson came down from Cambridge to bowl his medium pace to good effect, and he also strengthened the tail, for he could be a very hard-hitting batsman. He and Sydenham were to share a ferocious last-wicket partnership the following season.

Surrey's decline in the late 1950s and early 1960s coincided with a time when cricket itself was going through an uncertain period.

257

Crowds were dropping, and the financial structure of the game was threatened. There seemed to be a dullness shadowing much that happened, and there were constant administrative manoeuvrings in search of brighter cricket. The early 1960s were to see the elimination of the distinction between amateur and professional, and so the end of fixtures between Gentlemen and Players, and the introduction of the one-day game. In 1961 and 1962, one of the sillier experiments was to abolish the follow-on. This certainly cost Surrey at least one victory in 1962 when Stewart, 200, and Barrington, 130, shared an unbroken second-wicket partnership of 316 against Essex at The Oval. It was a dazzling partnership, full of rich strokes. Essex made 139, but Surrey had to bat again. Stewart declared at 132 for two, and although Essex lost eight wickets they held out.

On the brighter side in 1962 was the form of Arnold Long in his first full season as Surrey's wicket-keeper. He accounted for 90 batsmen in all matches, 73 caught, 17 stumped, and so established a Surrey record at the first attempt. It was not to be his last.

The change in attitude in the game took its toll. May had retired from Test cricket because he felt he had never really played as well since his illness as he had done before his operation. Test cricket had become less enjoyable for all concerned, and he was a sensitive man who, in the position of captain, had taken more knocks than most. At the end of the 1962 season with Surrey, May went home and reviewed his life. He felt that he was not enjoying the game as much as he once did:

> Perhaps it was anticlimax after the glorious years of the 1950s, beer after champagne, as it were. I was not playing up to the high standards which I had always set myself.

He did indeed set himself the very highest of standards, and there was no dissuading him. He resigned the captaincy, but said that he would be pleased to play when on holiday from his work in the City or when the County felt that they particularly needed him. He never played one-day cricket, for which, one feels, he was probably thankful. If he had done, he would not have violated the aesthetic as many find it necessary to do. He played three times for Surrey in 1963, twice at Guildford, against Cambridge University and Sussex, and against Northamptonshire at The Oval. He scored four against Cambridge for whom Richard Hutton, son of his predecessor as captain of England made 163 not out, and 85 against Sussex. In his last match, against Northamptonshire, he made 1 and nought:

> Because of everything that had gone before, a great deal was expected of me and I knew that, without the constant competitive

cricket on which I had thrived, I would not be able to produce it. I did not enjoy the idea of letting people down.

Peter May never let anybody down, least of all himself, but when he took over as chairman of Test selectors in the early 1980s cricketers and press were speaking a different language. That was their failing, not his, and the game would be better if we could return to the standards he knew and upheld.

May was confident in his successor as Surrey captain, Micky Stewart, and rightly so. Stewart took over at a difficult time and held the side together most ably in a transitional period. The 1963 season saw the last of Lock and Loader, both of whom went to settle in Australia, and of Parsons who decided to follow a business career. The season also saw the County establish a record when, in the first Test

Captain, manager and restructurer of Surrey cricket, Micky Stewart. (Allsport)

match against West Indies at Old Trafford, they supplied the first three England batsmen, Stewart, Edrich and Barrington. This was the first time in a Test match in England that one county had provided the first three batsmen for the England side.

Their absence for between three and five Tests, and Lock's for three, put extra pressure on a developing side which had other problems, notably the loss of Arnold Long with appendicitis halfway through the season. Three men were called upon to deputise for him, one of them being coach Arthur McIntyre. The other two were Owen Kember and Nicholas Majendie, neither of whom appeared for Surrey again after 1963.

With leading batsmen absent for much of the season, Willett and Tindall shouldered responsibility well, although Tindall's off-breaks showed little improvement. Indeed, the Surrey attack, until recently so strong in spin, was now reliant more and more upon medium-pace bowling. Gibson enjoyed a better season, Storey showed promise as an all-rounder and Geoff Arnold, 18 years old, made the first of his 218 appearances for the County.

His career began in the second Championship match of the season when Surrey beat Derbyshire by an innings. He dismissed top-scorers Oates and Buxton in the first innings and, opening the bowling, had Swallow caught in the second. He conceded only 40 runs in 16 overs. He finished the year with a creditable 18 wickets in his six matches, and he was seen by many as the natural successor to Alec Bedser although they were dissimilar in many ways.

Of the pace bowlers, the one to enjoy the most successful season was David Sydenham, who was the only one to take 100 Championship wickets. He also contributed a useful batting performance in an astonishing game at Northampton. The home side hit 301 for three in their first innings and bowled Surrey out for 106. With the follow-on rule operative again, Surrey slumped to 186 for seven in their second knock. Jefferson joined Lock, and 66 were added in an hour, Lock hitting 56 of them. He was bowled by Crump who bowled Loader ten runs later so that when Sydenham joined Jefferson the score was 262 for nine.

Jefferson then took over. Attacking the bowling without taking unnecessary risks, he showed remarkable control in hitting his first Championship century. Three 6s and twenty-one 4s were included in his 136, scored in just under three hours. Sydenham gave fine support and this remarkable stand of 138, the highest for the last wicket against Northamptonshire, occupied only an hour-and-three-quarters.

Sydenham's contribution was 15 not out.

Richard Jefferson was a medium-pace bowler and hard-hitting batsman who got his blue at Cambridge in 1961. He was an enterprising player who hit 100 not out in 100 minutes against Derbyshire at Buxton in 1964, an innings which included six sixes and nine fours, but he could never hold a regular place in the side, so rich were Surrey in seam bowlers, and it was generally felt that the County did not make the best use of his services.

While there were several contenders for the use of the new ball the successors to Lock and Laker were harder to find, but there was some encouraging bowling from the 21-year-old slow left-arm spinner Roger Harman. In 1963, he was still deputy to Lock, yet he produced some remarkable bowling when given the opportunity. At Blackheath, Kent, needing 102 to win, were 91 for two when Harman bowled Wilson. Two balls later, he caught and bowled Luckhurst, and Denness suffered the same fate next ball, which was the last of the over. With the first ball of his next over he bowled Leary so completing the hat-trick and a spell of four wickets in five balls.

These were isolated individual performances, however, in a season in which a changing side, finding its shape, finished 11th in the Championship and was comprehensively beaten in the first round of the first Gillette Cup competition.

Far better luck attended Surrey in the second year of the competition, when they beat Cheshire at Hoylake, Sydenham taking four for 6 and the individual award, Gloucestershire at The Oval, with Edrich hitting 96, and Middlesex at The Oval before going down to Sussex at Hove in the semi-final.

The improved form was not restricted to the one-day knock-out tournament, for, in 1964, a young and eager Surrey side finished fourth in the Championship, although it would be true to say that they never seriously threatened the leaders. Harman had a magnificent season, taking 136 wickets at 21.01 runs each in all matches and suggesting immediately that he could prove a worthy successor to Tony Lock. He had a high action, flighted the ball intelligently and spun it considerably. Twice in the season he took eight wickets in an innings. His spell at Trent Bridge turned what looked likely to be a defeat into victory. Surrey trailed by 68 runs on the first innings, and Nottinghamshire were 63 for one in their second when Harman joined the attack and produced figures of 17.1-10-12-8. Against Kent at The Oval, he took eight for 32, and Surrey again won a match in which they had been trailing.

So much was expected of Harman. It seemed to those close to the game that he was certain to become an England player so talented was he, but the second season is always more difficult than the first. When batsmen began to read him he seemed to lack the spark of aggression that had characterised Lock and Laker, and, delightful man that he was, he became dispirited. Never again was he to produce the form of 1964, and he left Surrey at the end of the 1968 season.

Before the end of the 1964 season, Harman had been joined in the Surrey attack by Pat Pocock, a 17-year-old off-spinner. He took six wickets against Cambridge University, and, in his first Championship match, against Nottinghamshire in the Bank Holiday game at The Oval, he had Moore caught at slip before he had conceded a run and finished with three for 68 and three for 44. He was recognised as an off-spinner of exceptional ability, and he was to confirm that opinion over the next 22 years.

Sydenham, although missing many matches through injury, was always threatening, and he began the season with nine for 70 against Gloucestershire at The Oval after Stewart had put the visitors in to bat. It was the best performance of his career, and Surrey won by eight wickets. A balanced and aggressive attack was forming, and the batting was as strong as ever.

Ken Barrington, 'The Colonel', in his benefit year, topped Club, national and Test averages. Stewart had a splendid season with a career best 227 not out against Middlesex at The Oval in July. This was a strange match. Surrey were bowled out for 119 in their first innings, and Willett hit 73 not out. Middlesex made 365, and they seemed set for victory. The left-handed Bill Smith and Stewart began Surrey's second innings with a partnership of 219. Smith, a stylish player, was out for 91, and Edwards and Tindall followed so that three were down for 310. Willett joined Stewart in a stand of 149 in 80 minutes, and of these Willett hit 102 to record the fastest century of the season. While all this was going on Ken Barrington was hitting 256 for England against Australia at Old Trafford.

Willett, always a forceful player, had his best season for the Club, but a cartilage operation was to cause him to miss much of the following season. Edrich was as resolute as ever, and Storey's advance as a batsman was most marked. A young man named Roope made his first appearance for the County, but his great deeds lay ahead, just as those of Bernard Constable lay behind him. Constable, now 43 and the only survivor from before the war, played his last innings for Surrey on 2 September when he took a delightful 61 not out off the Warwickshire bowling. It was his 434th match for the County on whose history he had printed his name indelibly.

Arnold Long, recovered from his appendicitis operation and with his career still in its infancy, established a world record some two months before Constable left the game. Against Sussex at Hove, on 18–21 July, he caught seven batsmen in the first innings and four in the second. His seven catches stood as a record for an English wicket-keeper until beaten by David East of Essex in 1985, and his eleven catches has since been equalled, by Marsh and Bairstow, but not beaten.

Over the years Long was to give remarkably fine service to Surrey. A thoughtful man, quietly efficient and tactically sound, he was able, with his captain, to galvanise the field and help to maintain the high standards for which Surrey had become noted, and only on rare occasions did those standards lapse. Unfortunately, one such occasion was the Gillette Cup Final of 1965.

Gibson had blossomed into a fine all-rounder by this time, and Storey was not far behind him, but a slight falling away by Sydenham and Harman's loss of form and confidence saw Surrey fall to eighth in the Championship. In the Gillette Cup, however, they carried all before them, until 4 September.

They had a bye in the first round and entertained Glamorgan in the second. They followed what was becoming the norm by omitting their spinners, Harman and Pocock, and playing an all-seam attack. It was successful in that Glamorgan were bowled out for 146 in 46.1 overs. Surrey won by five wickets with 18 overs to spare, and John Edrich's 65 earned him the individual award, although many thought that Geoff Arnold's four for 26 had actually decided the match.

Northamptonshire were the visitors in the quarter-final and again the award went to a batsman, Ron Tindall, who hit 11 fours in his 73 after four wickets had fallen for 79, but Surrey also owed much to Storey, who took four for 14 as Northants were bowled out for 97.

The semi-final paired Surrey with Middlesex, who hit 250 for eight in their 60 overs. They had begun slowly, scoring only 77 for three in 32 overs, but Eric Russell, Murray, Brearley and Titmus had hit lustily to present Surrey with a formidable target. Stewart and Edrich gave Surrey a solid start, but the match-winning stand was between Barrington and Edwards, who added 83 in ten overs. This was the start of a period in which Surrey had ascendancy over Middlesex in one-day matches. It is worth noting that there was 'delight' that 8,000 people had paid to see this game, a reflection of the economic decline which cricket suffered in the late 1950s and early 1960s.

Surrey were favourites for the final against Yorkshire at Lord's, a match which was watched by 25,000 people. They were a young side, good in the field with an accurate pace attack, and strong in batting, but little went right on the day.

Stewart won the toss, and he asked Yorkshire to bat first. It was an understandable decision, for the ground was wet after overnight rain, and Surrey benefited by the early dismissal of Taylor and by Yorkshire's slow start, but Close joined Boycott in a partnership of 192. Boycott had had an indifferent season in which, incredibly, he had

263

failed to hit a first-class century, but in that Gillette Cup Final he played what many consider to be the best innings of his career. He hit three sixes and 15 fours, and the Surrey bowling and fielding, generally so tight and so keen, wilted. Twenty-three years later, Boycott's 146 remains the highest score in a 60-over final.

Facing a total of 317 for four, Surrey looked to be without heart. Stewart hit 33 and Tindall 57, but in 40.4 overs they were bowled out for 142. The memories of that final revolve around the batting of Boycott and Close.

There had been a change in the administration at The Oval in 1965 for Brian 'Bob' Babb had retired as secretary and been succeeded by Geoffrey Howard, formerly with Lancashire and formerly Assistant Secretary at The Oval. Surrey gave trials to two left-handed batsmen in the match against the South African tourists, Ian Finlay and Younis Ahmed. Younis hit 21 and 66, so beginning a rather turbulent career.

Younis had to be content with second eleven cricket in 1966 as he qualified for the County, and his performances in the Second Eleven, scoring more than 1,000 runs, must have made Surrey wish they could play him, for the batting of the side seemed to lose confidence.

There were niggling injuries and illnesses to Gibson, Barrington and Arnold, and the team as a whole played with an uncharacteristic lack of flair. There were exceptions. John Edrich was now a power in the land. He had hit 310 not out for England against New Zealand the previous summer, and his batting had a resolution that was awesome. Michael Edwards, born in Balham and educated at Alleyns and Cambridge where, surprisingly, he had failed to get a blue, was moved up the order to open with Edrich, Stewart dropping down. The move was an instant success, and the cultured Edwards, relishing the extra time and composure he was allowed as an opener, responded with a maiden century against Gloucestershire at The Oval and 1,000 runs in a season for the first time.

Just as encouraging was the form of Stewart Storey, who became the first Surrey player since Freddie Brown in 1932 to do the 'double', yet, in a sense, Storey's achievement was symptomatic of so much of Surrey's cricket in the mid-1960s in that it promised more than it ever really fulfilled. The side which had looked excitingly young, eager and balanced fell apart before it ever came to maturity. Sydenham had retired, and Gibson, Tindall, Jefferson, Willett and Harman all left the game in the space of a couple of years, plagued by injury or unrealised potential.

There were, of course, compensations. Geoff Arnold had developed into a Test match bowler, and, in 1966, Robin Jackman arrived with 22 Championship wickets. Pat Pocock had made a tremendous advance as an off-spinner to the extent that, in 1968, he made his Test debut at the age of 22 and claimed Clive Lloyd as his first Test victim. Roope, too, was maturing into a very capable all-round cricketer, but, as yet, it seemed that Surrey was like a jigsaw puzzle that was tantalisingly incomplete.

Hopes were raised in 1967 when, with Pocock, Arnold and Storey bowling well, and the batting, boosted by the arrival of Younis, looking more adventurous and exciting, Surrey finished fourth in the Championship. Edrich hit his highest score for Surrey, 226 not out against Middlesex at The Oval when he and Barrington shared a fourth wicket stand of 297 in four-and-a-half hours, but a bad start to the season had really destroyed any chance that the County had of making a serious challenge for the title.

The hopes were not realised. In 1968, Surrey played some of the worst cricket in their history. They were dull and unenterprising, gripped by a corporate malaise. Only Edrich hit a century in the Championship. Arnold missed practically the whole season with injury, and Storey fell away sadly. Jim Cumbes, lively, cheerful, with a good, high action, used the new ball well when he was released from his soccer commitments; Jackman bowled, as he was to do all his career, with tireless energy and enthusiasm; Pocock consistently displayed his precocious talent; and Roope, and, occasionally, Knight, showed encouraging all-round form, but the batting was both listless and disappointing. Most alarming was the decline of Barrington. Only some months later, when he collapsed in Australia with heart trouble, did the reason for his decline become apparent. He was forced to retire, and this came as a shattering blow to Surrey, and England. A man of wit and cheerful charm, he taught many of those around him the meaning of professional application, and his influence on a side was enormous and always for the good. As a batsman he seemed to be hewn out of granite, his nose and chin defiantly projecting his immovability.

The loss of Barrington coming hard upon a season in which things had gone so badly as for Surrey to plunge to 15th in the Championship and make no impact on the Gillette Cup caused some reassessment of staff and attitudes at The Oval and an examination, too, of whether the County was coming to terms with the game as it was now ordered. In 1968, the rule allowing immediate registration of an overseas player had been introduced, but not all counties, Surrey included, had grasped the significance of the impact that this would have on the game. While Procter, Barry Richards and Sobers paraded their talents elsewhere Surrey offered no new fare. There were, too, the increasing demands of the one-day game and, with the arrival of the John Player Sunday League in 1969, its growing popularity.

Surrey woke up to these changes, and, for the 1969 season, they enlisted the aid of Intikhab Alam, the Pakistani leg-spinner and hard-hitting batsman. It was something of an anachronism to sign a leg-spinner in an age when they had all but ceased to exist, but it was an inspired move, for here was a cricketer of modesty and lavish talent, adaptable to all forms of cricket, and loved by friend and foe alike. Surrey cricket had received the blood transfusion that it needed.

Intikhab Alam, Pakistani Test captain and all-rounder, and Surrey's first long-serving 'overseas' player, was a popular figure at The Oval for 12 years.

Intikhab was one of four players to be capped by the County in 1969; Younis, Roope and Derek Taylor, who was to depart to become Somerset's wicket-keeper, and a very fine one, at the end of the season, were the others. A wonderful team effort brought victory over Hampshire at Southampton with seven balls to spare and took Surrey into the quarter-final of the Gillette Cup, where they lost to Yorkshire at The Oval before a disappointingly small crowd. Some enterprising cricket was played in the John Player League, and Surrey finished fifth, a position which they have never bettered, and in the Championship they were once again a team to be reckoned with.

Edrich, Roope, Younis, Stewart and Edwards all found their form with the bat, and they were ably supported by Intikhab and, when available, Roger Knight. An injured heel took Arnold out of the attack in the closing weeks of the season, and this cost the County dearly in the run-in to the Championship in spite of the pounding efforts of a raw, tear-away fast bowler named Bob Willis.

On 20 June, and with only two victories to their credit, Surrey were top of the County Championship, eight points ahead of Warwickshire who had a game in hand and who, like Surrey, were unbeaten. By 2 July, with still only two victories and no defeats, Surrey had dropped to fourth, and their strength was easily discernible with Younis and Edrich first and fourth in the national batting averages. By the end of July, Edrich was first and Younis second. Surrey were third, still unbeaten and with four wins.

The two wins had come in a ten-day period towards the end of the month. The first was a thrilling victory over Leicestershire at The Oval. Surrey had been well on top in the early stages of the match, with Stewart hitting 97 and Roope 75 and Stewart declaring at 324 for seven. Arnold and Cumbes made quick inroads into the Leicestershire batting, but at 161 for six, Birkenshaw and Dudleston came together, and with Birkenshaw hitting 131, they added 148, and Leicestershire took a first innings lead of 40. McKenzie then took five wickets, and Leicestershire were left to score 137 in 105 minutes. At 108 for four, this did not seem an arduous task, but clever bowling by Intikhab changed the course of the match. He sent back four batsmen in quick succession, and when he began the last over Leicestershire needed five to win with one wicket to fall. On the fifth ball, a fine throw by Pocock ran out Dudleston and gave Surrey victory by two runs.

Victories over Sussex and Essex kept up the Surrey challenge, but in late August, in spite of beating Yorkshire at Scarborough, they began to tire, and they suffered their only Championship defeat of the season when Essex won at The Oval. Pocock and Intikhab had bowled well throughout the season, but now, without Arnold to act as strike bowler, the challenge faded, and Surrey finished third.

The 1970 season followed an identical pattern. Five wins, four draws and one defeat in the first ten Championship matches kept them well to the fore in mid-June. Six points from a draw with Gloucestershire at The Oval took them top of the table on 8 August, but defeats at Bradford and Blackheath heralded a falling away, and Surrey finished fifth.

There was general frustration and criticism. It was now 12 years since Surrey had won anything, and many found this unacceptable, for it seemed that the County possessed the best balanced side in the country. They were so strong that Roger Knight had moved to Gloucestershire to get regular cricket, and Willis, fast, furious and raw, was to move on in 1971 for the same reason. Storey had refound his form as a batsman and joined Edwards, Younis, Roope, Stewart and Edrich on 1,000 runs. There was a balanced and lively attack, with two potent spinners in Pocock and Intikhab, yet the County had nothing to show for all this talent.

There were allegations that Stewart was not getting the best out of his men, and that his tactics were unenterprising. The Oval pitches came in for severe criticisms, and there was unrest and anger.

Micky Stewart was well aware of the frustration and criticism, much of which he felt himself. He announced early in the 1971 season that he would resign the captaincy at the end of the campaign. He felt that there was too big a gap between committee and players, and he was critical of the sluggish pitches at The Oval and at the lack of atmosphere at the old ground. He was voicing a view that many now felt. Gone were the days when crowds flocked on trams to see Hobbs and Sandham. Gone, although only by 15 years, were the days when 50,000 swarmed through the turnstiles in three days to see Surridge and his men take on Middlesex or Yorkshire. The world had changed, and Surrey had not always kept pace with the fresh demands that now came from the game, its players and spectators. Social and environmental factors had taken their toll, too, and Kennington, blitzed by traffic and the intersection of main road arteries, was no longer the fashionable King's Town of the nineteenth century. It is easy to consider these points at the distance of 15 or 20 years; harder to assess their effect when you are living through the changes themselves. To what amounted to a crisis of identity, Surrey responded in the best possible way.

They began the 1971 season in fine form, beating Lancashire and, as it transpired, most importantly, Warwickshire in two of their first three matches. In the early stages of the season, they were always in a challenging position, but by the first week in August, they had begun to fall apart, and it seemed that a familiar pattern was emerging.

On 10 August, Surrey stood seventh in the table with six wins and two defeats in 17 matches. They were 37 points behind Warwickshire at the top of the table, but they had two games in hand. No one saw them as potential Champions. On Saturday, 14 August, they began their three-day match with Middlesex at Lord's. Brearley declared at 242 for seven, and Stewart declared twelve runs in arrears, having settled for the three batting points that they had earned. In 1971, the system in operation gave one point for each 25 runs scored after 150 within the space of 85 overs and one point for each two wickets taken in the same period. Batting again, Middlesex were routed by Pocock and Arnold, and Surrey won by five wickets. A week later, with Arnold taking nine wickets in the match, Surrey crushed Northamptonshire in two days at Kettering, and followed this with an innings victory over Yorkshire in Arnold Long's benefit match.

Surrey needed all the bonus points they could get, and they got nine. The basis of their innings came in a second-wicket stand of 130 between Stewart and Roope, and Roope played a magnificent innings of 171, which was the highest of his career. Roope was a lovely player to watch when in full flow, his driving free and eloquent. Like many Surrey players, he was a fine footballer, and this, no doubt, contributed to his outstanding fielding. He became a close-to-the-wicket catcher on a par with the Locks and Surridges of the 1950s. Tim Lamb, of Middlesex and Northamptonshire and later an astute administrator with Middlesex and TCCB, once proffered the remark that he had wished he had spent all his career bowling with Roope at slip or close in on the leg side.

Roope's 171 helped Surrey to 381 against Yorkshire, who were twice bowled out by Intikhab and Pocock. Intikhab had joined the side late, for he had been captaining the Pakistan side against England, but Chris Waller, slow left-arm, had served Surrey well in the earlier part of the year.

Derbyshire proved stiffer opposition than Yorkshire, and Surrey were reeling at 70 for five before being rescued by a most impressive innings of 164, the highest of his career, by Stewart Storey. Since doing the 'double' in 1966, Storey had had a somewhat fluctuating career, and he was now more of a bits and pieces player than a full-fledged all-rounder, for his medium pace was used less in the first-class game than it had been although, of course, he was invaluable as an all-rounder in the one-day game. His 164 against Derbyshire came at a time when it was needed most, for Edrich was absent with a back injury, and Surrey needed all the runs they could muster. Derbyshire were eventually left with the task of scoring 205 in 165 minutes to win the match. They were never in with a chance. Willis, bowling very quickly, took two wickets in his second over, and Pocock and Intikhab came into the attack to destroy the lower order and give Surrey victory by 40 runs with ten minutes to spare.

This was Surrey's fifth win in succession, for Gloucestershire had been beaten at Bristol just before the triumph over Yorkshire, and they now stood second in the Championship. Warwickshire had finished their programme and had nine victories and 255 points. Surrey already had eleven victories so that they needed only to draw level on points with Warwickshire to snatch the title. With two matches to play, they had 244 points, which was seven more than Kent had gained in winning the Championship the previous year.

The first of Surrey's two remaining games was against Glamorgan at The Oval. Glamorgan, runners-up in 1970, had plummeted in 1971, but they were never easy opposition. Stewart gave his side the ideal start with a chanceless century on the first day, and Dudley Owen-Thomas, an attractive and aggressive batsman, scored well towards the close, but the pitch was sluggish, and Surrey managed only three batting points. On the second day, Intikhab and Pocock troubled all the Glamorgan batsmen and bowled their side to an 82-run lead. Edrich and Roope added 107 in brisk time so that Stewart was able to declare and give his bowlers five hours in which to bowl out Glamorgan, who were set a target of 287.

For much of the time, Glamorgan looked likely winners. They were 186 for three, and Majid Khan and Roy Fredericks had made their task look a light one, but the Surrey bowlers persevered and when the ninth wicket went down Glamorgan were 44 runs short of their target. There was still 80 minutes to play, but Roger Davis, back in the side after a terrible injury earlier in the year when he was hit on the head fielding at short leg, and Lawrence Williams held out as eight Surrey fieldsmen clustered round the bat watched by an excited but modest crowd.

The failure to beat Glamorgan was a disappointment, for it left Surrey still six points short of the Championship with one game to play in uncertain weather. Happily the sun shone at Southampton, and Edrich and Stewart gave Surrey a rollicking start with a partnership of 109. Roope, too, played well, but the middle order fell apart. Surrey were 240 for three and going well, but they crashed to 269 all out, so missing a fifth bonus point by six runs at a time when they had hopes of gaining six points. One of the big disasters came when Pocock ran out John Edrich who had made 113 and on whom, naturally enough, hopes rested for the fifth and sixth points. As it was, Surrey did not even last the 85 overs.

They spent a worrying weekend, and when the game resumed the worries were not eased. Hampshire had a formidable batting line-up – Barry Richards, Gordon Greenidge, David Turner, Roy Marshall, Richard Gilliatt, Peter Sainsbury and Trevor Jesty being the first seven. Arnold and Willis removed the first two for one run, but Turner and Marshall added 101 before Turner was bowled by Willis.

There seemed, as Pat Pocock expressed years later in his autobiography:

> ... an agonising wait, and then Intikhab flicked the edge of Richard Gilliatt's bat, Arnold Long held the catch at the wicket and as I ran in from fine leg I knew that this was the most marvellous moment I would ever know in county cricket. Micky's wife, Sheila, ran on to embrace him. Stuart Surridge, then the chairman of cricket, strode on to the field to congratulate the entire side.

The players drank champagne on the field, and Surrey had come in from the cold. It was an outstanding success against considerable odds, not least of which was the placid Oval pitch. At the beginning of the season, Geoffrey Howard had said that groundsman Ted Warn was striving to make faster wickets, but none could yet be sure of the outcome of his endeavours, and, in 1971, The Oval wickets proved to be as slow as ever. Evidence of this is seen in the figures of Geoff Arnold, who took 83 wickets in the season, less than a third of them at The Oval.

The quality of Stewart's achievement was that he welded together a side of disparate personalities into a competitive unit. Arnold and Roope were men who needed constant encouragement, surprising in two such dedicated and talented cricketers, while Younis needed a firm hand. He was a glorious batsman, and one remembers watching him late in his career when playing for Glamorgan against Sussex when he was so technically and stylistically superior to the rest on view that it was almost an embarrassment, but he was a man with a fatal flaw. Initially, it seemed an arrogance which could be harnessed into displays of contemptuous ease when batting, but later it manifested itself in acts of naive misjudgement, like betting against his own side when at Worcestershire, which led him to part company with three counties in less than happy circumstances.

The committee met Micky Stewart at Southampton and asked him to reconsider his decision to resign and to remain as captain. He considered the position for two months and then agreed on the understanding that the reasons for disquiet that he had forwarded should be investigated.

Bob Willis could not be persuaded to change his mind, and he left the County to join Warwickshire. He had been flown out to Australia as a replacement for Derbyshire's Ward in 1970–71 and had played Test cricket without being a capped county player. He bowled very fast, and he was wild in line and length, and Surrey could not agree to ensuring him a regular first-team place against the competition of such superb professionals as Arnold, Jackman and Storey. Both England and Surrey were right. England selectors recognised him as a great Test fast bowler; Surrey had doubts about his strength and stamina for continuous county cricket. He did become one of the greatest of Test match fast bowlers; his county record was less impressive.

Perhaps it was a mistake that Stewart, 'the epitome of the English professional', allowed himself to be persuaded to lead the side for one more year, for it was hard to sustain the momentum that had taken Surrey to the title at a time when cricket was in a state of flux. To accommodate the new Benson and Hedges Cup, the Championship was reduced to 20 matches in 1972, and as Surrey did not win a Championship match until they beat Hampshire at Guildford on 14 July, their 11th encounter, their final position of 12th came as no surprise.

Jackman, Intikhab and Pocock carried the bowling, for Arnold had hamstring trouble. Edrich could play in only 11 matches because of Test calls, and of the other batsmen, only Roope and Younis hit reliable form, although Lewis was an able deputy for Edwards, once seen as unlucky not to be opening for England, now showing something of a decline.

When he came down from Cambridge University Dudley Owen-Thomas batted with considerable panache, and he was named as Young Cricketer of the Year, but some rather exaggerated claims were made for him. One writer considered that, with his uncoached background and his complete lack of nerves, he was Bradmanesque and should be considered for England, but his brief career was not to blossom to quite that extent. Interestingly, Surrey gave debuts to two young players, Alan Butcher and New Zealander Geoff Howarth. Butcher was played primarily as a left-arm medium-pace bowler, and it was his six for 48 in the first innings against Hampshire at Guildford that set up Surrey's first victory. Ironically, it was to remain the best bowling performance of a career that was to be spent mostly in the plundering of runs.

The most memorable match of a season in which Surrey failed to make progress in any of the four competitions was at Eastbourne. Chasing a target of 205 in 135 minutes, Sussex seemed well set for victory at 187 for one with three overs remaining. Pocock then began one of the most remarkable bowling spells in cricket history. He bowled Gordon Greenidge with the first ball of what was his 15th over, having taken none for 58 in his first 14. Michael Buss played the second ball, but was bowled by the third. Jim Parks took two off the fourth ball, failed to score off the fifth and was caught and bowled off the sixth. The score was 189 for four so that Sussex needed 16 off the last two overs.

Prideaux and Griffith took eleven runs off the penultimate over of the match, bowled by Jackman, so that five were needed off Pocock's last over. The off-spinner had Prideaux caught by Jackman with his first ball, Griffith caught by Lewis with the next and Morley stumped by Long with the third to make him the third Surrey bowler to take four wickets in four balls. Spencer took a single off the fourth ball of the over, but Pocock bowled Tony Buss with the fifth. This meant that Joshi had to hit the last ball for four to win the match. He took a wild swipe and was run out going for a second run.

There were several records in this remarkable achievement. Sussex had lost five wickets in one over. Pocock had taken a world record six wickets in nine balls, seven wickets in eleven balls and five wickets in six balls, which equalled the world record. The last over had taken ten minutes to bowl, and Sussex, on the brink of victory, had lost eight wickets for 15 runs in 18 balls and drawn. Pocock's final analysis, 16-1-67-7, hid those remarkable final overs which read:

W . W2 . W
W W W1 W1

It was sad that Stewart should end on a low note. Cheerful, honest, reliable and unquenchably enthusiastic, he had led Surrey with great integrity through a most difficult period which had witnessed all the major changes in the modern game. He had tasted success in the great side of the 1950s, and he knew the discipline and endeavour that was needed to produce a Championship-winning team. He reached the pinnacle in 1971 after nine years of hard work, and he could never call on the wealth of talent that had been available to Surridge and May. His days with Surrey were far from over, for he was to return within a decade to manage the County and to bring them further benefit with his wisdom, experience and total professionalism.

MODERN TIMES

JOHN EDRICH WAS APPOINTED CAPTAIN of Surrey in succession to Micky Stewart. In the circumstances, it was the only logical appointment. He was 36 years old, the senior professional and had first played for Surrey 15 years earlier. Edrich was a genuinely great player with 83 first-class centuries to his credit, and 59 England caps, yet the very qualities that made him an outstanding Test opening batsman with an average of 43.54 were not necessarily those that would equip him to lead a county side.

He was a chunky, strong left-hander whose success was founded on unwavering concentration, self-discipline and a phlegmatic temperament. Like the legendary Herbert Sutcliffe, he revealed no emotion if struck or beaten by a ball. He would simply take up his stance again and quite likely nudge the next delivery for four as if nothing had happened. His innings did not always live in the memory as being full of beautifully executed shots, but they have endured in the record books, and many a lost cause was won because of John Edrich.

The problem was that the characteristics of his batting demanded almost a retreat into himself so that he remained undistracted by all else around him, which is why he was able to accumulate so many runs, but this necessary remoteness was not conducive to good leadership. Boycott was another to find this, but it should be emphasised that in no way was Edrich egocentric.

At the beginning, things did not go well. Once again Surrey were eliminated in the zonal round of the Benson and Hedges Cup. They lost their first match in the Gillette Cup, and the John Player League again proved to be a competition in which Surrey could find no successful formula.

The County Championship programme began disastrously. Three of the first nine games were lost; the other six drawn. On 10 July, Surrey beat Warwickshire at The Oval to record their first win, and this moved them up to ninth in the table. The game included a sparkling century by John Jameson for Warwickshire, two fine innings from Younis, and a sheet-anchor 100 from Edrich as well as some excellent bowling by Jackman and the under-rated Waller.

In the next match, Yorkshire were totally humiliated at The Oval. Jackman took seven for 36 as they were bowled out for 60, and Pocock six for 11 when they were bowled out for 43 in their second innings. Younis hit his second century in successive matches, and Surrey won by an innings. A third win came at Chesterfield.

Two draws were followed by six wins in the last six matches. The second of the two draws, with Middlesex at Lord's, took Surrey to sixth place, 49 points behind the leaders, Hampshire. It was too big a leeway to make up, but Surrey's dramatic finish took them into second place, 31 points behind the Champions.

Edrich could have every cause for satisfaction in his first season as captain, but, as Pocock revealed some years later, many of the players were not totally satisfied and asked that Edrich should be relieved of the captaincy, not out of any dislike for him, but because they felt that he was not the right man for the job. The committee chose to ignore their application. This decision caused no rift as the players had indicated at the outset that they would support whoever the County chose as captain, although they felt that their communication with Edrich was not what it should be. Pocock felt, for the reasons outlined earlier in this chapter, that Edrich was unable to give the job the total concentration that it needed. Edrich believed that he could do the job and responded in the way that he did when just beaten by a ball that had shaved the off stump. He set about the next task.

That was not easy because, in 1974, Edrich missed more than half the Championship matches as did, for various reasons, Intikhab and Arnold. On top of this, to the bewilderment of many, Chris Waller could not be persuaded to stay, and moved to Sussex. With Intikhab absent so much, he would have been invaluable, for, although Roope bowled more, the attack was almost entirely in the hands of Pocock, Jackman, wonderfully exciting in all that he did, and Arnold.

Storey was used sparingly, but he batted as well as anyone and was the only man in the side to hit two Championship centuries. Surprisingly, and perhaps as a result of the pre-season unrest, he retired at the end of the season, only to reappear with Sussex and Arnold Long left a couple of years later. Edwards, too, who had lost his form suddenly and unexpectedly, retired, and if he never did make the England side as was once anticipated he left a memory of some cultured batting.

The Championship and the John Player League were soon out of reach, but the Gillette Cup held promise. Victory over Lincolnshire was followed by a quarter-final tie against Somerset at Taunton. Put in to bat in humid conditions, Surrey batted vigorously. Edrich, Younis and Storey all batted well, and 254 for seven seemed to have assured them of success, but, before a capacity crowd of 10,000, Somerset were inspired by Denning's 112 and won with ten balls to spare. Their winning score, at the time, was the highest ever made in the competition by a side batting second.

This left the Benson and Hedges Cup, which had not been a happy competition for Surrey. Neither did it seem that it would be again when Kent won by 14 runs at Canterbury in spite of a Younis century. An expected win over Cambridge University was followed by a fine win over Essex at The Oval, and when Sussex were trounced at Hove Surrey found themselves in the quarter-finals for the first time.

Their opponents, at The Oval, were Yorkshire. Geoff Howarth was the backbone of the Surrey innings, and his 80 won him the Gold Award, but, decisively, Jackman bowled Boycott in the fourth over and captured three more wickets as Surrey won by 24 runs.

The semi-final took Surrey to Old Trafford where, on a difficult pitch in uncertain conditions, John Edrich batted throughout the morning session to defy Lancashire after Edwards had gone early. Jackman, who had an impressive year with the bat, and was always willing to hit the ball, scored freely towards the end of the innings, and Surrey reached a commendable, if not invincible, 193 for eight. Barry Wood began at a furious rate, but Butcher's 11 overs cost only 11 runs and brought him the wickets of David Lloyd, Pilling and Hayes. This was a match-winning performance, and Roope, Storey and Pocock maintained the pressure for Surrey to win with remarkable ease by 63 runs. Lancashire lost their last six wickets for 37 runs.

In the third Benson and Hedges Cup Final, Surrey found themselves opposed to Leicestershire, the first winners of the trophy. Edrich won the toss and elected to bat. Lonsdale Skinner, preferred to the out-of-form Edwards, soon fell to Higgs, but Edrich batted with caution to ensure that there was no further breakthrough, and Howarth batted with confidence. It was Howarth who played the forcing shots, but Booth, fast-medium, made the ball lift awkwardly on occasions and had the New Zealander caught behind at 36.

Edrich still played the anchor role as Younis batted with some fluency for the highest score of the day. Shortly before lunch he mistimed a ball from Illingworth and was caught by Dudleston.

Roope was out of touch, and Edrich had scored only 18 in the first 24 overs, but his caution was necessary and eventually decisive. When he was out for 40 in the 36th over the Surrey innings trembled. It might well have collapsed completely had Booth not dropped Jackman at mid-off in the 44th over. Jackman had scored six at the time. He was to hit 30 more furious runs which, in the context of the match, was a vast amount. Jackman was last out, but in the penultimate over Higgs did the hat-trick when he dismissed Butcher, Pocock and Long with successive deliveries. Higgs finished with four for 10 and four of his quota of overs unused, something on which Leicestershire might have reflected later.

Defending a moderate total, Surrey needed an early strike and this was provided by Arnold who had Dudleston lbw with the first ball of the innings. Steele and Norman added 46 in 19 overs to give the Leicestershire challenge a substantial base, but after Norman was lbw to Roope a collapse ensued, and four wickets fell for 19 runs.

Steele was run out in an horrendous mix-up which saw him and Davison at the same end, and four runs later, Tolchard fell to Roope. Much was expected of Davison, and he drove Arnold majestically through the covers. Edrich reinforced the off-side field by moving Howarth into cover, and next ball Davison slashed the ball chest high into Howarth's hands.

Butcher had bowled a tight spell, and he now gave way to Pocock who bowled with a demanding accuracy that frustrated Leicestershire. The loss of four quick wickets had sapped their courage, and neither Balderstone nor the limping Illingworth could take too many chances with Pocock. Balderstone was bowled by Pocock, who had McKenzie very well stumped down the leg side next ball. Illingworth heaved at Arnold and was bowled, and the match ended when Booth lofted to cover, but Surrey had long taken a grip on the game by then.

The Gold Award was given by adjudicator Freddie Brown to John Edrich in recognition of both his solid innings and his tight field settings. It must be remembered that the rule stipulating that four fielders must be inside the circle was not in operation at this time. There were those in the press in July and August 1974, who were advocating Edrich as captain of England.

The triumph at Lord's was joyful not only for the players but for all those associated with the Club, Geoffrey Howard in particular. He had been assistant secretary at The Oval from 1947 to 1949 when he had moved to Lancashire. He had returned to The Oval as secretary in 1965, and he retired at the end of 1974. He was a most accomplished secretary, and a man of great dignity and charm. Always a keen follower of the fortunes of Surrey, he was named as president for 1989.

Lt-Col W. H. Sillitoe was named as Howard's successor. Having been concerned with security in Northern Ireland, he could have expected some respite from that onerous duty when he arrived at The Oval, but things did not go as smoothly as he might have wished. The Benson and Hedges Cup victory, the prize money from which was eaten into by fines for slow over-rate, did not bring the new dawn that had been anticipated. The Club's financial position was far from happy. There was a running sore relating to plans to redevelop The Oval which had first been mooted in 1966. There were constant delays in granting planning permission, and these frustrations forced the committee to reconsider their whole strategy. The initial redevelopment was limited to a modest replacement of old seating, and the desire to modernise the ground and bring it in line with contemporary needs and comforts dragged into another decade.

On the playing side, fortunes fluctuated. In 1975, interest in the one-day tournaments quickly evaporated, and the first weeks of the County Championship offered equally cold comfort. By mid-August,

BENSON AND HEDGES CUP FINAL
SURREY *v* LEICESTERSHIRE

Played at Lord's, 20 July 1974

SURREY WON BY 27 RUNS

SURREY

*J. H. Edrich	c and b Steele	40
L. E. Skinner	lbw b Higgs	0
G. P. Howarth	c Tolchard b Booth	22
Younis Ahmed	c Dudleston b Illingworth	43
G. R. J. Roope	b McKenzie	13
S. J. Storey	lbw b Illingworth	2
R. D. Jackman	c Tolchard b McKenzie	36
A. R. Butcher	c Tolchard b Higgs	7
P. I. Pocock	b Higgs	0
†A. Long	c Tolchard b Higgs	0
G. G. Arnold	not out	0
Extras	lb 5, nb 2	7
Total	(54.1 overs)	170

Fall: 1-4, 2-36, 3-99, 4-111, 5-118, 6-137, 7-168, 8-168, 9-168

BOWLING	O	M	R	W
McKenzie	10.1	0	31	2
Higgs	7	2	10	4
Booth	8	1	30	1
McVicker	8	1	25	0
Illingworth	11	0	36	2
Steele	10	0	31	1

LEICESTERSHIRE

B. Dudleston	lbw b Arnold	0
J. F. Steele	run out	18
M. E. J. C. Norman	lbw b Roope	24
B. F. Davison	c Howarth b Arnold	13
†R. W. Tolchard	lbw b Roope	0
J. C. Balderstone	b Pocock	32
*R. Illingworth	b Arnold	23
N. M. McVicker	c Edrich b Pocock	10
G. D. McKenzie	st Long b Pocock	0
P. Booth	c Arnold b Jackman	5
K. Higgs	not out	8
Extras	b 1, lb 5, nb 4	10
Total	(54 overs)	143

Fall: 1-0, 2-46, 3-46, 4-50, 5-65, 6-113, 7-129, 8-129, 9-131

BOWLING	O	M	R	W
Arnold	10	4	20	3
Jackman	11	1	34	1
Roope	11	2	30	2
Butcher	11	1	23	0
Pocock	11	1	26	3

Umpires: W. E. Alley and H. D. Bird

*Captain; †Wicket-keeper

a run of three successive victories took Surrey into the top three, but defeat at Bristol ended dreams of grandeur and prize money, and sixth place was not an unfair reflection of the side's performance.

In a fine summer, the four main bowlers worked hard, and Butcher became a batsman who bowled rather than the reverse. He was moved up to open the innings with Aworth, just down from Cambridge. Chris Aworth, like Butcher and Edrich a left-hander, began his Surrey career in sensational manner, hitting 115 against Middlesex at The Oval when deputising for Edrich in July. It was to be his only century for the County, and, like Owen-Thomas, he faded from the scene after a couple of seasons despite showing so much initial promise. Edrich dropped down the order to number three and still scored heavily, as did Roope and Younis, and, on occasions, Intikhab.

One of the strangest decisions was to select Lonsdale Skinner as wicket-keeper ahead of Arnold Long, who moved to Sussex at the end of the season. Long was 35 years old and still a fine keeper while his left-handed batting had become increasingly useful. Skinner had potential as a batsman which was never fully realised, but his wicket-keeping was neither as efficient nor as consistent as one would have hoped for. The departure of Long, like that of Knight, began to cast doubts on what was happening at The Oval as Long began to prosper at Sussex.

This was a gloomy time at The Oval, and results on the field began to mirror events off it so that Harold Abel could write in *Wisden* that few were sorry to see the Hobbs Gates close for the last time on the 1976 season. Edrich, who had taken a terrible battering from the West Indian fast bowlers in a courageous Test farewell, Howarth, who found his most elegant touch, Younis, Roope and Butcher all scored their runs. Jackman, Pocock and Arnold, when fit, took their wickets, but an appearance in the semi-final of the Benson and Hedges Cup, where they lost narrowly to Kent, was the best that could be shown for an unhappy season.

Jackman, Baker and Skinner were injured in a car accident when travelling from Manchester to Worcester for a Sunday League game. Arnold went down first with Achilles tendon trouble and then with a hamstring injury. Edrich pulled a leg muscle as he went for the run which gave him his 99th first-class century, against Middlesex at The Oval on 1 September. Next day, Middlesex celebrated winning the Championship. The pendulum of power in London had swung firmly to the north.

These mishaps seemed only to emphasise the predicament in which the Club now found itself. The hopes of making The Oval into a ground with amenities fitting for its status as a Test centre and into a place where local inhabitants could enjoy their leisure were finally dashed. Although agreement had seemed close in 1975, the procrastinations of the GLC, the local authority and the Duchy of Cornwall had meant that the variety of schemes were no longer economically viable. Harold Abel wrote:

> The outcome meant that the Surrey Club were left with the responsibility of improving a ground of about nine and a half acres, including a square measuring 88 yards across and on which 93 days cricket were played in 1976. Every inch belonged to the Duchy of Cornwall, so nothing was saleable, and there was never any chance that a county club by its normal sources of income could even start to think about alterations on the scale of those envisaged by the developers. They entailed an estimated £7 million.

There was no lightening of the gloom. Fred Titmus, formerly of Middlesex, was appointed coach. This was a break with tradition, for men like Morice Bird, 'Razor' Smith, Alan Peach, Andrew Sandham and Arthur McIntyre, Surrey men, had formerly held the post, and now the County had crossed the river and engaged one of the old enemy. Titmus was contracted for three years, 1977–1979, but he served only two years of his term before resigning. Titmus was with Surrey at what was probably the most difficult time in the Club's history, and his appointment was never really a success, but, in his two years with the County, he unearthed Jack Richards, Andy Needham, David Thomas and Monte Lynch, and, shortly before his departure, signed Sylvester Clarke.

Titmus was not the only one to leave, for secretary Sillitoe resigned in 1977, which was John Edrich's last year as captain, and Geoff Arnold's last as a Surrey player before moving across to Sussex.

'Horse', as Arnold became nick-named because of his initials, had been a tireless worker in spite of his constant trouble with injuries. He could swing and cut the ball viciously and was as dangerous as any new-ball bowler in England. Strongly built, he bowled closer to fast-medium than fast and would have earned many more wickets had he not had to bowl at The Oval in the 1970s. As it was, he took well over 1,000 wickets in his career, and claimed 115 in 34 Tests. He had a considerable impact on Sussex and, with Long, helped to revive their fortunes. This put further pressure on Surrey as Selvey, who had played for Surrey before going up to university, and Emburey, who had played for Surrey Young Cricketers, thrived for Middlesex, and other players rejected by the County prospered elsewhere.

In the midst of the dissension and controversy and the criticism that was being levelled at the standard of cricket that Surrey were providing, and the paucity of entertainment, John Edrich hit his 100th hundred. It came against Derbyshire at The Oval on 12 July 1977, when, although the game was destined to be drawn, Eddie Barlow agreed to play on. At 5.32 pm, Edrich tucked Alan Hill away for four to equal the achievement of Hayward, Hobbs and Sandham. Few people were watching, and it had nothing of the drama that had attended Hobbs's milestone, but nothing should detract from the feat, which had come after years of resolution, utmost concentration and exemplary courage. Edrich was to play one more season after he had resigned the captaincy, and then leave the game quietly and with dignity while still a very good player.

Ian Scott-Browne succeeded Sillitoe as secretary, and Roger Knight, after his travels to Gloucestershire and Sussex, returned to the county of his birth to take over as captain. It would be difficult to imagine a more unpropitious time at which to take on such a job.

Knight's first season as captain, 1978, is remembered with shudders of horror. It represents the nadir of Surrey's fortunes. They finished second from bottom in the County Championship, the lowest position in their history, and made no impact whatsoever on the three one-day competitions. Younis left the Club, and there was considerable uncertainty over the future of other players. David Smith had been sacked the previous September, but was re-engaged. Andy Mack, a tall left-arm pace bowler, went off to Glamorgan. Medium-pace bowler Ray Baker was not re-engaged, but Butcher, dropped for a time, returned to show his best form, and the reprieved Smith and Lynch hit their maiden first-class hundreds. These, like the bowling of Pocock, Intikhab and Jackman, were sparks in the darkness. The Club was in the throes of radical change.

Derek Newton succeeded Subba Row as chairman. Newton was able to bring a shrewd business acumen to the job and free Raman Subba Row to concentrate on cricketing matters. Surridge has always admired Subba Row's determined, sharp and professional approach to matters. 'I don't always agree with him, but he gets things done. He's professional, and he's efficient.'

Derek Newton brought with him a dedication to Surrey cricket, business experience at the highest level with C. E. Heath, the international insurance brokers, and the ability to listen, a gift given to too few in the latter part of the twentieth century. Pocock, as a senior professional, approached Newton when Titmus resigned and asked him to bring Micky Stewart back to The Oval as manager.

Stewart was marketing manager of a sports company, but his heart was with cricket and, in particular, with Surrey, who had been his life. Pocock believed that Stewart's appointment was necessary because attitudes at Surrey had grown lax, even irresponsible, and the outlook was bleak unless the playing side of the Club could be revitalised. There was a sense, too, that more expertise was needed on the business side, particularly in the selling of tickets for Test matches and other notable events. Anne Bickerstaff was brought in as office manager, and later on as Assistant to the Secretary. She had spent her life in the theatre, stage managing such West End successes as *Oh Calcutta!* and dealing with all financial aspects of a big production. She was brought to The Oval to put the sale of tickets on a proper foundation. What she found on the playing side, initially, disturbed her, for the players are always any club's main asset.

She had come from a profession where in order to survive ambition is everything; what she found at The Oval was complacency. Second-team players seemed content to remain second-team players; first-team players were going through the motions with seemingly little fun or joy in what they did. Her findings echoed Pocock's view that 'the attitude of many first-team players was irresponsible; the second-team players were even worse'.

Under Ian Scott-Browne's guidance, Anne Bickerstaff organised The Oval ticket office to make it the most efficient in cricket, and Ian worked away from first thing in the morning and made himself readily available to members at all times. They were supported by a committee totally aware of the economic necessities of the time, sensitive to marketing and sales, experienced in business and management and concerned for players and spectators.

There are still great debates as to whether or not a manager of a county cricket club is either necessary or advisable; for Surrey in 1979 and for the years immediately after, Micky Stewart was essential. In no way is this a slight on Roger Knight, who had quickly proved himself to be a most capable leader and, as befits a vigorous Christian, strong in resolve. But Knight needed the backing of a dedicated and seasoned professional who could link the traditions of Surrey's past to the needs of the present and future. Stewart was acutely aware that the attitudes to all sport had changed considerably since the days when he was both a footballer and a cricketer. In those long-remembered days of the 1950s, crowds packed into grounds to catch a glimpse of Compton or Hutton or May; the result to many mattered little, for there was only one competition to win, and that was almost exclusively in the hands of Surrey or Yorkshire. People paid to watch cricket. By the 1980s, people paid to watch their side win, and when a side failed to win a trophy the people stopped paying to watch any more. This was the harsh reality of a materialistic society – and Stewart was completely aware of it.

Before the start of the 1979 season, Surrey took a three-week trip to the Far East. This helped to bring the side together, and for Stewart to form an assessment of the players. He set them targets; to reach the knock-out stages of the Benson and Hedges Cup and to finish in the first six of the County Championship. He laid down other aims:

Roger Knight played first for Surrey in 1968, and after spells with Gloucestershire and Sussex in the 1970s returned to captain the side from 1978 to 1983. (George Herringshaw)

'Returning to The Oval, it was very easy to identify the first problem that existed among the majority of the Surrey players. They had been starved of success and were certainly not enjoying playing for Surrey. Therefore the first emphasis of the policy I laid down to the players was:

1. *enjoyment* – in playing the game
2. *pride* – in the club and individual performance
3. *responsibility* – of producing acceptable individual and team results
4. *good image* – on and off the field in dress and conduct
5. *to be a winner* – this habit is essential these days.'

283

Stewart engaged David Gibson as assistant coach, and each player's technique, however august the individual, was closely scrutinised and faults worked upon. Stewart saw this as the first part of his job, 'to begin to groom and develop the professional playing staff, the shop window of Surrey cricket, so that the game was played to the necessary standards, standards acceptable to our supporters'. The second part of his job he saw as developing a structure of cricket throughout the county so that young players from school and clubs would be recognised and encouraged. In this, he was aided by his liaison with Mike Verney of the Surrey Schools' Cricket Association, a man who did an immense amount for schools' cricket, in Surrey and the country as a whole.

A further aid came from the fact that Harry Brind was now groundsman at The Oval and wickets were once more fast and true. Like Bert Lock, Harry Brind was to take The Oval wickets to a standard envied by all others and, again, like Bert Lock, he was to be called upon by those who govern the game to give assistance and advice to others.

Stewart's strength was that he did not see cricket in a vacuum. His

Harry Brind, groundsman supreme, and Lucy, The Oval cat, inspect the Kiwi mascot.

position as UK Sales Manager for Slazengers, where he controlled a large sales force and was responsible for millions of pounds, had made him realise that the playing performance of a county club had to be good otherwise there was no product to market, and that spelled disaster, for finance was any club's greatest problem:

> The situation was very different to the first-class game to which I was introduced in the 1950s when the Club put a strict limit on membership and was proud to say it had a waiting list of four figures.

If one has personalised these views as being those of Micky Stewart, it is because it was his job to transmit them to the players. They were, in fact, the philosophy of the Club, expounded by chairman Derek Newton and his committee, uppermost in the minds of Subba Row and the cricket committee, and publicised by presidents like Stuart Surridge, Brigadier Rimbault, Sir George Edwards, Alf Gover and other dedicated and energetic men.

Surrey cricket was electrified. Essex ran away with the Championship in a wet summer, and there was never any hope of catching them, so other counties jostled for second place. Surrey held that position in the closing weeks of the season, but they had the misfortune to meet Essex in the match after that county had won the title. The Chelmsford ground was packed as the Essex supporters came to acclaim their heroes. Geoff Howarth hit a delightful 100, but Surrey trailed by 13 runs on the first innings. Jackman and Wilson bowled Essex out for 101 in their second innings, but Lever and Phillip, of whom Surrey were to learn more later, bowled out Surrey for 99, and Essex won by 15 runs. This defeat condemned Surrey to third place, but after the horrors of the previous season this was paradise, indeed.

Essex figured largely in Surrey's season. The County made little progress in the Gillette Cup or the John Player League, but the Benson and Hedges Cup saw them fulfil the target Stewart had set them. Recovering from the loss of three wickets for 48, Surrey reached 205 for four against Northants at Northampton, thanks largely to a fine innings of 92 not out by Roger Knight. The game dragged into a third day, and Surrey eventually won by five runs. Combined Universities were beaten with some ease, and Essex were overcome by seven runs with five balls to spare. The defeat by Sussex did not matter, for Surrey had already qualified for the quarter-final.

The draw took them to Worcester, where Younis hit 107 in his first appearance against his old county, but Butcher, Lynch, Howarth and Knight all scored consistently and Surrey reached their target of 200 with five overs to spare and for the loss of only three wickets. The semi-final at Derby was a much closer affair.

This match revealed the positive qualities of Knight's leadership and the new-found spirit of Surrey cricket. Batting first on a slow pitch, Surrey were given a good start by Butcher and Lynch, who put on 52. Butcher was out hooking, and Howarth was caught at slip. Knight lobbed a gentle catch to Hendrick at mid-on, and Roope drove at Miller to be spectacularly caught by Tunnicliffe diving to his right. Lynch was caught behind one short of his 50, Jackman was run out, and when Clarke was lbw to Miller Surrey were 108 for seven, and Lord's seemed but a mirage.

David Smith and Jack Richards struck out purposefully to add 50, but Surrey's 166 for eight hardly looked a match-winning score. Both Derbyshire openers were soon out to the tall and fast Hugh Wilson, but Peter Kirsten took complete command in an innings of 70, and with 20 overs remaining, Derbyshire were 114 for two and seemingly cruising to victory.

All through this period Knight had maintained attacking fields with three men clustered round the bat, and the pressure began to tell on the batsmen. Kirsten's award-winning innings ended when he snicked Jackman to Richards. Wilson bowled Steele, and Jackman bowled Borrington. Then Sylvester Clarke took over.

This was his first season with Surrey. He had arrived from Barbados, a little-known fast bowler with 22 first-class matches and 78 wickets behind him, but by the end of that first season with Surrey he had become the most feared bowler in England. He has the reputation ten years later. He tends to fit the description of a once-famous film star: 'Mean, Moody and Magnificent'. He missed half the first season with a leg injury, but he was just what Surrey had needed. He bowled out his eleven overs against Derbyshire and sent back Miller, Barnett and Walters before limping off the field by which time Derbyshire were 141 for eight.

Taylor and Tunnicliffe tried to squeeze out runs against a fielding side that had never lost faith in itself and a captain who had attacked throughout the innings. Roope was used as the sixth bowler and bowled Tunnicliffe, 157 for nine. Derbyshire now needed ten runs to win, and Roger Knight took on the responsibility of bowling himself for the final stages. Hendrick scored three and then went for a big hit off Knight that would have levelled the scores had he connected, but he did not and was bowled. The Surrey players leaped in the air in undisguised delight. This had been a noble victory.

There were many things stacked against Surrey in the final, not the least of which was Sylvester Clarke's inability to play because of his leg injury. The young left-arm bowler David Thomas was also unfit, Wilson and Knight had been injured, and Jackman played under a severe handicap. Sentiment and the neutral observer was also very

Sylvester Clarke, 'Mean, Moody and Magnificent.' (David Munden)

much on the side of Essex, who had never won a trophy and who were appearing in a Lord's final for the first time.

Knight won the toss and asked Essex to bat first. Gooch and Denness gave them a bright start, and, later, Gooch and McEwan played champagne cricket. Jackman was obviously struggling, and Pocock had not been in the best of form, and both bowlers suffered. Hugh Wilson took four wickets, but his inexperience showed, and Knight and Intikhab, of the Surrey bowlers, exerted most restraint on the Essex batsmen. Essex's score of 290 for six was the highest ever made in a Benson and Hedges Final.

That Surrey were beaten by only 35 runs was a credit to their undying spirit and courage. Howarth and Knight batted splendidly,

287

adding 91 at a rate which compared favourably to that of Gooch and McEwan, but Roope was left high and dry at the end of an outstanding match.

The resurgence in Surrey cricket was obvious from the zest with which the players approached the game after the arrival of Stewart. Experienced players had a new spring in their step; new players, like Clinton, who had joined the side from Kent, were quick to settle. The form of 1979 proved to be no false dawn, for the following season saw the side finish fifth in the John Player League, so equalling their highest position, reach the quarter-final of the Benson and Hedges Cup, where they again bowed the knee to Essex to end as beaten Lord's finalists for the second year in succession. This time they were runners up in the last 60-over knock-out competition to be sponsored by Gillette. Their run to the final was not without incident and excitement.

The first round match against Northamptonshire at The Oval produced some of the finest bowling that the competition had ever known. Clarke bowled at a sizzling pace and was unerringly accurate. His first seven overs cost only two runs, and his final figures were one for 9 in 12 overs, seven of them maidens. His fire was of considerable assistance to Robin Jackman who dismissed Larkins and Williams with successive balls and tore the heart out of the Northants batting with the result that they lost the first six in their order for 28 runs, five of them to Jackman, who later dismissed Sharp and finished with six for 28. Facing a total of 141, Surrey were never in real danger and won by seven wickets with 17 overs to spare.

Jackman was again to the fore in the second-round match against Gloucestershire at The Oval, this time as an all-rounder. Butcher and Clinton gave Surrey a good start, but they fell within one run of each other, and from 71 for no wicket, the County slipped to 117 for five. Jackman helped Knight to add 66 in 13 overs, and Surrey eventually reached 200 off the final ball of the innings. The visitors lost half their side to Knight and Jackman for 66, but Procter and David Graveney effected a recovery, and it needed the return of Jackman to end resistance and give Surrey victory by eight runs.

The quarter-final at Chelmsford produced one of the most incredible matches ever seen in one-day cricket. Surrey began poorly and were 58 for three, but Clinton (who had settled and become a much freer batsman with a wider range of strokes at Surrey than he had ever shown at Kent) hit a resolute 58, and with David Smith playing with customary force for 37, the County reached 195 for seven in their 60 overs, a far better score than had looked possible earlier in the day. They seemed to take a grip on the game when, with Jackman menacing and marauding, they reduced Essex to 35 for four,

Gooch and McEwan among those back in the pavilion. Hardie and Keith Pont put on 65, and although Turner went quickly, Norbert Phillip hit fiercely, and he and Hardie took the score to 185. With five overs remaining, Essex needed only 11 runs to win and had four wickets standing, including those of Hardie and Phillip, who were in full flow. An Essex victory appeared to be a formality, but Hardie hit lazily to cover to give Jackman his fifth wicket, Phillip was insanely run out and Clarke wrecked Neil Smith's stumps. The last over began with Essex needing two to win, and the last pair at the wicket. David Thomas, who had conceded 55 runs in his previous ten overs was the bowler, and when Ray East took a single to level the scores the game still seemed to be with Essex for the taking. With two balls remaining, Lever pushed Thomas to mid-off and East came charging down the wicket. He was beaten by Knight's under-arm throw, and Surrey had won by virtue of having lost fewer wickets with the scores level.

The semi-final was less invigorating. It spread into two days, and Yorkshire were bowled out on a newly laid Oval pitch in poor light for 135. Ray Illingworth, their manager, was not pleased. Surrey won by four wickets with 12.1 overs to spare.

Following the drama of the earlier rounds, the final was something of an anti-climax. Surrey were put in to bat on a sluggish wicket and scored only 21 in the first eleven overs. A late assault by David Smith and Intikhab, in his penultimate season with Surrey, brought 62 in eight overs, but the final score of 201 was not too daunting for Middlesex, who won by seven wickets.

Middlesex's victory completed a double for them, for they had also taken the County Championship where, from mid-season, Surrey were their only real challengers. Each side won ten matches, but Surrey lost two to Middlesex's four, although Middlesex claimed 13 more bonus points than Surrey, which was the margin between the two sides. Nottinghamshire, in third place, were 67 points behind Surrey and won just six matches.

There was a storming finish to the season by Surrey who won five of their last six matches, and also beat the Australians, who were on a short tour for the Centenary Test.

Crucially, Middlesex beat Surrey by an innings at Lord's, and the return match at The Oval was ruined by rain. Just as crucial was the game at Derby on 16–19 August when the home side inflicted on Surrey the only defeat that they suffered in those last six matches. Knight won the toss and put Derbyshire in to bat. Jackman took five for 43, and the last six Derbyshire wickets went down for 12 runs. The Surrey batsmen fared even worse on an uncertain pitch and, bowled out for 129, they trailed by 65 on the first innings and eventually lost by 174 runs.

In spite of being a frustrating and serious defeat for Surrey, the match was memorable in that Jackman became the first bowler in England to reach 100 wickets for the season. Doshi of Warwickshire reached the target in the last game of the campaign. Jackman's figures for the year were 746.2 overs, 220 maidens, 1,864 runs, 121 wickets, average 15.40. On top of this one must consider his constant success in one-day cricket, where he took another 36 wickets, including one for England in the Prudential Trophy against Australia. He was everybody's bowler of the year, except the selectors, who did not pick him for a Test nor for England's tour of the West Indies although he was later sent there with unfortunate repercussions.

Robin Jackman had a lust for life that permeated his cricket. He enjoyed every ball he bowled, batted and fielded, and it showed. His father was a regular army officer, full of vitality, and Robin was born in Simla where his father was spending the last months of his army career. His uncle, on his mother's side, was the actor Patrick Cargill, and it may be from his mother that he inherited some of his irrepressible humour and energy. He could bowl for hours without a sign of weariness and without losing control or the ability to move the ball. It was not just that he was willing; he hated it when he was taken off.

Jackman was the first to admit that the arrival of Clarke had brought an extra dimension to his own bowling, for now batsmen could no longer afford to attempt simply to survive against Jackman's fast-medium line and length and movement off the seam. There was no respite at either end, and Clarke's pace and hostility was frightening to many. If the England players like Gooch and Gatting had had a free choice to select the MCC side that played Rest of the World to celebrate MCC's Bicentenary in 1987, Clarke would have been first on the list.

The arrival of Clarke had made things difficult for Howarth, although not intentionally. He began 1980 in indifferent form and dropped down to the Second Eleven to regain confidence. In the meantime, Intikhab had replaced Giles Cheatle, slow left-arm, whose form had lapsed, and Howarth was unable to regain his place because Surrey had their quota of two overseas cricketers. It was not to be the last time that Howarth encountered this problem.

Roope, Knight, Butcher, who had a splendid season, and Clinton forged all the runs that were needed, and Surrey were a side, talented, balanced and so obviously enjoying their cricket. Roger Knight was an unostentatious cricketer, and an undemonstrative captain, but a strong one. David Acfield, the Essex off-spinner and later BBC commentator, once said of Knight that when you bowled to him you were not particularly troubled because he did not seem to be hitting

Robin Jackman's enthusiasm and endeavour were bywords at The Oval during his 338 matches for the Club. (Allsport)

you about, but then you glanced at the score-board and you saw that he had already got forty-odd to his credit. His bowling was in the same category, medium-pace, wobbling a little, but naggingly accurate, and, in one-day cricket, in particular, lethal. His record as an all-rounder in limited-overs cricket in the early 1980s was second to none.

Knight had been in such fine form, and Surrey had done so well, that there was disappointment in 1981 that the County did not carry off a trophy. In a wet summer, there was some good cricket, but not as good as Micky Stewart felt the side was capable of playing, and there was some bad luck. The misfortune was the injury which kept Clarke out of the side for much of the season; the disappointment was in the form of Pocock and Knight as bowlers and in the lesser performances of batsmen like Roope and Smith.

Clarke played in only nine Championship matches, but he took 44 wickets at 15.43 runs each, and, against Glamorgan at Swansea, he hit his maiden first-class 100, in 62 minutes, the fastest of the season.

The loss of Clarke was devastating, well as Butcher, Knight, Clinton and the exciting Lynch batted, and encouraging as was the bowling of Thomas. In spite of a good spell in August, with Butcher in fine form, Surrey slipped to sixth in the Championship. They were knocked out of the NatWest Bank Trophy in a ten-over slog against Leicestershire, and they faded in the Sunday League, yet none of these failings was as disappointing as the fact that they reached a Lord's final for the third year in succession, and lost again.

The survival through the zonal round of the Benson and Hedges Cup was soggy and precarious, two abandonments, a defeat and a win over Minor Counties being enough to take Surrey into the quarter-finals for the match against Nottinghamshire at Trent Bridge.

Rice won the toss and asked Surrey to bat. The response was a solid, consistent batting performance founded on a second wicket stand of 104 between Knight and Clinton. Knight hit 70, followed it with the wickets of Rice and Birch for 36 and took the Gold Award. It was his tenth individual award in one-day competitions, a fact which emphasises his worth as a limited-overs all-rounder.

Clarke soon bowled both Nottinghamshire openers, Todd and Robinson, and Thomas had Hassan caught at slip by the incomparable Roope. Randall and Rice flattered briefly, but Jackman accounted for Randall, and finished with four wickets as Surrey won by 47 runs, Nottinghamshire being dismissed for 179 in 49.4 overs.

The semi-final was an altogether more tense affair. Roger Knight chose to bat first on The Oval wicket when he won the toss, and Clinton and Richards, now promoted to opener for one-day matches, gave Surrey a good start against the formidable Leicestershire pace attack. In the early stages runs came at four an over, but the steadiness of the bowling, supported by tight fielding, restricted progress when Surrey would have been looking to increase the rate, and it took a late 55 not out from Graham Roope to take the home side to 191 for nine in their 55 overs. It looked an indefensibly small total.

The Surrey score shrank as Balderstone and Steele passed 50 for the first wicket. Payne bowled Balderstone at 56, and at 84, he dismissed

Gower and Davison with successive deliveries. Pocock had Steele caught in the next over to swing the game in favour of Surrey. Briers and Garnham added 30 before Briers was bowled by Pocock, but Garnham and Roberts, realising that there was now much to do began to attack the bowling. The score climbed to 153 at which point four wickets fell as only 12 runs were scored. Thomas took three of the wickets, including Garnham and Roberts, who had added 39 in five overs, Roberts falling to a spectacular catch by Roope. When the last pair, Higgs and Parsons, came together, Leicestershire needed 27 runs to win. When Jackman began the last over 12 were wanted. Parsons pulled the third ball over mid-wicket for six, and the next ball went for two so that Leicestershire now had a very real chance of winning, but an unwise attempt at a run off the fifth ball of the over saw Higgs run out at the bowler's end by Pocock, and Surrey victorious by three runs.

The hero of the win over Leicestershire had been Ian Payne, deputising for the injured Clarke, but he could find no place in the side for the final when Clarke was pressed into service again. Butcher was also omitted, and Richards was once more used as an opener, but he struggled painfully against Garner and Botham after Rose, the Somerset captain, had asked Surrey to bat first. The first 17 overs produced only 16 runs, for Clinton, too, was out of touch. This put great pressure on the later batsmen, and Knight and Howarth did their best to rectify matters, but Howarth was also not at his best, and his attempted big hits against Marks did not always connect. Monte Lynch shone briefly before being caught in the deep by Garner, and Knight unobtrusively shouldered the responsibility for his side. He had hit 92 when a ball from Garner looped off his glove to wicket-keeper Taylor, capped by Surrey twelve years earlier.

Surrey's 194 for seven hardly looked likely to be a winning score against a side of Somerset's batting power, but Jackman and Clarke raised great hopes when they bowled Rose and Denning in the first three overs of the innings. That was really the last spark of comfort for Surrey. Richards, having played himself in, began to clout the ball in all directions. Roebuck helped him to add 105, and then Viv Richards and Ian Botham hit off the last 87 runs at a very brisk pace to bring Somerset victory with 10.3 overs to spare.

It was a very disappointing showing by Surrey in what was something of a sad season. They had led the Championship at the end of June, but then came Clarke's injury and decline. Butcher finished the season with a glorious flourish, but had been unable to score runs in the middle, and neither Clinton nor Knight had found true consistency. Jackman, inevitably, had worked hard, but missed Clarke's support, and Pocock had had a poor season. Intikhab was the

Alan Butcher arrived at The Oval as a slow bowler and became one of the most dashing opening batsmen in the country during the 1970s and 1980s. (Allsport)

leading wicket-taker, and it was the last season for the courteous, sporting, highly talented Pakistani who had been such a wonderful asset and team-man for Surrey.

The disappointment in 1981 was compounded into sadness by the deaths at an early age of both Tom Clark and Ken Barrington. Barrington's death in West Indies where he was assistant manager of the touring England side shocked the cricket world, and Surrey set up an appeal so that his name should be ever-remembered at The Oval in a way in which he would have liked, giving pleasure and help to others.

Micky Stewart was quite clear at the end of the 1981 season as to what had to be done to span the gap between near-miss and triumph. In his annual report, he presented five points which were Surrey's aims for 1982 – to keep Sylvester Clarke fit, to see that each individual accepted his own responsibilities, to increase Pat Pocock's quota of wickets at The Oval, to find a replacement for the number of wickets that Intikhab had taken, and to be positive and confident at all times. In these aims, Surrey were partly successful.

Mackintosh, Needham and Thomas went some of the way to filling the gap left by Intikhab's retirement. Clarke, as ferocious and fast as ever, steered clear of serious injury for the first time since joining Surrey, and he and Jackman were the most formidable opening attack in the country. The side was positive and confident for most of the season, but, frustratingly, Pocock could play in only a third of the Championship matches because of a back injury. This meant that after the hard work of Jackman and Clarke in breaking down early opposition there was an inadequate spin attack to consolidate the position and grasp opportunities that were offered on certain types of wickets.

Andy Needham offered considerable promise as an off-spinner and as a batsman, but he and Duncan Pauline violated what Stewart saw as the individual's responsibilities and paid the price. In the game against Lancashire at Old Trafford on 10, 12 and 13 July, Surrey were 152 for nine when Jackman joined Needham. By the close of play on the Saturday, the pair were still together, and the score was 260. On the Monday, they took it to 324 before Jackman was bowled by David Hughes for 60. Needham finished with 134 not out, the first century of his career, and the last wicket stand of 172 was only one run short of the record set up by Ducat and Sandham in 1921.

Needham's day of glory did not end there, for he followed this with five for 91, a career best, with his well-flighted off-breaks. He suffered somewhat in the second innings when Clive Lloyd and Abrahams punished him mercilessly, and Lancashire won by four wickets. It was later revealed that, in celebrating Needham's fine all-round performance, the player himself and Duncan Pauline, who was also in the side, had stayed out beyond the prescribed hour. Both were omitted from the next match in punishment. There were some who thought it harsh, but Stewart, Knight and the Surrey administration were firm and clear in the standards that they required of their players, and there were no complaints from the players' side.

The injury to Pocock, the retirement of Intikhab and niggling injuries to Clinton as well as some inconsistencies in the batting militated against Surrey being a serious challenger in the Championship. They were always in the top five, and, briefly in July, they were second, but the final position of fifth was realistic. In the Benson and Hedges Cup, they failed to progress past the zonal round. The story in the NatWest Bank Trophy was different.

There were some tremors at The Oval in the first round match against Durham when Simon Davis, an Australian pace bowler, sent back Pauline, Clinton and Knight for 16 runs in his first six overs, but Monte Lynch, 129, and Graham Roope, 77, added 166 in 107 minutes for the fifth wicket, and Surrey reached 279. Durham could not match the rate of scoring required and were prepared to concede the game when a violent thunderstorm saturated the ground at 7.30 pm with eight overs still to be bowled. Both sides agreed to come back on to the field at 8.30 pm, and Lynch and Clinton bowled out the remaining overs in rather eerie conditions.

Lynch was now a firm favourite at The Oval. His cheerful attitude to the game manifested itself in his gloriously aggressive batting and exciting fielding, and he won friends wherever he went. In the second round, he had to play second fiddle to David Smith who hit 103 not out in wintry conditions to take Surrey to victory over Northants at The Oval with seven balls to spare.

At Southampton, Surrey gained great advantage from winning the toss. It had been decided to start the NatWest Bank Trophy quarter-final matches on 4 August at 10.00 am, and Knight had no hesitation in asking Hampshire to bat first on a pitch that was to remain damp for two to three hours under a sky that was overcast. Having the conditions to exploit is one thing, however; having the bowlers to exploit them is another. Jackman used them to great advantage, finishing with six for 22, while Graham Monkhouse, in particular, gave able support. David Turner battled bravely for his 51, but Hampshire were all out for 119, and Surrey went on to win by eight wickets in mid-afternoon. They were now only one match away from their fourth final in four years.

Only 14 overs were possible on the first day at The Oval when Brearley had won the toss for Middlesex and put Surrey in to bat. Howarth played at a wide ball from Daniel and was caught behind, but on the resumption, Butcher and Smith scored freely until Butcher was run out. Knight flattered briefly, but Smith looked good until he was bowled by Edmonds. Lynch was subdued, and the fireworks were provided by Thomas, but in spite of his blows, Surrey made only 205 for nine, which did not look to be a winning score. Within the first 11 overs of the Middlesex innings, however, the match was decided in favour of Surrey. Clarke, bowling with considerable menace, had

Brearley caught behind, Tomlins lbw, Slack caught behind and Gatting taken at short leg by Butcher. In six overs, Clarke had taken four for 8.

Radley suggested recovery, but he was bowled by a lovely ball from Monkhouse, and Roland Butcher swatted briefly before he skied a ball to square leg where Richards ran to take the catch. Middlesex crumbled to 80 all out.

The National Westminster Bank Trophy Final of 1982 will not be remembered as one of the classic games, but for Surrey, it was a total triumph. They arrived at Lord's with a settled side in good form. Knight won the toss and asked Warwickshire to bat. It was a pleasant morning, but the early atmosphere was heavy. The atmosphere played no part in the fall of the first wicket in the fourth over. Lloyd shuffled across his wicket to Jackman and was lbw.

Kallicharran took no risks and it was eight overs before Warwickshire reached double figures. Clarke bowled with great hostility, and Jackman nagged away relentlessly. When they were replaced by Thomas and Monkhouse, David Smith seemed relieved at the change and hit Monkhouse for two straight fours. It was a dying gesture. In the next over, he turned Thomas to leg and, looking for the single, he slipped his foot back and dislodged a bail. He left the wicket looking back in anguish.

Amiss fretted a little and then played across the line to Thomas. Humpage edged the same bowler and was superbly caught by the diving Richards. Oliver set off on an insane run and was sent back by Kallicharran, but he had reached the point of no return and was run out by four yards.

Kallicharran played a couple of exquisite shots before flashing wildly at Knight to be brilliantly taken by Howarth at slip. Ferreira was leg before to Clarke, and Lethbridge was taken high and one-handed by Howarth at slip, a second magnificent catch. In the 28th over, Warwickshire were 74 for eight.

The game had really been turned by Knight – who only bowled himself because Monkhouse had failed to settle – and by Thomas, a left-arm bowler who could generate a fair pace, but who, ultimately, never achieved quite as much as he had promised.

Small and Asif Din restored some pride for Warwickshire with a ninth wicket stand of 62 in 24 overs, and 158 was certainly a better score than had looked possible at 11.30 am.

There was no nonsense about the batting of Butcher and Howarth. Helped by a generous sprinkling of no-balls, they reached 20 inside four overs and 30 inside six. Howarth played some magnificent shots off the back foot, and his driving square of the wicket was regal. His downfall was an anti-climax, for he played a wretched shot at a bad ball and was caught by mid-on diving forward. Butcher batted on in majestic fashion, and it was fitting that he should on-drive Kallicharran for four and the winning hit. Warwickshire had been outclassed.

Graham Roope was not re-engaged for the 1983 season so ending 20 years of entertaining batting and brilliant fielding with Surrey. If he never shone as an outstanding batsman in his 21 Test matches, he had a fine international record, averaging 30.71 with the bat and taking 35 catches. Another loss before the start of the 1983 season was the decision by Robin Jackman that he would retire from first-class cricket and settle in South Africa.

The departure of Jackman severely affected Surrey's chances of enjoying the successful season that had been predicted for them, and for the first time since Stewart had become manager and Gibson had become coach, Surrey failed to make a serious challenge in any of the competitions. Kevin Mackintosh, who had been expected to assume Jackman's role, was injured and, in fact, disappeared from the side. The bowling was carried by Clarke, Monkhouse, Thomas and Pocock, and even Clarke took time to get into his stride.

It was a season not without trauma, but not without hope. A wet May saw Surrey make an inglorious exit from the Benson and Hedges Cup, and, on the 30th of that month, they were bowled out for the lowest score in their history. At Chelmsford, Essex hit 287 on the Monday after a blank first day. Surrey began their innings with 67 minutes to play. Butcher was caught behind off Foster off the first ball of the third over. Two overs later, Foster bowled Needham. Knight lasted only three balls before being lbw to Phillip, and Lynch was out the same way in the ninth over by which time Surrey were 8 for four. Three more wickets fell at the same score, and only a clout for four by Clarke off Foster and an edged two by Monkhouse prevented the score from being the lowest in first-class history. Surrey were out for 14: Clinton 6, Clarke 4, Phillip six for 4, Foster four for 10.

The next day, after being 18 for two, Surrey drew the match, Knight hitting 101 not out and sharing an unbroken third wicket partnership of 167 with Clinton.

The rest of the season was not quite as damaging as that although some would argue that the nine-wicket defeat by Warwickshire in the second round of the NatWest Trophy was equally traumatic, but there were problems in other directions. Disturbed by his side's poor form, Roger Knight called for extra effort and arranged extra practice. The response was good, the improvement obvious, but there had been trouble with David Smith, who seemed unable to accept the authority of his captain. In mid-August, it was announced that Surrey had accepted his resignation. He later joined Worcestershire, but was

NATIONAL WESTMINSTER BANK TROPHY FINAL
SURREY *v* WARWICKSHIRE

Played at Lord's, 4 September 1982

SURREY WON BY 9 WICKETS

WARWICKSHIRE

K. D. Smith	hit wkt b Thomas	12
T. A. Lloyd	lbw b Jackman	2
A. I. Kallicharran	c Howarth b Knight	19
D. L. Amiss	b Thomas	0
†G. W. Humpage	c Richards b Thomas	0
P. R. Oliver	run out	2
M. Asif Din	lbw b Jackman	45
A. M. Ferreira	lbw b Clarke	8
C. Lethbridge	c Howarth b Knight	4
G. C. Small	c Richards b Clarke	33
*R. G. D. Willis	not out	8
Extras	b 8, lb 11, nb 6	25
Total	(57.2 overs)	158

Fall: 1-3, 2-32, 3-42, 4-48, 5-51, 6-52, 7-67, 8-74, 9-136

BOWLING	O	M	R	W
Clarke	11.2	5	17	2
Jackman	12	2	27	2
Thomas	11	1	26	3
Monkhouse	8	0	36	0
Knight	12	3	14	2
Mackintosh	3	0	13	0

SURREY

A. R. Butcher	not out	86
G. P. Howarth	c Oliver b Lethbridge	31
D. M. Smith	not out	28
*R. D. V. Knight		
M. A. Lynch		
†C. J. Richards		
D. J. Thomas		
G. Monkhouse		
S. T. Clarke		
R. D. Jackman		
K. S. Mackintosh		
Extras	lb 4, nb 10	14
Total	(33.4 overs, for 1 wkt)	159

Fall: 1-80

BOWLING	O	M	R	W
Willis	7	0	23	0
Small	8	0	60	0
Ferreira	6	0	16	0
Lethbridge	6	1	23	1
Kallicharran	6.4	1	23	0

Umpires: H. D. Bird and B. J. Meyer

Man of the Match: D. J. Thomas.

*Captain; †Wicket-keeper

299

to return to The Oval, somewhat unexpectedly, in 1987 only to leave again after two seasons.

Stewart and others at The Oval in 1983 were sorry that Smith had had to leave. A tall, upright player, he was a punishing batsman with a particular disdain for fast bowling, but, like Younis, he had a fatal flaw. Stewart's statement on Smith's departure was simple:

> In a highly competitive team game the right standard of discipline and codes of conduct have to be maintained for the good of cricket, the Surrey Club and all its players, in order to achieve success. David found this difficult to accept.

On the brighter side, there was the exciting but controlled form of Monte Lynch, a show of promise from Duncan Pauline which was never maintained either in his remaining days with Surrey or, briefly, at Glamorgan, and the advance of Alec Stewart. Stewart had made his debut in 1981, and he was now forcing his way more regularly into a side which had need, among other things, of his brilliant fielding although he was also a highly competent wicket-keeper. A handsome and aggressive batsman, he hit a maiden hundred, 118 not out in three hours, against Oxford University at The Oval in June 1983. It was a happy sign for the future.

Roger Knight resigned the captaincy at the end of the season, but he agreed to play for one more year under the new skipper Geoff Howarth before taking up a teaching appointment. He served Surrey well as player and captain. His calm and authority did much to re-establish order and discipline at a time when it was necessary that they should be re-established.

As young players like Alec Stewart, Chris Bullen and Mark Feltham began to force their way into the side, there were other exciting developments at The Oval. The Ken Barrington Appeal was launched in June 1983, in an attempt to develop the Barrington Cricket Centre at the Vauxhall End of the ground. After years of struggling with bureaucrats and politicians, the Club began a period of reconstruction on the ground. The perimeter wall on the gasometer side, the entrances by the Hobbs Gate and administrative offices to control the flow of the crowd had all been set in process of reconstruction, and, most ambitiously, close to the pavilion a new executive suite and restaurant was developed which was opened in time for the 1984 season. With plans for development of the Vauxhall End and the introduction of colourful, comfortable bucket seats, the efforts of many worthy men and women who struggled long to bring the facilities at The Oval to a standard acceptable to the demands of the second half of the 20th century began to bear fruit.

The unveiling of the executive suite did not coincide with a marked

Monte Lynch, an exuberant and exhilarating middle-order batsman, always scoring quickly. (Allsport)

run of success on the field. Surrey did qualify for the quarter-finals of the Benson and Hedges Cup where they were beaten by Nottinghamshire, but only after a frighteningly close one-wicket win over Combined Universities at Oxford. Pat Pocock and Sylvester Clarke scored the 13 needed for the last wicket to win the match. In the NatWest Trophy, a good victory over Essex at Chelmsford was followed by a resounding quarter-final defeat at Edgbaston. Neither the County Championship nor the John Player League offered much comfort after a moderate start, and Surrey finished eighth in both. The season was accepted as disappointing, and it was apparent that too much responsibility in the bowling was being thrust on Pocock, who, to the delight of all, won his way back into the England side, and Clarke, who needed quicker, more hostile and more consistent support at the other end. The batting was generally good and entertaining, if a little inconsistent.

Judged entirely on first team results and the capturing of trophies, the modern yardstick, the 1984 season was disappointing, yet to the keen observer there was excitement bubbling close to the surface. Surrey broke new ground by staging a game against Cambridge University at Banstead at the end of June. Some of the senior players

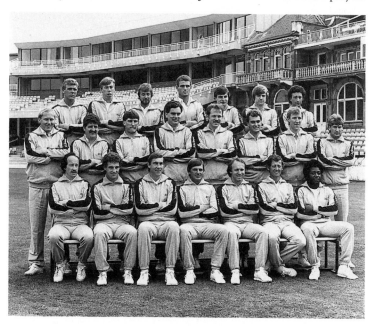

Surrey, 1984. Back row: Stewart, Ward, Needham, Taylor, Falkner, Medlycott, Pauline. Middle row: Monkhouse, Payne, Mackintosh, Bullen, Curtis, Waterman, Feltham, Thomas. Front row: Clinton, Richards, Knight, Howarth, Butcher, Pocock, Lynch.

stood down, and with Howarth out for nothing, Surrey were struggling at 172 for seven when Keith Medlycott joined Nick Falkner. Both players were making their first-class debuts. In 138 minutes, they shared an unbroken stand of 189, 15 runs short of the County record for the eighth wicket. Medlycott, primarily a slow left-arm bowler who had come up through all the youth structure from the Surrey Schools side at the age of eleven, hit a six and 13 fours in his 117. Falkner, who was playing on his own club ground, took 233 minutes for his 101 and hit three sixes and 11 fours. It was the first occasion in a first-class match when two batsmen have scored a century in the same innings on their first-class debuts.

Falkner was not in the side when Surrey played Kent at Canterbury and Gloucestershire at Cheltenham in August, yet, remarkably, for the first time in their history, Surrey fielded 11 players all of whom had hit a first-class century – Butcher, Clinton, Knight, Lynch, Needham, Richards, Monkhouse, Thomas, Clarke, Howarth and Medlycott. The medium-pace 'Farmer' Monkhouse had hit 100 when batting as a night-watchman against Kent at The Oval earlier in the season while Thomas had hit a fierce century against Notts at The Oval in 1983.

Scratching deeper, there was more cause for Surrey elation, for, with Geoff Arnold now back at The Oval as coach, the Second Eleven finished second in the Second Eleven Championship and the Under-25 Trophy came to Surrey after a thrilling one-run win over a strong Middlesex side at The Oval.

There was abounding hope for the 1985 season, but the hope was dashed almost before the season began. It was found that Sylvester Clarke was suffering from disc trouble and that he would not be able to play at all during the season. The loss of Clarke was a shattering blow for, in effect, he was the Surrey attack. A replacement was urgently needed, and Surrey signed Tony Gray, a 6ft 8in fast bowler, who had just taken 36 wickets for Trinidad in the Shell Shield in his first full season. The registering of another overseas player meant that, under the current regulations, Gray and Howarth could not appear in the same side. Howarth, even though he was captain, had to stand down.

It must be emphasised that Howarth was fully supportive of all that was done. It was he who insisted that Surrey's need was a fast bowler, and that they needed Gray's bowling more than they needed his batting. In fact, Geoff Howarth's last contribution to Surrey cricket was an act of chivalrous self-sacrifice. He did not appear in a Championship match, and he faded quietly from the scene.

Howarth's greatest contribution will always be seen as what he did for New Zealand cricket, for he led the Kiwis through the most successful period in their cricket history. They looked upon him as a 'bit of a toff' according to one of his team-mates, and they would have died for him on the cricket field. Strangely, he was something of a rebel in his early days at The Oval, but Surrey cricket taught him much, and this man of quiet humour, great dignity and gentle charm repaid the Club in full for all that they had done for him.

Pocock led the side for a few matches, and then Trevor Jesty, who had just joined the County from Hampshire, was appointed captain for the rest of the season when it was apparent that Howarth would not be able to take his place in the side. Jesty was signed to give middle order experience to the team. Ian Greig was to say of Jesty: 'He was the model professional. In dress and manners, he was everything for a young player to model himself on, both on and off the field.' He was not, however, an adventurer. His captaincy was always safe. He did not make mistakes, but he took few chances.

Jesty begun with a cascade of runs, but the captaincy affected him to some extent. However, he still passed 1,000 runs in Championship matches as did Lynch, who played with excitement and maturity, Clinton, a battered and bruised model of consistency, Needham, for the first time, and Butcher. Butcher and Clinton, a left-handed double act, were as good as any opening pair in the country, and the batting that followed was enterprising. For the first two months of the season, Surrey were in the top four in the Championship, and wins with maximum points over Warwickshire and Derbyshire took them to third at the beginning of August, but four frustrating draws followed, and in at least two of these matches, more penetrative bowling might have forced victories. Statistically, Surrey could still have won the Championship when they began their penultimate match against Sussex at The Oval on 4 September. Harry Brind, honoured for preparing the best wickets in the country, had given the sides a beautiful track on which to play. Sussex asked Surrey to bat first on a cold, overcast day. The wonderfully dependent Clinton hit his third Championship century of the season, and Jesty played a delightful innings of 82 and declared at 349 for five. Green hit a career best 133 for Sussex who declared when they reached 300 in 76 overs. On the last morning, Surrey were 37 for five, but they were rescued by a brave, positive 81 not out from Alec Stewart, and Jesty set Sussex to score 248 in 48 overs. They were 94 for four before Imran and le Roux hit 72 in 11 overs. Imran was superbly stumped by Richards off Monkhouse, and le Roux and Alan Wells also fell, but Ian Gould and Ian Greig scored 40 off 31 balls to bring victory to Sussex with eight balls to spare.

This defeat ended Surrey's Championship hopes, and they finished sixth. Thomas reappeared in this match after being absent through injury, and a catalogue of injuries to Monkhouse, Feltham and others clouded the season, yet the event which typified Surrey's fortunes most in 1985 happened to the Second Eleven.

With Bullen, Doughty, Falkner, Ward, Taylor and an impressive young fast bowler, Martin Bicknell, prominent, they played cricket of character and imagination and believed that they had won the Second Eleven Championship. However, TCCB deducted the 24 points they had won at Hove where, it was alleged, they had played an ineligible player, and this put them in second place, 0.1 behind Nottingham-shire.

The season ended with Stewart, Gray and Needham all receiving their county caps. Gray had taken 79 first-class wickets and proved to be an excellent acquisition. It is worth noting that Graham Gooch believed that at the end of May, when he played against Gray at The Oval, Gray was no more than medium pace, but by the time he came to Chelmsford in late August, he was very quick indeed.

With Clarke fit again, Surrey were able to call upon both West Indian fast bowlers in 1986 although not in tandem because of the overseas player regulations. It did mean, however, that they always had available a potent leader of the attack, and the pair captured 99 wickets between them. Excitingly, Martin Bicknell, 17 years old, very quick and eager to learn, forced his way into the side and belied his years and inexperience with some good performances. Tall, dark and slender, with a fine action, he took 27 wickets and would have taken more but for injury.

Pocock had taken over the captaincy in what was to be his last season, and with Micky Stewart now more involved with the England side, Geoff Arnold's position as coach involved the first team while Chris Waller, another Surrey faithful, took over the Second Eleven. Three wins in four matches at the end of July and beginning of August took Surrey into a challenging position for the Championship, but four draws followed, and it was victory in the last match against Leicestershire at The Oval that enabled them to climb into third place, 39 points behind Essex, the winners. They had never really recovered from a poor June when they were beaten four times.

There was much exciting cricket being played, not consistently, but there was disquieting news of dressing-room disharmony. Monte Lynch was suspended from a Sunday League game at the end of July, and there were constant rumblings for the rest of the season which could not have made things easy for Pocock, who strode through all with his usual cheerful manner.

Pat Pocock played for Surrey for 22 years. He knew good times and bad, and he transcended the bad because he never lost his love of the game. He had a lovely high action, and his off-spin was shot with variety and experiment. Like Laker, he worked his fingers red and

An appealing Pat Pocock, long-serving off-break bowler and eventual skipper,
whose most famous feat was seven Sussex wickets in 11 balls.

blistered, and if he had a fault, it was that he often turned the ball too
much. Ever cheerful, delighted in his art, he was always optimistic and
refreshingly open.

Perhaps it was a little too late for him when he became captain of
Surrey. He missed his old comrades, especially Intikhab, Howarth,
Knight and Jackman, and the values they represented. He said of
Jackman that if anybody could find a way of bottling his energy, zest
and commitment, then the future of cricket would be safe for the next
century. Like Jackman, Pocock believed in the game, and one
wonders if, when he wrote of his friend Jackman: 'He loved cricket as
he loved life, indeed he rarely drew a distinction', he was really writing

of himself. Cricket was an emptier game after he had been clapped off the field at The Oval on the evening of Tuesday, 16 September. Surrey had just beaten Leicestershire by an innings, and Pat Pocock's long love affair with the game was over.

He came close to leading Surrey to a Lord's final in his last month, but he was to be denied in a game which few who saw it will ever forget. A rather close win over Cheshire had brought a tie with Derbyshire who were convincingly beaten. Nottinghamshire, too, were brushed aside, and Surrey found themselves at home to Lancashire in the semi-final of the NatWest Bank Trophy.

Pocock won the toss and asked Lancashire to bat first. His reasoning was soon to become apparent, for a torrid first over from Sylvester Clarke produced a single which took Mendis to face Bicknell's first ball. The Lancashire opener slashed it into the hands of Clarke at gully. Clarke claimed the next wicket himself when he made a ball rear nastily at Fowler who fended it off only to be caught one-handed by Richards, diving wide to his left down the leg side. It was a breathtaking catch.

In the 15th over, Abrahams missed an in-swinger from Feltham and Lancashire were 28 for three. Bicknell and Clarke had troubled Clive Lloyd with their pace and left him floundering, but he survived. Fairbrother did not. He fell to Thomas in the 25th over, and Lancashire were 59 for four. Against less hostile bowling than that of Clarke and Bicknell, Lloyd and O'Shaughnessy added 99 in 21 overs. It was to prove to be a vital stand.

Lloyd was caught behind cutting at Pocock. Hayhurst fell to Butcher who bowled seven tidy overs. Maynard hit a belligerent 22 before falling to Feltham, but any hopes Lancashire had of increasing their score significantly were blighted by the return of Clarke who had O'Shaughnessy taken at slip, Allott at extra cover and bowled Simmons with the third ball of the 59th over. Lancashire were all out for 229.

Surrey were soon in trouble. Butcher hooked Allott unwisely and was caught at long leg, and Clinton edged to slip off the same bowler. Stewart was lbw to Watkinson, and Surrey were 30 for three. Lynch and Jesty suggested recovery until Lynch insanely ran himself out. Jesty was driving handsomely, but there was much wantonness at the other end. At 173 for seven, the game was tilted in favour of Lancashire, but Clarke played a couple of thunderous shots before swatting rashly to square-leg, and when Pocock was bowled by Allott Surrey were 24 runs short of victory with only Martin Bicknell to support the limping Jesty. Having reached 76, Jesty pulled a leg muscle and had batted with a runner since that time. The restrictions imposed upon him by the injury gave an added lustre to his stroke-play. His driving was majestic. Always a neat, elegant, unruffled batsman, he stood now like a wounded hero against the invading hordes. Young Bicknell gave him the support that any valiant squire should give to his knight.

When Hayhurst began the penultimate over Surrey needed seven to win, and Jesty was on strike. He hit the first ball for two, and on the fifth he attempted a long, lofted drive towards the pavilion, but Fowler, sprinting round the boundary from long-on, held the ball as he dived and rolled over and over. Jesty had made 112 off 139 deliveries with a six and 14 fours. There was no better innings played on any ground in any competition in 1986, but Surrey had lost by four runs. For Jesty, 20 years in the game and never an appearance in a Lord's final, it was a sad moment. For Pocock, it was, perhaps, the most exciting memory of his last season.

Nothing could dim the brightness that was shining from the young players on the staff. The Second Eleven was exciting, eager and successful. Its members, as they should, were pressing for first team places, and with this in mind, the County released the durable and faithful Butcher, who went to give good service to Glamorgan, Doughty, later to return briefly, and Monkhouse. With both captain and vice-captain gone, Surrey needed a leader.

In 1986, Geoff Arnold had phoned Ian Greig in Australia asking him to join Surrey as a medium-pace bowler and late middle-order batsman, for it was felt that his talents were what was needed to supplement the team and give it a boost that was required. A few weeks later, the call was repeated, but this time Greig was offered the captaincy.

Ian Greig had spent much of his career in the shadow of his brother Tony who had captained both England and Sussex and been prominent in the Packer Revolution which, whatever else it did, certainly raised the income and status of the professional cricketer and, indirectly, encouraged a great deal of sponsorship into cricket. Ian Greig was 31, had been born in South Africa and educated at Cambridge University, although his interests were sporting rather than academic, and had played for Sussex from 1980 to 1985. He had played twice for England, and many believed he should have played more, and he had left Sussex in strange circumstances when, before the end of the 1985 season, they had announced that they would not be retaining him as they could not afford him. Other rumours suggested political infighting. He left Sussex and England to run an indoor sports centre in Brisbane where all the Greigs now lived. His wife is Australian.

When he was offered the Surrey captaincy Ian Greig sought the advice of his elder brother Tony, for whom he has the greatest

Ian Greig, South African born and former Sussex and England all-rounder, was an inspired choice to lead Surrey in 1988. (Allsport)

admiration. Tony Greig put three points to his brother by which he could determine whether or not the job was right for him:

If you want to take the job just because it is a good financial offer, don't take it.

If you want to be captain of Surrey just to get back at Sussex because of the way they treated you, don't take it.

If you want to captain Surrey because you want to get back to the game you love and you think you can do a good job, say yes and start packing.

The news of Ian Greig's appointment took all by surprise. His name had never been mentioned outside the committee room and administrative circles, but whoever first mooted the idea was responsible for one of the most inspired moves in recent cricket history.

Ian Greig is transparently honest and open. It is a quality that tends to humble those with whom he comes in contact. He was aware that the dressing room atmosphere had been bad, that there had been too much back-biting, and dealing with this became his first priority. All disagreements, all complaints and grievances would be talked through in the open, face to face. Failures or weaknesses in a match were to be discussed, blame apportioned and accepted. His passion for the game and his own disarming frankness made this policy totally acceptable.

Greig revealed, too, that vital spark of captaincy that so many have lacked, the belief that one does not deserve to win a game unless one is prepared to chance losing it. He proved ready to make a decision and stand by it. He proved tough, warm and encouraging, and he won the respect of his men and all those who came in contact with him.

Surrey moved to seventh in the Sunday League, not in itself a position at which to rejoice overmuch, but certainly far better than the County had known for some years and the product of some pulsating cricket on occasions. Against Northamptonshire at Guildford on 28 June, Surrey were defending a total of 220. When the last over arrived the visitors needed four runs to win with six wickets in hand. Greig handed the ball to Monte Lynch who had not bowled an over of his off-breaks in a limited-overs match all season. It was a stroke of genius. Lynch had Harper caught behind, Williams stumped, and Geoff Cook was run out on the last ball of the match to give Surrey victory by one run.

Surrey went through to the quarter-finals of the Benson and Hedges Cup, having won all four of their zonal round matches. In the quarter-final, they met Worcestershire at The Oval. The visitors reached an impressive 233 for eight. Darren Bicknell, a left-hander of immense promise, and David Smith, recently returned to the fold, put on 58 for the first wicket. Stewart and Lynch went quickly, but Jesty and Smith added the 159 needed for victory. Smith hit 110, Jesty 85. It was positive, confident cricket, yet the confidence did not always appear to be there, and they lost the semi-final to Yorkshire with an immature and ragged display.

Northamptonshire, relying on spin, won the second round NatWest Trophy tie at Northampton, but Surrey's challenge for the Championship in 1986 was a serious one. The lapse came at the beginning of August when defeat at Cheltenham was followed by four fruitless draws, two of which should have been wins.

The first of these was against Kent at The Oval. Surrey were 191 for six when Keith Medlycott joined Jack Richards. Both batsmen proceeded to hit the highest scores of their careers, Richards 172 not out, Medlycott 153. They added 262 at a rate of more than five runs an over and so established a Surrey record for the seventh wicket. Greig was able to declare before close of play, but Kent did not lose a wicket, and next day they took their score to 341 for six. Having scored at more than six an over, Surrey reached 184 for five, and Greig declared setting Kent the task of scoring 317 in 70 overs. Medlycott took five wickets, and Kent were 219 for nine with 12.1 overs to go, but Igglesden and Jarvis held out.

In the next match, also at The Oval, against Somerset, Surrey needed 11 off the last over, but they lost three wickets for five runs and Clinton had to bat with a broken finger and save the game.

Wins over Glamorgan, Essex and Northants took Surrey to within reach of the leaders, but defeat at Old Trafford in the last match meant fourth place.

Clarke and Gray took 110 wickets between them, and Martin Bicknell continued to show exciting promise, but the maturation of one of the spinners was needed to transform Surrey into a Championship-winning side. The batting promised excitement without ever convincing that it totally believed in itself. At the end of the year, it was decided not to retain Jesty and he moved to Lancashire. This was a hard decision, for he was well liked by all, an exemplary professional who had served the Club nobly, but he was 39, and there were so many good young batsmen like David Ward, Darren Bicknell, Atkins and Robinson jostling for places that room had to be made. Falkner, realising the abundance of talent at The Oval, moved to Sussex where he felt he would have more opportunity.

A new and exciting Surrey side was emerging from the chrysalis. Most of the players were products of the youth policy which had initially been formulated by Micky Stewart, yet before the 1988 season had begun, the Club was again confronted by an off-the-field crisis. For over 30 years, on and off, the County had been bedevilled by the vagaries of politicians, and again they fell foul. The extensive phase of planned redevelopment of The Oval had led the committee to work towards raising a million pounds to pay for the project, believing that the government would also provide funds for the scheme as it would bring jobs and wealth to an area in need of both. The government failed to provide those funds, and so Raman Subba Row launched the Save The Oval appeal, for the historic and noble ground was truly under threat. Sir Leonard Hutton and John Paul Getty junior became patrons of the appeal, and many worked long and hard hours so that the rebuilding could begin on schedule in September 1988. It is the latest chapter in the tale of passion and dedication which has surrounded the Club for close to 150 years.

Into this new crisis came a new secretary. Ian Scott-Browne, who had not been in the best of health, retired after ten faithful years. He was succeeded by David Seward, a man of tremendous vitality, enthusiasm and commercial expertise who came with experience at both Somerset and Nottinghamshire.

Far from producing an air of crisis, the Save The Oval Appeal generated a feeling of energy and excitement. It was proof to all that The Oval and Surrey were quick and alive.

That sense of activity was transmitted on the field. There was a constant challenge in the Sunday League, and until August it seemed that Surrey would finish in the top four and so qualify for the new Refuge Assurance Cup, but they were thwarted by a defeat at the hands of lowly Somerset and they had to settle for fifth position, so equalling once more their highest position in the league. At Chelmsford, in May, they swamped Essex in astonishing fashion. They reached their target of 139 with 33 balls to spare, and Jack Richards hit 106 of the 139.

Surrey failed to reach the knock-out stage of the Benson and Hedges Cup, but they died bravely. Knowing that they needed a fast run rate, they scored at more than seven an over against Sussex and just lost.

Three victories in August took them to fourth place again in the County Championship. They would have done infinitely better in a season where they looked so good in the field but dropped so many catches had they held on to some of those chances.

Yet the year was not without its unhappier side. David Smith did not play again after Guildford week where he hit 157 not out against Hampshire, and once more his contract with the Club was terminated. Greig had supported him after incidents the previous season, just as he supported Clarke when he erred, but Smith had once more failed to live up to the professional standards set by Surrey. More disturbing to some people, but not totally unexpected, was the news that Jack Richards was not to be re-engaged.

At times a brilliant wicket-keeper and thrilling batsman, Richards was a highly talented player, but for one who could give much pleasure, at times he seemed to draw little pleasure from the game itself and gave the impression of one who felt the world was against him. He had achieved much, and like Strudwick, McIntyre, Wood and Pooley, he had played for England. A player who is unhappy and discontented, however, can imbue others with that discontent, and however good the individual, cricket is a team game. When one remembers Jack Richards and Surrey one wants only to remember things like the catch that accounted for Fowler in the NatWest semi-final of 1986 or the 100 against Essex in his last season. Those are warm and happy memories.

Inevitably, too, in 1988, Surrey had their share of injuries. Gray played in only two matches. Clarke, Stewart, Clinton and Martin Bicknell, who took the season's best, nine for 45 against Cambridge, all suffered breaks, pulls or bruises, and Monte Lynch had knee trouble. On the positive side, pace bowlers Peters and Frost caught the eye with some excellent performances, Feltham hinted that determination and self-belief were now being allied to an immense talent, and by the end of the year there were press cries of Medlycott for England.

Staffordshire, Essex, in a tense game, and Glamorgan were beaten to take Surrey to the NatWest Bank Trophy semi-final yet again. Middlesex were the visitors to The Oval. They began briskly, but in the fifth over, Carr was caught down the leg side by Richards off Clarke, who was not fully fit. Bullen frustrated Needham and then had him caught, and Gatting was run out in bizarre fashion, but Butcher and Downton played with sensible aggression, and, aided by four dropped catches, Middlesex made 258 for seven.

Surrey began bleakly in reply. Clinton and Atkins could not get going even though Simon Hughes encouraged them with a sprinkling of wides. Lynch was hampered by his injury, and Greig, seeking urgency, was run out. Alec Stewart made 107 not out, but it was never going to be a match-winning innings. Surrey were bowled out for 188.

Two years earlier, when they lost to Lancashire, there had been bitter disappointment. Now there was honesty and realism. We played badly. We did not deserve to win. And, ultimately, from Keith Medlycott, we are a young side. We are learning with every match. We have some wonderful young players here.

There is a spirit of youth abroad at The Oval. The traditions are revered. The ghosts of Hobbs and Hayward and the rest make happy visitations, and those who wear the chocolate cap today are fully aware of the trust they hold and the standards the masters have set them and which they hope one day to emulate. The policy on and off

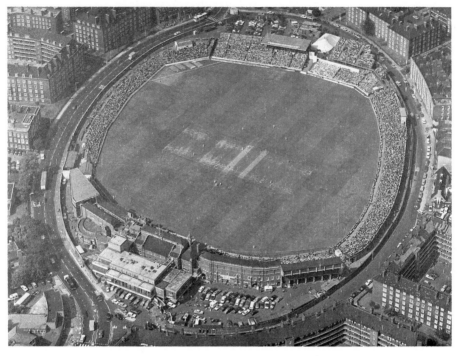

'A certain Blank piece or parcel of Ground intended to be left void in a certain Oval'.

the field is fresh and invigorating; and as the new buildings take shape alongside the pavilion and another phase of redevelopment begins one wonders what William Clayton of Harleyford, Bucks, would think if he could see today that 'certain Blank piece or parcel of Ground intended to be left void in a certain Oval' which he reserved for his own use when he leased it from the Duchy of Cornwall in 1790.

STATISTICAL SECTION

BIOGRAPHICAL DETAILS OF SURREY PLAYERS

The following individuals played in first-class matches, 1839 to 1988

NAME AND EXTENT OF CAREER	BIRTHPLACE	DATE OF BIRTH	DATE OF DEATH
Abbott, Charles James *1844*		c1815	6. 1.1889
Abbott, William *1873*	Walton-on-Thames	28.10.1856	22.12.1935
Abel, Robert *1881–1904*	Rotherhithe	30.11.1857	10.12.1936
Abel, Thomas Ernest *1919–1920*	Kennington	10. 9.1890	23. 1.1937
Abel, William John *1909–1926*	South Bermondsey	29. 8.1887	23. 3.1934
Adams, Donald *1902*	Ockley	8. 6.1880	8. 1.1976
Adams, Henry James *1887–1889*	Croydon	25. 4.1852	21. 2.1922
Akroyd, Bayly Nash *1872–1873*	Streatham	27. 4.1850	24.11.1926
Akroyd, Swainson Howden *1869–1878*	Streatham	13.11.1848	5.12.1925
Alexander, George Caledon *1869*	Epsom	4.10.1842	8. 4.1913
Allom, Anthony Thomas Carrick *1960*	Bletchingly	21.10.1938	
Allom, Maurice James Carrick *1927–1937*	Northwood	23. 3.1906	
Altham, Harry Surtees *1908–1912*	Camberley	30.11.1888	11. 3.1965
Anstead, Walter Henry *1870–1872*	Twickenham	26. 2.1845	14. 5.1933
Arnold, Geoffrey Graham *1963–1977*	Earlsfield	3. 9.1944	
Ashby, David (Alexander) *1874*	Beddington	11. 6.1852	2. 6.1934
Atkins, Paul David *1988*	Aylesbury	11. 6.1966	
Avory, Henry Kemp *1876*	Clapham	4.10.1848	16. 4.1918
Aworth, Christopher John *1974–1976*	Wimbledon	19. 2.1953	
Ayres, George White *1892–1896*	Thames Ditton	5. 7.1871	28. 8.1934
Baggallay, Thomas Weeding *1865–1874* (later known as T. W. Weeding)	St Pancras	11. 6.1847	19.12.1929
Baily, Robert Edward Hartwell *1904–1906*	Godstone	6. 6.1885	19. 9.1973
Bainbridge, Herbert William *1883–1885*	Gowhatti, India	29.10.1862	3. 3.1940
Baker, Albert *1900–1907*	Farnham	28.11.1872	17. 4.1948
Baker, Raymond Paul *1973–1978*	Carshalton	9. 4.1954	
Baker, William Danby *1847–1851*	Kennington	c1806	11. 3.1885
Baldwin, Charles *1892–1898*	Bury St Edmunds	29.12.1864	2. 5.1947
Baldwin, Herbert George *1922–1930*	Hartley Wintney	16. 3.1893	7. 3.1969
Bale, Ernest William *1904*	Mitcham	18. 9.1878	6. 7.1952
Barker, Kenneth Edgar Mylne *1899–1903*	Godstone	27.10.1877	6. 8.1938
Barker, W- *1882*			
Barling, Henry Thomas *1927–1948*	Kensington	1. 9.1906	
Barnato, Joel Woolf *1928–1930*	Westminster	27. 9.1895	27. 7.1948
Barratt, Edward *1876–1885*	Stockton-on-Tees	21. 4.1844	27. 2.1891
Barrington, Kenneth Frank *1953–1968*	Reading	24.11.1930	14. 3.1981
Bartlett, Hugh Tryon *1933–1935*	Balaghat, India	7.10.1914	26. 6.1988
Barton, Michael Richard *1948–1954*	Dereham	14.10.1914	

Batchelar, Arthur *1862*	Brockham	11. 3.1831	6. 1.1912
Bayford, Robert Augustus *1860–1861*	Albury	13. 3.1838	24. 8.1922
Bayley, John *1839–1847*	Mitcham	17. 5.1794	7.11.1874
Bayley, Morton *1866*	Mitcham	7. 5.1843	6. 3.1926
Beard, Thomas Arthur *1857–1858*		c1817	1903
(later Beard de Beauchamp)			
Beauchamp, John *1854–1855*	Chertsey	20.10.1825	30. 5.1911
Beaumont, John *1885–1890*	Armitage Bridge	16. 9.1854	1. 5.1920
Bedser, Alec Victor *1939–1966*	Reading	4. 7.1918	
Bedser, Eric Arthur *1939–1961*	Reading	4. 7.1918	
Bell, Roland *1876*	Bishops Stortford	16. 5.1857	29. 1.1935
Bennett, Cecil Tristram *1922*	Tulse Hill	10. 8.1902	3. 2.1978
Bennett, Nigel Harvie *1946*	Walton-on-Thames	23. 9.1912	
Berrington, Edwin Henry *1872*	Lambeth	1850	1880
Berry, Fred *1934–1939*	Kirkheaton	13. 2.1910	
Bickley, John *1852*	Keyworth	16. 1.1819	15.11.1866
Bicknell, Darren John *1987–1988*	Guildford	24. 6.1967	
Bicknell, Martin Paul *1986–1988*	Guildford	14. 1.1969	
Bigwood, Alfred *1878*	Mortlake	3. 8.1857	12. 9.1940
Bird, Morice Carlos *1909–1921*	Liverpool	25. 3.1888	9.12.1933
Birley, Francis Hornby *1879*	Manchester	14. 3.1850	1. 8.1910
Blacklidge, Henry George *1908–1913*	Stoughton	14. 7.1884	23. 5.1917
Blackman, Arthur *1878*	Dartford	13.10.1853	6. 4.1908
Blamires, Nimrod *1878–1881*	Bradford	31. 7.1850	22. 3.1886
Block, Spencer Allen *1928–1933*	Esher	15. 7.1908	7.10.1979
Bloomfield, Horace Orlando *1921–1922*	Brixton	15. 7.1891	31. 5.1973
Boardman, Alfred Joseph *1878–1880*	Islington	11. 5.1859	1928
Boiling, James *1988*	New Delhi, India	8. 4.1968	
Boult, Farrington Holker *1872–1873*	Bath	12. 6.1852	21. 5.1882
Boultbee, St John *1867*	Bedford	30. 4.1843	4. 9.1898
Bowden, Montague Parker *1883–1888*	Stockwell	1.11.1865	19. 2.1892
Bowley, Thomas *1885–1891*	Basford	28. 2.1857	9.11.1939
Box, Thomas *1849*	Ardingly	7. 2.1808	12. 7.1876
Braund, Leonard Charles *1896–1898*	Clewer	18.10.1875	22.12.1955
Bray, Edward *1870–1878*	Shere	19. 8.1849	19. 6.1926
Brazier, Alan Frederick *1948–1954*	Paddington	7.12.1924	
Bridges, John Henry *1876*	Horsham	26. 3.1852	12. 2.1925
Bristow, John *1867–1873*	Esher	13. 4.1840	25. 1.1912
Brockwell, George *1844–1857*	Kingston-on-Thames	14. 8.1811	12.12.1876
Brockwell, William *1886–1903*	Kingston-on-Thames	21. 1.1865	1. 7.1935
Brooks, Edward William John *1925–1939*	Camberwell	6. 7.1898	10. 2.1960
Brooks, Richard *1889*	Sutton-on-Sea	29. 7.1863	9. 4.1927
Brown, Frederick Richard *1931–1948*	Lima, Peru	16.12.1910	
Brown, Graham Elliott *1986–1988*	Balham	11.10.1966	
Brown, Thomas *1868–1874*	Rusper	9. 8.1845	
Bryant, James Mark *1852*	Caterham	24.10.1826	10.12.1881

Buckle, Frederick *1867–1872*	Thames Ditton	25. 9.1849	1884
Budgen, Harry *1904–1909*	Reigate	1. 4.1879	13. 3.1944
Bullen, Christopher Keith *1982–1988*	Clapham	5.11.1962	
Bullock, Burnett (Wedlake) *1922–1924*	Redhill	5.10.1896	22.12.1954
Burbidge, Arthur *1857*	Camberwell	c1836	18.12.1890
Burbidge, Frederick *1854–1866*	Camberwell	23.11.1832	12.11.1892
Burls, Charles William *1873–1880*	Peckham Rye	8. 3.1847	17.12.1923
Burnett, John David *1862*	Vauxhall	25. 2.1840	18. 6.1878
Burrows, Montagu Brocas *1921*	Reigate	31.10.1894	17. 1.1967
Burton, Henry (Herbert) *1904*	Lambeth	1874	4. 2.1964
Bush, Frederick William *1879–1885*	East Dulwich	27. 2.1852	8. 1.1937
Bush, Harry Stebbing *1901–1912*	Dulwich	7.10.1871	18. 3.1942
Bush, Robert (Thompson) *1864–1868*	Kennington	14. 1.1839	24.12.1874
Bushell, Robert Hitchens *1857–1858*		c1836	13. 7.1883
Busher, Sydney Edmund *1908*	Solihull	19.12.1882	6.1953
Buss, Clarence Harold Henry *1934*	Weybridge	19. 2.1913	6.12.1974
Butcher, Alan Raymond *1972–1986*	Croydon	7. 1.1954	
Butcher, Douglas Harry *1900–1913*	Mitcham	15. 5.1876	4. 7.1945
Butcher, Martin Simon *1982*	Thornton Heath	17. 5.1958	
Caesar, Frederick Bowles *1859–1862*	Godalming	11.10.1827	5.10.1882
Caesar, Julius *1848–1867*	Godalming	25. 3.1830	6. 3.1878
Caesar, William Cecil *1922*	Clapham	25.11.1899	5. 4.1988
Caffarey, James *1881–1882*	Mitcham	c1861	12.1913
Caffyn, Walter Waller *1844*	Reigate	28.11.1814	26. 1.1895
Caffyn, William *1849–1873*	Reigate	2. 2.1828	28. 8.1919
Calvert, Charles *1868*	Isleworth	21. 3.1833	7. 4.1905
Campbell, Gerald Victor *1912*	Kensington	29. 4.1884	26. 3.1950
Campbell, Ian Percy Fitzgerald *1910–1927*	Palampur, Kangra Valley, Punjab	25.11.1890	25.12.1963
Carmichael, John *1876–1881*	Howden	4. 7.1858	24. 8.1914
Carter, William John *1871–1874*	Kennington	21. 1.1841	18.11.1888
Carver, George James *1907*	Long Ditton	4. 5.1879	1.10.1912
Cattley, Arthur Cyril *1882*	Croydon	27.11.1861	21. 9.1895
Cattley, Stephen Wildman *1879–1883*	Croydon	28.10.1860	11. 4.1925
Chandler, Allen *1873–1877*	Kensington	5.12.1849	25.12.1926
Charman, William *1875*	Epsom	23. 9.1850	1914
Cheatle, Robert Giles Lenthall *1980–1983*	Paddington	31. 7.1953	
Chenery, Charles John *1872–1873*	Lambourne	1. 1.1850	
Chester, Arthur *1873–1883*	Kingston-on-Thames	18.12.1851	13. 5.1915
Chester, James *1846–1858*	Kingston-on-Thames	30. 5.1823	23. 6.1888
Chinnery, Esme Fairfax *1906*	Hatchford	28. 3.1886	15. 1.1915
Chinnery, Harry Brodrick *1897–1904*	Teddington	6. 2.1876	28. 5.1916
Christy, Alfred *1857*	Southwark	17. 1.1818	23. 3.1876
Clark, Thomas Henry *1947–1959/60*	Luton	4.10.1924	14. 6.1981
Clarke, Alfred Ferrier *1890–1892*	Farnworth	12. 8.1865	1935
Clarke, Charles Frederick Carlos *1873–1882*	Welton	26. 4.1853	29. 1.1931
Clarke, Morice Carlos *1875–1886*	Welton	1852	14. 7.1887

Clarke, Sylvester Theophilus *1979–1988*	Lead Vale, Barbados	11.12.1954	
Clarke, William *1852*	Nottingham	24.12.1798	25. 8.1856
Clifford, George *1871–1878*	Barnes	19. 4.1852	1941
Clinton, Grahame Selvey *1979–1988*	Sidcup	5. 5.1953	
Clode, Harry Pile *1899–1903*	Kensington	7. 9.1877	1964
Cobbett, James *1839*	Frimley	12. 1.1804	31. 3.1842
Collett, William Eustace *1869–1874*	Lambeth	23. 9.1839	2. 5.1904
Collyer, William James *1866–1869*	Chobham	1. 6.1841	1. 9.1908
Colman, Stanley *1882*	Clapham	6. 1.1862	27. 2.1942
Coltson, Charles *1847–1851*	Kennington	1813	15. 3.1852
Comber, George *1880–1885*	Redhill	12.10.1856	18.10.1929
Comber, Robert Harrison *1851*	Mitcham	1816	28. 5.1858
Constable, Bernard *1939–1964*	East Molesey	19. 2.1921	
Cook, William Thomas *1921–1933*	Brixton	6.12.1891	22. 9.1969
Cooper, Sydney Hyde *1936*	Carshalton	5. 2.1913	20. 1.1982
Cosh, Nicholas John *1969*	Denmark Hill	6. 8.1946	
Cowderoy, John *1876*	Battersea	19. 4.1851	1934
Cox, Dennis Frank *1949–1957*	Bermondsey	21.12.1925	
Crawford, John Neville *1904–1921*	Cane Hill	1.12.1886	2. 5.1963
Crawford, Vivian Frank Shergold *1896–1902*	Leicester	11. 4.1879	21. 8.1922
Crouch, Henry Russell *1946*	Calcutta, India	10.12.1914	
Cumberlege, Charles Farrington *1872*	Kurreebee, India	29. 7.1851	12. 2.1929
Cumbes, James *1968–1969*	East Didsbury	4. 5.1944	
Curtis, Ian James *1983–1984*	Purley	13. 5.1959	
Curwen, Wilfred John Hutton *1909*	Beckenham	14. 4.1883	9. 5.1915
Cuthbertson, John Leyton *1963*	Bombay, India	24. 2.1942	
Daily, Charles Edwin *1923–1929*	Ockley	28. 4.1900	30. 6.1974
Daley, John Valiant *1936–1938*	Beccles	1. 2.1906	1986
Dalmeny, Lord *1903–1908* (Albert Edward Harry Mayer Archibald Primrose)	Westminster	8. 1.1882	30. 5.1974
Davies, Alec George *1985*	Rawalpindi, Pakistan	14. 8.1962	
Davis, James *1850*			
Davis, William Ernest *1903–1911*	Wimbledon	26.11.1880	27. 1.1959
Day, Daniel *1846–1852*	Streatham	14. 6.1807	22.11.1887
Deane, Marmaduke William *1880*	Petersham	25. 3.1857	1936
Dible, William Guy *1882* (known as William Charles Dible)	Stoneham	5.11.1861	15. 8.1894
Dickinson, Patrick John *1939*	Upper Barian, India	28. 8.1919	28. 5.1984
Diver, Edwin James *1883–1886*	Cambridge	20. 3.1861	27.12.1924
Dolbey, Hugh Owen *1899–1902*	Sutton	27.11.1879	14. 7.1936
Doughty, Richard James *1985–1987*	Bridlington	17.11.1960	
Douglas, Archibald Philip *1887*	Norwood Green	7. 6.1867	24. 1.1953
Douglas, Robert Noel *1890–1891*	Norwood Green	9.11.1868	27. 2.1957
Dowson, Edward *1860–1870*	Camberwell	17. 2.1838	29. 4.1922
Dowson, Edward Maurice *1900–1903*	Weybridge	21. 6.1880	22. 7.1933

Driver, Burrell Neale *1847–1852*	Southwark	c1820	25. 5.1877
Druce, Norman Frank *1895–1897*	Denmark Hill	1. 1.1875	27.10.1954
Ducat, Andrew *1906–1931*	Brixton	16. 2.1886	23. 7.1942
Dunn, John *1881*	Hobart, Tasmania	8. 6.1862	10.10.1892
Earle, Guy Fife *1911–1921*	Newcastle-on-Tyne	24. 8.1891	30.12.1966
Earnshaw, Alfred *1897*	Bloomsbury	7. 8.1814	8. 3.1895
Earnshaw, George Russell Bell *1880*	Clapham	5. 5.1857	29.12.1894
Edrich, John Hugh *1958–1978*	Blofield	21. 6.1937	
Edwards, Frank *1909*	Merstham	23. 5.1885	10. 7.1970
Edwards, Michael John *1961–1974*	Balham	1. 3.1940	
Eglington, Richard *1938*	Esher	1. 4.1908	20. 3.1979
Elliott, George Frederick *1875–1880*	Farnham	1. 5.1850	23. 4.1913
Estridge, George Tyler *1859–1860*	Carshalton	11. 8.1835	6. 6.1862
Falkner, Nicholas James *1984–1987*	Redhill	30. 9.1962	
Farmer, Arthur Augustus *1839*	London	22. 2.1815	17. 4.1897
Feltham, Mark Andrew *1983–1988*	St John's Wood	26. 6.1963	
Fender, Percy George Herbert *1914–1935*	Balham	22. 8.1892	15. 6.1985
Fenley, Stanley *1924–1939*	Kingston-on-Thames	4. 1.1896	2. 9.1972
Fielding, Felix *1889*	Lewisham	24. 2.1858	4. 2.1910
Finlay, Ian William *1965–1967*	Woking	14. 5.1946	
Fishlock, Laurence Barnard *1931–1952*	Battersea	2. 1.1907	26. 6.1986
Fletcher, David George William *1946–1951*	Sutton	6. 7.1924	
Fox, Charles John McDonald *1876*	Dum Dum, India	5.12.1858	1. 4.1901
Franklin, Henry William Fernehough *1921*	Ford End	30. 6.1901	25. 5.1985
Freeman, Albert *1871–1875*	Croydon	3. 6.1844	27. 3.1920
Freeman, Albert James *1919*	Kennington	9. 7.1887	1945
Frost, Mark *1988*	Barking	21.10.1962	
Gamble, Frederick Charles *1933–1935*	Charing Cross	29. 5.1905	15. 5.1965
Gamble, George (F–) *1906*	Leicester	24.10.1877	1949
Game, William Henry *1871–1883*	Stoke Newington	2.10.1853	11. 8.1932
Garland, Edward *1846*	Kennington	c1826	4. 9.1882
Garland-Wells, Herbert Montandon *1928–1939*	Brockley	14.11.1907	
Garth, Richard *1844*	Lasham	11. 3.1820	23. 3.1903
Geary, Albert Charles Taylor *1922–1931*	Croydon	11. 9.1900	
Gentry, Jack Sydney Bates *1922–1923*	Wanstead	4.10.1899	16. 4.1978
Gibson, David *1957–1969*	Mitcham	1. 5.1936	
Gilbert, Charles Arthur William *1877–1878*	Melton Mowbray	9. 1.1855	28. 9.1937
Gillespie, Francis Sydney *1913*	Croydon	26. 3.1889	18. 6.1916
Gilligan, Arthur Edward (Robert) *1919*	Denmark Hill	23.12.1894	5. 9.1976
Goatly, Edward Garnett *1901–1914*	Twickenham	3.12.1882	12. 2.1958
Gooder, Leonard Montague Harry *1901–1905*	Paddington	11. 2.1876	26.11.1928
Gordon, John Harvey *1906–1907*	Reigate	15. 6.1886	23. 4.1933
Gore, Spencer William *1874–1875*	Wimbledon	10. 3.1850	19. 4.1906
Gover, Alfred Richard *1928–1947*	Epsom	29. 2.1908	
Graburn, William Turbett *1894*	Filey	16. 3.1865	13.12.1944
Gray, Anthony Hollis *1985–1988*	Port of Spain, Trinidad	23. 5.1963	
Green, W– *1883*			

Greenfield, George Price *1867–1869*	Winchester	24. 1.1843	3. 9.1917
Greenwood, John Frederick *1874*	Epsom	10. 3.1851	31. 8.1935
Gregory, John Constable *1870–1871*	Marylebone	17. 8.1842	28. 6.1894
Gregory, Robert James *1925–1947*	Croydon	26. 8.1902	6.10.1973
Greig, Ian Alexander *1987–1988*	Queenstown, South Africa	8.12.1955	
Griffin, Neville (Featherstone) *1963*	Croydon	17.12.1933	
Griffith, George *1856–1871*	Ripley	20.12.1833	3. 5.1879
Griffith, Stewart Cathie *1934*	Wandsworth	16. 6.1914	
Groom, Robert *1846*	Shoreditch	15. 4.1816	
Gunn, Thomas William *1863–1869*	Croydon	10. 7.1843	4. 5.1908
Haden, J– V– *1882*			
Hadfield, George Hugh *1903–1904*	Edmonton	1880	30.11.1935
Hadingham, Anthony Wallace Gwynne *1932*	Mentone, France	1. 3.1913	14. 7.1986
Hall, Charles John *1868–1873*	Kingston-on-Thames	12. 8.1848	18.11.1931
Hall, John Keith *1958–1962*	West Wickham	29. 7.1934	
Hammersley, William Josiah *1848–1850*	Ash	25. 9.1826	15.11.1886
Hanbury, Edwin Charles *1871*	Clapham Park	23. 6.1848	1914
Hankey, Reginald *1855*	Marylebone	3.11.1832	25. 8.1886
Hansell, Thomas Michael Geoffrey *1975–1977*	Sutton Coldfield	24. 8.1954	
Harman, Roger *1961–1968*	Hersham	28.12.1941	
Harper, Leonard Vyse *1904*	Balham	12.12.1880	13. 1.1924
Harris, Stanley Shute *1904*	Clifton	19. 7.1881	4. 5.1926
Harrison, Harry Starr *1909–1923*	Cheam	12. 4.1883	8.12.1971
Hartley-Smith, Hartley *1880*	Kensington	1852	1905
Hartnell, Edward George *1853*	Balham	13. 8.1823	28.12.1897
Harwood, Frederick *1851–1865*	Mitcham	1. 6.1828	11.12.1887
Hayes, Ernest George *1896–1919*	Peckham	6.11.1876	2.12.1953
Hayward, Daniel Snr *1839–1847*	Mitcham	25. 8.1808	29. 5.1852
Hayward, Daniel Jnr *1854*	Chatteris	19.10.1832	30. 5.1910
Hayward, Thomas Walter *1893–1914*	Cambridge	29. 3.1871	19. 7.1939
Hearsum, John *1871*	Chelsea	2.11.1852	21. 7.1931
Heartfield, James *1860–1867*	Mitcham	19. 1.1823	1891
Heath, John *1846–1854*	Lambeth	12.11.1807	7.11.1878
Heath, Walter Hodsoll Gordon *1919*	Streatham	3.12.1897	4.12.1965
Henderson, Robert *1883–1896*	Newport	30. 3.1865	28. 1.1931
Hillyer, William Richard *1849*	Leybourne	5. 3.1813	8. 1.1861
Hinkly, Edmund *1848–1853*	Benenden	12. 1.1817	8.12.1880
Hitch, John William *1907–1925*	Radcliffe	7. 5.1886	7. 7.1965
Hoare, Arthur Malortie *1846–1847*	Blandford	18. 9.1821	26. 2.1894
Hoare, Charles Hugh *1846–1853*	Mitcham	24.10.1819	4. 4.1869
Hoare, Charles Twysden *1871–1874*	Mitcham	10.11.1851	22. 1.1935
Hobbs, John Berry *1906–1934*	Cambridge	16.12.1882	21.12.1963
Holland, Frederick Charles *1894–1908*	Battersea	10. 2.1876	5. 2.1957
Holmes, Errol Reginald Thorold *1924–1955*	Calcutta, India	21. 8.1905	16. 8.1960
Hooper, John Michael Mackenzie *1967–1971*	Milford	23. 4.1947	
Hore, Fraser Salter *1861*	Wimbledon	c1835	7. 7.1903
Horner, Charles Edward *1882–1886*	Dulwich Common	9. 4.1857	4. 9.1925
Howarth, Geoffrey Philip *1971–1985*	Auckland, N.Z.	29. 3.1951	

Howell, Leonard Sidgwick *1869–1880*	Dulwich	6. 8.1848	7. 9.1895
Howell, Miles *1919–1925*	Thames Ditton	9. 9.1893	23. 2.1976
Howell, Reginald *1878–1879*	Streatham	16. 4.1856	3. 8.1912
Humphrey, Richard *1870–1881*	Mitcham	12.12.1848	28. 2.1906
Humphrey, Richard Geoffrey *1964–1970*	Hampstead	17. 9.1936	
Humphrey, Thomas *1862–1874*	Mitcham	16. 1.1839	3. 9.1878
Humphrey, William *1864*	Mitcham	15. 9.1843	24. 2.1918
Hyndson, James Gerard Wyndham *1927*	Cape Town, S.A.	25. 4.1892	23. 2.1935
Intikhab Alam Khan *1969–1981*	Hoshiarpur, India	28.12.1941	
Jackman, Robin David *1966–1982*	Simla, India	13. 8.1945	
Jackson, McIvor Tindall *1903–1907*	Merton	24. 5.1880	15. 6.1936
Jardine, Douglas Robert *1921–1933*	Bombay, India	23.10.1900	18. 6.1958
Jeacocke, Alfred *1920–1934*	Islington	1.12.1892	25. 9.1961
Jefferson, Richard Ingleby *1961–1966*	Frimley	15. 8.1941	
Jennings, Thomas Shepherd *1921–1924*	Exeter	3.11.1896	7. 9.1972
Jephson, Digby Loder Armroid *1894–1904*	Clapham	23. 2.1871	19. 1.1926
Jesty, Trevor Edward *1985–1987*	Gosport	2. 6.1948	
Johnson, Fredrick *1878–1883*	Rolvenden	14. 3.1851	24.11.1923
Jones, George Gregory *1875–1888*	Mitcham	8. 1.1856	1. 4.1936
Judd, Peter *1960*	Balham	29. 4.1938	
Jupp, Henry *1862–1881*	Dorking	19.11.1841	8. 4.1889
Jupp, William Thomas *1876*	Dorking	11.11.1851	3. 8.1878
Keene, John William *1897*	Mitcham	25. 4.1873	3. 1.1931
Kelleher, Henry Robert Albert *1955*	Bermondsey	3. 3.1929	
Kember, Owen David *1962–1963*	Lingfield	23. 1.1943	
Kendrick, Neil Michael *1988*	Bromley	11.11.1967	
Kenrick, Jarvis *1876*	Chichester	13.11.1852	29. 1.1949
Kersley, Tom *1899*	Surbiton	9. 2.1879	1927
Key, Kingsmill James *1882–1904*	Streatham	11.10.1864	9. 8.1932
Killick, William *1876*	Reigate	14. 5.1855	2. 4.1938
King, Kenneth Charles William *1936–1938*	Beddington	4.12.1915	
King, Percival *1871*	Stockwell	9.12.1835	29.10.1910
Kingsford, Robert Kennett *1872–1874*	Sydenham	23.12.1849	14.10.1895
Kirby, Geoffrey Norman George *1948–1953*	Reading	6.11.1923	
Kirk, Ernest Charles *1906–1921*	Clapham	21. 3.1884	19.12.1932
Knight, Donald John *1911–1937*	Sutton	12. 5.1894	5. 1.1960
Knight, Roger David Verdon *1968–1984*	Streatham	6. 9.1946	
Knox, Frank Pery *1899–1902*	Clapham	23. 1.1880	1. 2.1960
Knox, Neville Alexander *1904–1910*	Clapham	10.10.1884	3. 3.1935
Lagden, Reginald Bousfield *1912*	Maseru, Basutoland	15. 4.1893	20.10.1944
Laker, James Charles *1946–1959*	Frizinghall	9. 2.1922	23. 4.1986
Lane, Charlton George *1856–1861*	Kennington	11. 6.1836	2.11.1892
Lane, William Ward Claypon *1868–1870*	Kennington	1. 8.1845	31. 3.1939
Lawrence, Charles *1854–1857*	Hoxton	16.12.1828	6. 1.1917
Leaf, Herbert *1877*	Norwood	10.10.1854	13. 2.1936
Lee, Frederick *1861*	Finsbury	11. 8.1840	13.11.1922
Lee, John Morley *1847–1850*	London	12.10.1825	20. 1.1903
Lees, Walter Scott *1896–1911*	Sowerby Bridge	25.12.1875	10. 9.1924
Leveson-Gower, Henry Dudley Gresham *1895–1920*	Limpsfield	8. 5.1873	1. 2.1954

Name	Place	Born	Died
Lewis, Roy Markham 1968–1973	Bromley	29. 6.1948	
Lindsay, William 1876–1882	India	3. 8.1847	15. 2.1923
Loader, Peter James 1951–1963	Wallington	25.10.1929	
Lock, Graham Anthony Richard 1946–1963	Limpsfield	5. 7.1929	
Lock, Herbert Christmas 1926–1932	East Molesey	8. 5.1903	19. 5.1978
Lock, Norman William 1934	Ham Common	13. 3.1912	
Lockton, John Henry 1919–1926	Peckham	22. 5.1892	29. 6.1972
Lockwood, William (Henry) 1889–1904	Old Radford	25. 3.1868	26. 4.1932
Lockyer, Thomas 1849–1866	Croydon	1.11.1826	22.12.1869
Lohmann, George Alfred 1884–1896	Kensington	2. 6.1865	1.12.1901
Long, Arnold 1960–1975	Cheam	18.12.1940	
Long, Robert 1870	Richmond	9.11.1846	6. 8.1924
Longman, Henry Kerr 1901–1908	Kensington	8. 3.1881	7.10.1958
Lowe, Ronald Francis 1923	Shepherd's Bush	28. 7.1905	29. 8.1960
Lowles, George William 1887	Whitechapel	1865	1940
Lowther, Hon. Henry Cecil 1839	Lowther Castle	27. 7.1790	6.12.1867
Lucas, Alfred Perry 1874–1882	Westminster	20. 2.1857	12.10.1923
Lucas, Arthur Charles 1874	Lowestoft	22. 5.1853	14. 6.1915
Luff, Alfred 1867	Kew	5. 4.1846	1925
Lutterlock, Edward 1874	Stockwell	26. 2.1852	1938
Lynch, Monte Alan 1977–1988	Georgetown, British Guiana	21. 5.1958	
Lyons, Godfrey Louis 1880	Fleetwood	23. 5.1854	1931
Lywood, Lewis William 1927–1928	Walthamstow	23.12.1906	31.10.1971
McCanlis, Maurice Alfred 1926–1927	Quetta, India	17. 6.1906	
McDonell, Harold Clark 1901–1904	Wimbledon	19. 9.1882	23. 7.1966
McEntyre, Kenneth Brinsley 1965–1966	Chester	24. 3.1944	
Machin, Reginald Stanley 1927–1930	Weybridge	16. 4.1904	3.11.1968
McIntyre, Arthur John William 1938–1963	Kennington	14. 5.1918	
Mack, Andrew James 1976–1977	Aylsham	14. 1.1956	
McKelvey, Patrick George 1959–1960	Barnet	25.12.1935	
Mackintosh, Kevin Scott 1981–1983	Surbiton	30. 8.1957	
McMahon, John William Joseph 1947–1953	Balaclava, S. Australia	28.12.1919	
McMurray, Thomas 1933–1939	Belfast	24. 7.1911	24. 3.1964
Macniven, Edward 1851	Offley	1. 6.1827	4. 1.1858
Majendie, Nicholas Lionel 1963	Cheltenham	9. 6.1942	
Marriott, Dennis Alston 1965–1967	Annotto Bay, Jamaica	24.11.1939	
Marshal, Alan 1907–1910	Warwick, Queensland	12. 6.1883	23. 7.1915
Marshall, Alexander 1849–1857	Godalming	31.10.1820	28. 9.1871
Marshall, Charles 1893–1899	Woodville	1.10.1863	20.11.1948
Marshall, Henry 1853–1854	Godalming	22. 4.1831	30. 4.1914
Marten, William George 1871–1872	Tunbridge Wells	5. 9.1845	25.11.1907
Martingell, William 1839–1859	Nutfield	20. 8.1818	29. 9.1897
Mathews, Frederick John 1883	Thames Ditton	7. 3.1861	9. 2.1950
May, Peter Barker Howard 1950–1963	Reading	31.12.1929	
May, Percy Robert 1902–1909	Chertsey	13. 3.1884	6.12.1965
Mayo, Henry Edward 1868–1870	South Lambeth	13.11.1847	30.10.1891
Mays, Christopher Sean 1987–1988	Brighton	11. 5.1966	

Name	Place	Born	Died
Meads, James Wilford *1905* (known as James Wilfred)	Calverton	28.10.1877	3.11.1957
Medlycott, Keith Thomas *1984–1988*	Whitechapel	12. 5.1965	
Merrall, John Edwin *1932–1933*	Shipley	7. 1.1909	
Meymott, Charles *1847*	Southwark	8. 1.1813	24. 6.1867
Miller, Frederick Peel *1851–1867*	Clapham	29. 7.1828	22.11.1875
Miller, Neville *1899–1903*	Shanghai, China	27. 8.1874	3. 3.1967
Mills, Charles Henry *1888*	Peckham	26.11.1867	26. 7.1948
Mills, Edwin *1885–1887*	Coddington	6. 3.1857	25. 1.1899
Mobey, Gerald Spencer *1930–1948*	Surbiton	5. 3.1904	
Molony, Trevor James *1921*	Kensington	6. 7.1897	3. 9.1962
Money, Walter Baptist *1869*	Sternfield	27. 7.1848	1. 3.1924
Monkhouse, Graham *1981–1986*	Long Wathby	26. 4.1954	
Montgomery, William *1901–1904*	Staines	4. 3.1878	14.11.1952
Morgan, Charles *1871*	Greenwich	29. 1.1839	17. 7.1904
Morris, Norman *1873*	Peckham	1849	20. 1.1874
Mortlock, William *1851–1870*	Kennington	18. 7.1832	23. 1.1884
Morton, Philip Howard *1884*	Tallerford	20. 6.1857	13. 5.1925
Moulder, John Hardie *1902–1906*	Richmond	29. 9.1881	13.10.1933
Mudie, William *1856–1865*	Kennington	26. 4.1836	25. 1.1871
Myers, Edwin Bertram *1910–1914*	Blackheath	5. 7.1888	15. 9.1916
Naumann, Frank Charles Gordon *1919–1921*	Lewisham	9. 4.1892	30.10.1947
Needham, Andrew *1977–1986*	Calow	23. 3.1957	
Nevell, William Thomas *1939*	Balham	13. 6.1916	25. 8.1978
Newman, Frederick Charles William *1919–1921*	Luton	2. 2.1896	1. 1.1966
Newnham, Stanley William *1932*	New Cross	7. 4.1910	2.12.1985
Nice, Ernest Herbert Leonard *1895–1905*	Redhill	1. 8.1875	6. 6.1946
Nightingale, James *1868*	Reigate	10. 8.1840	9. 2.1917
Noble, Charles *1868*	Kennington	9. 2.1850	1927
Noble, John Wilson *1866–1869*	Kennington	4. 8.1845	20. 4.1889
O'Gorman, Joseph George *1927*	Walworth	24. 7.1890	26. 8.1974
Oliver, Frederick William *1855–1856*	Mayfair	4. 1.1836	9. 7.1899
Owen, Joseph Glyn *1930–1933*	Llanelly	23. 1.1909	17. 2.1978
Owen-Thomas, Dudley Richard *1970–1975*	Mombassa, Kenya	20. 9.1948	
Palmer, William Thomas *1872–1876*	Canterbury	5. 1.1847	2. 9.1906
Parfitt, James John Alexander *1881–1882*	Brecon	23.12.1857	17. 5.1926
Parker, John Frederick *1932–1952*	Battersea	23. 4.1913	26. 1.1983
Parr, George *1852*	Radcliffe-on-Trent	22. 5.1826	23. 6.1891
Parsons, Arthur Brian Douglas *1958–1963*	Guildford	20. 9.1933	
Pauline, Duncan Brian *1979–1985*	Aberdeen	15.12.1960	
Payne, Ian Roger *1977–1984*	Kennington	9. 5.1958	
Peach, Herbert Alan *1919–1931*	Maidstone	6.10.1890	8.10.1961
Penfold, Alexander George *1929*	Kenley	14. 5.1901	28. 9.1982
Peters, Nicholas Howard *1988*	Guildford	21. 2.1968	
Peto, John *1847*	Guildford	c1810	22. 2.1874
Pickering, Edward Haynes *1844*	Clapham	21. 5.1807	19. 5.1852
Pickering, William Percival *1844–1848*	Clapham	25.10.1819	16. 8.1905
Pierpoint, Frederick George *1936–1946*	Walworth	24. 4.1915	
Piggott, Julian Ito *1910–1913*	Tokyo, Japan	25. 3.1888	23. 1.1965

Pilch, Fuller *1844*	Horningtoft	17. 3.1803	1. 5.1870
Pilkington, Alfred Frederick *1926*	Camberwell	22. 4.1901	10.1986
Platt, George (John) William *1906–1914*	Richmond	9. 6.1881	14. 4.1955
Pocock, Patrick Ian *1964–1986*	Bangor	24. 9.1946	
Ponsonby, Hon Frederick George Brabazon *1839*	London	11. 9.1815	12. 3.1895
Ponsonby, Hon Spencer Cecil Brabazon *1844–1853*	Marylebone	14. 3.1824	1.12.1915
Pontifex, Dudley David *1881*	Bath	12. 2.1855	27. 9.1934
Pooley, Edward *1861–1883*	Richmond	13. 2.1838	18. 7.1907
Pooley, Frederick William *1876–1877*	Richmond	7. 4.1852	14. 9.1905
Potter, Charles Warren *1869–1871*	Albury	18. 4.1851	6. 6.1895
Potter, Joseph *1875–1881*	Northampton	13. 1.1839	2. 6.1906
Powell, Ernest Ormsby *1882*	Liverpool	19. 1.1861	28. 3.1928
Pratt, Derek Edward *1954–1957*	Balham	31.10.1925	
Pratt, John *1867*	Mitcham	4. 2.1834	6. 6.1886
Pratt, Ronald Charles Ernest *1952–1959*	Balham	5. 5.1928	1. 6.1977
Pretty, Harold Cooper *1899*	Fressingfield	23.10.1875	31. 5.1952
Price, Vincent Rains *1919*	Sutton	22. 5.1895	29. 5.1973
Ransom, Victor Joseph *1951–1955*	New Malden	17. 5.1917	
Raphael, John Edward *1903–1909*	Brussels, Belgium	30. 4.1882	11. 6.1917
Ratcliff, John *1876*	Richmond	31.12.1848	11. 8.1925
Ratcliffe, Alan *1932–1935*	Dulwich	31. 3.1909	21. 8.1967
Read, Frederick Hurrell *1881*	Thames Ditton	26.12.1855	4. 5.1933
Read, Holcombe Douglas *1933*	Woodford Green	28. 1.1910	
Read, John Maurice *1880–1895*	Thames Ditton	9. 2.1859	17. 2.1929
Read, Walter William *1873–1897*	Reigate	23.11.1855	6. 1.1907
Reay, Gilbert Martin *1913–1923*	Wallington	24. 1.1887	31. 1.1967
Redgewell, Louis John *1922–1923*	Battersea	13.10.1894	17. 2.1966
Reeves, Edmund *1848–1852*	Kennington	27.11.1821	10.12.1906
Reiner, Charles Frederick *1906*	Sutton	15. 2.1884	9. 1.1947
Richards, Clifton James *1976–1988*	Penzance	10. 8.1958	
Richards, James Henry *1881*	Brixton	1855	24. 8.1923
Richardson, Harold Bamford *1899*		10. 3.1873	
Richardson, Thomas *1892–1904*	Byfleet	11. 8.1870	2. 7.1912
Ricketts, George William *1887*	Allahabad, India	2. 6.1864	16. 6.1927
Roberts, Desmond *1921*	Hampstead	5. 2.1894	11. 1.1968
Roberts, Frederick *1867–1868*	Kennington	24. 9.1848	1903
Robertson, Frederick Marrant *1877*	Ramble, Jamaica	1843	28. 3.1920
Robinson, Jonathan David *1988*	Epsom	3. 8.1966	
Rogers, George Russell *1870*	West Brixton	20. 4.1847	14.12.1905
Roller, Charles Trevor *1886*	Clapham	28. 2.1865	15.11.1912
Roller, William Eyton *1881–1890*	Clapham	1. 2.1858	27. 8.1949
Roope, Graham Richard James *1964–1982*	Fareham	12. 7.1946	
Rose, John *1878*	Warwick	24.12.1853	6.11.1920
Rudd, William James *1904*	Little Amwell	29. 6.1880	27. 3.1971
Rushby, Thomas *1903–1921*	Cobham	6. 9.1880	13. 7.1962
Rushworth, William Robert *1946*	Dulwich	4.11.1914	19. 1.1966
Russell, Stephen George *1967*	Sutton	13. 3.1945	
Rutty, Arthur William Forder *1910*	Reading	22. 8.1872	10. 1.1932

Sadiq, Zahid Asa *1988*	Nairobi, Kenya	6. 5.1965	
Sadler, William Cecil Holborn *1928–1925*	Kings Cross	24. 9.1896	12. 2.1981
Sandham, Andrew *1911–1937*	Streatham	6. 7.1890	20. 4.1982
Sarel, William Godfrey Molyneaux *1904–1909*	Dover	15.12.1875	5. 4.1950
Selvey, Michael Walter William *1968–1971*	Chiswick	25. 4.1948	
Sewell, Thomas snr *1839–1849*	Mitcham	5. 5.1806	1.11.1888
Sewell, Thomas jnr *1859–1868*	Mitcham	15. 3.1830	13. 6.1871
Sewell, William Humphrey *1844*	Mitcham	7. 8.1808	1865
Shadwell, Francis Bradby *1880*	Barnes	4. 5.1851	9. 2.1915
Sharpe, John William *1889–1893*	Ruddington	9.12.1866	19. 6.1936
Sheffield, Edward James *1930–1932*	New Eltham	20. 6.1908	28. 4.1971
Shepherd, Thomas Frederick *1919–1932*	Headington	5.12.1889	13. 2.1957
Shepherd, William *1864–1865*	Kennington	9. 8.1841	27. 5.1919
Sheppard, Robert Alexander *1904–1905*	Croydon	24. 8.1879	28. 1.1953
Sherman, Thomas *1847–1870*	Mitcham	1.12.1825	10.10.1911
Shuter, John *1877–1909*	Thornton Heath	9. 2.1855	5. 7.1920
Shuter, Leonard Allen *1876–1883*	Thornton Heath	25. 5.1852	13. 7.1928
Simmonds, Arthur *1872–1873*	Godalming	1. 2.1848	2. 8.1933
Skinner, Edward Alfred *1871–1881*	Mitcham	18. 1.1847	10. 2.1919
Skinner, Lonsdale Ernest *1971–1977*	Plaisance, British Guiana	7. 9.1950	
Slater, Philip Hugh *1911*	Canterbury	1876	20. 8.1958
Smith, David Mark *1973–1988*	Balham	9. 1.1956	
Smith, Edward *1858*	London	1. 6.1832	16. 6.1899
Smith, Frank Ernest *1893–1908*	Bury St Edmunds	13. 5.1872	3.12.1943
Smith, Gilbert Oswald *1896*	Croydon	25.11.1872	6.12.1943
Smith, Thomas *1876*	Guildford	6. 4.1854	
Smith, William Albert *1961–1970*	Salisbury	15. 9.1937	
Smith, William Charles *1900–1914*	Oxford	4.10.1877	15. 7.1946
Snow, Henry *1839*	London	2.1811	20. 1.1874
Soden, Frederick Brewer *1870–1871*	Clapham Common	30. 3.1846	13. 4.1877
Southerton, James *1854–1879*	Petworth	16.11.1827	16. 6.1880
Spicer, William Baldwin *1870*	Kensington	18. 5.1846	1892
Spring, William Amos *1906–1913*	Dulwich	17. 5.1880	14. 3.1958
Squires, Harry Stanley *1928–1949*	Kingston-on-Thames	22. 2.1909	24. 1.1950
Stacey, Charles Frederick *1901*	Chalfont St Giles	27. 4.1878	1950
Stafford, James Pratt *1864*	Godalming	1844	24. 8.1919
Staveley, Miles *1870*	St Pancras	12. 8.1846	
Stedman, Frederick *1899–1908*	Cobham	4. 3.1872	5. 2.1918
Stephenson, Heathfield Harman *1853–1871*	Esher	3. 5.1833	17.12.1896
Stevens, John *1874–1875*	Guildford	5.10.1854	
Stewart, Alec James *1981–1988*	Merton	8. 4.1963	
Stewart, Michael James *1954–1972*	Herne Hill	16. 9.1932	
Stockley, Anthony John *1968*	Kingston-on-Thames	4. 4.1940	
Stoner, Arthur *1899–1900*	Streatham	11. 5.1871	
Storey, Stewart James *1960–1974*	Worthing	6. 1.1941	
Strachan, George *1872–1880*	Prestbury	21.11.1850	29.12.1901

Strahan, William *1839–1849*	Westminster	21. 8.1807	2. 7.1886
(born William Snow)			
Streatfeild, Edward Champion *1890–1892*	Nutfield	16. 6.1870	22. 8.1932
Street, Alfred Edward *1892–1898*	Godalming	7. 7.1869	18. 2.1951
Street, James *1863–1878*	Cranleigh	10. 3.1839	17. 9.1906
Stroud, Eric Gundry *1930*	Caterham	11. 7.1904	14. 8.1944
Strudwick, Herbert *1902–1927*	Mitcham	28. 1.1880	14. 2.1970
Subba Row, Raman *1953–1954*	Croydon	29. 1.1932	
Sullivan, Dennis *1914–1921*	Mitcham	28. 1.1883	28.12.1968
Surridge, Stuart Spicer *1978*	Westminster	28.10.1951	
Surridge, Walter Stuart *1947–1959/60*	Herne Hill	3. 9.1917	
Swan, John James *1870–1876*	Oadby	24. 9.1848	22. 2.1924
Swetman, Roy *1954–1961*	Croydon	25.10.1933	
Sydenham, David Alfred Donald *1957–1972*	Surbiton	6. 4.1934	
Tabor, Arthur Sydney *1878*	Trent	9.11.1852	14.10.1927
Tanner, William *1866–1868*	Weybridge	11. 4.1841	
Taylor, Andrew *1865*	Camberwell	20. 4.1838	1901
Taylor, Derek John Somerset *1966–1969*	Amersham	12.11.1942	
Taylor, Edward Fairfax *1865–1867*	Holborn	10. 7.1845	27. 1.1902
Taylor, Nicholas Simon *1984–1985*	Holmfirth	2. 6.1963	
Taylor, William *1852–1855*	Dorking	17. 5.1821	29. 3.1878
Teesdale, Hugh *1906–1908*	Staines	12. 2.1886	31. 3.1971
Thain, Caryl *1923*	Portsmouth	11. 4.1895	24. 9.1969
Thomas, David James *1977–1987*	Solihull	30. 6.1959	
Thompson, Herbert *1894–1919*	Norwood	6.12.1869	22.10.1947
Thorpe, Graham Paul *1988*	Farnham	1. 8.1969	
Tillard, Charles *1874–1875*	Wimbledon	18. 4.1851	7. 3.1944
Tindall, Ronald Albert Ernest *1956–1966*	Streatham	23. 9.1935	
Titmus, Frederick John *1978*	St Pancras	24.11.1932	
Topley, Thomas Donald *1985*	Canterbury	25. 2.1964	
Trodd, Thomas *1879–1880*		1852	26. 7.1908
Trodd, William *1869*	Stoke-next-Guildford	7. 8.1836	9. 4.1880
Trollope, William Stapleton *1877–1882*	Lambeth	31. 7.1854	20. 9.1895
Trouncer, Charles Albert *1888*	Uckfield	14. 8.1866	13. 3.1938
Tufnell, Neville Charsley *1922*	Simla, India	13. 6.1887	3. 8.1951
Verrinder, Alan Otto Charles *1974–1976*	Henley-on-Thames	28. 7.1955	
Vigar, Herbert Evelyn *1906–1911*	Redhill	29.11.1883	27.10.1946
Vince, John *1870*	Hackbridge	31.12.1849	1886
Vincett, John Herbert *1921*	Hastings	24. 5.1883	28.12.1953
Von Ernsthausen, Adolph Christian *1900–1901*	Belsize Park	17.10.1880	29. 5.1928
(later A. C. E. Howeson)			
Voss, Ralph *1883–1886*	Croydon	30. 3.1860	16.11.1900
Vyse, Edmund Waller *1857*	Luton	20. 2.1831	11. 4.1890
Wait, Owen John *1950–1951*	Dulwich	2. 8.1926	26. 4.1981
Walker, Livingstone *1900–1903*	Urmston	14. 6.1879	10.10.1940
Waller, Christopher Edward *1967–1973*	Guildford	3.10.1948	
Walter, Clarence Richard *1859*	Guildford	16. 4.1838	1918
Wanostrocht, Nicholas *1846–1852*	Camberwell	5.10.1804	3. 9.1876
(N. Felix)			
Ward, David Mark *1985–1988*	Croydon	10. 2.1961	
Waterman, Peter Andrew *1983–1985*	Pinner	26. 3.1961	

Watney, James *1851*	Beddington	19. 5.1832	2.11.1886
Watts, Edward Alfred *1933–1949*	Peckham	1. 8.1911	2. 5.1982
Watts, George Herbert *1890–1892*	Cambridge	18. 2.1867	22. 4.1949
Watts, Thomas *1922–1926*	Kennington	21. 8.1899	19. 1.1976
Weeks, Donald *1933*	Lewisham	5. 2.1903	1967
Wellings, Evelyn Maitland *1931*	Alexandria, Egypt	6. 4.1909	
Wells, Cyril Mowbray *1892–1893*	St Pancras	21. 3.1871	22. 8.1963
Westerman, Peter *1949–1951*	East Sheen	12. 8.1920	
Whale, George *1861–1867*	Guildford	27. 3.1833	1896
Wheatley, Garth Angus *1947*	Twickenham	28. 5.1923	
Wheeler, Alfred *1872–1873*	Croydon	2.10.1845	
Wheeler, Walter Charles *1875*	Newport IOW	30.12.1841	10.10.1907
White, Capt. – *1850*			
White, A– C– *1881*			
White, Charles *1850*	Southwark	c1823	18. 2.1873
White, Jack *1926*	Putney	9. 7.1893	6.11.1968
Whitfield, Edward Walter *1930–1939*	Clapham	31. 5.1911	
Whitley, Robert Thomas *1873*	Pimlico	1837	26.10.1887
Whittaker, Geoffrey James *1937–1953*	Peckham	29. 5.1916	
Whyting, Charles Henry *1939*		c1812	23. 4.1866
Wilkinson, Cyril Theodore Anstruther *1909–1920*	Durham	4.10.1884	16.12.1970
Willett, Michael David *1955–1967*	Norwood	21. 4.1933	
Willis, Henry *1868*	Sydenham	17. 3.1841	29. 9.1926
Willis, Robert George (Dylan) *1969–1971*	Sunderland	30. 5.1949	
Wilson, Claude William *1881*	Banbury	9. 9.1858	7. 7.1881
Wilson, Ernest Frederick *1928–1936*	Caterham	24. 6.1907	3. 3.1981
Wilson, Peter Hugh L'Estrange *1978–1982*	Guildford	17. 8.1958	
Wiltshire, Edgar *1902–1903*	Addiscombe	25. 9.1877	25. 8.1912
Wingfield, W– *1881*			
Winlaw, Roger de Winton Kelsall *1932–1934*	Morden	28. 3.1912	31.10.1942
Winterborne, Gary *1986*	Hammersmith	26. 6.1967	
Wood, Henry *1884–1900*	Dartford	14.12.1853	30. 4.1919
Wood, W– *1883*			
Woodgate, Thomas William *1877*	Holborn	5.1857	30. 1.1929
Wyatt, George Nevile *1877–1879*	Chumparum, India	25. 8.1850	16. 2.1926
Wyld, William George *1879–1887*	Stirling	3.12.1859	16. 7.1900
Yates, G– *1851–1854*			
Yeatman, Rex Herbert *1946–1947*	Kew	4.10.1919	
Younis Ahmed *1965–1978* (formerly Mohammed Younis)	Jullundur, India	20.10.1947	

CAREER RECORDS
OF SURREY PLAYERS 1839–1988

The statistics below do not include the following matches: A Surrey XI v The Rest (1949); Surrey v The World (played in Australia 1861/62); Players of Surrey v Gents of South (1863); Surrey Club matches. (★ = not out).

Name	Inns	NO	Runs	HS	Avge	100s	Runs	Wkts	Avge	Best	5wI
Abbott, C. J.	1	0	2	2	2.00	0					
Abbott, W.	5	0	9	5	1.80	0					
Abel, R.	813	59	27605	357★	36.61	64	5966	256	23.30	6/15	3
Abel, T. E.	13	1	224	50★	18.67	0	718	23	31.22	3/30	0
Abel, W. J.	245	29	4984	117	23.07	1	5685	184	30.90	5/28	3
Adams, D.	2	0	26	14	13.00	0	83	1	83.00	1/28	0
Adams, H. J.	7	4	25	9	8.33	0					
Akroyd, B. N.	12	0	108	30	9.00	0	14	0	—		
Akroyd, S. H.	40	0	622	87	15.55	0					
Alexander, G. C.	1	0	0	0	0.00	0					
Allom, A. T. C.	1	1	0	0★	—	0	53	0	—	—	—
Allom, M. J. C.	107	17	952	64	10.58	0	7546	333	22.66	7/71	18
Altham, H. S.	14	2	237	51	19.75	0					
Anstead, W. H.	12	2	61	17	6.10	0	542	48	11.29	6/27	5
Arnold, G. G.	217	52	2302	63	13.95	0	14857	745	19.94	8/41	32
Ashby, D.	2	0	0	0	0.00	0	8	0	—	—	—
Atkins, P. D.	11	1	357	114★	35.70	1					
Avory, H. K.	4	0	82	42	20.50	0					
Aworth, C. J.	47	4	965	115	22.44	1	353	5	70.60	2/23	0
Ayres, G. W.	33	1	407	44	12.72	0	27	0	—	—	—
Baggallay, T. W.	13	0	178	82	13.69	0					
Baily, R. E. H.	10	0	155	61	15.50	0					
Bainbridge, H. W.	17	1	175	32	10.94	0	89	2	44.50	1/18	0
Baker, A.	162	18	3729	155★	25.90	5	34	1	34.00	1/3	0
Baker, R. P.	56	30	563	91	21.65	0					
Baker, W. D.	6	0	48	16	8.00	0	2942	104	28.29	6/29	1
Baldwin, C.	126	12	2757	234	24.18	3	87	0	—	—	—
Baldwin, H. G.	46	8	509	63★	13.39	0	321	3	107.00	2/83	0
Bale, E. W.	1	0	6	6	6.00	0					
Barker, K. E. M.	8	0	141	52	17.63	0	25	0	—	—	—
Barker, W.	2	0	1	1	0.50	0	40	0	—	—	—
Barling, H. T.	605	54	18995	269	34.47	34	530	7	75.71	3/46	0
Barnato, J. W.	8	1	23	7	3.29	0					
Barratt, E.	210	48	1403	67	8.66	0	12227	706	17.32	8/28	62
Barrington, K. F.	564	99	19197	207	41.28	43	4729	133	35.55	5/46	4
Bartlett, H. T.	5	1	86	61	21.50	0					
Barton, M. R.	183	13	3975	132	23.38	5					
Batchelar, A.	3	1	11	8★	5.50	0	20	1	20.00	1/20	0
Bayford, R. A.	6	0	24	10	4.00	0					
Bayley, J.	7	4	38	17★	12.67	0	+19	—	—	5/?	2
Bayley, M.	1	1	8	8★	—	0	19	0	—	—	—
Beard, T. A.	6	1	29	10	5.80	0					
Beauchamp, J.	10	1	56	30	6.22	0					

Name	Inns	NO	**Batting** Runs	HS	Avge	100s	Runs	**Bowling** Wkts	Avge	Best	5wI
Beaumont, J.	120	38	738	60	9.00	0	6222	404	15.40	8/40	28
Bedser, A. V.	429	148	4108	126	14.62	1	27918	1459	19.14	8/18	72
Bedser, E. A.	669	78	14148	163	23.94	9	19831	797	24.88	7/33	24
Bell, R.	2	0	4	3	2.00	0					
Bennett, C. T.	6	0	82	26	13.67	0					
Bennett, N. H.	45	2	688	79	16.00	0	25	1	25.00	1/1	0
Berrington, E. H.	2	0	16	8	8.00	0	4	0	—	—	—
Berry, F.	64	11	1004	104*	18.94	1	2192	75	29.23	5/61	1
Bickley, J.	1	0	0	0	0.00	0	63	8	7.88	5/33	1
Bicknell, D. J.	39	4	943	105	26.94	1	19	0	—	—	—
Bicknell, M. P.	37	12	222	33	8.88	0	3108	119	26.11	9/45	3
Bigwood, A.	2	1	5	4	5.00	0					
Bird, M. C.	203	8	4880	151	25.03	4	2858	114	25.07	5/48	2
Birley, F. H.	2	0	7	6	3.50	0					
Blacklidge, H. G.	9	2	100	45	14.29	0	334	10	33.40	4/26	0
Blackman, A.	2	0	5	3	2.50	0					
Blamires, N.	55	12	406	31	9.44	0	2576	127	20.28	8/77	9
Block, S. A.	46	3	1135	117	26.40	1	21	2	10.50	1/0	0
Bloomfield, H. O.	7	2	180	107*	36.00	1					
Boardman, A. J.	17	2	157	33	10.47	0	37	0	—	—	—
Boiling, J.	2	1	9	8*	9.00	0	40	0	—	—	—
Boult, F. H.	41	0	536	65	13.07	0	1117	52	21.48	5/32	1
Boultbee, St.J.	4	1	20	10	6.67	0	76	3	25.33	2/54	0
Bowden, M. P.	109	11	1880	189*	19.18	2	14	0	—	—	—
Bowley, T.	100	26	695	46	9.39	0	4182	256	16.34	7/64	9
Box, T.	4	0	48	19	12.00	0					
Braund, L. C.	28	2	409	85	15.73	0	193	2	96.50	1/12	0
Bray, E.	26	4	184	36	8.36	0	742	48	15.46	7/32	4
Brazier, A. F.	56	11	979	92	21.76	0	7	0	—	—	—
Bridges, J. H.	2	0	9	8	4.50	0					
Bristow, J.	58	8	514	79	10.28	0	1503	73	20.58	7/45	5
Brockwell, G.	58	7	605	57	11.86	0	136	5+33	27.20	4/?	0
Brockwell, W.	472	45	11830	225	27.70	20	12273	500	24.55	8/22	21
Brooks, E. W. J.	437	96	4437	70	13.01	0	6	0	—	—	—
Brooks, R.	1	0	4	4	4.00	0					
Brown, F. R.	159	16	3982	212	27.85	9	10548	429	24.59	8/34	30
Brown, C. E.	11	8	59	13*	19.66	0					
Brown, T.	15	2	58	10	4.46	0	123	7	17.57	4/16	0
Bryant, J. M.	3	2	8	5	8.00	0	65	2	32.50	2/54	0
Buckle, F.	25	4	156	31	7.43	0	165	6	27.50	2/40	0
Budgen, H.	4	0	58	30	14.50	0	213	3	71.00	3/112	0
Bullen, C. K.	31	5	573	65	22.03	0	984	34	28.94	6/119	1
Bullock, B. W	8	1	121	40	17.29	0					
Burbidge, A.	4	0	24	8	6.00	0					
Burbidge, F.	68	9	799	101	13.54	1					
Burls, C. W.	17	0	99	16	5.82	0					
Burnett, J. D.	2	0	9	5	4.50	0					
Burrows, M. B.	2	1	26	24*	26.00	0	117	3	39.00	2/58	0
Burton, H. H.	6	1	126	48*	25.20	0					
Bush, F. W.	12	0	70	22	5.83	0	216	6	36.00	1/13	0
Bush, H. S.	109	7	2532	135	24.82	4	161	2	80.50	1/12	0

Name	Inns	NO	Runs	HS	Avge	100s	Runs	Wkts	Avge	Best	5wI
			Batting				**Bowling**				
Bush, R. T.	4	1	21	8*	7.00	0					
Bushell, R. H.	4	0	23	17	5.75	0					
Busher, S. E.	1	0	52	52	52.00	0	92	7	13.14	4/41	0
Buss, C. H. H.	2	0	47	42	23.50	0	143	2	71.50	2/90	0
Butcher, A. R.	479	43	14571	216*	33.41	29	4689	125	37.51	6/48	1
Butcher, D. H.	11	1	187	71	18.70	0					
Butcher, M. S.							2	0	—	—	—
Caesar, F. B.	13	1	95	23	7.92	0	6	0	—	—	—
Caesar, J.	202	17	3314	132*	17.91	2	123	5	24.60	2/1	0
Caesar, W. C.							38	0	—	—	—
Caffarey, J.	5	0	18	6	3.60	0	44	0	—	—	—
Caffyn, W.	154	15	3226	103	23.21	2	4299	321+10	13.39	8/25	29
Caffyn, W. W.	2	0	1	1	0.50	0					
Calvert, C.	23	2	266	67*	12.67	0	27	1	27.00	1/9	0
Campbell, G. V.	1	0	1	1	1.00	0	26	0	—	—	—
Campbell, I. P. F.	39	0	829	88	21.26	0					
Carmichael, J.	24	1	243	47	10.57	0	9	0	—	—	—
Carter, W. J.	12	3	77	21*	8.56	0	41	4	10.25	2/15	0
Carver, G. J.	2	0	36	36	18.00	0	42	1	42.00	1/42	0
Cattley, A. C.	2	0	45	45	22.50	0					
Cattley, S. W.	41	1	562	89	14.05	0	13	0	—	—	—
Chandler, A.	47	0	633	74	13.47	0					
Charman, W.	2	0	11	7	5.50	0	24	0	—	—	—
Cheatle, R. G. L.	13	9	62	27*	15.50	0	894	27	—	5/28	2
Chenery, C. J.	22	2	298	40*	14.90	0	48	1	48.00	1/11	0
Chester, A.	27	2	272	54*	10.88	0					
Chester, J.	45	2	625	64	14.53	0	4	0+15	—	3/?	—
Chinnery, E. F.	1	0	47	47	47.00	0					
Chinnery, H. B.	47	2	957	149	21.27	1	212	6	35.33	4/51	0
Christy, A.	2	0	0	0	0.00	0					
Clark, T. H.	421	35	11458	191	29.68	12	2233	73	30.59	5/23	1
Clarke, A. F.	8	2	61	30	10.17	0					
Clarke, C. F. C.	16	1	103	19	6.87	0	84	2	42.00	1/12	0
Clarke, M. C.	17	1	115	26	7.19	0					
Clarke, S. T.	155	18	2130	100*	15.54	1	11226	591	18.99	8/62	37
Clarke, W.	2	1	12	11	12.00	0					
Clifford, G.	28	1	255	45	9.44	0	355	13	27.31	3/15	0
Clinton, G. S.	320	43	9676	192	34.93	19	192	2	96.00	2/77	0
Clode, H. P.	56	6	596	50*	11.92	0	2884	111	25.98	6/31	6
Cobbett, J.	1	0	37	37	37.00	0		0+3	—	3/?	—
Collett, W. E.	8	0	44	19	5.50	0					
Collyer, W. J.	34	3	386	69	12.45	0					
Colman, S.	10	0	81	63	8.10	0					
Coltson, C.	16	1	122	24*	8.13	0					
Comber, G.	11	2	44	19	4.89	0					
Comber, R. H.	2	0	20	17	10.00	0					
Constable, B.	681	81	18224	205*	30.37	26	2585	49	52.76	3/68	0
Cook, W. T.	52	3	1032	84	21.06	0	48	1	48.00	1/1	0
Cooper, S. H.	2	1	11	11*	11.00	0					
Cosh, N. J.	9	1	165	55	20.63	0					

Name	Inns	NO	Runs	HS	Avge	100s	Runs	Wkts	Avge	Best	5wI
			Batting				**Bowling**				
Cowderoy, J.	2	0	4	2	2.00	0	11	0	—	—	—
Cox, D. F.	52	17	660	57	18.86	0	2316	68	34.06	7/22	2
Crawford, J. N.	182	22	5217	232	32.60	8	8765	450	19.48	8/24	27
Crawford, V. F. S.	164	15	4280	159	28.72	8	246	3	82.00	2/18	0
Crouch, H. R.	1	0	4	4	4.00	0					
Cumberlege, C. F.	4	0	30	26	7.50	0					
Cumbes, J.	22	13	76	25*	8.44	0	1989	93	21.39	6/35	5
Curtis, I. J.	11	5	23	7	3.83	0	726	18	40.33	6/28	1
Curwen, W. J. H.	7	0	23	8	3.28	0					
Cuthbertson, J. L.	9	3	118	34	19.67	0	204	3	68.00	1/13	0
Daily, C. E.	60	4	998	91	17.82	0	11	1	11.00	1/11	0
Daley, J. V.	34	24	75	26*	7.50	0	1942	67	28.99	6/47	3
Dalmeny, Lord	151	5	3386	138	23.19	2	73	3	24.33	2/16	0
Davies, A. C.	1	1	26	26*	—	0					
Davis, J.	2	0	0	0	0.00	0					
Davis, W. E.	176	12	3419	112	20.85	3	823	13	63.31	2/34	0
Day, D.	36	10	127	19	4.89	0	657	47+86	13.98	8/?	14
Deane, M. W.	2	0	1	1	0.50	0					
Dible, W. G.	2	0	8	4	4.00	0	5	0	—	—	—
Dickinson, P. J.	12	1	132	49*	12.00	0	70	0	—	—	—
Diver, E. J.	122	4	2643	143	22.40	1	103	0	—	—	—
Dolbey, H. O.	6	2	21	18*	5.25	0	235	7	33.57	4/96	0
Doughty, R. J.	33	4	631	65	21.75	0	2047	66	31.01	6/33	1
Douglas, A. P.	2	1	63	51*	63.00	0					
Douglas, R. N.	4	0	92	72	23.00	0					
Dowson, E.	90	5	1394	87	16.40	0					
Dowson, E. M.	71	6	1669	123	25.68	3	2185	56	39.02	7/72	4
Driver, B. N.	4	0	11	10	2.75	0					
Druce, N. F.	16	1	286	51*	19.07	0					
Ducat, A.	657	59	23108	306*	38.64	52	903	21	43.00	3/12	0
Dunn, J.	8	1	85	38*	12.14	0					
Earle, G. F.	6	0	124	48	20.67	0	389	13	29.92	5/137	1
Earnshaw, A.	8	0	50	15	6.25	0					
Earnshaw, G. R. B.	4	1	31	13*	10.33	0	4	0	—	—	—
Edrich, J. H.	716	80	29305	226*	46.08	81	16	0	—	—	—
Edwards, F.	2	0	8	6	4.00	0	54	3	18.00	3/31	0
Edwards, M. J.	415	24	10581	137	27.06	12	34	0	—	—	—
Eglington, R.	3	0	59	34	19.67	0					
Elliott, G. F.	80	5	1037	53	13.83	0	472	8	59.00	1/2	0
Estridge, G. T.	8	1	89	34	12.71	0					
Falkner, N. J.	24	3	734	102	34.95	2	9	1	9.00	1/3	0
Farmer, A. A.	1	0	3	3	3.00	0					
Feltham, M. A.	68	22	974	76	21.17	0	4792	156	30.71	5/45	4
Fender, P. G. H.	556	52	14117	185	28.01	17	38200	1586	24.08	8/24	86
Fenley, S.	111	45	396	26	6.00	0	345	8	8/69	19	
Fielding, F.	2	0	76	75	38.00	0					
Finlay, I. W.	35	3	654	103	20.44	1	56	1	56.00	1/19	0
Fishlock, L. B.	588	41	22138	253	40.47	50	433	9	48.11	4/62	0
Fletcher, D. G. W.	494	40	13646	194	30.06	21	0	0	—	—	—
Fox, C. J. M.	2	0	4	4	2.00	0					

Name	Inns	NO	Runs	HS	Avge	100s	Runs	Wkts	Avge	Best	5wI
			Batting					**Bowling**			
Franklin, H. W. F.	2	1	22	12	22.00	0					
Freeman, A.	54	5	399	32	8.14	0	458	8	57.25	2/47	0
Freeman, A. J.	1	1	0	0*	—	0	67	0	—	—	—
Frost, M.	4	0	11	7	2.75	0	326	10	32.60	4/56	0
Gamble, F. C.	25	10	132	29	8.80	0	1555	40	38.88	4/82	0
Gamble, G. F.	8	4	28	7	7.00	0	470	18	26.11	5/78	1
Game, W. H.	71	4	1084	84*	16.18	0	226	2	113.00	1/31	0
Garland, E.	1	0	0	0	0.00	0					
Garland-Wells, H. M.	185	11	3617	103	20.79	1	4137	97	42.65	5/25	2
Garth, R.	2	0	16	10	8.00	0					
Geary, A. C. T.	90	27	670	40	10.63	0	6068	198	30.65	6/50	6
Gentry, J. S. B.	11	4	65	13	9.29	0	761	36	21.14	4/36	0
Gibson, D.	211	45	3143	98	18.93	0	12213	550	22.21	7/26	26
Gilbert, C. A. W.	4	1	25	17*	8.33	0					
Gillespie, F. S.	11	0	249	72	22.64	0					
Gilligan, A. E. R.	5	0	33	15	6.60	0	247	3	82.33	2/59	0
Goatly, E. G.	198	21	4419	147*	24.97	3	733	19	38.58	4/48	0
Gooder, L. M. H.	29	2	312	35	11.56	0	1862	54	34.48	5/66	3
Gordon, J. H.	5	1	118	69*	29.50	0					
Gore, S. W.	3	0	52	36	17.33	0	51	0	—	—	—
Gover, A. R.	386	154	2170	41*	9.35	0	34101	1437	23.73	8/34	87
Graburn, W. T.	1	0	39	39	39.00	0					
Gray, A. H.	32	6	223	35	8.57	0	3568	180	19.82	8/40	11
Green, W.	2	0	2	2	1.00	0					
Greenfield, G. P.	5	1	115	102	28.75	1	67	4	16.75	3/38	0
Greenwood, J. F.	5	0	17	8	3.40	0					
Gregory, J. C.	35	5	630	70	21.00	0	12	0	—	—	—
Gregory, R. J.	622	76	18978	243	34.76	38	13877	434	31.97	6/21	11
Greig, I. A.	63	7	1416	104*	25.28	1	2400	84	28.57	6/34	2
Griffin, N. F.	2	1	90	83*	90.00	0	45	0	—	—	—
Griffith, G.	288	15	4604	142	16.86	2	9148	550	16.63	9/130	45
Griffith, S. C.	1	0	19	19	19.00	0					
Groom, R.	4	1	11	4	3.67	0					
Gunn, T. W.	11	3	52	13	6.50	0					
Haden, J. V.	10	0	42	22	4.20	0					
Hadfield, G. H.	4	1	21	10	7.00	0	419	14	29.93	5/52	1
Hadingham, A. W. G.											
Hall, C. J.	13	1	71	15	5.92	0	13	1	13.00	1/4	0
Hall, J. K.	11	3	19	5	2.38	0	787	36	21.86	5/30	1
Hammersley, W. J.	7	0	68	27	9.71	0	11	0	—	—	—
Hanbury, E. C.	6	2	44	17	11.00	0					
Hankey, R.	2	0	5	5	2.50	0	26	0	—	—	—
Hansell, T. M. G.	26	5	319	54	15.19	0	0	0	—	—	—
Harman, R.	144	50	924	34	9.83	0	8708	369	23.59	8/12	18
Harper, L. V.	9	0	145	67	16.11	0					
Harris, S. S.	2	0	9	8	4.50	0					
Harrison, H. S.	254	33	5226	155*	23.65	2	726	20	36.30	2/14	0
Hartley-Smith, H.	2	0	17	11	8.50	0					
Hartnell, E. G.	2	0	5	3	2.50	0					
Harwood, F.	5	1	8	5	2.00	0	158	7	22.57	3/39	0

Name	Inns	NO	Batting Runs	HS	Avge	100s	Bowling Runs	Wkts	Avge	Best	5wI
Hayes, E. G.	802	45	25062	276	33.11	45	12761	473	26.98	8/22	12
Hayward, D. snr	5	1	76	43	19.00	0					
Hayward, D. jnr	1	0	1	1	1.00	0					
Hayward, T. W.	932	79	36175	315*	42.41	88	9342	436	21.43	8/89	17
Hearsum, J.	4	0	43	25	10.75	0	59	0	—	—	—
Heartfield, J.	13	2	24	10*	2.18	0	338	21	16.10	6/28	2
Heath, J.	19	35	4	218	35		7.03	0			
Heath, W. H. G.	5	1	82	58*	20.50	0					
Henderson, R.	219	28	3466	106	18.15	1	1248	59	21.15	6/17	1
Hillyer, W. R.	4	1	71	30	23.67	0	—	+18	—	7/?	2
Hinkly, E.	3	2	11	7*	11.00	0	91	8	11.38	4/24	0
Hitch, J. W.	423	41	6765	107	17.71	3	26550	1232	21.55	8/38	90
Hoare, A. M.	3	0	77	59	25.67	0					
Hoare, C. H.	27	3	308	58	12.83	0					
Hoare, C. T.	7	0	98	35	14.00	0					
Hobbs, J. B.	956	80	43554	316*	49.72	144	1948	86	22.65	7/56	3
Holland, F. C.	425	29	10323	171	26.07	12	570	13	43.85	2/20	0
Holmes, E. R. T.	298	40	8837	206	34.25	15	6135	173	35.46	6/16	3
Homer, C. E.	80	26	468	37*	8.67	0	3630	217	16.73	8/35	14
Hooper, J. M. M.	36	10	406	41*	15.62	0	10	1	10.00	1/10	0
Hore, F. S.	1	1	8	8*	—	0					
Howarth, G. R.	323	25	9284	183	31.15	18	848	18	53.00	3/20	0
Howell, L. S.	24	5	330	96	17.37	0					
Howell, M.	55	8	1117	99	23.77	0	6	0	—	—	—
Howell, R.	5	1	31	10	7.75	0					
Humphrey, R.	268	16	4433	116*	17.59	1					
Humphrey, R. G.	2	1	63	58	63.00	0					
Humphrey, T.	289	10	5215	144	18.69	4	2285	107	21.35	6/29	5
Humphrey, W.	6	0	49	18	8.17	0	148	2	74.00	1/19	0
Hyndson, J. G. W.	2	0	19	18	9.50	0	125	4	31.25	2/30	0
Intikhab Alam	338	45	5707	139	19.47	4	18871	629	30.00	8/74	25
Jackman, R. D.	386	132	4823	92*	18.98	0	26969	1206	22.36	8/58	61
Jackson, M. T.	17	8	21	9	2.33	0	660	33	20.00	7/96	3
Jardine, D. R.	194	36	7037	167	44.54	14	916	25	36.64	2/13	0
Jeacocke, A.	205	15	5608	201*	29.52	8	576	14	41.14	2/24	0
Jefferson, R. I.	106	23	1663	136	20.04	2	5582	206	27.10	6/25	7
Jennings, T. S.	7	3	194	37*	13.86	0	1094	37	29.57	6/51	3
Jephson, D. L. A.	237	32	6566	213	32.03	9	5747	249	23.08	7/51	10
Jesty, T. E.	102	14	3288	221	37.36	7	884	29	30.48	6/81	1
Johnson, F.	32	8	158	21*	6.58	0	1302	51	25.53	6/42	4
Jones, G. G.	156	23	1155	63	8.68	0	5406	321	16.84	7/20	15
Judd, P. E.							14	0	—	—	—
Jupp, H.	467	40	11452	165	26.82	12	316	7	45.14	3/75	0
Jupp, W. T.	3	1	25	11	12.50	0	57	0	—	—	—
Keene, J. W.	2	1	3	3	3.00	0	174	4	43.50	3/61	0
Kelleher, H. R. A.							179	12	14.08	5/23	2
Kember, O. D.	7	2	56	19*	11.20	0					
Kendrick, N. M.	1	1	8	8*	—	0	97	1	97.00	1/92	0
Kenrick, J.	1	0	11	11	11.0	0	44	1	44.00	1/26	0
Kersley, T.	4	1	23	15*	7.67	0	145	7	20.71	3/36	0

334

Name	Inns	NO	Runs	HS	Avge	100s	Runs	Wkts	Avge	Best	5wI
			Batting					**Bowling**			
Key, K. J.	423	55	9654	179	26.23	8	195	5	39.00	2/36	0
Killick, W.	2	0	3	3	1.50	0					
King, K. C. W.	39	8	334	64	10.77	0	1148	33	34.79	4/38	0
King, P.	2	0	16	13	8.00	0	18	0	—	—	—
Kingsford, R. K.	5	0	80	30	16.00	0					
Kirby, G. N. G.	17	8	141	32	15.67	0					
Kirk, E. C.	50	7	406	43	9.44	0	3079	128	24.05	7/130	6
Knight, D. J.	159	11	4390	146	29.66	9	2	3	0.67	2/0	0
Knight, R. D. V.	290	32	8712	142	33.76	15	5549	163	34.04	5/44	2
Knox, F. P.	12	2	196	42	19.60	0	223	8	27.88	3/28	0
Knox, N. A.	106	30	670	27*	8.82	0	7269	347	20.95	8/48	31
Lagden, R. B.	1	0	3	3	3.00	0					
Laker, J. C.	387	70	5531	113	17.45	2	24236	1395	17.37	10/88	93
Lane, C. G.	30	3	487	72	18.04	0	63	3	21.00	3/31	0
Lane, W. W. C.	4	0	56	36	14.00	0	7	0	—	—	—
Lawrence, C.	3	0	42	22	14.00	0	35	2	17.50	1/8	0
Leaf, H.	2	0	8	7	4.00	0					
Lee, F.	2	0	42	30	21.00	0					
Lee, J. M.	11	2	140	40	15.56	0		0+2	—	2/?	—
Lees, W. S.	488	68	7237	137	17.23	2	28542	1331	21.44	9/81	92
Leveson-Gower, H. D. G.	174	27	3308	155	22.50	2	211	2	105.50	1/12	0
Lewis, R. M.	68	9	1746	87	29.59	0	7	0	—	—	—
Lindsay, W.	62	5	987	74	17.32	0					
Loader, P. J.	291	87	1827	81	8.96	0	20685	1108	18.67	9/17	65
Lock, G. A. R.	451	100	5391	70	15.36	0	29835	1713	17.42	10/54	123
Lock, H. C.	29	8	89	20*	4.24	0	2381	75	31.75	4/34	0
Lock, N. W.	2	1	1	1	1.00	0					
Lockton, J. H.	34	9	409	77*	16.36	0	2071	78	26.55	5/80	1
Lockwood, W.	446	33	9299	165	22.52	14	21266	1182	17.99	9/59	105
Lockyer, T.	197	31	2588	108*	15.59	1	1742	93	18.73	6/33	9
Lohmann, G. A.	269	25	5070	115	20.78	2	16108	1221	—	9/67	128
Long, A.	409	90	4999	92	15.67	0					
Long, R.	4	0	0	0	0.00	0	20	0	—	—	—
Longman, H. K.	8	0	98	33	12.25	0					
Lowe, R. F.	11	3	15	7	1.88	0	557	26	21.42	5/15	1
Lowles, G. W.	2	1	1	1*	1.00	0					
Lowther, H. C.	1	0	13	13	13.00	0					
Lucas, A. C.	2	0	50	29	25.00	0					
Lucas, A. P.	76	6	1721	115	24.59	2	1011	62	16.31	5/23	2
Luff, A.	6	1	25	8	5.00	0	111	2	55.50	1/28	0
Lutterlock, E.	6	0	23	8	3.83	0					
Lynch, M. A.	358	43	11353	152	36.04	27	972	22	44.18	3/6	0
Lyons, G. L.	2	0	8	8	4.00	0					
Lywood, L. W.	2	0	7	7	3.50	0	177	1	177.00	1/22	0
McCanlis, M. A.	3	2	44	19*	44.0	0	209	3	69.67	1/41	0
McDonell, H. C.	22	3	269	46	14.16	0	892	41	21.76	7/44	2
McEntyre, K. B.	3	0	33	15	11.00	0					
Machin, R. S.	9	2	33	17	4.71	0					
Mackintosh, K. S.	12	9	117	31	39.00	0	1135	36	31.52	6/61	1

335

Name	Inns	NO	Runs	HS	Avge	100s	Runs	Wkts	Avge	Best	5wI
			Batting				**Bowling**				
McIntyre, A. J. W.	544	75	10893	143*	23.23	7	180	4	45.00	1/10	0
Mack, A. J.	9	0	42	16	4.67	0	760	7	108.57	2/50	0
McKelvey, P. G.							19	1	19.00	1/7	0
McMahon, J. W. J.	106	52	344	23*	6.37	0	6903	234	29.50	8/46	9
McMurray, T.	54	6	892	62	18.58	0	23	1	23.00	1/3	0
Macniven, E.	1	0	8	8	8.00	0					
Majendie, N. L.	6	1	11	6	2.20	0					
Marriott, D. A.	13	6	88	24*	12.57	0	1244	43	28.93	4/45	0
Marshal, A.	158	11	4195	176	28.54	7	2121	101	21.00	7/41	6
Marshall, A.	23	5	146	23*	8.11	0					
Marshall, C.	60	13	341	42	7.26	0					
Marshall, H.	4	0	20	8	5.00	0					
Marten, W. G.	42	13	163	18	5.62	0	1672	79	21.16	6/11	3
Martingell, W.	81	12	643	49	9.32	0	1513	130+54	11.64	8/37	13
Mathews, F. J.	3	0	14	9	4.67	0					
May, P. B. H.	327	46	14168	211*	50.42	39					
May, P. R.	19	4	188	32	12.53	0	988	22	44.91	6/88	1
Mayo, H. E.	27	1	246	53	9.46	0	112	4	28.00	2/13	0
Mays, C. S.	3	2	20	13*	20.00	0	303	3	101.00	1/36	0
Meads, J. W.	4	0	9	4	2.25	0	135	7	19.28	4/36	0
Medlycott, K. T.	83	18	1624	153	24.98	2	4691	159	29.50	8/52	10
Merrall, J. E.	2	0	10	5	5.00	0	153	6	25.50	3/24	0
Meymott, C.	2	0	0	0	0.00	0					
Miller, F. P.	132	14	1540	105	13.05	1	2708	130+1	20.83	6/36	2
Miller, N.	12	1	346	124	31.45	1	114	1	114.00	1/28	0
Mills, C. H.	3	0	6	4	2.00	0	17	0	—	—	—
Mills, E.	12	2	54	11*	5.40	0	344	15	22.93	5/33	1
Mobey, G. S.	105	19	1526	75	17.74	0					
Molony, T. J.	4	0	2	2	0.50	0	89	4	22.25	3/11	0
Money, W. B.	4	0	50	19	12.50	0	203	4	50.75	4/136	0
Monkhouse, G.	85	33	1158	100*	22.26	1	4589	170	26.99	7/81	2
Montgomery, W.	19	2	60	12	3.53	0	580	22	26.36	4/17	0
Morgan, C.	7	0	31	15	4.43	0	170	2	85.00	1/36	0
Morris, N.	10	0	177	64	17.70	0					
Mortlock, W.	236	22	4125	106	19.28	3	2339	128	18.27	7/42	7
Morton, P. H.	3	1	20	19*	10.00	0	79	4	19.75	2/26	0
Moulder, J. H.	34	4	451	48	15.03	0	203	8	25.38	3/41	0
Mudie, W.	56	9	547	79	11.64	0	748	47	15.91	7/61	3
Myers, E. B.	17	1	217	40	13.56	0	211	3	70.33	1/10	0
Naumann, F. C. G.	17	1	216	52	13.50	0	610	15	40.67	5/51	1
Needham, A.	132	17	2620	138	22.78	4	4429	104	42.58	6/30	5
Nevell, W. T.	1	0	5	5	5.00	0	35	0	—	—	—
Newman, F. C. W.	7	0	123	54	17.57	0					
Newnham, S. W.	1	0	4	4	4.00	0	13	2	6.50	2/13	0
Nice, E. H. L.	96	10	1247	66	14.50	0	4394	174	25.25	8/83	5
Nightingale, J.	1	1	2	2*	—	0	8	0	—	—	—
Noble, C.	7	0	53	17	7.57	0					
Noble, J. W.	45	2	521	71	12.12	0	268	12	22.33	4/36	0
O'Gorman, J. G.	4	3	106	42*	106.00	0	167	4	41.75	2/49	0
Oliver, F. W.	4	0	71	30	17.75	0					

Name	Inns	NO	Runs	HS	Avge	100s	Runs	Wkts	Avge	Best	5wI
Owen, J. G.	13	3	196	54	19.60	0	710	16	44.38	3/15	0
Owen-Thomas, D. R.	118	14	2604	112	25.04	3	6	0	—	—	—
Palmer, W. T.	36	0	289	54	8.03	0	15	0	—	—	—
Parfitt, J. J. A.	16	2	111	23	7.93	0	477	25	19.08	7/33	1
Parker, J. F.	512	70	14068	255	31.83	20	15387	538	28.60	6/34	8
Parr, G.	2	1	4	4	4.00	0					
Parsons, A. B. D.	203	18	5307	125	28.69	3	4	0	—	—	—
Pauline, D. B.	76	6	1803	115	25.75	1	595	16	37.18	5/52	1
Payne, I. R.	37	5	338	43	10.56	0	1127	26	43.34	5/13	1
Peach, H. A.	411	50	8497	200*	23.54	4	20261	778	26.04	8/60	30
Penfold, A. G.	4	1	12	6	4.00	0	201	13	15.46	4/36	0
Peters, N. H.	15	8	83	125	12.08	0	954	34	28.05	6/31	1
Peto, J.	2	1	12	7	12.00	0					
Pickering, E. H.	1	0	0	0	0.00	0					
Pickering, W. P.	4	0	23	21	5.75	0					
Pierpoint, F. G.	11	7	15	4	3.75	0	592	13	45.54	3/60	0
Piggott, J. I.	5	1	153	84	38.25	0					
Pilch, F.	2	0	22	11	11.0	0					
Pilkington, A. F.	1	0	4	4	4.00	0	29	1	29.00	1/29	0
Platt, G. J. W.	49	8	396	49	9.66	0	2042	102	20.02	6/61	6
Pocock, P. I.	503	144	4400	75*	12.25	0	35594	1399	25.44	9/57	53
Ponsonby, F. G. B.	1	0	7	7	7.00	0					
Ponsonby, S. C. B.	6	1	12	12	2.40	0					
Pontifex, D. D.	17	1	303	89	18.94	0	13	0	—	—	—
Pooley, E.	453	37	6642	97	15.97	0	371	6	61.83	2/39	0
Pooley, F. W.	4	0	13	11	3.25	0					
Potter, C. W.	31	3	385	31	13.75	0	17	1	17.00	1/17	0
Potter, J.	62	12	325	27*	6.50	0	1961	98	20.01	7/31	7
Powell, E. O.	7	0	95	53	13.57	0					
Pratt, D. E.	12	4	171	33	21.38	0	392	13	30.15	6/119	1
Pratt, J.	2	0	10	9	5.00	0	12	0	—	—	—
Pratt, R. C. E.	102	14	1900	120	21.59	1	138	3	46.00	1/8	0
Pretty, H. C.	11	0	233	124	21.18	1	15	0	—	—	—
Price, V. R.	1	0	25	25	25.00	0	179	1	179.00	1/156	0
Ransom, V. J.	2	0	3	2	1.50	0	82	1	82.00	1/21	0
Raphael, J. E.	64	7	1614	111	28.32	1	49	0	—	—	—
Ratcliff, J.	8	0	69	27	8.63	0					
Ratcliffe, A.	10	2	142	34	17.75	0	8	0	—	—	—
Read, F. H.	1	0	4	4	4.00	0					
Read, H. D.	2	1	0	0*	0.00	0	152	6	25.33	4/26	0
Read, J. M.	450	35	10840	186*	26.12	8	1610	64	25.15	6/41	1
Read, W. W.	580	41	17683	338	32.81	31	2830	84	33.69	4/27	0
Reay, G. M.	34	2	410	54	12.81	0	1859	89	20.89	5/22	3
Redgewell, L. J.	4	2	5	4	2.50	0					
Reeves, E.	14	2	125	25	10.42	0					
Reiner, C. F.	2	0	50	26	28.00	0					
Richards, C. J.	328	79	7142	172*	28.68	7	219	5	43.80	2/42	0
Richards, J. H.	4	0	9	8	2.25	0	89	2	44.50	2/40	0
Richardson, H. B.	31	5	585	72	22.50	0	1	0	—	—	—
Richardson, T.	396	106	2853	69	9.84	0	31732	1775	17.88	10/45	169

337

Name	Inns	NO	Batting Runs	HS	Avge	100s	Bowling Runs	Wkts	Avge	Best	5wI
Ricketts, G. W.	5	0	48	26	9.60	0	12	0	—		
Roberts, D.	2	0	15	14	7.50	0	31	1	31.00	1/31	0
Roberts, F.	7	2	20	7	4.00	0	159	9	17.67	7/72	1
Robertson, F. M.	2	1	7	4	7.00	0	49	2	24.50	2/32	0
Robinson, J. D.	5	2	55	20	18.33	0	105	3	35.00	2/41	0
Rogers, G. R.	10	1	34	18	3.78	0					
Roller, C. T.	2	0	15	14	7.50	0					
Roller, W. E.	162	10	3343	204	21.99	7	3190	164	19.45	6/44	4
Roope, G. R. J.	554	118	16226	171	37.21	22	7725	211	36.61	5/14	3
Rose, J.	2	0	0	0	0.00	0	2	1	2.00	1/2	0
Rudd, W. J.	2	0	4	4	2.00	0					
Rushby, T.	289	129	1192	58*	7.45	0	19544	954	20.49	10/43	58
Rushworth, W. R.	1	0	0	0	0.00	0	86	2	43.00	1/15	0
Russell, S. G.							77	2	38.50	2/63	0
Rutty, A. W. F.	2	2	18	12*	—	0					
Sadiq, Z. A.	6	0	135	64	22.50	0					
Sadler, W. C. H.	65	22	646	68	15.02	0	3907	167	23.40	6/50	7
Sandham, A.	830	71	33312	292*	43.89	83	386	16	24.13	3/27	0
Sarel, W. G. M.	8	0	120	57	15.00	0	46	1	46.00	1/20	0
Selvey, M. W. W.	8	4	19	14*	4.75	0	445	21	21.19	6/58	1
Sewell, T. snr	16	1	96	25	6.40	0					
Sewell, T. jnr	179	39	1756	62	12.54	0	4835	248	19.49	8/54	11
Sewell, W. H.	2	1	19	11	19.00	0					
Shadwell, F. B.	2	0	16	15	8.00	0	18	0	—	—	—
Sharpe, J. W.	79	27	503	36	9.67	0	4183	275	15.21	9/47	19
Sheffield, E. J.	17	3	176	64*	12.57	0	1492	68	21.94	7/123	2
Shepherd, T. F.	520	60	18254	277*	39.68	41	13478	439	30.70	6/78	12
Shepherd, W.	17	6	56	18	5.09	0	709	38	18.66	8/49	2
Sheppard, R. A.	16	1	356	82	23.73	0	526	20	26.30	4/33	0
Sherman, T.	81	19	422	32	6.81	0	1781	125 + 107	14.25	8/?	20
Shuter, J.	447	19	9369	135	21.89	8	37	0	—	—	—
Shuter, L. A.	65	2	1040	89	16.51	0	75	1	75.00	1/10	0
Simmonds, A.	12	0	149	50	12.42	0					
Skinner, E. A.	6	1	37	10	7.40	0	112	3	37.33	2/33	0
Skinner, L. E.	115	14	2255	93	22.33	0					
Slater, P. H.	1	0	1	1	1.00	0					
Smith, D. M.	260	57	6723	160	33.11	11	1463	27	54.18	3/40	0
Smith, E.	2	1	18	9*	18.00	0					
Smith, F. E.	69	18	492	45	9.65	0	3121	169	18.47	6/12	9
Smith, G. O.	5	0	17	9	3.40	0					
Smith, T.	2	0	16	13	8.00	0	20	0	—	—	—
Smith, W. A.	242	18	5024	103	22.43	2	1	0	—	—	—
Smith, W. C.	318	62	3193	69*	12.47	0	17616	1036	17.00	9/31	92
Snow, H.	1	0	3	3	3.00	0					
Soden, F. B.	6	1	35	18*	7.00	0	17	2	8.50	1/2	0
Southerton, James	261	77	1665	82	9.05	0	13793	994	13.57	8/34	115
Spicer, W. B.	2	0	16	14	8.00	0	17	1	17.00	1/17	0
Spring, W. A.	106	13	1968	135	21.16	2	2093	71	29.48	6/38	3
Squires, H. S.	643	44	18636	236	31.11	36	10496	297	35.34	8/52	7
Stacey, C. F.	1	1	0	0*	—	0	148	1	148.00	1/78	0

Name			Batting					Bowling			
	Inns	NO	Runs	HS	Avge	100s	Runs	Wkts	Avge	Best	5wI
Stafford, J. P.	2	0	0	0	0.00	0	31	0	—	—	—
Staveley, M.	2	0	3	3	1.50	0	51	1	51.00	1/24	0
Stedman, F.	184	67	1484	62	12.68	0	53	0	—	—	—
Stephenson, H. H.	312	24	5338	119	18.53	2	3340	190	17.58	7/58	12
Stevens, J.	4	0	36	16	9.00	0					
Stewart, A. J.	183	19	6029	166	36.76	10	143	1	143.00	1/18	0
Stewart, M. J.	844	91	25007	227*	33.21	48	48	1	48.00	1/4	0
Stockley, A. J.	2	0	5	5	2.50	0	194	10	19.40	4/74	0
Stoner, A.	9	0	98	61	10.89	0	344	14	24.57	4/16	0
Storey, S. J.	468	58	10402	164	25.57	12	12903	490	26.33	8/22	11
Strachan, G.	93	5	1186	84	13.48	0	2087	118	17.68	6/33	5
Strahan, W.	5	0	14	8	2.80	0					
Streatfeild, E. C.	13	1	185	39	15.42	0	231	19	12.16	5/26	1
Street, A. E.	66	6	1356	161*	22.60	1	393	15	26.20	3/44	0
Street, J.	239	70	1280	50	7.57	0	11435	534	21.41	7/141	36
Stroud, E. G.	7	3	63	22*	15.75	0	526	23	22.87	4/17	0
Strudwick, H.	695	197	5485	93	11.01	0	60	0	—	—	—
Subba Row, R.	58	11	1663	128	35.38	3	131	1	131.00	1/10	0
Sullivan, D.	10	4	34	12*	5.67	0					
Surridge, S. S.	1	1	2	2*	—	0					
Surridge, W. S.	316	32	3697	87	13.02	0	13753	464	29.64	7/49	19
Swan, J. J.	59	5	637	62	11.80	0	83	2	41.50	1/15	0
Swetman, R.	178	29	3073	93	20.62	0					
Sydenham, D. A. D.	131	64	483	24*	7.21	0	9548	481	19.85	9/70	26
Tabor, A. S.	2	0	0	0	0.00	0					
Tanner, W.	4	2	2	1*	1.00	0	26	0	—	—	—
Taylor, A.	1	0	1	1	1.00	0	13	1	13.00	1/13	0
Taylor, D. J. S.	8	1	137	56	19.57	0					
Taylor, E. F.	4	0	48	27	12.00	0	135	7	19.29	4/59	0
Taylor, N. S.	9	4	63	21*	12.60	0	833	28	29.75	7/44	1
Taylor, W.	6	1	15	10	3.00	0	43	1 + 1	43.00	1/23	0
Teesdale, H.	3	0	65	26	21.67	0					
Thain, C.	2	1	4	4*	4.00	0	88	3	29.33	3/38	0
Thomas, D. J.	172	35	2850	119	20.80	2	10155	303	33.51	6/36	6
Thompson, H.	20	4	138	44*	8.63	0	663	31	21.39	5/59	2
Thorne, C. P.	6	2	158	100*	39.50	1	77	4	19.25	2/53	0
Tillard, C.	4	0	51	22	12.75	0	149	7	21.29	3/10	0
Tindall, R. A. E.	256	38	5383	109*	24.69	2	4846	150	32.31	5/41	2
Titmus, F. J.	2	2	4	4*	—	0	35	1	35.00	1/35	0
Topley, T. D.	1	1	6	6*	—	0	64	2	32.00	2/42	0
Trodd, J. T.	8	5	10	5	3.33	0	70	4	17.50	2/13	0
Trodd, W.	11	0	65	16	5.91	0	146	3	48.67	2/38	0
Trollope, W. S.	14	0	154	35	11.00	0	99	4	24.75	2/2	0
Trouncer, C. A.	5	1	51	26	12.75	0	25	0	—	—	—
Tufnell, N. C.	2	0	9	7	4.50	0	5	0	—	—	—
Verrinder, A. O. C.	2	0	0	0	0.00	0	105	4	26.25	2/42	0
Vigar, H. E.	21	2	226	33*	11.89	0					
Vince, J.	22	1	60	10*	2.86	0	454	15	30.26	4/58	0
Vincett, J. H.	4	1	31	23*	10.33	0	50	2	25.00	2/46	0
Von Emsthausen, A. C.	3	0	24	13	8.00	0	95	1	95.00	1/37	0

Name	Inns	NO	Runs	HS	Avge	100s	Runs	Wkts	Avge	Best	5wI
Voss, R.	5	2	10	7	3.33	0	53	2	26.50	2/31	0
Vyse, E. W.	4	0	34	24	8.50	0					
Wait, O. J.	9	3	11	4	1.83	0	400	14	28.57	3/27	0
Walker, L.	93	8	1609	84	18.93	0	354	8	44.25	3/54	0
Waller, C. E.	31	13	173	47	9.61	0	2195	96	22.86	7/64	4
Walter, C. R.	1	0	0	0	0.00	0					
Wanostrocht, N. (Felix)	38	1	659	82	17.81	0		0+1	—	1/?	—
Ward, D. M.	62	10	1499	143	28.82	2	31	0	—	—	—
Waterman, P. A.	6	3	7	6*	2.33	0	727	18	40.38	3/22	0
Watney, J.	2	0	9	8	4.50	0					
Watts, E. A.	350	68	6005	123	21.29	2	18757	722	25.98	10/67	24
Watts, G. H.	16	2	79	20	5.64	0	21	0	—	—	—
Watts, T.	8	5	42	21*	14.00	0	327	8	40.88	2/32	0
Weeks, D.	2	0	2	1	1.00	0	165	2	82.50	1/25	0
Wellings, E. M.	4	1	33	10	11.00	0	195	2	97.50	1/30	0
Wells, C. M.	7	1	49	20	8.17	0	216	15	14.40	7/31	1
Westerman, P.	12	5	25	10*	3.57	0	596	21	28.38	5/49	2
Whale, G.	6	0	40	26	6.67	0	288	5	57.60	3/94	0
Wheatley, G. A.	7	1	119	37*	19.83	0					
Wheeler, A.	3	0	15	9	5.00	0					
Wheeler, W. C.	10	1	33	13	3.67	0	88	5	17.60	2/10	0
White, Capt	2	0	3	3	1.50	0					
White, A. C.	2	1	15	9*	15.00	0					
White, C.	1	0	0	0	0.00	0					
White, J.							103	1	103.00	1/56	0
Whitfield, E. W.	157	21	3498	198	25.72	6	1354	31	43.68	4/63	0
Whitley, R. T.	2	0	8	5	4.00	0					
Whittaker, G. J.	183	18	4584	185*	27.78	6	47	1	47.00	1/31	0
Whyting, C. H.	1	1	14	14*	—	0					
Wilkinson, C. T. A.	76	8	1734	135	25.50	3	706	23	30.70	6/43	1
Willett, M. D.	273	45	6535	126	28.66	8	1105	23	48.04	3/36	0
Willis, H.	2	0	7	7	3.50	0					
Willis, R. G. D.	34	20	228	33	16.29	0	2428	96	25.29	5/78	1
Wilson, C. W.	2	0	10	9	5.00	0					
Wilson, E. F.	120	12	2516	110	23.30	1	43	0	—	—	—
Wilson, P. H. L.	23	15	80	15	10.00	0	1814	55	32.98	4/39	0
Wiltshire, E.	22	2	219	33	10.95	0					
Wingfield, W.	6	0	13	5	2.17	0					
Winlaw, R. de W. K.	26	5	650	91	30.95	0	13	0	—	—	—
Winterborne, C.							47	0	—	—	—
Wood, H.	378	89	4948	83	17.12	0	29	0	—	—	—
Wood, W.	4	0	9	8	2.25	0	44	1	44.00	1/22	0
Woodgate, T. W.	2	0	11	11	5.50	0					
Wyatt, G. N.	18	0	251	58	13.94	0	17	0	—	—	—
Wyld, W. G.	16	1	169	34*	11.26	0	113	3	37.67	1/12	0
Yates, G.	3	0	9	6	3.00	0					
Yeatman, R. H.	8	1	53	21	7.57	0	18	0	—	—	—
Younis Ahmed	448	63	14112	183*	36.65	19	602	17	35.41	4/10	0

RESULTS OF SURREY COUNTY
CHAMPIONSHIP MATCHES 1846 to 1988

Year	C	D	E	Ga	Go	H	K	La	Le	M	Nr	No	So	Su	Wa	Wo	Y	M	W	L	D	A	Pos
1846							WD											2	1	0	1	–	
1847							TL											2	0	1	0*	–	
1848					no major inter-county matches played																		
1849														WL				2	1	1	0	–	
1850							W–			WW								4	4	0	0	–	
1851										W–			W–				WW	4	4	0	0	–	
1852							L–			LL			LD					5	0	4	1	–	
1853							W–			L–								2	1	1	0	–	
1854[1]										WW			WD					4	3	0	1	–	
1855										LL								2	0	2	0	–	
1856							–W						WW					3	3	0	0	–	
1857	WW						W–						WW					5	5	0	0	–	
1858	W–												W–					2	2	0	0	–	
1859													L–					1	0	1	0	–	
1860													LW	DW				4	2	1	1	–	
1861	LD						LL			WW							WL	8	3	4	1	–	
1862[2]	WL						WW			DL							WL	8	4	3	1	–	
1863							WW			D–			WD				DL	7	3	3	1	–	
1864							WW						WW	DW			WD	8	6	0	2	–	
1865						WL	WW			LD			WL	WD			WW	12	7	3	2	–	
1866						WL	WL	DW		LL				WL				10	4	5	1	–	
1867							DW	DD		DW				WL			LL	10	3	3	4	–	
1868							LL	WL		TL			WL	WW			LW	12	5	6	0*	–	
1869							DL	WL		WL			LL	WD			LL	12	3	7	2	–	
1870[3]					LL		WL	WL		LW			LW	LW		LL		14	5	9	0	–	
1871	D–				LL		LD			LD			LL	LL			LD	13	0	9	4	–	
1872					WL		WW			WW			DD	LW			LW	12	7	3	2	–	
1873					LD		WL	LL		WL			LL	WD			LL	14	3	9	2	–	
1874					WL					LW			LL	WD			LL	10	3	6	1	–	
1875					WL					WW			LD	DL			LL	10	3	5	2	–	
1876					LD		WL			TL			LL	WL			LL	12	2	8	1*	–	
1877					LL		DW			WW			WL	DW			DW	12	6	3	3	–	
1878					WD		DL			DL			LL	WW			LL	12	3	6	3	–	
1879					LD		WW			LL				WD			DL	10	3	4	3	–	
1880					WL		DL	LL		LD			LD	WD			LD	14	2	7	5	–	
1881					LL		WW	LL		LL			WL	WD			LL	14	4	9	1	–	
1882					DL		WW	LD		WL			LL	LW			LD	14	4	7	3	–	
1883		WL				WW	DW	DD	WL			WL	DL	WW	WW		DL	20	10	5	5	–	
1884	WW					WD	WW	DL	LW			LW		DL	WW		DD	18	9	4	5	–	
1885	WW					LL	WW	DW	WD			WW	DD	WW	WW		LL	20	12	4	4	–	
1886	WW					WW	WW	WL	WW			LD		LW			WW	16	12	3	1	–	
1887	WW					WW	DW	LW	LW			WW		DW			WW	16	12	2	2	–	
1888						WD	WW	LW	WW			WW		WW			WW	14	12	1	1	–	
1889						WD	WW	LL	WW			WL		WW			WW	14	10	3	1	–	
1890						WW	LD	WW	WW			WL		WW			LD	16	9	3	2	–	1st
1891						WW	WW	DW	WL			WW	WL	DW			WW	16	12	2	2	–	1st
1892						WW	WW	WD	WW			LL	WW	WW			WW	16	13	2	1	–	1st
1893						WL	DL	LW	LL			WW	LW	LW			WL	16	7	8	1	–	5th
1894						WW	WL	TW	WL			WW	WW	WW			WW	16	13	2	0*	–	1st
1895		DW	WW			WD	WW	WW	LW	LW		DW	DW	WL	WW	WD	LW	26	17	4	5	–	1st
1896		WW	WL			WD	WW	LL	WW	LW		WW	WL	LW	WW		WD	26	17	7	2	–	4th
1897		WW	DW			LW	WD	WW	WW	WW		WD	LL	WD	WW	WW	DL	26	17	4	5	–	2nd
1898	AW	WL				WL	DW	WD	DD	WD		DL	DD	WD	WW	WA	WL	26	11	4	9	2	4th
1899	WW	DW				DW	WL	WD	WD	DL		DD	DD	DD			DD	26	10	2	14	–	4th
1900	DW	LW				WL	WW	DD	WL	DW		LL	DW	DD	DW		DD	28	9	7	12	–	7th
1901[4]	WW	DD				WD	DD	LL	DL	DW		DD	LL	WD	WW	AD	DL	28	7	6	14	1	6th
1902	WD	DW				DD	DL	WL	DD	DW		DD	DD	DW	DD		DL	28	8	5	15	–	4th
1903	DL	LL				WL	AW	LD	DL	WW		LL	LD	WD	DD	LD	DL	28	7	11	9	1	11th
1904	LW	LW				DW	WD	DL	LL	WD		LL	LL	LL	DD	DD	DL	28	6	12	10	–	11th
1905	WW	WW				DL	WW	TL	AW	DD	WL	WW		WD	DD	WD	LL	28	14	6	6*	1	4th
1906	WW	DW				WW	WW	LL	LD	WW	DW	WW	DL	WW	WD	WD	WL	28	18	4	6	–	3rd
1907	WW	WW				WL	WW	WL	WL	WW	DD	DD	DL	WD	DD	DD	DD	28	12	4	12	–	4th
1908	WW	WD				DL	WW	WL	AW	DW	WD	DW	WD	DD	WW	LL	LL	30	13	4	12	–	3rd
1909	WW	DW				DW	WW	LL	LL	DW	DW	WW	WL	WL	DD	WD	WL	30	16	7	7	–	5th
1910[5]	DW	DW				LW	WL	WD	WD	LW	WD	WL	WL	WW	DL	WW	DL	30	16	7	7	–	2nd
1911	WW	DW				WD	WD	WL	DD	WW	LL	WW	LL	WD	WW	WD	LL	30	15	7	8	–	5th

341

Year	C	D	E	Ga	Go	H	K	La	Le	M	Nr	No	So	Su	Wa	Wo	Y	M	W	L	D	A	Pos
1912		WW				WA	DD	LL	DL	DD	DD	DL	DL	WW	WD	WD	DA	26	7	5	12	2	7th
1913		WD	WW	WW	WL	DL	WW	DL	DW	WL				WL	DD	DD	LW	26	13	5	8	–	3rd
1914[6]			LW	WW	DW	WD	WW	AW	DD	DD	DD	WW	WA	WL	WD	WW		28	15	2	9	2	1st
1919[7]		DW			LD	WL	DD			DW		DD	WW	WD	WD		DL	20	7	3	10	–	4th
1920		WW				WD	WL	WW	WW	LL	WW	LW	DL	WL	WD	WW	WW	24	15	6	3	–	3rd
1921		WW				DW	WD	DD	WW	WL	WW	DL	WW	WD	WW		DW	24	15	2	7	–	2nd
1922		DD	WW	WD	DL	WW	WW	WW	WD			DW	WW	WD	DW		DD	24	13	1	10	–	3rd
1923		WW	WW	WD	DD	DW	DD	WD	DW				DL	WW	DD		DL	26	11	2	13	–	4th
1924	WW	AW	WW	WD	DL	DD	DD	WA	DD			DD	DD	DW			WD	26	9	1	14	2	3rd
1925		WD	WD	WW	WW	DW	WL	DW	DD			DD	WW	DW	WW		DL	26	14	2	10	–	2nd
1926		DW	DL	WW	DD	DD	DL	WD	DW				WD	WD	LD	DD	DL	26	7	4	15	–	5th
1927		WW	WD	DD	DL	WD	DD	DW	DW				DL	DW	WD	DD	DL	26	8	3	15	–	6th
1928		DW	DD	DL	DD	WD	LD	DD	DD	WW		DW	DD	DL	DD		DD	28	5	3	20	–	6th
1929		DD	WW	DD	DL	WD	DL	DL	DL	LD	WL	DL	WW	WL	WD		DD	28	8	7	13	–	10th
1930[8]	LD	DD	DD	DL		DD	DD	WL			AD	DD	DD	DD	WL	DW		28	3	4	20	1	8th
1931	DD	DW	WL	LD	DW	DW	DD	WD				LD	DD	DW	WA	DD	DL	28	6	4	17	1	8th
1932	WD	WW	DD	DW	WW	DD	DA			WW	DW	DD		DD	DD		DL	28	9	2	16	1	5th
1933		WL			WL	DD	DL	DD	WD	WW	DD	DD	WD	DD	DD		DL	26	6	5	15	–	9th
1934	WD	LL	LD	WL	WD	DL	DD			WL		DW	DD	WL	DD		LD	26	6	8	12	–	11th
1935	LD	DL			DD	WW	LW	LL		DD		DD	DW	DD	WD	WW	DL	26	7	5	14	–	11th
1936	DL	LW	DW	WL	DD	DW	WD	DD	DL			LD	WD	DW	LW	WD	DL	30	9	7	14	–	6th
1937	DD	DD	WD	LD	LW	WD	WD			LD		DL	WW	DW	WD		DL	26	8	5	13	–	8th
1938	WL	WL			DW	WW	WW	LD		WD		DW	WD	DW	LD	LD	WL	26	12	6	8	–	3rd
1939[9]	LD	DL	DW	WL	DD	LD	DW			WD		DL	WW	WW	WW	WL	DL	28	11	7	10	–	8th
1946[10]	DL	L–	DL		L–	DD	DL		–W	LL	DW	WD	DW	L–		–D	LL	26	6	11	9	–	11th
1947[11]	WA	–W	WL	L–	–L	WW	DD	W–	LL	DD	LD	WW	DL	–W	D–	DW	LL	26	10	7	8	1	6th
1948		–W	LW	–L	WD	DW	WW	W–	DW	LL	W–	WL	–W	D–	WW	LL	LL	26	13	9	4	–	2nd
1949	W–	DW	D–	LW	WL	WD	–L	DL	WW	–D	DL	W–	–D	LW	WL	WL	LL	26	11	8	7	–	5th
1950	W–	LW	DD	WW	D–	WL	DD	WD	WW	WD	WW	WW	–W	–W	WW	LL	LL	28	17	4	7	–	1st
1951	–D	LD	LW	DW	–D	DW	DL	DL	DW	LW	DW	LD	D–	D–	WD	DD		28	7	7	15	–	6th
1952	WW	WD	–D	WW	WW	WW	L–	DD	WW	DW	WW	W–	WW	WL	–W	WL		28	20	3	5	–	1st
1953	WL	DD	W–	DL	WW	WD	–W	WD	WD	DD	WD	–W	LD	WL	W–	WD		28	13	4	11	–	1st
1954	–W	WD	LD	WW	W–	DD	WD	DW	DW	WW	WD	WD	–W	L–	WW	LD		28	15	3	10	–	1st
1955	W–	WW	WW	WW	–L	LW	WW	WW	WW	WL	WW	WW	W–	–L	WW	WL		28	23	5	0	–	1st
1956	DD	WW	–W	DL	WL	WW	D–	WW	WW	LL	DL	W–	WW	AD	–D	WW		28	15	5	7	1	1st
1957	DW	WL	W–	WL	WW	WW	–W	WW	DW	LW	WW	–W	DW	WW	W–	WD		28	21	3	4	–	1st
1958	–D	DL	DW	WD	D–	WL	WW	WL	WW	WW	DD	WW	DL	–W	LW	WL		28	14	5	9	–	1st
1959	D–	WD	DW	WW	–D	DW	LL	DD	DD	LD	WD	WW	W–	–L	WW	WL	WW	28	12	5	11	–	2nd
1960	D–	AD	WL	–D	WD	WD	LD	–W	LL	D–	WW	WW	DL	DD	WD	LD		28	9	6	12	1	7th
1961	–L	DD	LL	D–	LL	DD	LD	L–	LW	–W	LL	LW	DD	DL	DD	DD		28	4	13	11	–	15th
1962	W–	DD	WD	–W	DD	WD	WL	–W	DW	DW	LW	LD	LD	DD	DD	DD		28	10	3	15	–	5th
1963	WD	DD	–L	DD	LD	WL	D–	DD	WD	LD	DL	W–	WD	DL	–D	DD		28	5	6	17	–	11th
1964	WD	DD	W–	WW	DW	WD	–D	DA	DD	DL	DW	L–	WW	WL	D–	WD		28	11	3	13	1	4th
1965	–W	DD	DL	WD	D–	DD	DD	DW	LW	DW	–W	DD	DW	DL	DL	DW		28	7	4	17	–	8th
1966	L–	WD	DW	DW	–D	DD	WD	DD	WD	D–	DD	DL	WD	–W	DL	DW		28	8	3	17	–	7th
1967	DD	DD	L–	WD	LD	LD	–D	WD	DD	WD	DD	–W	WW	DD	WL	–D		28	8	4	16	–	4th
1968	DW	DW	–L	DD	DD	DW	D–	DD	DL	WL	DD	D–	DD	LL	–D	LL		28	4	7	17	–	15th
1969	D–	LW	D–	WD	D–	WD	D–	W–	WD	–D	DD	–D	WD	–D	DD	DW		24	7	1	16	–	3rd
1970	–D	WD	–D	DD	–W	DL	D–	–D	DW	L–	WW	W–	DD	LD	DD	DW		24	6	4	14	–	5th
1971	W–	D–	D–	–W	DL	DL	–W	DD	LW	–W	–W	DD	WW	WD	W–	WD		24	11	3	10	–	1st
1972	D–	–L	D–	–D	W–	DD	–D	–L	DD	–D	W–	L–	DD	–L	D–	WL		20	3	5	12	–	12th
1973	–W	L–	D–	L–	–D	DD	W–	D–	WD	W–	–D	–L	WW	W–	–D	WW		20	9	3	8	–	2nd
1974	–W	–D	D–	L–	D–	LD	–D	–W	DL	–W	W–	DW	–D	DL	D–	DL		20	6	4	10	–	7th
1975	D–	W–	–W	L–	–W	DD	D–	W–	DD	W–	–D	–D	WW	L–	–W	LD		20	8	3	9	–	6th
1976	–L	LD	D–	W–	–D	DD	D–	–W	W–	–L	D–	–D	W–	–D	W–	DW		20	6	4	10	–	9th
1977	D–	DL	–W	–D	WD	DD	DA	L–	DL	D–	–D	–L	DL	W–	D–	–L		22	3	6	12	1	12th
1978	–W	WL	W–	L–	DL	LL	DD	–D	LD	–D	D–	D–	DD	–D	L–	L–		22	3	7	12	–	16th
1979	D–	AL	–W	–W	WW	DW	DD	D–	DD	D–	–D	DL	W–	L–	–D	DL		22	6	3	12	1	3rd
1980	–L	WL	W–	D–	DW	WD	DD	–D	DL	–W	L–	W–	WW	–D	–W	D–		22	10	4	8	–	2nd
1981	D–	WD	–W	–L	AW	LD	WD	D–	WL	D–	–L	–D	WD	D–	W–	–L		22	7	5	9	1	6th
1982	–D	DL	W–	LW	WD	DL	–L	DL	–W	W–	L–	DD	–D	D–	–D	D–		22	6	6	10	–	5th
1983	D–	WD	–L	WD	–D	DW	D–	DD	LL	D–	WW	–D	LD	D–	WW	–D		22	7	4	13	–	8th
1984	WD	LD	DD	–D	W–	DL	–D	L–	WW	LL	–L	WD	–D	D–	W–			24	6	6	12	–	8th
1985	–W	WD	L–	D–	DD	LD	WD	–D	DD	D–	D–	LD	WL	–D	DW	DD		24	5	5	14	–	6th
1986	W–	DD	–D	DL	–L	WD	W–	WL	DW	L–	DL	–W	WD	W–	DD	–L		24	8	6	10	–	3rd
1987	WD	DW	WW	–L	D–	DD	–L	L–	WD	WD	–D	DD	WD	–L	D–	D–		24	7	4	13	–	4th
1988	D–	DL	–D	–W	LW	DL	WD	D–	LD	D–	–W	–L	WW	W–	D–	–D		22	7	5	10	–	4th

Notes

M denotes the total number of matches arranged for the season, but it should be noted that in some seasons the 'official' county championship table does not include matches in which there was no result on first innings.

A denotes matches in which no play at all took place.

*plus one tie.

Although some very rudimentary form of 'County Championship' took place in the 18th century, the matches involving Surrey at that period are not included in the above table. The table therefore commences after the formation of the present Surrey County Cricket Club.

The position in the County Championship table is given only from 1890. Prior to this Surrey were the Champion County in 1864, 1887, 188 and tied for the title in 1889.

[1] In 1854 both matches against Sussex were staged at Brighton, owing to a dispute between Surrey CCC and the proprietor of The Oval.

[2] In 1862 the match against Middlesex is entitled Surrey Club *v* Middlesex and is not included above as a Championship game.

[3] In 1870 both Middlesex matches were played at The Oval as the Middlesex Ground at Lillie Bridge was deemed unsuitable.

[4] In 1901 the Surrey *v* Yorkshire championship match at The Oval was totally washed out. The teams re-played the fixture later in the season, but it ws not included as a championship match.

[5] In 1910, the home matches against Derbyshire and Essex were prematurely ended due to the death and then funeral of King Edward VII.

[6] In 1914 the matches against Leicestershire at home and Sussex away were abandoned due to the outbreak of war. Also the home matches *v* Kent and Yorkshire were both played at Lord's, since The Oval had been requisitioned.

[7] In 1919 Surrey played Middlesex twice at The Oval, the second match, which was drawn was not counted in the Championship.

[8] In 1930, 1931 and 1932 two home and away friendly first-class matches were played against counties. Middlesex being the opponents in 1930 and 1931, Sussex in 1932. These matches are not included in the table.

[9] In 1939 the home match *v* Lancashire was played at Old Trafford.

[10] In 1946 Surrey played Hampshire at Guildford, as a second home match against that county, but not part of the Championship.

[11] In 1947 a friendly first-class match *v* Essex at The Oval was not included in the Championship.

RESULTS OF ALL SUNDAY LEAGUE MATCHES 1969 to 1988

Year	D	E	Ga	Go	H	K	La	Le	M	Nr	Nt	So	Su	Wa	Wo	Y	M	W	L	T	A	Pts	Pos
1969	W	W	W	L	L	W	L	W	L	W	L	L	A	W	W	W	16	9	6	0	1	37	5th
1970	L	A	W	L	L	L	W	L	L	W	W	W	W	L	A	W	16	7	7	0	2	30	7th
1971	L	L	W	W	W	W	L	L	L	W	W	L	L	W	L	W	16	8	8	0	0	32	7th
1972	W	L	W	W	L	L	W	L	W	A	W	A	L	L	W	L	16	7	7	0	2	30	9th
1973	L	W	W	A	W	L	A	W	A	L	L	W	L	W	T	L	16	6	6	1	3	29	9th
1974	W	W	W	A	W	W	L	L	W	L	L	L	L	W	L	L	16	7	8	0	1	30	10th
1975	L	L	L	L	L	W	W	W	W	W	W	L	L	L	L	L	16	6	10	0	0	24	12th
1976	W	W	W	W	L	L	L	L	L	W	L	L	W	W	L	W	16	8	8	0	0	32	8th
1977	L	L	W	L	L	L	W	L	W	W	L	L	L	A	W	A	16	5	9	0	2	24	13th
1978	A	W	W	L	W	L	L	L	A	L	L	L	W	W	L	W	16	6	8	0	2	28	10th
1979	A	A	L	L	W	L	L	L	W	W	L	L	W	W	L	L	16	5	9	0	2	24	12th
1980	W	L	A	L	W	W	W	W	L	W	W	L	A	L	L	W	16	8	6	0	2	36	5th
1981	W	L	A	W	L	L	W	W	L	L	W	L	A	L	W	W	16	7	7	0	2	32	7th
1982	W	L	L	W	T	L	L	W	L	L	W	L	L	W	L	W	16	6	9	1	0	26	12th
1983	A	W	L	A	L	L	L	W	W	L	A	A	L	L	W	A	16	4	7	0	5	26	11th
1984	W	L	W	L	W	A	W	W	L	W	L	L	A	L	L	W	16	7	7	0	2	32	8th
1985	A	A	W	L	L	L	W	L	A	L	L	L	W	W	L	L	16	4	9	0	3	22	17th
1986	L	W	W	W	L	T	L	W	L	L	L	A	L	A	W	L	16	5	8	1	2	26	12th
1987	A	W	A	L	L	L	A	A	W	W	L	W	W	W	L	L	16	6	6	0	4	32	7th
1988	T	W	L	W	W	W	W	W	A	W	L	L	W	A	L	L	16	8	5	1	2	38	5th

RESULTS OF ALL GILLETTE CUP/ NATWEST TROPHY CUP MATCHES 1963 to 1988

1963 Lost in first round to Worcestershire
1964 Beat Cheshire, Gloucestershire, Middlesex; lost in semi-final to Sussex
1965 Beat Glamorgan, Northamptonshire, Middlesex; lost in final to Yorkshire
1966 Beat Leicestershire; lost in third round to Hampshire
1967 Beat Derbyshire; lost in third round to Kent
1968 Lost in second round to Middlesex
1969 Beat Hampshire; lost in third round to Yorkshire
1970 Beat Yorkshire, Glamorgan, Middlesex; lost in semi-finals to Sussex
1971 Beat Hertfordshire, Middlesex; lost in third round to Gloucestershire
1972 Beat Durham; lost in third round to Worcestershire
1973 Lost in second round to Gloucestershire
1974 Beat Lincolnshire; lost in third round to Somerset
1975 Lost in first round to Somerset
1976 Lost in second round to Derbyshire
1977 Beat Lancashire; lost in third round to Glamorgan
1978 Beat Shropshire; lost in second round to Essex
1979 Lost in second round to Northamptonshire

1980 Beat Northamptonshire, Gloucestershire, Essex, Yorkshire; lost in final to Middlesex
1981 Lost in second round to Leicestershire
1982 Beat Durham, Northamptonshire, Hampshire, Middlesex and Warwickshire to win Cup
1983 Beat Lincolnshire; lost in second round to Warwickshire
1984 Beat Ireland, Essex; lost in quarter-finals to Warwickshire
1985 Lost in first round to Kent
1986 Beat Cheshire, Derbyshire, Nottinghamshire; lost in semi-finals to Lancashire
1987 Beat Hertfordshire; lost in second round to Northamptonshire
1988 Beat Essex, Glamorgan; lost in semi-finals to Middlesex

RESULTS IN THE BENSON AND HEDGES CUP 1972 to 1988

1972 Failed to qualify for knock-out section
1973 Failed to qualify for knock-out section
1974 Second in South Zone; beat Yorkshire in quarter-finals; Lancashire in semi-finals and Leicestershire in final to win Cup
1975 Failed to qualify for knock-out section
1976 Second in Group D; beat Essex in quarter-finals; lost to Kent in semi-finals
1977 Failed to qualify for knock-out section
1978 Failed to qualify for knock-out section
1979 Second in Group C; beat Worcestershire in quarter-finals; Derbyshire in semi-finals; lost to Essex in final
1980 Second in Group D; lost to Essex in quarter-finals
1981 Second in Group D; beat Nottinghamshire in quarter-finals; Leicestershire in semi-finals; lost to Somerset in final
1982 Failed to qualify for knock-out section
1983 Failed to qualify for knock-out section
1984 Second in Group D; lost to Nottinghamshire in quarter-finals
1985 Failed to qualify for knock-out section
1986 Failed to qualify for knock-out section
1987 First in Group D; beat Worcestershire in quarter-finals; lost to Yorkshire in semi-finals
1988 Failed to qualify for knock-out section

INDIVIDUAL RECORDS

SCORES OF OVER 200 FOR SURREY IN FIRST-CLASS CRICKET

Score	Batsman	Opponents	Venue	Year
357*	R. Abel	Somerset	The Oval	1899
338	W. W. Read	Oxford University	The Oval	1888
316*	J. B. Hobbs	Middlesex	Lord's	1926
315*	T. W. Hayward	Lancashire	The Oval	1898
306*	A. Ducat	Oxford University	The Oval	1919
292*	A. Sandham	Northamptonshire	The Oval	1921
290*	A. Ducat	Essex	Leyton	1921
282*	A. Sandham	Lancashire	Manchester	1928
277*	T. F. Shepherd	Gloucestershire	The Oval	1927
276	E. G. Hayes	Hampshire	The Oval	1909
273*	E. G. Hayes	Derbyshire	Derby	1904
273	T. W. Hayward	Yorkshire	The Oval	1899
271	A. Ducat	Hampshire	Southampton	1919
269	H. T. Barling	Hampshire	Southampton	1933
261	J. B. Hobbs	Oxford University	The Oval	1926
255	J. F. Parker	New Zealanders	The Oval	1949
253	L. B. Fishlock	Leicestershire	Leicester	1948
250	R. Abel	Warwickshire	The Oval	1897
248*	A. Sandham	Glamorgan	Cardiff	1928
247	W. W. Read	Lancashire	Manchester	1887
244*	W. W. Read	Cambridge University	The Oval	1887
243	R. J. Gregory	Somerset	The Oval	1938
239	A. Sandham	Glamorgan	The Oval	1937
236	H. S. Squires	Lancashire	The Oval	1933
235	A. Ducat	Leicestershire	The Oval	1926
234	C. Baldwin	Kent	The Oval	1897
234	T. F. Shepherd	Cambridge University	The Oval	1930
233*	H. T. Barling	Nottinghamshire	The Oval	1946
232	J. N. Crawford	Somerset	The Oval	1908
231	R. Abel	Essex	The Oval	1896
230	A. Sandham	Essex	The Oval	1927
229*	T. W. Hayward	Derbyshire	Derby	1896
227*	M. J. Stewart	Middlesex	The Oval	1964
226*	J. H. Edrich	Middlesex	The Oval	1967
226	J. B. Hobbs	Nottinghamshire	The Oval	1914
225	W. Brockwell	Hampshire	The Oval	1897
221	R. Abel	Worcestershire	The Oval	1900
221	J. B. Hobbs	West Indians	The Oval	1933
221	T. E. Jesty	Essex	The Oval	1986
219	R. Abel	Kent	The Oval	1898
219	T. W. Hayward	Northamptonshire	The Oval	1906
219	A. Sandham	Australians	The Oval	1934

*not out

Score	Batsman	Opponents	Venue	Year
218	E. G. Hayes	Oxford University	The Oval	1906
218	A. Ducat	Nottinghamshire	Nottingham	1930
217	R. Abel	Essex	The Oval	1895
216*	A. R. Butcher	Cambridge University	Fenner's	1980
216	J. H. Edrich	Nottinghamshire	Nottingham	1962
215	R. Abel	Nottinghamshire	The Oval	1897
215	J. B. Hobbs	Essex	Leyton	1914
215	J. B. Hobbs	Warwickshire	Edgbaston	1925
215	A. Sandham	Somerset	Taunton	1932
213	D. L. A. Jephson	Derbyshire	The Oval	1900
212	T. F. Shepherd	Lancashire	The Oval	1921
212	F. R. Brown	Middlesex	The Oval	1932
211	P. B. H. May	Nottinghamshire	Nottingham	1954
210*	T. F. Shepherd	Kent	Blackheath	1921
210	H. S. Squires	Derbyshire	The Oval	1949
210	L. B. Fishlock	Somerset	The Oval	1949
209*	A. Sandham	Somerset	The Oval	1921
208	T. W. Hayward	Warwickshire	The Oval	1906
208	A. Ducat	Essex	Leyton	1928
207*	T. F. Shepherd	Kent	Blackheath	1925
207	P. B. H. May	Cambridge University	The Oval	1954
207	K. F. Barrington	Nottinghamshire	The Oval	1964
206	E. R. T. Holmes	Derbyshire	Chesterfield	1935
205*	R. Abel	Middlesex	The Oval	1901
205*	J. B. Hobbs	Australian Imp. Forces	The Oval	1919
205*	B. Constable	Somerset	The Oval	1952
205*	J. H. Edrich	Gloucestershire	Bristol	1965
205	J. B. Hobbs	Hampshire	The Oval	1909
204*	T. W. Hayward	Warwickshire	The Oval	1909
204*	A. Ducat	Northamptonshire	Northampton	1921
204*	J. F. Parker	Derbyshire	The Oval	1947
204	W. E. Roller	Sussex	The Oval	1885
204	J. B. Hobbs	Somerset	The Oval	1929
204	A. Sandham	Warwickshire	Edgbaston	1930
203*	J. B. Hobbs	Nottinghamshire	Nottingham	1924
203	A. Ducat	Sussex	The Oval	1920
202	E. G. Hayes	Middlesex	The Oval	1907
202	T. W. Hayward	Derbyshire	The Oval	1911
202	J. B. Hobbs	Yorkshire	Lord's	1914
201*	A. Jeacocke	Sussex	The Oval	1922
200*	H. A. Peach	Northamptonshire	Northampton	1920
200*	J. B. Hobbs	Warwickshire	Edgbaston	1928
200*	M. J. Stewart	Essex	The Oval	1962
200	A. Sandham	Essex	Leyton	1923
200	J. B. Hobbs	Hampshire	Southampton	1926
200	H. S. Squires	Cambridge University	The Oval	1931

*not out

347

CENTURIES IN LIMITED-OVERS MATCHES

John Player/Refuge Assurance League

Score	Batsman	Opponents	Venue	Year
136	M. A. Lynch	Yorkshire	Bradford	1985
122	G. P. Howarth	Gloucestershire	The Oval	1976
120*	G. R. J. Roope	Worcestershire	Byfleet	1973
113*	A. R. Butcher	Warwickshire	Edgbaston	1978
113	Younis Ahmed	Warwickshire	Edgbaston	1976
113	C. J. Richards	Somerset	The Oval	1987
111	A. R. Butcher	Leicestershire	Leicester	1983
108*	J. H. Edrich	Derbyshire	Derby	1972
106	A. R. Butcher	Middlesex	The Oval	1979
106	G. P. Howarth	Hampshire	The Oval	1976
105*	G. S. Clinton	Yorkshire	Scarborough	1981
105*	C. J. Richards	Essex	Chelmsford	1988
103*	A. R. Butcher	Derbyshire	The Oval	1976
103	M. A. Lynch	Northamptonshire	Northampton	1984

Benson & Hedges Cup

Score	Batsman	Opponents	Venue	Year
121*	G. S. Clinton	Kent	The Oval	1988
115*	G. R. J. Roope	Essex	Chelmsford	1973
112*	M. A. Lynch	Kent	The Oval	1987
110*	D. M. Smith	Worcestershire	The Oval	1987
106*	G. S. Clinton	Middlesex	Lord's	1985
101*	Younis Ahmed	Kent	Canterbury	1974

Gillette Cup/NatWest Trophy

Score	Batsman	Opponents	Venue	Year
146	G. S. Clinton	Kent	Canterbury	1985
129	M. A. Lynch	Durham	The Oval	1982
112	T. E. Jesty	Lancashire	The Oval	1986
107*	A. J. Stewart	Middlesex	The Oval	1988
105*	C. J. Richards	Lincolnshire	Sleaford	1983
103*	D. M. Smith	Northamptonshire	The Oval	1982
101	M. J. Stewart	Durham	Chester-le-Street	1972

CARRYING BAT THROUGH A COMPLETED FIRST-CLASS INNINGS

Batsman	Score	Total	Opponents	Venue	Year
R. Abel (5)	88	(198)	Gloucestershire	Cheltenham	1885
	151*	(425)	Middlesex	Lord's	1890
	136*	(300)	Middlesex	The Oval	1894
	357*	(811)	Somerset	The Oval	1899
	151*	(263)	Sussex	The Oval	1902
A. Baker	55*	(110)	Gloucestershire	Bristol	1905
W. Brockwell	76*	(158)	Leicestershire	Leicester	1898
T. H. Clark	81*	(135)	Yorkshire	The Oval	1956
G. S. Clinton (2)	113*	(260)	Derbyshire	The Oval	1984
	84*	(171)	Yorkshire	Leeds	1986

*not out

Batsman	Score	Total	Opponents	Venue	Year
J. H. Edrich (2)	79*	(122)	Northamptonshire	The Oval	1963
	61*	(108)	Essex	Southend	1978
L. B. Fishlock	81*	(141)	Australians	The Oval	1948
D. G. W. Fletcher	127*	(271)	Yorkshire	Bradford	1947
T. W. Hayward (7)	156*	(287)	Philadelphians	The Oval	1903
	188*	(321)	Kent	Canterbury	1904
	129*	(286)	Australians	The Oval	1905
	144*	(225)	Nottinghamshire	Nottingham	1906
	114*	(190)	Lancashire	The Oval	1907
	90*	(156)	Somerset	Taunton	1909
	96*	(178)	Australians	The Oval	1909
J. B. Hobbs (4)	60*	(155)	Warwickshire	Birmingham	1907
	205*	(344)	AIF	The Oval	1919
	172*	(294)	Yorkshire	Leeds	1921
	133*	(300)	Yorkshire	The Oval	1931
M. Howell	15*	(73)	Kent	Blackheath	1920
R. Humphrey	30*	(60)	Nottinghamshire	The Oval	1872
T. Humphrey	43*	(95)	Sussex	Brighton	1867
H. Jupp (11)	94*	(297)	Hampshire	The Oval	1866
	90*	(222)	Yorkshire	Sheffield	1868
	27*	(95)	Lancashire	Manchester	1870
	50*	(88)	Gloucestershire	Clifton	1870
	51*	(113)	Nottinghamshire	The Oval	1873
	43*	(95)	Yorkshire (1st inns)	The Oval	1874
	109*	(193)	Yorkshire (2nd inns)	The Oval	1874
	37*	(74)	Yorkshire	Sheffield	1876
	73*	(268)	Kent	The Oval	1876
	91*	(264)	Kent	The Oval	1877
	117*	(284)	Yorkshire	Sheffield	1880
A. P. Lucas	36*	(121)	Gloucestershire	Clifton	1877
A. B. D. Parsons	30*	(71)	Leicestershire	The Oval	1961
W. W. Read	196*	(413)	Sussex	The Oval	1892
A. Sandham (6)	123*	(323)	Hampshire	Portsmouth	1922
	155*	(330)	Somerset	The Oval	1923
	96*	(158)	Cambridge University	The Oval	1924
	125*	(282)	Northamptonshire	Northampton	1930
	113*	(221)	Hampshire	Bournemouth	1931
	169*	(333)	Hampshire	The Oval	1933

CARRYING BAT THROUGH COMPLETE LIMITED-OVERS INNINGS

John Player/Refuge Assurance League

Batsman	Score	Total	Opponents	Venue	Year
G. S. Clinton (2)	105*	(243)	Yorkshire	Scarborough	1981
	92*	(206)	Yorkshire	The Oval	1986
J. H. Edrich	64*	(175)	Sussex	Hove	1973
G. R. J. Roope (2)	120*	(200)	Worcestershire	Byfleet	1973
	74*	(205)	Derbyshire	Derby	1982

*not out

Benson & Hedges Cup

Batsman	Score	Total	Opponents	Venue	Year
G. R. J. Roope (2)	115★	(234)	Essex	Chelmsford	1973
	97★	(210)	Cambridge University	The Oval	1974

Nat West Trophy/Gillette Cup

None

A HUNDRED IN EACH INNINGS OF A FIRST-CLASS MATCH

Scores		Batsman	Opponents	Venue	Year
186	118★	K. F. Barrington	Warwickshire	Birmingham	1959
117★	114	A. R. Butcher	Glamorgan	The Oval	1984
112	124	J. H. Edrich	Nottinghamshire	Nottingham	1959
143	113★	J. H. Edrich	Worcestershire	Worcester	1970
111	124	J. H. Edrich	Warwickshire	The Oval	1971
140	115	J. H. Edrich	Kent	The Oval	1977
131★	100★	L. B. Fishlock	Sussex	The Oval	1936
113	105	L. B. Fishlock	Yorkshire	The Oval	1937
129	112	L. B. Fishlock	Leicestershire	Leicester	1946
111	118	L. B. Fishlock	Nottinghamshire	Nottingham	1949
106	112	T. W. Hayward	Sussex	Hove	1904
144★	100	T. W. Hayward	Nottinghamshire	Nottingham	1906
143	125	T. W. Hayward	Leicestershire	Leicester	1906
(scored in successive matches)					
160	100	J. B. Hobbs	Warwickshire	Birmingham	1909
104	143★	J. B. Hobbs	Cambridge University	The Oval	1925
101	101★	J. B. Hobbs	Somerset	Taunton	1925
112	104	J. B. Hobbs	Hampshire	The Oval	1927
137	111★	J. B. Hobbs	Glamorgan	The Oval	1930
113	119★	J. B. Hobbs	Essex	The Oval	1932
114	101	D. J. Knight	Yorkshire	The Oval	1919
167	103★	P. B. H. May	Essex	Southend	1951
109	103★	G. R. J. Roope	Leicestershire	Leicester	1971
121	101★	T. F. Shepherd	Leicestershire	The Oval	1926
131	102	H. S. Squires	Oxford University	The Oval	1932

A HUNDRED ON FIRST-CLASS DEBUT FOR SURREY

Score	Batsman	Opponents	Venue	Year
107★	H. O. Bloomfield	Northamptonshire	Northampton	1921
101★	N. J. Falkner	Cambridge University	Banstead	1984
117★	K. T. Medlycott	Cambridge University	Banstead	1984
124	N. Miller	Sussex	Hove	1899
124	H. C. Pretty	Nottinghamshire	The Oval	1899
114★	P. D. Atkins	Cambridge University	The Oval	1988

Note: M. R. Barton scored 124 *v* MCC (Lord's) 1948 on his first-class debut for Surrey having previously played first-class cricket

★not out

2,000 RUNS IN A SEASON FOR SURREY

Batsman	Runs	Average	Year
T. W. Hayward	3,246	72.13	1906
R. Abel	2,849	52.75	1901
T. W. Hayward	2,734	55.79	1904
J. B. Hobbs	2,499	62.47	1914
A. Sandham	2,417	60.42	1928
T. W. Hayward	2,407	53.48	1901
R. Abel	2,404	55.90	1899
J. B. Hobbs	2,399	54.52	1913
T. W. Hayward	2,349	54.62	1900
A. Sandham	2,348	53.36	1929
J. B. Hobbs	2,331	66.60	1925
L. B. Fishlock	2,322	44.65	1950
R. J. Gregory	2,278	55.66	1934
L. B.Fishlock	2,219	43.50	1949
A. Sandham	2,161	51.45	1930
K. F. Barrington	2,158	56.78	1959
R. J. Gregory	2,149	46.71	1937
J. H. Edrich	2,142	51.00	1962
L. B. Fishlock	2,130	50.71	1946
R. Abel	2,100	56.75	1900
T. W. Hayward	2,087	48.53	1911
A. Ducat	2,067	49.21	1930
A. Sandham	2,056	57.11	1925
R. Abel	2,050	45.55	1902
P. B. H. May	2,048	58.51	1953
A. Sandham	2,025	61.36	1927
J. B. Hobbs	2,015	80.60	1928
H. T. Barling	2,014	43.78	1946
J. B. Hobbs	2,005	54.18	1919

RECORD WICKET PARTNERSHIPS
IN FIRST-CLASS MATCHES

First wicket (Qualification 250)

Score	Batsmen	Opponents	Venue	Year
428	J. B. Hobbs and A. Sandham	Oxford University	The Oval	1926
379	R. Abel and W. Brockwell	Hampshire	The Oval	1897
364	R. Abel and D. L. A. Jephson	Derbyshire	The Oval	1900
352	T. W. Hayward and J. B. Hobbs	Warwickshire	The Oval	1909
313	T. W. Hayward and J. B. Hobbs	Worcestershire	Worcester	1913
290	J. B. Hobbs and T. W. Hayward	Yorkshire	Lord's	1914
277	G. S. Clinton and A. R. Butcher	Yorkshire	The Oval	1984
270*	R. Abel and W. Brockwell	Kent	The Oval	1900
266	A. Sandham and A. Jeacocke	Northamptonshire	The Oval	1921
266	A. R. Butcher and G. S. Clinton	Cambridge University	Fenner's	1980
265	R. Abel and W. Brockwell	Warwickshire	The Oval	1898

*not out

351

Score	Batsmen	Opponents	Venue	Year
264	J. B. Hobbs and A. Sandham	Somerset	Taunton	1932
260	L. B. Fishlock and E. A. Bedser	Somerset	The Oval	1949
255	R. C. E. Pratt and M. J. Stewart	Cambridge University	Guildford	1956
253*	J. B. Hobbs and A. Sandham	West Indians	The Oval	1928

Second wicket (Qualification 250)

371	J. B. Hobbs and E. C. Hayes	Hampshire	The Oval	1909
344	A. Sandham and R. J. Gregory	Glamorgan	The Oval	1937
316*	M. J. Stewart and K. F. Barrington	Essex	The Oval	1962
316*	A. R. Butcher and D. M. Smith	Warwickshire	Birmingham	1982
299	A. Sandham and A. Ducat	Lancashire	Manchester	1928
291	A. Sandham and H. S. Squires	Yorkshire	The Oval	1933
281	A. Sandham and A. Ducat	Nottinghamshire	Nottingham	1930
276	J. B. Hobbs and R. J. Gregory	Hampshire	Southampton	1926
272	R. Abel and E. G. Hayes	Worcestershire	The Oval	1900
259	T. W. Hayward and E. G. Hayes	Yorkshire	The Oval	1911
256*	G. P. Howarth and R. D. V. Knight	Cambridge University	Cambridge	1978

Third wicket (Qualification 250)

353	A. Ducat and E. G. Hayes	Hampshire	Southampton	1919
317	A. Ducat and T. F. Shepherd	Essex	Leyton	1928
306	R. Abel and F. C. Holland	Cambridge University	The Oval	1895
305	W. E. Roller and W. W. Read	Lancashire	Manchester	1887
297	J. H. Edrich and K. F. Barrington	Middlesex	The Oval	1967
267	R. J. Gregory and H. T. Barling	Nottinghamshire	The Oval	1946
263	D. G. W. Fletcher and H. S. Squires	Nottinghamshire	Nottingham	1947
261	A. Ducat and T. F. Shepherd	Leicestershire	The Oval	1926
261	B. Constable and P. B. H. May	Nottinghamshire	Nottingham	1958

Fourth wicket (Qualification 250)

448	R. Abel and T. W. Hayward	Yorkshire	The Oval	1899
334	R. Abel and T. W. Hayward	Somerset	The Oval	1899
293	H. T. Barling and H. S. Squires	Oxford University	The Oval	1932
289	A. Ducat and T. F. Shepherd	Gloucestershire	The Oval	1927
270	J. B. Hobbs and D. R. Jardine	Middlesex	Lord's	1926
256	R. Abel and F. C. Holland	Essex	The Oval	1895
250	T. H. Clark and R. C. E. Pratt	Kent	The Oval	1953

Fifth wicket (Qualification 225)

308	J. N. Crawford and F. C. Holland	Somerset	The Oval	1908
288	H. A. Peach and A. Ducat	Northamptonshire	Northampton	1920
287	R. Abel and W. H. Lockwood	Lancashire	The Oval	1899
262	A. Jeacocke and W. J. Abel	Cambridge University	The Oval	1923
256*	R. Abel and D. L. A. Jephson	Gloucestershire	The Oval	1898
252	A. J. Stewart and M. A. Lynch	Kent	Canterbury	1985
250	T. W. Hayward and D. L. A. Jephson	Derbyshire	The Oval	1901
247*	J. F. Parker and E. R. T. Holmes	Nottinghamshire	Nottingham	1947
230	C. Baldwin and D. L. A. Jephson	Kent	The Oval	1897

*not out

Sixth wicket (Qualification 225)

Score	Batsmen	Opponents	Venue	Year
298	A. Sandham and H. S. Harrison	Sussex	The Oval	1913
294	D. R. Jardine and P. G. H. Fender	Yorkshire	Bradford	1928
260	J. N. Crawford and Lord Dalmeny	Leicestershire	The Oval	1905

Seventh wicket (Qualification 200)

262	C. J. Richards and K. T. Medlycott	Kent	The Oval	1987
200	T. F. Shepherd and J. W. Hitch	Kent	Blackheath	1921

Eighth wicket (Qualification 175)

204	T. W. Hayward and L. C. Braund	Lancashire	The Oval	1898
198	K. F. Barrington and J. C. Laker	Gloucestershire	The Oval	1954
197	H. T. Barling and A. V. Bedser	Somerset	Taunton	1947
189*	N. J. Falkner and K. T. Medlycott	Cambridge University	Banstead	1984
188	H. S. Bush and V. F. S. Crawford	Lancashire	Manchester	1902
182	R. Abel and W. E. Roller	Kent	The Oval	1883
175	E. Pooley and J. Southerton	MCC	The Oval	1871

Ninth wicket (Qualification 150)

168	E. R. T. Holmes and E. W. J. Brooks	Hampshire	The Oval	1936
161	G. J. Whittaker and W. S. Surridge	Glamorgan	The Oval	1951
156	A. E. Street and F. E. Smith	Leicestershire	Leicester	1895
155	F. R. Brown and M. J. C. Allom	Middlesex	The Oval	1932
155	S. J. Storey and R. D. Jackman	Glamorgan	Cardiff	1973

Tenth wicket (Qualification 100)

173	A. Ducat and A. Sandham	Essex	Leyton	1921
172	A. Needham and R. D. Jackman	Lancashire	Manchester	1982
138	R. I. Jefferson and D. A. D. Sydenham	Northamptonshire	Northampton	1963
133*	A. Sandham and W. J. Abel	Middlesex	The Oval	1919
131	D. L. A. Jephson and F. Stedman	Lancashire	The Oval	1900
130	H. Strudwick and J. W. Hitch	Warwickshire	Birmingham	1911
129	E. G. Goatly and F. Stedman	South Africans	The Oval	1904
128	W. Mudie and T. Sewell jr	Kent and Sussex	The Oval	1859
119*	E. A. Watts and J. V. Daley	Hampshire	Bournemouth	1936
118	C. Calvert and T. Sewell jr	Sussex	Hove	1868
113*	E. W. Whitfield and J. F. Parker	Indians	The Oval	1932
111	J. F. Parker and A. R. Gover	Indians	The Oval	1936
105	W. Brockwell and T. Richardson	Gloucestershire	The Oval	1893
104	F. R. Brown and J. F. Parker	Kent	Blackheath	1932

JOHN PLAYER/REFUGE ASSURANCE LEAGUE

First wicket (Qualification 125)

Score	Batsmen	Opponents	Venue	Year
218	A. R. Butcher and G. P. Howarth	Gloucestershire	The Oval	1976
145	A. R. Butcher and G. R. J. Roope	Yorkshire	The Oval	1978

*not out

Score	Batsmen	Opponents	Venue	Year
142	A. R. Butcher and G. P. Howarth	Derbyshire	The Oval	1976
132	A. R. Butcher and G. S. Clinton	Sussex	Hove	1985

Second wicket (Qualification 125)

187	A. R. Butcher and R. D. V. Knight	Leicestershire	Leicester	1983
145	D. B. Pauline and R. D. V. Knight	Worcestershire	Guildford	1983
130	G. R. J. Roope and Younis Ahmed	Leicestershire	Leicester	1973

Third wicket (Qualification 125)

158*	C. J. Richards and M. A. Lynch	Gloucestershire	Cheltenham	1988
130*	Younis Ahmed and G. R. J. Roope	Leicestershire	The Oval	1976

Fourth wicket (Qualification 125)

139*	D. M. Smith and T. E. Jesty	Northamptonshire	Guildford	1987

Fifth wicket

89	G. P. Howarth and J. H. Edrich	Derbyshire	Chesterfield	1975

Sixth wicket

78.	G. R. J. Roope and Intikhab Alam	Middlesex	Byfleet	1972

Seventh wicket

88*	G. S. Clinton and R. D. Jackman	Nottinghamshire	The Oval	1980

Eighth wicket

50	Intikhab Alam and A. Long	Yorkshire	The Oval	1974

Ninth wicket

45	C. K. Bullen and A. H. Gray	Worcestershire	Hereford	1987

Tenth wicket

39	G. G. Arnold and P. I. Pocock	Somerset	Guildford	1975

BENSON AND HEDGES CUP

First wicket (Qualification 125)

Score	Batsmen	Opponents	Venue	Year
155	J. H. Edrich and G. R. J. Roope	Essex	Chelmsford	1973
136	G. S. Clinton and D. M. Smith	Kent	The Oval	1988

Second wicket (Qualification 125)

147	D. M. Smith and M. A. Lynch	Kent	The Oval	1987

*not out

Third wicket (Qualification 100)

Score	Batsmen	Opponents	Venue	Year
119	A. R. Butcher and R. D. V. Knight	Somerset	Taunton	1980
105	G. P. Howarth and R. D. V. Knight	Essex	The Oval	1979

Fourth wicket (Qualification 100)

Score	Batsmen	Opponents	Venue	Year
159*	D. M. Smith and T. E. Jesty	Worcestershire	The Oval	1987

Fifth wicket (Qualification 100)

Score	Batsmen	Opponents	Venue	Year
105*	R. D. V. Knight and D. M. Smith	Northamptonshire	Northampton	1979

Sixth wicket

Score	Batsmen	Opponents	Venue	Year
64	J. H. Edrich and S. J. Storey	Kent	The Oval	1973

Seventh wicket

Score	Batsmen	Opponents	Venue	Year
69	J. H. Edrich and D. M. Smith	Essex	The Oval	1976

Eighth wicket

Score	Batsmen	Opponents	Venue	Year
50	D. M. Smith and C. J. Richards	Derbyshire	Derby	1979

Ninth wicket

Score	Batsmen	Opponents	Venue	Year
55	R. D. Jackman and G. Monkhouse	Kent	Canterbury	1982

GILLETTE CUP/NATWEST TROPHY

First wicket (Qualification 100)

Score	Batsmen	Opponents	Venue	Year
121	J. H. Edrich and M. J. Edwards	Hampshire	Southampton	1969
105	J. H. Edrich and W. A. Smith	Gloucestershire	The Oval	1964
105	J. H. Edrich and M. J. Edwards	Middlesex	The Oval	1970

Second wicket (Qualification 100)

Score	Batsmen	Opponents	Venue	Year
145	M. J. Edwards and M. J. Stewart	Derbyshire	The Oval	1967

Third wicket (Qualification 100)

Score	Batsmen	Opponents	Venue	Year
136	D. R. Owen-Thomas and Younis Ahmed	Lincolnshire	Lincoln	1974
105	J. H. Edrich and Younis Ahmed	Glamorgan	Swansea	1970
102	P. D. Atkins and M. A. Lynch	Glamorgan	The Oval	1988

Fourth wicket

Score	Batsmen	Opponents	Venue	Year
85	D. M. Smith and R. D. V. Knight	Northamptonshire	The Oval	1982

*not out

355

Fifth wicket (Qualification 100)

Score	Batsmen	Opponents	Venue	Year
166	M. A. Lynch and G. R. J. Roope	Durham	The Oval	1982
111	R. A. E. Tindall and W. A. Smith	Northamptonshire	The Oval	1965

Sixth wicket

83*	K. F. Barrington and M. J. Edwards	Middlesex	The Oval	1965

Seventh wicket

160*	C. J. Richards and I. R. Payne	Lincolnshire	Sleaford	1983

Eighth wicket

55	C. J. Richards and M. A. Feltham	Staffordshire	Burton	1988

Ninth wicket

44	D. J. Thomas and S. T. Clarke	Warwickshire	Birmingham	1984

Tenth wicket

26	A. Long and G. G. Arnold	Worcestershire	Worcester	1972

ALL-ROUND RECORDS
100 RUNS AND 10 WICKETS IN SAME MATCH

Player	Score	Analysis		Opponents	Venue	Year
E. A. Bedser	71 30	7-142	3-89	Gloucestershire	The Oval	1951
J. N. Crawford	148	7-85	4-63	Gloucestershire	Bristol	1906
P. G. H. Fender	104	3-48	7-76	Essex	Leyton	1926
R. J. Gregory	171	5-36	5-66	Middlesex	Lord's	1930
W. H. Lockwood	63 37	6-48	6-48	Lancashire	The Oval	1902

PLAYERS ACHIEVING THE 'DOUBLE'

Player	No. times	Year	Runs	Average	Wickets	Average
W. H. Lockwood	2	1899	1,113	37.10	106	19.26
		1900	1,266	32.46	124	19.41
J. N. Crawford	2	1906	1,064	29.55	111	19.54
		1907	1,061	35.36	118	16.02
P. G. H. Fender	2	1922	1,114	39.78	143	19.49
		1923	1,136	31.55	140	18.56
T. W. Hayward	1	1897	1,211	36.69	108	17.92
S. J. Storey	1	1966	1,013	24.70	104	18.39

*not out

BOWLING RECORDS
HAT-TRICKS

First-class matches

Year	Bowler	Opponents	Venue
1868	J. Street	Middlesex	The Oval
1885	W. E. Roller	Sussex	The Oval
1893	W. H. Lockwood	Cambridge University	Fenner's
1893	T. Richardson	Gloucestershire	The Oval
1896	T. Richardson	Leicestershire	The Oval
1897	W. S. Lees	Hampshire	Southampton
1898	T. Richardson	Warwickshire	The Oval
1898	T. Richardson	Sussex	Hove
1899	T. W. Hayward	Gloucestershire	The Oval
1899	T. W. Hayward	Derbyshire	Chesterfield
1900	W. Brockwell	Yorkshire	Sheffield
1901	W. H. Lockwood	Derbyshire	The Oval
1903	W. H. Lockwood	Yorkshire	Sheffield
1904	D. L. A. Jephson	Middlesex	The Oval
1908	W. C. Smith	Hampshire	The Oval
1910	W. C. Smith	Northamptonshire	The Oval
1911	J. W. Hitch	Cambridge University	The Oval
1914	J. W. Hitch	Warwickshire	The Oval
1914	P. G. H. Fender	Somerset	The Oval
1923	W. C. H. Sadler	Cambridge University	The Oval
1924	P. G. H. Fender	Gloucestershire	The Oval
1924*	H. A. Peach	Sussex	The Oval
1926	T. F. Shepherd	Gloucestershire	The Oval
1935*	A. R. Gover	Worcestershire	Worcester
1951	J. C. Laker	Gloucestershire	Gloucester
1953	J. C. Laker	Warwickshire	The Oval
1953	J. C. Laker	Cambridge University	Guildford
1953	A. V. Bedser	Essex	The Oval
1955	G. A. R. Lock	Somerset	Weston-super-Mare
1961	D. Gibson	Northamptonshire	Northampton
1963	P. J. Loader	Leicestershire	The Oval
1963	R. Harman	Kent	Blackheath
1965	S. J. Storey	Glamorgan	Swansea
1968	R. Harman	Derbyshire	Ilkeston
1971	R. D. Jackman	Kent	Canterbury
1971	P. I. Pocock	Worcestershire	Guildford
1972	Intikhab Alam	Yorkshire	The Oval
1972*	P. I. Pocock	Sussex	Eastbourne
1973	R. D. Jackman	Yorkshire	Leeds
1974	G. G. Arnold	Leicestershire	Leicester
1980	S. T. Clarke	Nottinghamshire	The Oval
1985	A. H. Gray	Yorkshire	Sheffield
1987	S. T. Clarke	Essex	Colchester

*Four wickets in four balls

Limited-Overs – Gillette Cup

1964	D. A. D. Sydenham	Cheshire	Hoylake

357

NINE WICKETS IN AN INNINGS FOR SURREY

Analysis	Bowler	Opponents	Venue	Year
10-43	T. Rushby	Somerset	Taunton	1921
10-45	T. Richardson	Essex	The Oval	1894
10-54	G. A. R. Lock	Kent	Blackheath	1956
10-67	E. A. Watts	Warwickshire	Edgbaston	1939
10-88	J. C. Laker	Australians	The Oval	1956
9-17	P. J. Loader	Warwickshire	The Oval	1958
9-28	P. J. Loader	Kent	Blackheath	1953
9-31	W. C. Smith	Hampshire	The Oval	1904
9-45	M. P. Bicknell	Cambridge University	The Oval	1988
9-47	J. W. Sharpe	Middlesex	The Oval	1891
9-47	T. Richardson	Yorkshire	Sheffield	1893
9-49	T. Richardson	Sussex	The Oval	1895
9-57	P. I. Pocock	Glamorgan	Cardiff	1979
9-59	W. H. Lockwood	Essex	Leyton	1902
9-67	G. A. Lohmann	Sussex	Hove	1889
9-70	T. Richardson	Hampshire	The Oval	1895
9-70	D. A. D. Sydenham	Gloucestershire	The Oval	1964
9-77	G. A. R. Lock	Oxford University	Guildford	1960
9-81	W. S. Lees	Sussex	Eastbourne	1905
9-94	W. H. Lockwood	Essex	The Oval	1900
9-105	W. H. Lockwood	Gloucestershire	Cheltenham	1899
9-130	G. Griffith	Lancashire	The Oval	1867

FIFTEEN OR MORE WICKETS IN A MATCH FOR SURREY

Analysis	Bowler	Opponents	Venue	Year
16-83	G. A. R. Lock	Kent	Blackheath	1956
15-83	T. Richardson	Warwickshire	The Oval	1898
15-95	T. Richardson	Essex	The Oval	1894
15-97	J. C. Laker	M.C.C.	Lord's	1954
15-98	G. A. Lohmann	Sussex	Hove	1889
15-113	T. Richardson	Leicestershire	The Oval	1896
15-154	T. Richardson	Yorkshire	Leeds	1897
15-155	T. Richardson	Hampshire	The Oval	1895
15-182	G. A. R. Lock	Kent	Blackheath	1958
15-184	W. H. Lockwood	Gloucestershire	Cheltenham	1899

SIX WICKETS IN LIMITED OVERS MATCH

John Player/Refuge Assurance League

Analysis	Bowler	Opponents	Venue	Year
6-25	Intikhab Alam	Derbyshire	The Oval	1974
6-34	R. D. Jackman	Derbyshire	Derby	1972

Benson and Hedges Cup

None

Gillette Cup/NatWest Trophy

Analysis	Bowler	Opponents	Venue	Year
7-33	R. D. Jackman	Yorkshire	Harrogate	1970
6-22	R. D. Jackman	Hampshire	Southampton	1982
6-32	R. D. Jackman	Northamptonshire	The Oval	1980
6-49	R. G. D. Willis	Middlesex	The Oval	1970

125 WICKETS IN A SEASON (100 SINCE 1969)

T. Richardson (6)	1894	196	W. S. Lees (4)	1907	135
	1895	252		1909	128
	1896	202	J. W. Hitch (4)	1911	137
	1897	238		1913	162
	1898	136		1914	126
	1901	159		1919	131
G. A. Lohmann (5)	1885	138	J. C. Laker (3)	1950	155
	1888	163		1951	128
	1889	143		1954	132
	1890	129	W. C. Smith (2)	1910	225
	1891	138		1911	156
A. R. Gover (5)	1934	126	P. G. H. Fender (2)	1922	143
	1935	133		1923	140
	1936	179	W. H. Lockwood	1892	134
	1937	168	A. V. Bedser	1955	131
	1939	129		1957	131
G. A. R. Lock (5)	1952	126	T. Rushby	1911	132
	1955	183	P. J. Loader	1962	131
	1956	138	E. Barratt	1883	144
	1957	187	N. A. Knox	1906	129
	1960	126	E. A. Watts	1938	129
W. S. Lees (4)	1905	184	R. Harman	1964	127
	1906	154	R. D. Jackman	1980	121

WICKET-KEEPING RECORDS
6 DISMISSALS IN AN INNINGS

No	Ct	St	Wicket-keeper	Opponents	Venue	Year
7	7	—	A. Long	Sussex	Hove	1964
6	5	1	E. Pooley★	Sussex	The Oval	1868
6	3	3	E. Pooley★	Sussex	The Oval	1868
6	4	2	E. Pooley	Yorkshire	The Oval	1870
6	1	5	E. Pooley	Kent	The Oval	1878
6	6	—	H. Strudwick	Sussex	The Oval	1914
6	6	—	E. W. J. Brooks	Kent	Blackheath	1935
6	6	—	G. N. G. Kirby	Cambridge University	Guildford	1949
6	6	—	R. Swetman	Kent	The Oval	1960
6	6	—	R. Swetman	Somerset	Taunton	1960

★Same match

No	Ct	St	Wicket-keeper	Opponents	Venue	Year
6	6	–	A. Long	Lancashire	Manchester	1967
6	5	1	A. Long	Northants	The Oval	1968
6	6	–	C. J. Richards	Warwickshire	The Oval	1988
6	6	–	A. J. Stewart	Lancashire	Southport	1988

8 DISMISSALS IN A MATCH

No	Ct	St	Wicket-keeper	Opponents	Venue	Year
12	8	4	E. Pooley	Sussex	The Oval	1868
11	11	–	A. Long	Sussex	Hove	1964
10	2	8	E. Pooley	Kent	The Oval	1878
10	9	1	C. J. Richards	Sussex	Guildford	1987
9	6	3	C. J. Richards	Glamorgan	Cardiff	1987
8	4	4	E. Pooley	Kent	Gravesend	1868
8	6	2	E. Pooley	Middlesex	The Oval	1875
8	4	4	E. Pooley	M. C. C.	Lord's	1876
8	7	1	H. Strudwick	Essex	Leyton	1904
8	7	1	E. W. J. Brooks	Somerset	The Oval	1933
8	8	–	C. J. Richards	Derbyshire	The Oval	1987

75 DISMISSALS IN A SEASON

No	Ct	St	Wicket-keeper	Year
90	73	17	A. Long	1962
87	71	16	F. Stedman	1901
87	66	21	A. J. W. McIntyre	1949
81	73	8	E. W. J. Brooks	1933
81	61	20	A. J. W. McIntyre	1955
80	63	17	H. Strudwick	1903
80	74	6	E. W. J. Brooks	1937
80	68	12	R. Swetman	1961
79	70	9	E. W. J. Brooks	1938
78	72	6	E. W. J. Brooks	1934
78	69	9	A. Long	1964
76	69	7	E. W. J. Brooks	1929
76	69	7	E. W. J. Brooks	1936
75	62	13	A. J. W. McIntyre	1950

400 DISMISSALS IN A CAREER

No	Ct	St	Wicket-keeper	Year
1,223	1,040	183	H. Strudwick	1902–1927
808	712	96	E. W. J. Brooks	1925–1939
805	702	103	A. Long	1960–1975
762	617	145	A. J. W. McIntyre	1938–1963
619	523	96	H. Wood	1884–1900
607	357	250	E. Pooley	1861–1883
600	534	66	C. J. Richards	1976–1988

FIELDING RECORDS

5 CATCHES IN AN INNINGS

No	Player	Opponents	Venue	Year
7	M. J. Stewart	Northamptonshire	Northampton	1957
5	R. Abel	Hampshire	Portsmouth	1898
5	E. G. Hayes	London County	The Oval	1901
5	G. A. R. Lock	Lancashire	Manchester	1953
5	W. S. Surridge	Lancashire	The Oval	1955
5	G. R. J. Roope	Cambridge University	Fenner's	1980

6 CATCHES IN A MATCH

No	Player	Opponents	Venue	Year
8	G. A. R. Lock	Warwickshire	The Oval	1957
7	J. F. Parker	Kent	Blackheath	1952
7	G. A. R. Lock	Lancashire	Manchester	1953
7	W. S. Surridge	Leicestershire	The Oval	1955
7	M. J. Stewart	Northamptonshire	Northampton	1957
6	R. Abel	Derbyshire	Derby	1884
6	J. M. Read	Hampshire	Southampton	1884
6	R. Abel	Hampshire	Portsmouth	1898
6	E. G. Hayes	Leicestershire	Leicester	1906
6	F. C. Holland	Leicestershire	Leicester	1908
6	P. G. H. Fender	Leicestershire	Leicester	1928
6	T. F. Shepherd	Kent	The Oval	1929
6	W. S. Surridge	Glamorgan	Cardiff	1956
6	R. C. E. Pratt	Sussex	Hastings	1956
6	M. J. Stewart	Sussex	Hove	1961
6	G. A. R. Lock	Australians	The Oval	1961
6	M. J. Edwards	Kent	Maidstone	1967

50 CATCHES IN A SEASON

No	Player	Year	No	Player	Year
77	M. J. Stewart	1957	54	K. F. Barrington	1958
64	K. F. Barrington	1957	53	M. J. Stewart	1959
59	G. R. J. Roope	1971	53	M. J. Edwards	1967
58	G. A. R. Lock	1957	52	M. J. Stewart	1955
58	M. J. Stewart	1958	51	W. S. Surridge	1952
55	W. S. Surridge	1955	50	E. G. Hayes	1906
54	W. S. Surridge	1956	50	G. A. R. Lock	1952

300 CATCHES IN A CAREER

No	Player	Years	No	Player	Years
604	M. J. Stewart	1954–1972	419	T. W. Hayward	1893–1914
560	E. G. Hayes	1896–1919	381	K. F. Barrington	1953–1968
532	G. A. R. Lock	1946–1963	360	W. S. Surridge	1947–1956
513	G. R. J. Roope	1964–1982	318	S. J. Storey	1960–1974
492	R. Abel	1881–1904	317	J. F. Parker	1932–1952
470	P. G. H. Fender	1914–1935	300	W. W. Read	1873–1897

TEAM RECORDS
HIGHEST AND LOWEST SCORES BY SURREY AGAINST EACH COUNTY

Opponents	Highest	Venue	Year	Lowest	Venue	Year
Derbyshire	611-9 dec	The Oval	1904	60	The Oval	1935
Essex	528-6 dec	The Oval	1947	14	Chelmsford	1983
Glamorgan	560-8 dec	The Oval	1947	59	Cardiff	1948
Gloucestershire	579	Bristol	1901	27	Cheltenham	1874
Hampshire	742	The Oval	1909	64	Basingstoke	1986
Kent	617	The Oval	1897	44	Maidstone	1884
Lancashire	634	The Oval	1898	33	The Oval	1873
Leicestershire	576	The Oval	1947	35	Leicester	1894
Middlesex	582-9 dec	The Oval	1919	35	Islington	1868
Northamptonshire	618-5 dec	Northampton	1920	58	The Oval	1913
Nottinghamshire	706-4 dec	Nottingham	1947	16	The Oval	1880
Somerset	811	The Oval	1899	35	The Oval	1957
Sussex	698	The Oval	1888	51	Petworth	1849
Warwickshire	634	The Oval	1906	61	The Oval	1962
Worcestershire	544	Worcester	1964	57	The Oval	1958
Yorkshire	560-6 dec	The Oval	1933	31	Holbeck	1883

HIGHEST AND LOWEST SCORES AGAINST SURREY BY EACH COUNTY

Opponents	Highest	Venue	Year	Lowest	Venue	Year
Derbyshire	386	Derby	1904	45	Derby	1907
Essex	616-5 dec	The Oval	1904	37	Leyton	1899
Glamorgan	550-6 dec	The Oval	1936	31	The Oval	1957
Gloucestershire	544	The Oval	1928	39	Clifton	1888
Hampshire	454-6	The Oval	1928	32	The Oval	1885
Kent	579-8 dec	The Oval	1935	20	The Oval	1870
Lancashire	588-4	Manchester	1928	27	Manchester	1958
Leicestershire	516-8 dec	The Oval	1929	35	Leicester	1897
Middlesex	563-9 dec	The Oval	1919	25	The Oval	1885
Northamptonshire	529-9	The Oval	1958	32	The Oval	1905
Nottinghamshire				40	The Oval	1955
Somerset	507-6 dec	Weston-super-Mare	1946	36	Weston-super-Mare	1955
Sussex	705-8 dec	Hastings	1902	40	Hove	1877
Warwickshire	585-7	The Oval	1905	45	The Oval	1953
Worcestershire	446-7	Guildford	1979	25	The Oval	1954
Yorkshire	704	The Oval	1899	26	The Oval	1909

Notes: The lowest total in all first-class cricket against Surrey is 15 by MCC in 1839
Leicestershire scored 35 in each innings of the match noted above
Sussex scored 19 v Surrey at Godalming in 1830 (before the period covered)

HIGHEST TOTALS IN LIMITED OVERS CRICKET BY SURREY

	Total	Opponents	Venue	Year
John Player/Refuge Assurance League	304-6	Warwickshire	The Oval	1985
Benson and Hedges Cup	276-6	Essex	The Oval	1982
Gillette Cup/NatWest Trophy	297-6	Lincolnshire	Sleaford	1983

LOWEST TOTALS IN LIMITED OVERS CRICKET BY SURREY

	Total	Opponents	Venue	Year
John Player/Refuge Assurance League	64	Worcestershire	Worcester	1978
Benson and Hedges Cup	89	Nottinghamshire	Nottingham	1984
Gillette Cup/NatWest Trophy	74	Kent	The Oval	1967

SURREY CAPTAINS

Date	Captain	Date	Captain
1846–1850	C. H. Hoare	1908–1910	H. D. G. Leveson-Gower
1851–1857	F. P. Miller	1911–1913	M. C. Bird
1858–1865	F. Burbidge	1914–1920	C. T. A. Wilkinson
1866	E. Dowson	1921–1931	P. G. H. Fender
1867	W. J. Collyer	1932–1933	D. R. Jardine
1968	C. Calvert	1934–1938	E. R. T. Holmes
1869–1870	S. H. Akroyd	1939–1945	H. M. Garland-Wells
1871	J. C. Gregory	1946	N. H. Bennett
1872–1875	G. Strachan	1947–1948	E. R. T. Holmes
1876	A. Chandler	1949–1951	M. R. Barton
1877–1878	G. Strachan	1952–1956	W. S. Surridge
1879	A. P. Lucas	1957–1962	P. B. H. May
1880–1893	J. Shuter	1963–1972	M. J. Stewart
1894–1899	K. J. Key	1973–1977	J. H. Edrich
1900–1902	D. L. A. Jephson	1978–1983	R. D. V. Knight
1903	L. Walker	1984–1985	G. P. Howarth
1904	Not appointed	1986	P. I. Pocock
1905–1907	Lord Dalmeny	1987–1988	I. A. Greig

SURREY PLAYERS' TEST RECORDS

Name	Country	Test career	M	Runs	Avge	Wkts	Avge
R. Abel	England	1888–1896	13	744	37.20	—	—
M. J. C. Allom	England	1929/30–1930/31	5	14	14.00	14	18.92
G. G. Arnold	England	1967–1975	34	421	12.02	115	28.29
K. F. Barrington	England	1955–1968	82	6806	58.67	29	44.82
A. V. Bedser	England	1946–1955	51	714	12.75	236	24.89
M. C. Bird	England	1909/10–1913/14	10	280	18.66	8	15.00
M. P. Bowden	England	1888/89	2	28	12.50	—	—
L. C. Braund	England	1901/02–1907/08	23	987	25.97	47	38.51
W. Brockwell	England	1893–1899	7	202	16.83	5	61.80
F. R. Brown	England	1931–1953	22	734	25.31	45	31.06
A. R. Butcher	England	1979	1	34	17.00	0	—
S. T. Clarke	West Indies	1977/78–1981/82	11	172	15.63	42	27.88
J. N. Crawford	England	1905/06–1907/08	12	469	22.33	39	29.48
N. F. Druce	England	1897/98	5	252	28.00	—	—
A. Ducat	England	1921	1	5	2.50	—	—
J. H. Edrich	England	1963–1976	77	5138	43.54	0	—
P. G. H. Fender	England	1920/21–1929	13	380	19.00	29	40.86
L. B. Fishlock	England	1936–1946/47	4	47	11.75	—	—
A. E. R. Gilligan	England	1922/23–1924/25	11	209	16.07	36	29.05
A. R. Gover	England	1936–1946	4	2	—	8	44.87
A. H. Gray	West Indies	1986/87	5	48	8.00	22	17.13
I. A. Greig	England	1982	2	26	6.30	4	28.50
S. C. Griffith	England	1947/48–1948/49	3	157	31.40	—	—
E. G. Hayes	England	1905/06–1912	5	86	10.75	1	52.00
T. W. Hayward	England	1895/96–1909	35	1999	34.46	14	36.71
J. W. Hitch	England	1911/12–1921	7	103	14.71	7	46.42
J. B. Hobbs	England	1907/08–1930	61	5410	56.94	1	165.00
E. R. T. Holmes	England	1934/35–1935	5	114	16.28	2	38.00
G. P. Howarth	New Zealand	1974/75–1984/85	47	2531	32.44	3	90.33
Intikhab Alam	Pakistan	1959/60–1976/77	47	1493	22.28	125	35.95
R. D. Jackman	England	1980/81–1982	4	42	7.00	14	31.78
D. R. Jardine	England	1928–1933/34	22	1296	48.00	0	—
H. Jupp	England	1876/1877	2	68	17.00	—	—
D. J. Knight	England	1921	2	54	13.50	—	—
N. A. Knox	England	1907	2	24	8.00	3	35.00
J. C. Laker	England	1947/48–1958/59	46	676	14.08	193	21.24
W. S. Lees	England	1905/6	5	66	11.00	26	17.96
H. D. G. Leveson-Gower	England	1909/10	3	95	23.75	—	—
P. J. Loader	England	1954–1959/59	13	76	5.84	39	22.51
G. A. R. Lock	England	1952–1967/68	49	742	13.74	174	25.58
W. H. Lockwood	England	1893–1902	12	231	17.76	43	20.55
G. A. Lohmann	England	1886–1896	18	213	8.87	112	10.75
A. P. Lucas	England	1878/79–1884	5	157	19.62	0	—
A. J. W. McIntyre	England	1950–1955	3	19	3.16	—	—
P. B. H. May	England	1951–1961	66	4537	46.77	—	—
C. H. Mills	South Africa	1891/92	1	25	12.50	2	41.50
P. I. Pocock	England	1967/68–1984/85	25	206	6.24	67	44.41

Name	Country	Test career	M	Runs	Avge	Wkts	Avge
J. M. Read	England	1882–1893	17	463	17.14	–	–
W. W. Read	England	1882/83–1893	18	720	27.69	0	–
C. J. Richards	England	1986/87–1988	8	285	21.92	–	–
T. Richardson	England	1893–1897/98	14	177	11.06	88	25.22
G. R. J. Roope	England	1972/73–1978	21	860	30.71	0	–
A. Sandham	England	1921–1929/30	14	879	38.21	–	–
M. W. W. Selvey	England	1976–1976/77	3	15	7.50	6	57.16
J. W. Sharpe	England	1890–1891/92	3	44	22.00	11	27.72
J. Shuter	England	1888	1	28	28.00	–	–
D. M. Smith	England	1985/86	2	80	20.00	–	–
J. Southerton	England	1876/77	2	7	3.50	7	15.28
M. J. Stewart	England	1962–1963/64	8	385	35.00	–	–
H. Strudwick	England	1909/10–1926	28	230	7.93	–	–
R. Subba Row	England	1958–1961	13	984	46.85	0	–
R. Swetman	England	1958/59–1959/60	11	254	16.93	–	–
F. J. Titmus	England	1955–1975/75	53	1449	22.29	153	32.22
N. C. Tufnell	England	1909/10	1	14	14.00	–	–
R. G. D. Willis	England	1970/71–1984	90	840	11.50	325	25.20
H. Wood	England	1888–1891/92	4	204	68.00	–	–
Younis Ahmed	Pakistan	1969/70–1986/87	4	177	29.50	0	–

GROUNDS USED BY SURREY 1846–1988

(First class matches only)

Ground	First	Last	M	W	L	D	A	T
Kennington Oval	1846	1988	1604	684	304	597	13	6
Broadwater Park, Godalming	1854		1	1	0	0	0	0
Reigate	1909		1	0	1	0	0	0
Lord's	1914		2	2	0	0	0	0
Guildford	1938	1988	60	31	7	22	0	0
Kingston	1946	1949	3	1	0	2	0	0
Banstead	1984		1	0	0	1	0	0
Total			1672	719	312	622	13	6

The above includes matches played by 'Surrey Club', which are given in the Association of Cricket Statisticians Guide to Important Matches played in the British Isles before 1864.

SELECT BIBLIOGRAPHY

Among the many books and periodicals referred to were:

A. T. Waghorn: *Cricket Scores, 1730–1773* (Blackwood, Edinburgh, 18889)

Lord Alverstone and C. W. Alcock eds.: *Surrey Cricket, its History and Associations* (Longmans, London, 1902)

David Kynaston: *Bobby Abel* (Secker & Warburg, London, 1982)

Anthony Meredith: *The Demon and the Lobster* (Kingswood Press, London, 1982)

G. B. Buckley: *Fresh Light on Eighteenth Century Cricket* (Cotterell & Co, Birmingham, 1935)

G. B. Buckley: *Fresh Light on Pre-Victorian Cricket* (Cotterell & Co, Birmingham, 1937)

Association of Cricket Statisticians: *First-Class Cricket Matches, 1864–1896*, 23 volumes

Benson and Hedges Cricket Year, ed. David Lemmon, seven volumes, 1982–1988 (Pelham Books, London)

Pelham Cricket Year, ed. David Lemmon, three volumes, 1979–1981 (Pelham Books, London)

P. Bailey, P. Thorn and P. Wynne-Thomas: *Who's Who of Cricketers* (Newnes Books, Feltham, 1984)

Wisden Cricketers' Almanack, various editors, 1898–1979

Pat Pocock: *Percy* (Clifford Frost, London, 1987)

Association of Cricket Statisticians: *Statistical Surveys* of 1864, 1865 and 1866

Richard Streeton: *P. G. H. Fender, A Biography* (Faber & Faber, London, 1981)

Louis Palgrave, *The Story of The Oval* (Cornish, Birmingham, 1949)

Roy Webber: *The County Cricket Championship* (SBC, London, 1958)

Association of Cricket Statisticians: *Surrey Cricketers, 1839–1980*

David Frith, ed.: *Guildford Jubilee, 1938–1988* (Guildford C.C., Guildford, 1988)

ACKNOWLEDGEMENTS

The author would like to thank the president, chairman, secretary and staff of the Surrey County Cricket Club for their patience, kindness, consideration and co-operation in the preparation of this work.

Special thanks are also due to Philip Bailey, who compiled the statistics section, and to the following: Brian Croudy, Peter Large, Peter Pickup, W. J. D. Hunt, R. H. Crowther-Smith, M. P. Murray, Robert Adams, J. S. Emsley, R. Taylor and Chris Roe.

The Statistical Section conforms to the Guides to First-Class Matches published by the Association of Cricket Statisticians.

David Lemmon
Leigh-on-Sea
1989

INDEX